BOOKS
THAT
HAVE
CHANGED
MAN'S
THINKING

THE
AENEID
OF
VIRGIL

*The poet Virgil, flanked by two muses,
in a second century A.D. mosaic
found near Carthage in North Africa.
As in this portrait, thought to have
been copied from a near-contemporary likeness,
Virgil was tall, with rugged features
and a dark complexion.*

THE
AENEID
OF
VIRGIL

Translated by
C. DAY LEWIS

With an Introduction by
C. DAY LEWIS
and an Appreciation by
JOHN POLLARD

Original Illustrations by
DAVID WHITFIELD

Distributed by
HERON BOOKS

Published by arrangement with
The Hogarth Press, Ltd., London

© *Editor's Foreword, Introduction, Appreciation and Illustrations*
Edito-Service S.A., Geneva

CONTENTS

LIST OF ILLUSTRATIONS

EDITOR'S FOREWORD

Virgil was the undisputed poet laureate of ancient Rome. The reader will discover, as he dips into the pages of the Aeneid, *that here is a masterpiece which is not only a great epic poem but also a moving and exciting story. For we have been fortunate in being able to use a highly readable, modern English translation from the Latin by C. Day Lewis, who appropriately enough is currently the poet laureate of England. He has also written for us a special introduction on the problems of the translator. In Mr. Day Lewis's hands the* Aeneid, *which for two thousand years without a break has been used mainly as a textbook, becomes once again a living, exciting and sentient work.*

In his Introduction, Mr. Day Lewis suggests that the reader should turn to classics like the Aeneid *in order " to make contact with the roots of his own civilization, to be reassured by this contact that, beneath all the chances of twenty centuries, there is a continuity of tradition." Virgil was a compassionate man, a man of peace, and he wrote in a period when Rome had just emerged from years of searing civil war. His feeling of compassion, of profound humanity, was something new in the literary expression of his day, and ties his great poem directly to our own longing for peace, for order, for the creating of a world in which men can live with dignity and confidence. Thus in the* Aeneid *we recognize, with surprise, our own attitudes, our own thoughts.*

In order to emphasize in his translation the modernity of the poem, Mr. Day Lewis asked himself before embarking on the project: " How would Virgil have told the story if he had been born in England, and in this present age?" His answer was to translate the Aeneid *in swinging, colloquial verse which, with its long, loosely flowing line, conveys most successfully the flavour, the urgency, as well as the humanity of the poem. In Book VI, for instance, Aeneas meets Dido, Queen of Carthage, in the Underworld, who had committed suicide for love of him:*

*Poor, unhappy Dido, so the message was true that came to me
Saying you'd put an end to your life with the sword and were dead?
Oh god! was it death I brought you, then? I swear by the stars,
By the powers above, by whatever is sacred in the Underworld,
It was not of my own will, Dido, I left your land...*

*Thus did Aeneas speak, trying to soften the wild-eyed,
Passionate-hearted ghost, and brought the tears to his own eyes.
She would not turn to him; she kept her gaze on the ground...
At last she flung away, hating him still, and vanished...
None the less did Aeneas, hard hit by her piteous fate,
Weep after her from afar, as she went, with tears of compassion.*

*Compassion, that is the mood that distinguishes this ancient poem;
compassion for stricken lovers, compassion for those who suffer in the
brutalities of war.*

*Thus out of this collaboration of two like-minded poets across the
centuries, each writing for his own time, has come a superb new
English version of an old classic that lies at the heart of the Western
literary tradition. And it is a classic that will continue for centuries
to come to speak to us movingly about the human condition.*

COURTLANDT CANBY
EDITOR OF THE SERIES

INTRODUCTION

*Aeneas, the hero of Virgil's epic, is constantly referred to as
" pius." The word carries slightly different meanings, according
to the context in which it is placed, and none of these can be accurately
given by the word " pious "—a word that for our modern ears
conveys a certain complacence or religiosity. When Virgil describes
Aeneas as " pius," he means essentially that his hero is motivated
and guided throughout by a sense of duty. His overmastering duty
is to lead the survivors out of vanquished Troy and to found with
them a new Troy in Italy, to which the gods have directed him.
Because he must be felt by the reader as an almost impersonal figure
of dutifulness, and because he is the son of a goddess, Aeneas must
sometimes appear to us a cold and almost repellent figure: he
lacks the human passions of Queen Dido, whom he seduces and
then betrays, or the human virtue and failings of Turnus, the prince
of Latium, who is his last and greatest opponent.*

*Although he suffers many ordeals and setbacks, we know that he
will win in the end, because he is semi-divine and because destiny
has ordained that he should survive even the implacable hostility of
Juno, the queen of the gods. Virgil put Aeneas, this abstract and
rather unsympathetic figure, at the centre of his epic for the reason
that he wished to glorify Rome—to give the Romans a noble origin
and pedigree. The* Aeneid *was written as, amongst other things, a
piece of propaganda for Rome and the virtues of its people: fortunately, it embodies many other things, for Virgil was a great poet
who could never be content with mere propaganda.*

*The chief of these other things is the quality which distinguishes
Virgil from Homer. In the* Iliad, *as in the British border ballads,
there is scarcely ever any emotional taking of sides: like them, the*
Iliad *is concerned with what happened and very seldom dilates upon
the feelings of those involved in the happenings. The* Iliad, *from
which, as from the* Odyssey *too, Virgil drew a good deal of material,
is the greatest of the pure epics; the* Aeneid *is an impure epic, the
first truly modern long poem in so far as it admits an element of*

subjectivism. This emerges signally in its pathos. I feel that, while Virgil crowded parts of his work with battle scenes in order to remind his readers of the ancestral Roman virtues of courage and endurance, he was ambivalent about them. Time and again " the pity of war " breaks through the glory of war. And nothing in Homer is comparable with the psychological insight Virgil shows in the passage between Aeneas and Dido, just as Homer could not have written the line, " Sunt lacrimae rerum et mentem mortalia tangunt "—" Tears in the nature of things, hearts touched by human transcience."

It is the strain between the conventional mythological elements— the quarrels of the gods, the legendary ordeals on sea and land—and the pristine note of humanism which we hear whispering through them, that makes the Aeneid *an imperfect epic but a giant stride in the progress of civilisation.*

The " piety " of Aeneas is composed from his sense of duty, his patriotism, his obligation to the past, his need to praise and protect his roots—or, being uprooted, to transplant them into another soil. This too is the translator's greatest problem; he has to transplant as much as he can of Virgil from an alien and dead language into the language of his own time and place. The language of poetry is always artificial; but Virgil's in the Aeneid *being so highly intricate, so different from ours in syntax, in the pattern and ordering of words, a translator cannot hope nowadays to produce an equivalent to Virgil's style while reproducing his meaning. It is seldom difficult to get at the meaning of what Virgil said; what is impossible is to convey the way in which he said it.*

Dr. Johnson, discussing Dryden's translation of the Aeneid, *remarked that " a translator is to be like his author: it is not his business to excel him." No translator today would worry unduly lest he might be excelling Virgil. Yet the rendering of works from foreign, sometimes dead, languages has not been so vigorously prac- tised in Britain since the Elizabethan age. So far as the great works in Latin or Greek are concerned, this must surely indicate two things :—the poet-translator's conviction that such translating will make his own style more flexible and more resourceful; and the reader's belief that, though he himself has no classical training, he can still get something valuable out of a great work, even in transla- tion. And this in its turn suggests that modern literature alone cannot directly satisfy one need of his—the need to make contact with the roots of his own civilisation, to be reassured by this contact that, beneath all the chances and changes of twenty centuries, there is a continuity of tradition. We can still find refreshment in the unique sources of European literature, even though they are piped from a long time away and inevitably lose much of their flavour in the process.*

The reader of this translation needs to know only two things— that it is a line-for-line version, and that each line has six beats. It has therefore an affinity with the Latin hexameter, the meter of the original. Unlike the Iliad, *the* Aeneid *was written to be read, not composed for oral recitation to be listened to. For this reason, it is more obviously a " literary " work than the* Iliad: *but the music, the sound-values of the original are none the less extremely delicate, varied and sophisticated. This is an aspect of the work to which a translator cannot do justice. He must make up for the deficiency by emphasising the narrative element. The* Aeneid *is much more than a narrative poem; but it is a good story, and the translator has failed if he cannot interest the reader in the story— its excitement, its grandeur and its pathos.*

My own translation was commissioned by the B.B.C., to be read aloud by a number of voices on the Third Programme. So, apart from my own preference for verse, a prose translation would not have suited the medium: it was essential to create the momentum, the rhythmical urgency which can only be achieved through verse. This momentum was necessary in order to carry the modern reader swiftly over the passages which could not be expected to hold his attention—the propagandist and antiquarian passages, with their clutter of place names, family names, customs even, which Virgil introduced for the glorification of his own people, to make them proud of their roots.

Again, since my translation was originally designed for public performance, I could follow my own bent to use words in ways that come natural to the modern ear. This had been relatively easy in my previous translation, of Virgil's Georgics, *which is a down-to-earth poem about farming and can be rendered in down-to-earth English. But the high style of the* Aeneid *loses a great deal when the translator is determined to avoid gross inversions and all the other aids to facile " poeticism " : here and there I used a modern colloquialism, even a slang expression, to prod the listener awake—and sometimes because such a phrase seemed to me the exact equivalent of Virgil's meaning. But all such devices are of minor importance. What matters most is that the reader should feel he is reading a poem which, however remote its subject and its detail, has been re-written into the language of his own day.*

He may well feel, as I did, in closest touch with Virgil in those numerous passages where the poet compares the action of his characters with some manifestation of nature. Virgil was a countryman: his close observation of nature time and again led him into those similes (the gathering of tribes for war compared with the swarming of bees or a forest fire), in which the action described disappears behind the vividness of the action to which it is compared. And Virgil was a peace-lover. He was sick of the civil wars which had raged in Italy: he genuinely believed that the reign of Augustus might bring in a millennium of peace, a new golden age. When, in praise of ancestral Roman virtue, bloodshed had to be described, he described it all the more vividly because he loathed it—shrank from it. This tenderness of Virgil's mind—the mind of a man of peace who could pay tribute to the warlike virtues but deprecated their results—made him the prophet of European humanism and brings him closest to the contemporary reader.

C. DAY LEWIS

THE AENEID
OF VIRGIL

Virgil's Mediterranean.

BOOK I

I tell about war and the hero who first from Troy's frontier,
Displaced by destiny, came to the Lavinian shores,
To Italy—a man much travailed on sea and land
By the powers above, because of the brooding anger of Juno,
Suffering much in war until he could found a city
And march his gods into Latium, whence rose the Latin race,
The royal line of Alba and the high walls of Rome.
Where lay the cause of it all? How was her godhead injured?
What grievance made the queen of heaven so harry a man
Renowned for piety, through such toils, such a cycle of calamity?
Can a divine being so persevere in anger?
There was a town of old—men from Tyre colonised it—
Over against Italy and Tiber mouth, but afar off,
Carthage, rich in resources, fiercely efficient in warfare.
This town, they say, was Juno's favourite dwelling, preferred
To all lands, even Samos: here were her arms, her chariot:
And even from the long-ago time she cherished the aim that this
Should be, if fate allowed, the metropolis of all nations.
Nevertheless, she had heard a future race was forming
Of Trojan blood, which one day would topple that Tyrian stronghold—
A people arrogant in war, born to be everywhere rulers
And root up her Libyan empire—so the Destiny-Spinners planned.
Juno, afraid of this, and remembering well the old war
Wherein she had championed the Greeks whom she loved against the
                                        Trojans—
Besides, she has other reasons for rage, bitter affronts
Unblotted as yet from her heart: deep in her mind rankle
The judgment of Paris, the insult of having her beauty scorned,
Her hate for Troy's origin, Ganymede taken and made a favourite—
Furious at these things too, she tossed all over the sea
The Trojans, the few that the Greeks and relentless Achilles had left,
And rode them off from their goal, Latium. Many years
They were wandering round the seven seas, moved on by destiny.

[Lines 1–32]

3

So massive a task it was to found the Roman race.
They were only just out of sight of Sicily, towards deep water
Joyfully crowding on sail and driving the foam-flocks before them,
When Juno, who under her heart nursed that inveterate wound,
Soliloquised thus:—
                    Shall I give up? own myself beaten?
Impotent now to foil the Trojan lord from Italy?
Fate forbids me, indeed! Did not Athene burn
The Argive fleet and drown the crews, because one man
Had given offence? because of the criminal madness of Ajax?
Why, she herself flung down Jove's firebolt from the clouds,
Blasted that navy and capsized the sea with a storm;
And Ajax, gasping flame out of his cloven breast,
She whisked up in the whirlwind, impaled him on a crag.
But I, who walk in majesty, queen of heaven, Jove's
Sister and consort, I must feud with a single nation
For all these years. Does anyone worship my divinity
After this, or pay my altar a suppliant's homage?

Such were the thoughts milling round in her angry heart as the goddess
Came to the storm-cloud country, the womb-land of brawling siroccos,
Aeolia. Here in a huge cavern King Aeolus
Keeps curbed and stalled, chained up in durance to his own will,
The heaving winds and far-reverberating tempests.
Behind the bars they bellow, mightily fretting: the mountain is
One immense murmur. Aeolus, aloft on his throne of power,
Sceptre in hand, gentles and disciplines their fierce spirits.
Otherwise, they'd be bolting off with the earth and the ocean
And the deep sky—yes, brushing them all away into space.
But to guard against this the Father of heaven put the winds
In a dark cavern and laid a heap of mountains upon them,
And gave them an overlord who was bound by a firm contract
To rein them in or give them their head, as he was ordered.
Him Juno now petitioned. Here are the words she used:—

Aeolus, the king of gods and men has granted
You the rule of the winds, to lull the waves or lift them.
A breed I have no love for now sails the Tyrrhene sea,
Transporting Troy's defeated gods to Italy.
Lash fury into your winds! Whelm those ships and sink them!
Flail the crews apart! Litter the sea with their fragments!

[*Lines 33–70*]

4

Fourteen nymphs I have—their charms are quite out of the common—
Of whom the fairest in form, Deiopea, I'll join
To you in lasting marriage and seal her yours for ever,
A reward for this great favour I ask, to live out all
The years with you, and make you the father of handsome children.
  Aeolus answered thus:—
                              O queen, it is for you to
Be fully aware what you ask: my duty is to obey.
Through you I hold this kingdom, for what it's worth, as Jove's
Viceroy; you grant the right to sit at the gods' table;
You are the one who makes me grand master of cloud and storm.
  Thus he spoke, and pointing his spear at the hollow mountain,
Pushed at its flank: and the winds, as it were in a solid mass,
Hurl themselves through the gates and sweep the land with tornadoes.
They have fallen upon the sea, they are heaving it up from its deepest
Abysses, the whole sea—East wind, South, Sou'-wester
Thick with squalls—and bowling great billows at the shore.
There follows a shouting of men, a shrilling of stays and halyards.
All of a sudden the storm-clouds are snatching the heavens, the daylight
From the eyes of the Trojans; night, black night is fallen on the sea.
The welkin explodes, the firmament flickers with thick-and-fast lightning,
And everything is threatening the instant death of men.
At once a mortal chill went through Aeneas and sapped him;
He groaned, and stretching out his two hands toward the stars,
Uttered these words:—
                              Oh, thrice and four times blessèd you
Whose luck it was to fall before your fathers' eyes
Under Troy's battlements! O Diomed, the bravest
Of the Greek kind, why could not I have fallen to death
On Ilium's plains and shed my soul upon your sword?
Fallen where Hector lies, whom Achilles slew, and tall
Sarpedon fell, and Simois our river rolls so many
Helmets and shields and heroes together down its stream?
  Even as he cried out thus, a howling gust from the North
Hit the front of the sail, and a wave climbed the sky.
Oars snapped; then the ship yawed, wallowing broadside on
To the seas: and then, piled up there, a precipice of sea hung.
One vessel was poised on a wave crest; for another the waters,

                                                      collapsing,
                              [*Lines 71–106*]

5

Showed sea-bottom in the trough: the tide-race boiled with sand.
Three times did the South wind spin them towards an ambush of rocks
(Those sea-girt rocks which Italians call by the name of "The Altars"),
Rocks like a giant spine on the sea: three times did the East wind
Drive them in to the Syrtes shoal, a piteous spectacle—
Hammering them on the shallows and hemming them round with
                                                      sandbanks.
One ship, which carried in her the Lycians and faithful Orontes,
Before Aeneas' eyes is caught by an avalanche wave
And pooped: her helmsman is flicked from off the deck and headlong
Sent flying; but three times the vessel is twirled around
By the wave ere the waters open and greedily gulp her down.
A man or two can be seen swimming the huge maelstrom,
With weapons and planks and Trojan treasure spilt on the sea.
Now Ilioneus' strong ship, now the ship of valiant Achates,
And the ships that carry Abás and aged Aletes go
Down to the gale; the ships have all sprung leaks and are letting
The enemy pour in through the loosened joints of their hulls.

    Meanwhile Neptune has felt how greatly the sea is in turmoil,
Felt the unbridled storm disturbing the water even
Down to the sea-bed, and sorely troubled has broken surface;
He gazes forth on the deep with a pacific mien.
He sees the fleet of Aeneas all over the main, dismembered,
The Trojans crushed by waves and the sky in ribbons about them:
Juno's vindictive stratagems do not escape her brother.
He summons the East and the West winds, and then proceeds to say:—
    Does family pride tempt you to such impertinence?
Do you really dare, you Winds, without my divine assent
To confound earth and sky, and raise this riot of water?
You, whom I——! Well, you have made the storm, I must lay it.
Next time, I shall not let you so lightly redeem your sins.
Now leave, and quickly leave, and tell your overlord this—
Not to him but to me was allotted the stern trident,
Dominion over the seas. His domain is the mountain of rock,
Your domicile, O East wind. Let Aeolus be king of
That castle and let him keep the winds locked up in its dungeon.

    He spoke; and before he had finished, the insurgent sea was calmed,
The mob of cloud dispersed and the sun restored to power.
Nereid and Triton heaving together pushed the ships off

    [*Lines 107–144*]

From the sharp rock, while Neptune levered them up with his trident,
And channelled a way through the sandbanks, and made the sea lie
                down—
Then lightly charioted off over the face of the waters.
Just as so often it happens, when a crowd collects, and violence
Brews up, and the mass mind boils nastily over, and next thing
Firebrands and brickbats are flying (hysteria soon finds a missile)—
That then, if they see some man whose goodness of heart and conduct
Have won their respect, they fall silent and stand still, ready to hear him;
And he can change their temper and calm their thoughts with a speech:
So now the crash of the seas died down, when Neptune gazed forth
Over their face, and the sky cleared, and the Father of ocean,
Turning his horses, wheeled away on an easy course.

   Aeneas' men, worn out, with a last effort make for
The nearest landing place; somewhere on the coast of Libya.
A spot there is in a deep inlet, a natural harbour
Formed by an island's flanks upon which the swell from the deepsea
Breaks and dividing runs into the land's recesses.
At either end of the lofty cliffs a peak towers up
Formidably to heaven, and under these twin summits
The bay lies still and sheltered: a curtain of overhanging
Woods with their shifting light and shadow forms the backdrop;
At the seaward foot of the cliffs there's a cave of stalactites,
Fresh water within, and seats which nature has hewn from the stone—
A home of the nymphs. Here, then, tired ships could lie, and need
No cable nor the hooking teeth of an anchor to hold them.
Here, with seven ships mustered, all that was left of his convoy,
Aeneas now put in: and the Trojans, aching for dry land,
Tumbled out of their ships onto the sands they craved so,
And laid their limbs, crusted with brine, upon the shore.
Then first of all Achates struck a spark from flint,
Nursed the spark to a flame on tinder, gave it to feed on
Dry fuel packed around it and made the flame blaze up there.
Sick of mischance, the men got ready the gifts and gear of
Ceres, setting themselves to roast on the fire and grind,
Though tainted it was with the salt water, what grain they had
                salvaged.

   While this was going forward, Aeneas scaled a crag
To get an extensive view of the sea, hoping to sight

                  [*Lines 145–181*]

Some Trojan ship—Antheus perhaps, safe from the storm,
Or Capys, or the tall ship displaying the shield of Caicus.
Ship there was none in view; but on the shore three stags
Caught his eye as they wandered with a whole herd behind them,
A straggling drove of deer which browsed along the valley.
Aeneas, where he stood, snatched up the bow and arrows—
The weapons he had borrowed just now from faithful Achates—
And aiming first at the leaders of the herd, which carried their heads
high
With branching antlers, he laid them low; then shot at the herd,
And his arrows sent it dodging all over the leafy woods.
Nor would he stop shooting until triumphantly
He had brought down seven beasts, one for each of his ships.
Then he returned to the harbour and shared them among his comrades.
And then he shared out the wine which good Acestes had casked
In Sicily and given them—a generous parting present,
And spoke these words of comfort to his sad-hearted friends:—

   Comrades, we're well acquainted with evils, then and now.
Worse than this you have suffered. God will end all this too.
You, who have risked the mad bitch, Scylla, risked the cliffs
So cavernously resounding, and the stony land of the Cyclops,
Take heart again, oh, put your dismal fears away!
One day—who knows?—even these will be grand things to look
back on.
Through chance and change, through hosts of dangers, our road still
Leads on to Latium: there, destiny offers a home
And peace; there duty tells us to build the second Troy.
Hold on, and find salvation in the hope of better things!

   Thus spoke Aeneas; and though his heart was sick with anxiety,
He wore a confident look and kept his troubles to himself.
The Trojans set to work, preparing the game for a banquet;
Hacked the chines apart from the ribs, and exposed the guts:
Some sliced the meat into steaks which they spitted with trembling
fingers,
Some set down cooking pots on the beach, and fed the fires.
Then they restored their strength with the food, sprawling at ease
On the grass they took their fill of the wine and the rich venison.
Afterwards, hunger appeased and the meal cleared away, for a long
time

[*Lines 182–216*]

8

They talked of their missing friends, longing to have them back,
Half-way between hope and fear, not knowing whether to deem them
Alive or utterly perished and far beyond human call.
True-hearted Aeneas grieved especially for the fate of
Ardent Orontes, and Amycus, and the cruel fate of Lycus,
Grieved for Gyas the brave and for the brave Cloanthus.

   At last they made an end. Jupiter from high heaven
Looked down at the flights of sails on the sea, and the earth beneath
                              him,
Its shores and its far-flung peoples: so, at the top of the morning
He stood, and presently focussed his gaze on the Libyan realm.
Now, as he deeply pondered the troubles there, came Venus,
Sadder than is her wont, her eyes shining with tears,
And spoke to him:—

                 Sir, you govern the affairs of gods and men
By law unto eternity, you are terrible in the lightning:
Tell me, what wrong could my Aeneas or his Trojans
Have done you, so unforgivable that, after all these deaths,
To stop them reaching Italy they are locked out from the whole world?
Verily you had promised that hence, as the years rolled on,
Troy's renaissance would come, would spring the Roman people
And rule as sovereigns absolute over earth and sea.
You promised it. Oh, my father, why have you changed your mind?
That knowledge once consoled me for the sad fall of Troy:
I could balance fate against fate, past ills with luck to come.
But still the same ill fortune dogs my disaster-ridden
Heroes. Oh when, great king, will you let their ordeal end?
Antenor, slipping away through the Greek army, could safely
Sail right up the Illyrian gulf, pass by the remote
Liburnians, and pass the source of river Timavus
Where tidal water, roaring aloud below rock, spouts up
Through nine mouths, and the fields are hemmed with a sound of the
                              sea.
He was allowed to found Padua, make a home for
Trojans there—could give his people a name, and nail up
His arms, could settle down to enjoy peace and quiet.
But we, your seed, for whom you sanction a place in heaven—
Our ships damnably sunk—because of one being's anger
We are cheated, and fenced afar from Italy.

                    [Lines 217–252]

Is this the reward for being true? Is it thus you restore a king?

The begetter of gods and men inclined towards her the smiling
Countenance which calms the sky and makes fair weather,
Gently kissed his daughter's mouth, and began to speak:—

Fear no more, Cytherea. Take comfort, for your people's
Destiny is unaltered; you shall behold the promised
City walls of Lavinium, and exalt great-hearted Aeneas
Even to the starry skies. I have not changed my mind.
I say it now—for I know these cares constantly gnaw you—
And show you further into the secret book of fate:
Aeneas, mightily warring in Italy, shall crush
Proud tribes, to establish city walls and a way of life,
Till a third summer has seen him reigning in Latium
And winter thrice passed over his camp in the conquered land.
His son Ascanius, whose surname is now Iulus—
Ilus it was, before the realm of Ilium fell—
Ascanius for his reign shall have full thirty years
With all their wheeling months; shall move the kingdom from
Lavinium and make Long Alba his sure stronghold.
Here for three hundred years shall rule the dynasty
Of Hector, until a priestess and queen of Trojan blood,
With child by Mars, shall presently give birth to twin sons.
Romulus, then, gay in the coat of the tawny she-wolf
Which suckled him, shall succeed to power and found the city
Of Mars and with his own name endow the Roman nation.
To these I set no bounds, either in space or time;
Unlimited power I give them. Even the spiteful Juno,
Who in her fear now troubles the earth, the sea and the sky,
Shall think better of this and join me in fostering
The cause of the Romans, the lords of creation, the togaed people.
Thus it is written. An age shall come, as the years glide by,
When the children of Troy shall enslave the children of Agamemnon,
Of Diomed and Achilles, and rule in conquered Argos.
From the fair seed of Troy there shall be born a Caesar—
Julius, his name derived from great Iulus—whose empire
Shall reach to the ocean's limits, whose fame shall end in the stars.
He shall hold the East in fee; one day, cares ended, you shall
Receive him into heaven; him also will mortals pray to.
Then shall the age of violence be mellowing into peace:

[*Lines 253–291*]

10

Venerable Faith, and the Home, with Romulus and Remus,
Shall make the laws; the grim, steel-welded gates of War
Be locked; and within, on a heap of armaments, a hundred
Knots of bronze tying his hands behind him, shall sit
Growling and bloody-mouthed the godless spirit of Discord.

So Jupiter spoke, and sent Mercury down from on high
To see that the land and the new-built towers of Carthage offered
Asylum to the Trojans, for otherwise might queen Dido,
Blind to destiny, turn them away. He aerially wafted,
Feathering his wings, and post-haste came down on Libyan soil.
Now he performs his mission; at the god's will that people
Puts by its haughty temper, the queen at once responds to
An intimation of peace and goodwill towards the Trojans.
True-hearted Aeneas, after a night spent on a treadmill
Of cares, when kindly dawn came, determined to reconnoitre
The strange terrain, find out to what land the storm had brought them
And who lived there—was it men or only beasts—for it looked like
A wilderness, and bring back a full report to his friends.
He saw that the ships were concealed in a woody creek, beneath
The overhang of the cliff, with trees and shifting shadows
About them; and then set forth, accompanied by Achates
Only, swinging a couple of broad-tipped spears in his hand.
There, from the heart of the woodland, his mother came to meet him
Guised as a maiden in face and dress, with a girl's weapons—
A Spartan girl, as it might be, or Thracian Harpalyce,
Outpacer of horses, swift outrunner of running rivers.
In huntress wise she had handily slung her bow from her shoulder,
And her hair was free to blow in the wind, and she went bare-kneed
With the flowing folds of her dress kilted up and securely knotted.
She spoke first:—

> Hullo there, young men! If you have seen
One of my sisters roving hereabouts or in full cry
After a foaming boar—she carries a slung quiver
And wears a spotted lynx-skin—please tell me where she went.

Thus Venus spoke; and the son of Venus began to reply thus:—

No sight or sound have I had of any of your sisters,
O—but what shall I call you, maiden? for your face is
Unmortal, and your speech rings not of humankind.
Goddess surely you are. A nymph? The sister of Phoebus?

[*Lines 292–329*]

11

Give luck, whoever you be! Lighten, I pray, our ordeal!
Tell me in what clime, upon what shores of the world
We are cast up: for, driven here by wind and wave,
We have no clue to the peoples or places of our wandering.
Tell this, and we will offer sacrifice at your altar.
  Then Venus said:—

                    Believe me, such titles are not my due:
It is the fashion for Tyrian girls to carry a quiver
And wear like this the high-laced, crimson hunting boot.
The kingdom you see is Carthage, the Tyrians, the town of Agenor;
But the country around is Libya, no folk to meet in war.
Dido, who left the city of Tyre to escape her brother,
Rules here—a long and labyrinthine tale of wrong
Is hers, but I will touch on its salient points in order.
Her husband was Sychaeus, a man of great estates
Among the Phoenicians and greatly loved by the ill-starred Dido
Whose father had given her in marriage to Sychaeus,
A virgin bride. Now the throne of Tyre was held by her brother,
Pygmalion, a monster who had no rival in wickedness.
Maniac evil stepped in. Pygmalion, blinded by love for
Gold, godlessly murdered the unsuspecting Sychaeus
In secret before the altar—no pang of compunction for her love;
And kept the deed dark for a long time, vilely inventive of fictions
To cheat with hollow hope her pining, loving heart.
But there came, one night as she slept, the phantom of her unburied
Husband, weirdly floating its clay-white face up to her,
Exposed the atrocious altar, the breast spitted with steel,
And took the cover off that crime hidden in the house.
Then the phantom urged her swiftly to fly the country,
And told her where she could find in the earth an old treasure, a secret
Hoard of gold and silver to help her on her way.
Dido, in great disquiet, organised her friends for escape.
They met together, all those who harshly hated the tyrant
Or keenly feared him: they seized some ships which chanced to be
                                                            ready
And loaded them with the gold: so was that treasure sailed
Out of Pygmalion's grasp: a woman led the exploit.
They came to this spot, where to-day you can behold the mighty
Battlements and the rising citadel of New Carthage,
  [*Lines 330–366*]

12

And purchased a site, which was named "Bull's Hide" after the bargain
By which they should get as much land as they could enclose with a
                                                                    bull's hide.
But now, tell me who you are, what land you have come from, and
                                                                    whither
Your journey leads.
                        So Venus questioned him; and Aeneas,
Sighing, drew up his voice as it were from the heart's depth:—
    Goddess, if I were to tell our tale right through from the start
And leisure there was to hear the chronicles of our labours,
Evening would close the sky and the day be asleep ere I finished.
We from old Troy (if ever the name of Troy has come to
Your ears) were voyaging, when the weather's caprice drove us
Off our course and piled us onto the Libyan shore.
I am true-hearted Aeneas; my fame has been heard of in heaven:
I carry my gods of Home which I rescued from the enemy.
I go to my own land, Italy, where Jove began our line.
With twenty ships I embarked on the Phrygian sea, my mother,
A goddess, showing the way, I following destiny's bidding:
But seven ships now are left us, battered by wind and wave.
I, a stranger and needy, now roam the Libyan desert,
Driven from Europe and Asia.
                        Venus could bear no longer
To hear him grieve, and so she broke in on his anguish, saying:—
    Whoever you are, you cannot breathe and live, I am sure,
Hateful to heaven, for soon you'll have reached the Tyrian city.
Do but fare on, press on from here to the queen's palace.
Unless what my parents taught me of signs and omens is meaningless,
I can declare your friends rallied to you, your missing
Ships brought back to haven here by a shift of the wind.
Look at those twelve swans flying in jubilant formation:
Just now an eagle, swooping from heaven, was scattering them
All over the sky: but see how, in a long line, they look down
Where to land or where their fellows already have landed.
Rallied they are, and romping aloft with their wings whooping,
And wheeling about the sky in company, and calling.
Even so it is with your ships and your young warriors—either
They're havened already or running free to the harbour mouth.
Do but fare on, and firmly step where the road leads you.
                                                    [*Lines 367–401*]

13

She spoke. She turned away; and as she turned, her neck
Glowed to a rose-flush, her crown of ambrosial hair breathed out
A heavenly fragrance, her robe flowed down, down to her feet,
And in gait she was all a goddess. Aeneas recognised
His mother, and as she passed from him, sent these words in her
wake:—

Must you too be cruel? Must you make game of your son
With shapes of sheer illusion? Oh, why may we not join
Hand to hand, or ever converse straightforwardly?
Thus he reproached her, and turned his steps toward the battlements.
But Venus folded them as they went in an opaque mist,
Magically poured round them an ample cloak of cloud,
Lest any should spy or encounter Aeneas and Achates,
Attempt to delay them or demand to know their business.
Then she herself was gone through the air to Paphos, joyfully
Homing again where her temple is, and a hundred altars
Glow with Sabaean incense and blow with fresh-breathed flowers.

Meanwhile the two pressed on apace, where the track pointed.
And now they were climbing a hill whose massive bulk looms over
The city and commands a prospect of soaring towers.
Aeneas marvels at great buildings, where once were shanties,
Marvels at city gates and the din of the paved streets.
The Tyrians are busy at work there, some extending the walls,
Manhandling blocks of stone and building the citadel,
Others choosing a site for a house and trenching foundations:
Laws are being made, magistrates and a parliament elected:
Here they dig out a harbour basin; here they are laying
Foundations deep for a theatre, and hewing from stone immense
Columns to grace one day a tall proscenium.
So in the youth of summer throughout the flowering land
The bees pursue their labours under the sun: they lead
A young brood from the hive, or press the flowing honey
And fill the cells to bursting with a delicious nectar;
Relieve incoming bees of their burden, or closing ranks
Shoo the drones, that work-shy gang, away from the bee-folds.
The work goes on like wild-fire, the honey smells of thyme.
"Ah, fortunate you are, whose town is already building!"
Aeneas said, and gazed up at the city's heights.
Then, in his cloak of darkness he went—a miraculous thing—
[*Lines 402–439*]

14

Into their midst and joined the crowds, but none perceived him.
    There was a grove, most genial its shade, at the city centre,
Just where the Carthaginians, after their rough passage,
First dug and found the sign which royal Juno had promised—
The skull of a spirited horse; it was a sign that henceforth
Their nation would thrive in wealth and war throughout the ages.
Dido was building here, in Juno's honour, a huge
Temple, made rich by offerings and the indwelling presence of Juno:
Bronze was its threshold, approached by a flight of steps; the door-posts
Were braced with bronze, and the door with its grinding hinges was
                                                                    bronze.
This grove had seen Dido's fear allayed by a chance of renewal
For the first time; and here Aeneas first dared to hope for
Salvation and believe that at last his luck was turning.
For, while he awaited the queen and his eyes roved over the detail
Of that immense façade, amazed by the town's good fortune,
Admiring the skill of the rival craftsmen, the scope of their work,
He noticed a series of frescoes depicting the Trojan war,
Whose fame had already gone round the world; the sons of Atreus
Were there, and Priam, Achilles too, hostile to both.
Aeneas stood; wept:—
                    Oh, Achates, is there anywhere,
Any place left on earth unhaunted by our sorrows?
Look!—Priam. Here too we find virtue somehow rewarded,
Tears in the nature of things, hearts touched by human transience.
Then cast off fear; the fame of our deeds will ensure your welfare.
    He spoke, and fed his soul on those insubstantial figures,
Heavily sighing, the large tears rivering down his cheeks.
Pictured there, he beheld scenes of the fight round Troy—
Here the Greeks fled with the Trojan warriors hard behind them,
Here fled the Trojans before the chariot of plumed Achilles.
He recognised through his tears, not far away, the snow-white
Tents of Rhesus taken by surprise, while all slept deep,
And wrecked with terrible slaughter by Diomed, man of blood,
And Diomed driving away to his camp the fiery horses
Before they could graze the meadows of Troy or drink the Xanthus.
Another scene was of Troilus in flight, his weapons gone
(Unhappy the lad, unequal the fight with Achilles): his horses
Are bolting; heels over head he hangs backwards out of the chariot,

[*Lines 440–476*]

15

Yet gripping the reins; his neck and his hair are being dragged along
Over the ground, and his trailing spearpoint scribbles in the dust.
Meanwhile to the shrine of their goddess, their foe's friend, the
                                                                Trojan women
Are walking to make intercession: their hair is unbound, they carry
The goddess' ritual robe, they mourn and beat their breasts:
But the goddess keeps her eyes on the ground and regards them not.
Thrice round the walls of Troy Achilles has dragged Hector
And now is demanding a ransom of gold for the lifeless body.
At this point Aeneas uttered a deep groan
To see the spoils, the chariot, the actual body of
His friend, and Priam's defenceless hands stretched out to Achilles.
He noticed himself, too, in the forefront of the battle,
Noticed the Aethiopian brigade and the arms of black Memnon;
Picked out Penthesilea leading the crescent shields of
The Amazons and storming through the ruck like a fire,
Her bare breast thrusting out over the golden girdle,
A warrior queen, a girl who braved heroes in combat.
   Now while Aeneas viewed with wonder all these scenes,
And stood at gaze, rooted in a deep trance of attention,
There came in royal state to the temple, a crowd of courtiers
Attending her, queen Dido, most beautiful to see.
As, by the banks of Eurotas or over the Cynthian slopes
Diana foots the dance, and a thousand Oreads following
Weave a constellation around that arrowy one,
Who in grace of movement excels all goddesses,
And happiness runs through the still heart of Latona—
So Dido was, even so she went her radiant way
Through the crowds, eager to forward the work and growth of her
                                                                realm.

Now, at the holy doors, under the temple porch,
Hedged by the spears of her guard, she throned herself on high;
Gave laws and ordinances, appointed the various tasks
In equitable proportions or else by drawing lots.
Just then, all of a sudden, Aeneas saw approaching
Amid the multitude Antheus, Sergestus, valiant
Cloanthus and other Trojans, whom the black hurricane
Had sundered at sea and driven afar to different beaches.
He and Achates together were thrilled through, were dumbfounded
   [*Lines 477–513*]

16

With anxious joy: they eagerly yearned to join hands with their friends,
But the mystery of the whole affair disquieted them.
So they keep dark, and peering out from their womb of cloud,
Speculate what befell these friends, where their ships are beached,
Why they are here: for spokesmen from each of the ships were coming
To sue the queen's favour, and shouting aloud as they neared the
temple.

When they had entered and Dido had granted to them an audience,
The eldest, Ilioneus, began in collected tones:—
    O queen, who, under God, have founded a new city
And curbed the arrogance of proud clans with your justice,
We hapless Trojans, wanderers over a world of seas,
Implore you, stop your people from wickedly burning our ships.
God-fearing men we are. Incline your heart to spare us.
We are not come as pirates to waste your Libyan homes
With the sword, and carry down their plunder to the beaches.
We've no mind for marauding; the conquered lack such effrontery.
There is a place—the Greeks call it Hesperia—
An antique land, well warded, possessed of a rich soil:
Oenotrians colonised it; whose heirs, so rumour says now,
Have named it, after their first founder, Italy.
That was our bourne. . . .
But rainy Orion rose, and the sea got up of a sudden:
We drove on chartless shoals, the winds wantonly pitched us
Far apart on the deep amid toppling waves and unchannelled
Reefs. A handful of us have drifted to your shores.
What manner of men are these? What land is this that allows them
Such barbarous ways? They bar us even from the sanctuary
Of the sands: they threaten, and forbid us to touch the hem of their
country.

If humankind and mortal arms mean nothing to you,
Think of the gods—they do not forget good deeds and bad.
Aeneas was our king: never was a man more just,
More duteous of heart, more adept in warlike arts, than he.
If destiny has preserved him, if still he breathes the air
Of day, and is not sleeping in death's unwelcome shade,
We need not fear; and you should have no cause to regret
That you were prompt to aid us. In Sicily, too, we have towns
And resources, and noble Acestes who comes of Trojan stock.

[Lines 514–550]

We pray you, let us lay up the vessels the storm shattered,
And shape new oars and timbers for them out of your forests;
So that, if we are meant to get back our friends and our king
And make for Italy, to Italy we may go;
But if that hope is lost—if the Libyan sea has drowned you,
Lord Aeneas, and there's no future for Iulus—
We may at least sail back to our last port of call, to Sicily,
Where homes are ready for us, and make Acestes our king.

  Ilioneus stopped speaking. A shout of assent rose from
The Trojans all. . . .
Then Dido, with her eyes downcast, addressed them briefly:—

  Trojans, put fear away from your hearts and forget your troubles!
Mine's a hard task, with a young country: that's why I have to
Do such things, to guard my frontiers everywhere.
Who has not heard of Troy and the men of Aeneas—their manly
Virtues, and all that famous conflagration of war?
We Carthaginians are not so insensitive of heart,
Nor is our city quite so out of the way or benighted.
Whether your choice is great Hesperia, land of Saturn,
Or you decide upon Sicily and king Acestes,
I will give you an escort there and what provision you need.
Or would you like to share my kingdom, on equal terms?
This city I am building—it's yours: draw up your ships, then;
There shall be no preference, I say, between you and us.
Oh, if only your king, Aeneas himself, could come here,
Fetched by the same storm. Well, I will send couriers abroad
With orders to comb the furthest corners of Libya, in case
He is wandering somewhere, in woods or towns, a castaway.

  Arrested by Dido's words, Aeneas and brave Achates
For some time now had been on fire to slough off their cloak
Of darkness. Achates first spoke urgently to Aeneas:—

  Tell me, goddess-born, what idea forms in your mind now.
All is saved, you can see, our fleet and our friends restored to us.
One only is missing, and him we saw drowned in the welter
Before our eyes: all else bears out what your mother told us.

  These words were hardly spoken, when in a flash the cloud-cloak
They wore was shredded and purged away into pure air.
Aeneas was standing there in an aura of brilliant light,
Godlike of face and figure: for Venus herself had breathed

[*Lines 551–589*]

18

Beauty upon his head and the roseate sheen of youth on
His manhood and a gallant light into his eyes;
As an artist's hand adds grace to the ivory he works on,
As silver or marble when they're plated with yellow gold.
So then Aeneas addressed the queen, and startling them all
At once began:—

               I am here, before you, the one you look for,
Trojan Aeneas, saved from out the Libyan sea.
O lady, you alone have pitied the tragic ordeal
Of Troy, and now you offer to share your home and city
With us, the remnant of Troy—men utterly spent by
Every disaster on land and sea, deprived of everything.
Dido, we have not the means to repay your goodness, nor have
Any of our kin, wherever they are, scattered over the world.
If spirits there be who look after the good, if indeed just dealing
And minds informed with the right mean anything to heaven,
May God reward you as you deserve! What happy age,
What great parentage was it gave life to the like of you?
So long as rivers run to the sea, and shadows wheel round
The hollows of the hills, and star-flocks browse in the sky,
Your name, your fame, your glory shall perish not from the land
Wherever I am summoned to go.

               He spoke: he stretched out
His right hand to Ilioneus, his friend, and his left to Serestus,
Then to others, brave Gyas and brave Cloanthus.
   Sidonian Dido, amazed first by the man's appearance
Then by the magnitude of his downfall, thus addressed him:—
   O goddess-born, what doom is pursuing you through so many
Hazards? What violent fate casts you on this harsh coast?
Are *you* the famed Aeneas, whom gentle Venus bore
To Trojan Anchises by the waters of Simois?
Indeed I well recollect Teucer coming to Sidon,
An exile from his homeland, and seeking a new kingdom
With the help of Belus: at that time Belus, my father, was sacking
Rich Cyprus and holding the island down in subjection to him.
Now from that time I have known about the fall of Troy,
And known your name, Aeneas, and the kings who led the Greeks.
Even their enemy held the Trojans in high esteem
And claimed blood kinship with the ancient line of Troy.

                    [*Lines 590–626*]

So, gentlemen, do not hesitate to come under my roof.
I too have gone through much; like you, have been roughly handled
By fortune; but now at last it has willed me to settle here.
Being acquainted with grief, I am learning to help the unlucky.

   She spoke: she led Aeneas into the royal palace,
And ordered a thanksgiving service to be held in the gods' temple.
Besides, she sent to his companions on the shore
Twenty bulls, a hundred head of bristle-backed swine,
A hundred fatted lambs together with their ewes,
And the good cheer of the Wine-god.
Within, the palace was being arrayed in all the glitter
Of regal luxury, and a banquet being made ready:
Richly embroidered the hangings of princely purple; a service
Of solid silver on the tables; and golden vessels chased
With the legends of family history—a long lineage of glory
Traced through many heroes right from its earliest source.

   Aeneas, whose love for his son would not allow a moment's
Delay, now sent Achates running down to the ships,
Bade him tell Ascanius the news and return with him,
Aeneas being always thoughtful for his dear son, Ascanius.
They were to bring back also some gifts, which had been salvaged
From Troy's ruins—a robe of stiff golden brocade
And a veil with a pattern of yellow acanthus round its border;
Argive Helen had worn them once, had brought them with her
Out of Mycenae when she eloped to Troy for that lawless
Marriage; they were a marvellous gift from her mother, Leda.
In addition to these, a sceptre which Ilione, the eldest
Daughter of Priam, had carried once, a pearl necklace,
And a double coronet of gold and precious stones.
With this commission Achates hurried down to the ships.

   But Venus was meditating a new and artful scheme,
Which was to substitute, for little Ascanius, Cupid
Changed into his likeness, and let Cupid inflame
The queen with those gifts and set a match to her very marrow:
For Venus felt uneasy about her hospitality
And Tyrian equivocation; the thought of Juno irked her,
Recurring at nightfall. So she talks to her winged Cupid:—

   My son, my only strength, sole agent of my powers,
My son, who laugh at the bolts of giant-killing Jove,

[*Lines 627–665*]

20

To you I come for à favour, petitioning your godhead.
Your own brother, Aeneas, is being tossed about
From shore to shore, a victim of Juno's brutal resentment—
This you know well and often have shared my grief at it.
Now Carthaginian Dido clings to him and delays him
With flattery. I fear the results of kindness inspired by
Juno: she'll not give up, when so much hinges on this.
Her I mean to forestall by rusefully taking the queen's heart
And throwing a cordon of fire round it: no deity
May swerve her if she is mine, possessed by love for Aeneas.
Now listen to my plan, how you can do this thing.
Sent for by his dear father, the royal child, the apple
Of my own eye, makes ready to go to Dido's city,
With gifts for her—things that escaped the sea and the blaze of Troy:
Him I shall hide away, drugged with sleep, in one of
My holy places, on high Cythera or on Idalium,
Lest he gain knowledge of my plot or interfere.
Do you impersonate him, for the space of one night only;
A boy yourself, put on that boy's familiar features,
So that, when Dido takes you joyfully into her lap
There at the banquet table with the wine passing round,
And when she hugs you close and pours sweet kisses upon you,
Then you may secretly fire her heart and inject your magic.
    Cupid obeyed the words of his dear mother: he took off
His wings, and walked rejoicing in the gait of young Ascanius.
But Venus showered a dew of peaceful sleep on the limbs of
Ascanius, snuggled him in her breast, and divinely bore him
Up to Idalian groves, where the tender marjoram puts him
To bed in a cradle of flowers and shade and entrancing fragrance.
And now, as his mother had bade him, Cupid was on his way
Carrying the kingly gifts and delighted to walk with Achates.
When he arrived, the queen had taken her place in the midst
And reclined on her golden couch beneath a magnificent awning.
Aeneas and his Trojan followers now assembled,
Disposed themselves upon the purple-upholstered couches.
Manservants brought round water to wash their hands, and offered
Bread in baskets, and gave out napkins of fine wool.
Within there were fifty maids, whose task it was by rote
To keep up the kitchen fire and a good supply of victuals:

[*Lines 666–704*]

21

A hundred maids and a hundred manservants, all of the same age,
Were there to load the banqueting tables and set the wine cups.
Carthaginians too, great numbers of them, were met
In the festive hall, invited to sit at the painted couches.
They admire the gifts of Aeneas, admire the boy Ascanius—
Or rather the radiant looks and plausible speech of Cupid—
Admire the robe and the veil with its pattern of yellow acanthus.
But above all poor Dido, fated to be destroyed,
Can't slake her soul with gazing, and in the gazing grows
Ever more ardent, moved alike by the boy and the gifts.
Cupid, when he had put his arms round Aeneas' neck
And been embraced, appeasing the love of his feigned father,
Went to the queen. With her eyes, with all her heart she devoured him,
Fondled him oft in her bosom—poor Dido, little she knew
The strength of him who was settling insidiously there. But Cupid,
Obeying his mother, began to efface little by little
The memory of Sychaeus from Dido's mind and tempt her
Disused, long-slumbering heart to awake to a living love.

When first there was a lull in the feast, and a course was removed,
Great bowls of wine were brought to the tables and garlanded.
A rumble of talk went up, the wide hall surged with voices:
The chandeliers that hung from the gold-fretted ceiling
Were lit, and cressets of torches subdued the night with their flames.
The queen now called for a goblet of gold, jewel-encrusted,
And filled it up with wine, a goblet Belus had used
And all his heirs; then did the company fall silent.

Jupiter—yours, they say, are the laws of hospitality—
Grant this be a happy day for the Carthaginians and those
Who come from Troy, a day that our children will remember!
May Bacchus, giver of joy, be here, and bounteous Juno!
And you, my people, bless our feast with friendly hearts!

With these words, Dido poured a libation of wine on the table,
And after the toast was first to touch her lips to the goblet;
Then passed it to Bitias with a challenge, who eagerly drained
The foaming golden cup, left not a drop within it.
Next, other chieftains drank. Then the long-haired Iopas,
A pupil of Atlas, made the hall hum with his golden zither:
He sang of the travelling moon and the sun's manifold labours;
He sang the creation of man and beast, of fire and water;

[*Lines 705–743*]

Arcturus he sang and the rainy Hyades and the twin Bears;
The reason why winter suns race on to dip in the ocean
And what slows down the long nights. Round after round of applause
Came from the Carthaginians; the Trojans followed suit.
Yes, and ill-starred Dido talked on into the small hours,
Talked over many things as she drank deep of love,
Asking over and over again about Priam and Hector,
Asking about the armour the son of Aurora had come in,
The points of Diomed's horses and the stature of great Achilles.
    But no, dear guest, tell us, please tell us from the beginning
The story of Greek stratagems, and how your comrades fell,
And your own wanderings; for now is the seventh summer
That over land and sea you have been widely wandering.

[Lines 744–756]

BOOK II

All fell silent now, and their faces were all attention
When from his place of honour Aeneas began to speak:—
    O queen, the griefs you bid me reopen are inexpressible—
The tale of Troy, a rich and a most tragic empire
Erased by the Greeks; most piteous events I saw with my own eyes
And played no minor part in. What Myrmidon or Thessalian,
What soldier of fell Ulysses could talk about such events
And keep from tears? Besides, the dewy night drops fast
From heaven, and the declining stars invite to sleep.
But if you want so much to know what happened to us
And hear in brief a recital of Troy's last agony,
Although the memory makes me shudder, and shrink from its sadness,
I will attempt it.
                    Broken in war and foiled by fate,
With so many years already slipping away, the Greek staff
Constructed a horse, employing the craft of the goddess Athene—
It was high as a hill, and its ribs were made from planks of pinewood—
To pay for their safe return to Greece, they pretended: this rumour
Got round. But, choosing warriors by lot, they secretly
Put them in on the blind side of the horse, until its vast
And cavernous belly was crammed with a party of armed men.
    In sight of Troy there's an island, a well-known island, Tenedos—
Rich and powerful it was, while Priam's empire stood;
Now, little but a bay, a roadstead unsafe for shipping.
Thither the Greeks sailed out, and hid on its desolate coast.
This was evacuation, we thought—they had sailed for Greece.
So all Troy threw off the chains of her long anguish.
We opened the gates, we enjoyed visiting the Greek camp,
Viewing the derelict positions on the abandoned beaches.
Here the Dolopes camped; there, ferocious Achilles:
Here was beached their navy, and here the battle raged.
Some of us gaped at the gift—so deadly—the Greeks had left for
Minerva, and its stupendous bulk. Thymoetes first,

[*Lines 1–32*]

25

Either from treachery or because Troy's fate now was sealed,
Urged that the horse be brought through the walls and placed in
                                                                    our citadel.

But Capys and all those of sounder views recommended
Hurling it into the sea or setting fire to it, as some
Booby-trap of the Greeks and not to be trusted—or else
Boring holes in its belly to see what might be inside it.
So the rank and file were violently torn between contraries.
Then out in front of them all, hundreds straggling behind him,
In a great temper Laocoon came tearing down from the citadel,
Crying from far:—
                        Citizens, are you all stark mad?
Do you really believe our foes are gone? Do you imagine
Any Greek gift is guileless? Is that your idea of Ulysses?
This thing of wood conceals Greek soldiers, or else it is
A mechanism designed against our walls—to pry into
Our homes and to bear down on the city; sure, some trick
Is there. No, you must never feel safe with the horse, Trojans.
Whatever it is, I distrust the Greeks, even when they are generous.

He spoke: he put forth his strength, and spun his huge great spear
At the flank of the monster, right into its belly's rounded frame.
The spear stuck quivering; the hollow womb of the creature
Grunted at the concussion and rumbled hollowly.
If destiny, if our own will had not been so contrary,
Laocoon would have made us rip open that cache of Greek troops—
There'd still be a Troy—O topless towers, you'd be standing now!

But listen, just at this moment some Trojan shepherds were noisily
Dragging a young man, handcuffed, into our king's presence.
The fellow had quite deliberately put himself in their path;
He was assured in nerve, and prepared one way or the other—
To bring off his underhand scheme (for they did not know him) or
                                                                    meet

A certain death: his game was to prise open Troy for the Greeks.
Eager to stare at him, the youth of Troy came mobbing
All round the man, and vied in jeering at him for being captured.
Now hear how the Greeks tricked us; learn from one case of their
                                                                    wickedness

What every Greek is like.
Well then, he came to a halt—stared at, worried, unarmed—
                                                                    [Lines 33–67]

Stood there, and ran his eyes round the Trojan spectators, and spoke:—
    O god! Is there now a single land or sea to accept me?
What awaits me now at the latter end? Oh, it is hopeless!
I have no foothold at all with the Greeks, and now the Trojans
Are my vindictive foes and they will have my blood.

    His pitiable tones produced a revulsion of feeling; our violence
Was checked: we encouraged him to tell us who he was,
What he could say for himself, and what he relied on in letting
Himself be taken. Finally, he laid aside fear, and spoke:—

    Sir, I will tell you all, of course, come what come may,
And tell you the whole truth. I will not deny that I am a Greek;
This first: if Fortune has cast Sinon for tragedy,
She shall not wantonly shape me into a liar as well.
Some talk has come to your ears, perhaps, about Palamedes
Of the family of Belus, and his bright reputation:
Him the Greeks framed on a monstrous charge of being a traitor,
And put him down to death, an innocent man, because
He was against the war. Now they are sorry they killed him.
Well, I was poor, so my father sent me to be his squire
At an early age, since he was a relative of ours.
While his authority was unshaken, his influence strong in
Our High Command, I too enjoyed a certain distinction
And honour. But when my kinsman, through the spiteful intrigues
                                                    of Ulysses
(I daresay you know the tale), was driven from the land of the living,
I was ruined; I dragged out the days under a cloud, grieving,
Bitter about the downfall of my innocent friend.
I had not the sense to keep quiet: I volunteered that if ever
We won and I got back to Greece, to my home, when a chance
                                                    offered,
I'd take revenge. Those words inspired a vicious hatred.
From then, my fortunes slipped; from then did Ulysses constantly
Persecute me with new slanders, dripping his subtle poison
Into the popular ear, and conspire to find allies against me.
Nor did he rest until, with Calchas under his influence—
But what's the point, I ask you, going on with the sorry tale
And delaying you, if you think all Greeks are alike, and merely
To be one condemns me? Take your long-due reprisal. Ulysses
Would love it: the sons of Atreus would pay you handsomely for it.
    [*Lines 68–104*]

27

Then of course we were all the more eager to find out the whole
of his story—
Greek cunning, evil on such a scale, being as yet beyond us.
So he went on, trembling, and spoke with pretended emotion:—
Often, sick of the way the war dragged on, the Greeks
Longed to withdraw from Troy, to sail home and be shut of fighting.
If only they'd done it! But always a stormy, vicious mood
Of the sea intervened and the South wind frightened them off sailing.
Especially when that horse, that fabric of maple, already
Was standing here, did the whole sky reverberate with storm clouds.
In this quandary, we sent Eurypylus to enquire
Of Phoebus' oracle; who brought back this message of gloom from
the shrine:—
With human sacrifice, O Greeks, with a young girl's blood
Did you appease the winds when first you sailed to Troy:
With human blood, with a Greek life, you must make sacrifice
If you're to get safe home. The words went round: our people's
Spirits were paralysed; an icy shuddering coursed through
Their bones—whom would fate fix on? whom does Apollo require?
At this stage Ulysses made a great scene, pulling the seer
Calchas into our midst, pestering him to tell us
The god's will. Yes, and already many surmised that I was
That heartless schemer's victim, and silently saw what was coming.
For ten days Calchas was dumb, stayed in retreat, and would not
Name or commit to death anyone by his utterance.
But at long last, as Ulysses got ever more importunate,
According to plan he broke silence and smelt me out for the altar.
They all approved: what each had feared for himself, was easy
To tolerate when it became the death of this one poor scapegoat.
And now the hideous day was here; the last rites made ready
For me—the salted meal, the headband to go round my temples.
I dodged away then from death, I confess it; I broke prison,
And lay all night concealed in the mud of a lake, among reeds,
Giving them time to sail, on the chance that indeed they would sail.
No more hope have I now of seeing the old country, seeing
My little sons or the father I yearn for: on them the Greeks
Maybe will exact reprisals because of my escape
And make them pay, poor things, with their life for what I have done.
Yet by the gods I beg you, by the high powers that are witness

[*Lines 105–141*]

28

To Truth, by Fidelity—if anywhere upon earth
She still can be found inviolate—I beg you to pity so dreadful
An ordeal, pity one who has too much to bear.
   We gave him his life for those tears: they even aroused our
                                        compassion.
Priam himself at once ordered the handcuffs, the cramping
Chains to be struck off the fellow, and spoke him a friendly word:—
   Whoever you are, from now on give up the Greeks, you are clear
                                          of them:
Be one of us, and answer these questions of mine truthfully.
Why did they build this huge monster of a horse? Who advised it?
Is their object religious? or was it to be some engine of war?
   So Priam spoke. Sinon, well up in the Greek art of trickery,
Raised to heaven his hands, free of the fetters, crying:—
   You everlasting lights, and your inviolate deity,
I call you to witness—the altar too, and the damnable knife
Which I escaped, and the holy headband I wore to be sacrificed!
No sin that I should relax the solemn code of the Greeks;
No sin to loathe them, or to disclose their secrets, if any
There are: I can have no guilt at law in my own land.
Only abide by your promise, Trojans, and with your preserver
Keep faith, if my words prove true and give good value for sparing me.
   All the hope of the Greeks, their assurance in starting the war,
Was sustained by the backing of Pallas Athene. But when the godless
Diomed and that master-craftsman of crime, Ulysses,
Set out to steal Troy's luck, Athene's image, away from
Her holy place, massacred the sentries high on the citadel,
Snatched up the sacred image, and dared to lay their bloodstained
Hands on her virginal headband—from that day forth, the hopes
Of the Greeks were caught in an undertow and carried away, their
                                          strength
Was shattered, for the goddess hardened her heart against them.
Unmistakeable were the signs of anger she gave us.
The image was hardly set up in our camp, when its eyes glared
Balefully glittering fire, salt sweat broke out all over it,
And thrice—oh, supernatural!—did the statue, untouched, dart forth
From her base, the spear and shield she carried quivering.
Straightaway, Calchas pronounced we must dare the sea and be gone,
For Troy would never now be destroyed by Greek weapons
   [*Lines 142–177*]

29

Unless we sailed back home to fetch new luck, and returned with
The gods' blessing as when we first sailed here in our fine ships.
So at this moment they're running free towards Mycenae
To get fresh force and the gods on their side again: they'll be back
Unexpectedly over the sea. So Calchas interprets the omens.
Thus advised, they built this horse to dispel the curse of
Guilt for stealing Athene's image and wounding her godhead.
But Calchas bade them build the horse of enormous size
With strong oak planks, a real sky-scraping monster, so that
It could not get through your gates or be towed within the walls,
And thus become your guardian, serving the old cult.
For if your hands had outraged this offering to Minerva,
It would be quite disastrous (may the omen sooner recoil
On its own prophet!) for Priam's rule and for the Trojans:
But if your hands should have got the horse up into the city,
Then would you carry Asia in war right up to the Grecian
Strongholds; such is the fate that is reserved for our children.

   Such was the artful, treacherous perjury Sinon used
To impose on us. We were tricked by cunning and crocodile tears—
We whom neither Diomed nor Larissaean Achilles
Could conquer, not in ten years, not with a thousand warships.
Just then another event, the most alarming yet,
Befell us wretches, muddling still further our hooded minds.
Laocoon, whom we'd elected by lot as Neptune's priest,
Was sacrificing a great bull at the official altar,
When over the tranquil deep, from Tenedos, we saw—
Telling it makes me shudder—twin snakes with immense coils
Thrusting the sea and together streaking towards the shore:
Rampant they were among the waves, their blood-red crests
Reared up over the water; the rest of them slithered along
The surface, coil after coil sinuously trailing behind them.
We heard a hiss of salt spray. Next, they were on dry land,
In the same field—a glare and blaze of bloodshot eyes,
Tongues flickering like flame from their mouths, and the mouths
                                                    hissing.

Our blood drained away at the sight; we broke and ran. The serpents
Went straight for Laocoon. First, each snake knotted itself
Round the body of one of Laocoon's small sons, hugging him tight
In its coils, and cropped the piteous flesh with its fangs. Next thing,

[*Lines 178–215*]

30

They fastened upon Laocoon, as he hurried, weapon in hand,
To help the boys, and lashed him up in their giant whorls.
With a double grip round his waist and his neck, the scaly creatures
Embrace him, their heads and throats powerfully poised above him.
All the while his hands are struggling to break their knots,
His priestly headband is spattered with blood and pitchy venom;
All the while, his appalling cries go up to heaven—
A bellowing, such as you hear when a wounded bull escapes from
The altar, after it's shrugged off an ill-aimed blow at its neck.
But now the twin monsters are gliding away and escaping towards
The shrine of relentless Minerva, high up on our citadel,
Disappearing behind the round of the goddess' shield, at her feet there.
Then, my god! a strange panic crept into our people's fluttering
Hearts: they argued Laocoon had got what he deserved
For the crime, the sacrilege of throwing his spear at the wooden
Horse and so profaning its holiness with the stroke.
"Bring the horse to Minerva's shrine! Pray for her goodwill!"
All of our people shouted.
We cut into our walls, laid open the heart of the city.
Everyone set about the task: we inserted rollers
Under its hooves, put hawsers of hemp around its neck,
And strained. The disastrous engine was jockeyed over our walls,
An army in its womb. Boys and unmarried maidens
Escorted it, singing psalms, joyfully gripping the traces.
The menace mounts, comes trundling into the city centre.
O, my country! O Ilium, home of the gods! O Troy town,
Famous through war! Four times the monster stopped at entrance,
And every time it stopped the accoutrements clanged in its belly.
Yet we persevered, with never a thought—we were madly blind—
Until we had lodged the ominous thing in our holy place.
Then, to cap all, Cassandra opened her mouth for prophecy—
She whom her god had doomed to be never believed by the Trojans.
But we poor fools, whose very last day it was, festooned
The shrines of the gods with holiday foliage all over the city.

  So now the sky rolled round, and night raced up from the ocean
Voluminously shrouding the earth and heaven's vault
And the villainous scheme of the Greeks. Not a sound from the
                                                    Trojans, supine

[*Lines 216–252*]

31

Along the walls, tired out, in the embrace of sleep.
And now the main Greek army was moving from Tenedos
In fleet formation, under the favouring silences
Of a quiet moon, towards the coast they knew so well.
Their leading galley had signalled with flame: Sinon, protected
By fate's injustice, stealthily unlocked the wooden horse
And let the Greeks out from its belly. The horse disgorged, the men
Burst revelling forth from its hollow flank into the fresh air—
Thessander and Sthenelus in the lead, with Ulysses the terrible,
Sliding down a rope they had lowered—Acamas, Thoas,
Neoptolemus son of Peleus, Machaon and Menelaus,
And Epeus—the man who had actually built the clever contraption.
They broke out over a city drowned in drunken sleep;
They killed the sentries and then threw open the gates, admitting
Their main body, and joined in the pre-arranged plan of attack.

   It was the hour when worn-out men begin to get
Some rest, and by god's grace genial sleep steals over them.
I dreamt, I seemed to behold our Hector standing before me,
Most woebegone and shedding great tears, just as he'd looked once
In death, after being dragged by the chariot, black with the dirt
And blood, his swollen feet pierced where the thongs had been
                                                        threaded.
Ah, god! what a sight he was! how terribly changed from the Hector
Who once came back arrayed in the armour of Achilles,
Who came back from bombarding the Greek navy with fire!
Now his beard is matted, clotted with blood his hair,
He exhibits the many wounds received while defending his country
In combat around the walls. I too am weeping. Unasked, I
Address him in my dream, force out these sorrowful words:—

   O light of Troy! O surest hope of the Trojans! What has
Been keeping you so long? What shores do you come from, Hector?
Long have we looked for you: how happily now we behold you—
We whom the death of many friends, the manifold ordeal
Of city and folk have exhausted! But why is your face, serene once,
So shamefully disfigured? Why do I see these wounds?

   He gave no heed at all to these futile questions of mine,
But heaving a heavy sigh from the depth of his heart, spoke out:—

   Goddess-born, you must go, you must save yourself from these
                                                        flames.

[*Lines 253–289*]

32

The enemy's within the gates. Troy's tower is falling, falling.
You owe no more to your country or Priam: if strong right hands
Could save our town, this hand of mine would have saved it long ago.
Her holy things, her home-gods Troy commends to your keeping:
Take these as partners in your fate, for these search out
The walls you are destined to build after long roaming the seaways.

    He spoke, he picked up the holy headbands, the puissant Vesta
And her undying fire from out the temple sanctuary.

    Meantime, Troy was shaken through and through by her last pangs—
Yes, more and more, although the house of my father, Anchises,
Lay far back from the street, detached, and screened by trees,
The sounds of death came clearly, the battle alarum swelled.
I shook myself out of sleep, and clambering onto the ridge
Of the roof, I stood up there, straining my ears to listen.
You know how it is when southerly gales are fanning a fire through
A cornfield, or when a torrent in spate with mountain water
Smears flat the fields, flattens the crops which the oxen have worked for,
Drags forests down in its course—how then a shepherd, perched on
A rock, hearing the noise, is bemused and quite at a loss.
Now what I saw in my dream came true, and the Greeks' treachery
Was plain to behold. Deiophobus' house flared up and hugely
Collapsed; the house of Ucalegon, next door, was blazing:
You could see the flames reflected all over the Sigean straits.
Everywhere rose the shouting of men, the braying of trumpets.
Madly I snatch up my arms, beyond thinking how best to employ
                                                          them;
Only I'm wild to rally some fighters and counter-attack
To relieve the citadel: blind rage and desperation
Drive me; one thought comes—that death in battle is a fine thing.

    But look, Panthus arrives, having got through the Greek barrage—
Panthus, the son of Othrys, Apollo's priest at the citadel:
Holding the hallows, his conquered divinities, and leading
His little grandson, he frantically has made his way to my doorstep.
Where is the core of the fighting? What is our rallying-point?
I had hardly spoken these words when he, with a sob, replied:—

    The very last day has come, the hour inevitable
For Troy. We Trojans, with Ilium and all its Teucrian glory,
Are things of the past; for cruel Jove has quite gone over
To the Greeks: the city's on fire; the Greeks are masters here.
    [*Lines 290–327*]

The towering horse which stands in the heart of the city spilt out
Armed men: and flushed with triumph, Sinon is stirring the blaze
Everywhere. There are Greeks packing the opened gates—
All who ever came in their thousands from Mycenae:
Wherever the roads are narrow, they're blocked by Greek detachments.
A front of steel stands there, the sword-points glitter, the swords
Are bared to kill. The sentries guarding our gates could hardly
Begin to resist or put up a fight in the blinding darkness.
    So Panthus spoke, revealing the will of heaven. His words
Drove me towards the burning, the fighting. I heard the call of
War's sombre Fury—a dull roar, and shouts flung up to heaven.
Now Rhipeus and champion Epytus, looming up in the moonlight,
Hypanis and Dymas were there to reinforce me
And fell in at my side, together with young Coroebus,
Son of Mygdon. Coroebus, it happened, had come to Troy
But recently, impelled by a crazy love for Cassandra,
Bringing a son-in-law's aid to Priam and the Trojans—
Hard luck that he did not listen to his prophetic Cassandra's
Warnings.
Well, when I saw them in close formation and good shape for battle,
I spoke to inspire them further. Men! dear hearts so vainly
Valiant! If you are set on following one who intends
To see the business through to the end, this is the picture:—
The gods, by whose grace our kingdom once stood, have washed
                                                    their hands of us,
Abandoning shrine and altar; the city you would relieve
Is ablaze: let us die, let us charge into the battle's heart!
Losers have one salvation—to give up all hope of salvation.
So I fired my men with the fury of desperation. Then, just like
Marauding wolves in a black fog, at a time when their rabid hunger
Has sent them blindly prowling, and the cubs they have left are waiting
At home, their gullets parched, so through the enemy barrage
We went as to certain death, we steadily made for the heart of
The city, and were engulfed in the black night's ambient shade.
That night!—what words can render its deaths and its disaster?
What tears can rise to the level of all that was suffered then?
An ancient city is falling, after long years of power:
So many motionless bodies prostrated everywhere
Along the streets, in the houses, on the gods' holy thresholds.

[*Lines 328–365*]

Not the Trojans alone paid their account in blood:
There were times when courage returned even though we knew we
were beaten,
And then the conquering Greeks fell. All over the town you saw
Heart-rending agony, panic, and every shape of death.

The first to cross our path was Androgeos, with a fair-sized
Body of Greeks around him: he thought, in his ignorance,
We were friends, and went so far as to hail us with comradely
words:—

Get going, men! Whatever has kept you so long? What do you
Mean by this slackness? The rest of the Greeks have been burning and
sacking
Ilium; and here are you only just turned up from the ships.

He spoke; and at once—for he got no satisfactory answer—
It dawned on him that the men he'd fallen in with were hostile.
Startled, he brought up sharp, checked speech, winced away.
Like one who, forcing his way through sharp briars, accidentally
Has trod on a snake, and in sudden panic shudders away from
Its angrily-rearing head, its gunmetal neck puffed out—
Androgeos, unnerved at the sight of us, made to retreat.
We went for him and his party, surrounded them; and since
They had no local knowledge and were paralysed with fear,
Picked them off one by one. So fortune favoured our first move.
Flown with success and in high spirits, Coroebus exclaimed:—

Comrades, let's follow up where fortune has first shown us
A way to survival, and play our luck while it is good!
Change shields with these dead Greeks, put on their badges and flashes!
Craft or courage—who cares, when an enemy has to be beaten?
The Greeks themselves shall equip us.
So saying, he put on
Androgeos' plumed helmet, his shield with its fine heraldic
Device, and fitted onto his side the Argive sword.
Rhipeus, and Dymas too, and all our warriors gleefully
Followed suit, each arming himself from the spoils just taken.
Then we went on through the press of the Greeks, under false favours
Of alien gods. Many a sharp engagement we fought
In the blindfold night, and many a Greek we despatched to Hades.
Some broke and ran for the ships, ran for the sure protection
The beaches gave: one lot, driven by sheer cowardice,

[*Lines 366–400*]

35

Climbed the horse again and returned to the womb they had come
from.
Ah well, there's no trusting the gods for anything, once they're
against you!—
Over there was Priam's daughter, Cassandra, her hair flying,
Being dragged away from Minerva's house, from its very sanctuary,
Her burning eyes uplifted to heaven, but in vain—
Her eyes, for she could not lift her delicate palms, they were pinioned.
Coroebus found this sight too much: in a passion of rage
He bores right into the thick of the foe; he wants to be killed.
We followed him, all of us, attacking in close order.
Now, we were first mown down by the fire of our own side, shooting
From the high temple roof; a deplorable slaughter began
Through mistaken identity—our Greek equipment and crests.
Next, the Greeks rallied, shouting with rage at the attempt to
Rescue Cassandra: they went for us—Ajax most vindictively,
And the two sons of Atreus, with the whole battalion of Dolopes:
So, when a hurricane breaks, you may get a clash and a tussle
Of winds—the West, the South, and the East wind roughriding
His orient steeds: then forests whine, and Nereus in wild rage
Churns the sea with his trident and raises it mountains-high.
More Greeks appeared now—the ones whom, in the confusing darkness
Of night, our ruse had routed and stampeded over the town.
These were the first to recognise our shields, our fraudulent weapons;
They noticed, too, the foreign tongue which gave us away.
Well, this was it. We were crushed by weight of numbers. Coroebus
Went down to Peneleus' sword at the altar of the war-puissant
Goddess; then Rhipeus fell, he who of all the Trojans
Was most fair-minded, the one who was most regardful of justice:
God's ways are inscrutable. Now Hypanis fell and Dymas
Shot by their own friends. And Panthus—not all his goodness
Nor the headband he wore as Apollo's priest saved him from death.
O ashes of Ilium! O flames that my world died in!
I call you to witness that I, at your setting, was facing the Greeks' fire,
Evading no danger in combat: if fate had meant me to die then,
I'd have earned that death by the way I fought. But soon myself,
Iphitus and Pelias were drawn away—Iphitus
Being old, and Pelias slowed down by a wound Ulysses had given
him—

[*Lines 401–436*]

36

Urgently summoned by war-cries we heard from the palace of Priam.
Here we beheld so tremendous a struggle as made it seem that
Nowhere else in the city could men be fighting and dying—
A bitter battle, the Greeks trying to scale the walls
And ramming a compact wedge of shields at the door they assaulted.
They advance ladders to the walls; hard by the very doorposts
They climb the rungs, with left hands holding their shields above them
To ward off missiles, and grasping the battlements with their right
hands.

The Trojans for their part are stripping the turrets and roof-tops,
Ready, since now the end is in sight, to use the material
For missiles, to put up a stern defence though death is upon them:
Yes, they throw down even the gilded beams, the pride of
Their ancestors; while others cluster to guard the doors
Below with a thick-set hedge of naked swords. Our courage
Rekindled now. We would seek to succour the king's palace,
Reinforce the defenders and lend our strength to the conquered.

    There was a door, a secret entrance by which you went
From one block to another, a postern out of the way
Behind the palace: by this, while our empire stood, Andromache—
Poor soul—would often come unattended to visit her husband's
Parents, bringing her child, Astyanax, to his grandsire.
Using this door, I got out onto the rooftop whence
The luckless Trojans were raining missiles, all to no purpose.
A tower stood over the sheer of the wall, its apex soaring
Skyward: this tower commanded a long-familiar prospect
Across Troyland to the Greek ships and the Achaean lines.
This we attacked with crowbars all round, where the weak joints of
Its flooring offered a purchase, prised it off from its deep bed
And pushed hard at it: the tower tottered and fell full length
With a sudden crash, bursting all over the massed attackers.
But still, others came on; still it rained spears and arrows
And stones and every missile unceasingly . . .

    Right on the very threshold of the entrance hall was Pyrrhus
In all his insolent glory, aglitter with bronze accoutrements.
So a snake comes out, full fed on malignant herbs—a snake
Which winter has kept underground sullenly brewing its poison,
But now it has sloughed its old skin, is young again and glistening;
It coils along on its slithering belly, and lifts to the sunlight

[*Lines 437–474*]

37

Its vertical throat and flickers a tongue like forked lightning.
With Pyrrhus were giant Periphas, and Achilles' old charioteer
Automedon, now a squire, and all the Scyrian brigade,
Assaulting the palace and tossing firebrands up at its roof.
Pyrrhus himself, in the lead, seized an axe, and battering the stout door
Smashed through it, and wrenched it away from its hinges, though
it was strengthened
With bronze: now he had hewed out a panel, and made a hole
In the tough wood, opening up a gap the size of a window.
Through this they are able to see the interior, the long gallery;
The private rooms of Priam and Troy's old kings are exposed,
And they see the armed defenders packing the doorway within.
    Inside the palace, all was confusion, groans, agony.
The echoing halls resounded through and through with the keening
Of women, whose wails and shrieks beat at the golden stars.
Mothers, distracted with fear, were wandering about the palace,
Clinging tight to its doorposts and kissing them goodbye.
Pyrrhus attacks, with his father's dash: neither the bolts
Nor the guards have the strength to withstand it: stroke upon stroke,
a ram
Weakens the door, till it's torn away from its hinges and falls in.
Brute force has made a breach; the Greeks go storming through,
Massacre those in their way, and the place overflows with soldiery.
More violent it was than when, banks broken, a foaming river
Pours through: the dykes have gone down to the thrust of the water,
and now
In a mass it raves forth over the fields, swirling the herds and
Their shippons across the plain. I had to watch Pyrrhus crazed with
Blood-lust, and the brothers Atrides, there on the threshold,
Hecuba with her hundred princesses, and Priam sullying
All over with blood the altar whose fire he had consecrated.
Those fifty bridal rooms, that promised a rich posterity—
Fallen flat were their doors, proudly adorned with eastern
Gold and with spoils. Wherever there was no fire, the Greeks were.
    I daresay you are wondering what happened to Priam then.
Once he had seen how the captured city was faring, seen
His doors were hacked away and the enemy deep in the palace,
Priam, though tremulous with old age, donned the armour
He had not worn for years—a pathetic gesture—strapped on

[*Lines 475–510*]

38

His useless sword, and was moving deathwards against the foe.
In the central court, beneath the uncovered sweep of the sky,
Stood a massive altar, and near it a very old laurel tree
Leaned over the altar, enfolding the home-gods with its shade.
Here Hecuba and her daughters, like a flock of doves dashed down
By a black storm, were sitting huddled about the altars
That would not protect them, and clasping the images of the gods.
Now, when she saw Priam dressed up in his youthful armour,
She cried:—

        Oh, my poor husband, what fatal intention has made you
Take up arms like this? Where are you running? Our present
Predicament is beyond such aid. Weapons won't save us,
Nor would they save us even if my own Hector was here now.
Please come back, over here: this altar shall guard us all,
Or else we will die together.

  This did she say, and taking
The old king to her, made him sit down in sanctuary.

  But picture it, Priam's son, Polites, had just avoided
A death-blow from Pyrrhus, and wounded was running the enemy
                                   gauntlet,
Running away down the long colonnades and across the great hall
Alone. Pyrrhus hotly pursued him, always about to strike,
Each moment seeming to have him, so close did the spearpoint come.
Just when Polites emerged before his parents' eyes,
He fell, and his life ebbed out in a deep river of blood.
Priam, though death now ringed him round, could not be passive,
Could not refrain from uttering his indignation. He cried:—

  Hear me, you criminal! If there is any justice in heaven,
Any eye for such things, may the gods pay you the due reward
And unstintingly show their gratitude for this most monstrous crime
You have committed—making me witness my son's death,
Fouling a father's eyes like this with the sight of murder!
You are poles apart from Achilles—your father, you lyingly claim.
He treated me differently far, though I was his foe; he respected
A suppliant's rights, gave up the bloodless remains of Hector
For burial, and gave me safe conduct back to my city.

  So saying, the old man flung his weapon, but harmlessly—
No strength behind it: a clang when the shield of Pyrrhus parried it,
And then the spear was dangling impotently from its centre.

  [*Lines 511–546*]

Pyrrhus replied:—

        All right, you shall go and carry a message
To my father Achilles. Remember to tell him how soft a milksop
His son has become, and what shocking deeds he has committed.
Now die!

        Even as he spoke, he dragged the old man, trembling,
And sliding in the pool of his son's blood, right to the altar;
Twined Priam's hair in his left hand, raised with his right the flashing
Sword, and sank it up to the hilt between his ribs.
Such was Priam's end, the close decreed by destiny—
That in his dying hour he should see Troy blazing, falling—
His Troy which boasted once such a wealth of lands and subjects,
The mistress of Asia once. A great trunk lies on the shore,
A head torn from the shoulders, a body without a name.

  Then first the full horror of it all was borne in upon me. I stood
In a daze: the picture of my dear father came to mind,
As I watched king Priam, a man of the same age, cruelly wounded,
Gasping his life away; I pictured my Creusa
Deserted, my home pillaged, and the fate of my little Ascanius.
I glanced round, wishing to see what force of men was left me.
All were gone: utter exhaustion and sickness of heart
Had made them drop from the roof to the ground or into the flames.

  Yes, I was now the one man left of my party. But just then,
Hugging close to the threshold of Vesta, speechlessly hiding there,
I noticed the daughter of Tyndareus, Helen. The blaze lit up
The whole scene as I wandered, peering this way and that.
Helen, the scourge of Troy and her own land alike,
In dread anticipation of Trojan wrath at Troy's
Downfall, of Greek revenge, of her cuckolded husband's anger,—
Helen, that hateful creature, was crouched by the altar, in hiding.
A fire broke out in my heart, a passion of rage to avenge
My country's fall and punish her crime by a crime upon her.
Was she going to get away with it? see Sparta again and her homeland?
Return as a queen, in triumph? be once more reunited
With husband, home, parents and children? use our Trojan
Ladies for her attendants and Trojan men for slaves?—
All this, with Priam put to the sword, and Troy in ashes,
And Troy's shore time and again bathed in a sweat of blood?
Not so, I said. For although to kill a woman earns one

[*Lines 547–583*]

40

No fame, and victory over a female wins no decorations,
I shall be praised for stamping out an iniquity, punishing
One who so richly deserves it; and I shall enjoy fulfilling
My soul with a flame of vengeance, appeasing my people's ashes.
Such were my thoughts, the insensate fury that drove me onward,
When to my view—and never before had I seen her so clear—
My gentle mother appeared: all glowing with light she came
Through the gloom, a goddess manifest, oh, high and handsome as
The heaven-dwellers know her. She laid a hand on mine,
Restraining me, then shaped these words with her rosy lips:—

My son, what anguish spurs you to this ungoverned rage?
What madness has driven all thought for love out of your heart?
Will you not first find out if your aged father, Anchises,
Is where you left him, and whether your wife, Creusa, be still
Alive, and little Ascanius? A whole Greek army is surging
Round them on every side, and but for my guardian care
The flames would have got them by now, the fell sword drained
their blood.

It is not the beauty of hated Helen, it is not Paris,
Though you hold him to blame—the gods, the gods, I tell you, are
hostile,
It's they who have undermined Troy's power and sent it tumbling.
Look! I shall wipe away the cloud which now occludes
And dulls your mortal vision, even as you gaze, the dank mist
Befogging you. Fear not to do whatever your mother
Tells you, and willingly be guided by me. Now, look at
That litter of masonry there, huge blocks, stone torn from stone,
And the dust-laden smoke billowing up from the debris—
It's Neptune's work: he gores and tosses with his great trident
The walls, the foundations, until the whole city is disembowelled.
Look over there! At the Scaean gate, panoplied Juno
Heads the shock-troops, and in a vindictive fury calls up
Her allies from the ships.
Look round! See Pallas Athene planted upon the citadel—
The storm-cloud is lurid about her, the Gorgon glares from her shield.
Jove supplies fresh courage and a victorious strength
To the Greeks, inciting the gods against the Trojan cause.
Escape then, while you may, my son, and end this ordeal.
I shall be with you, seeing you safe to your father's house.

[*Lines 584–620*]

41

She had spoken; and now she was vanished into the night's thick
darkness.

Terrible shapes loom up, set against Troy, the shapes of
Heaven's transcendent will.

   Then indeed I saw that all Ilium was subsiding
Into the flames, and Neptune's Troy quite overthrown.
Imagine a veteran ash-tree upon some mountain top,
When woodsmen are working to fell it, with blow upon blow of
their axes

Vigorously hacking: the tree seems always about to fall;
It nods, and the topmost leaves are shivered by each concussion:
Little by little their blows master it, till at last
With a great groan it snaps off and falls full length on the hillside.
Well, I went down from the roof, and divinely guided pressed on
Through flame and foe: the weapons gave way, the flames drew back
for me.

   But when I reached the door of my father's house, the ancestral
Home, my father Anchises, whom first I looked for, wishing
To get him away first to the safety of the hills—Anchises
Flatly refused to prolong his life, now Troy was finished,
Or to endure exile. He said:—
O you, whose blood
Is in the prime, who are strong enough to stand on your own feet,
Do you try for escape!
But as for me, if the gods had meant me to go on living,
They'd have preserved this place. Enough, more than enough
To have seen Troy ruined once and once have survived her capture.
Bid me farewell and leave, O leave this body of mine
Where it is! I shall find death in action. The foe will slay me
For pity, or spoils. And to bury me—that will not cost them much.
For years now I have been lingering, obnoxious to heaven and useless
To mankind, ever since the ruler of gods and men
Blasted me with the searing breath of his levin-flash.

   So he went on saying. We could not shift him, although
We implored him with floods of tears—I, and my wife Creusa,
Ascanius and the whole household—not to ruin everything,
Not to add his weight to the doom which was heavy upon us.
He refused: obstinately he clung to his house and his purpose.
Once again I am moved to fight, yearning for death in my misery,
[Lines 621–655]

42

Since neither luck nor forethought offered a way out now.
Father, I said, did you really think I could run away
And leave you? Did so shameful a notion escape your lips?
If it's the will of heaven that nothing be left of our city,
And if your mind's made up that you and your family
Shall perish, as well as Troy, a door to that death is wide open:
Pyrrhus is coming, all bathed in Priam's blood; he loves
Butchering sons in front of their fathers, fathers at the altar.
Was it for this, dear mother, you fetched me through fire and steel,—
That I should witness the enemy right in our house, witness
Ascanius and my father and my Creusa beside them
Lying slaughtered here in one another's blood?
To arms, my men! To arms! Their last hour calls the conquered.
Send me back to the Greeks! Let me go back and renew
The fight! It must never be said we died unavenged this day!

   My sword was at my side again; I was fitting my left arm
Through the strap of my shield, and on my way out of the house,
When Creusa clung to me at the door, gripping my ankles,
Holding little Ascanius up to his father, and crying:—
   If it's deathwards you go, take us with you! O take us, and come
                                                    what may!
But if your experience tells you that something is to be gained by
Fighting, protect this house first! Think what you're leaving us to—
Ascanius, your father, and me who loved to be called your wife once!
   Loudly she cried these words, and filled the house with her crying.
Just then a miracle happened, a wonderful miracle.
Imagine it!—our hands and our sad eyes were upon
Ascanius, when we beheld a feathery tongue of flame
Luminously alight on his head, licking the soft curls
With fire that harmed them not, and playing about his temples.
Anxious, in great alarm, his mother and I hurried to
Beat out, put out with water, that holy blaze on his hair.
But father Anchises, greatly heartened, lifted his eyes up,
Stretched up his hands to heaven, with words of prayer, saying:—
   O god omnipotent, if any prayers can sway you,
Give ear to mine. One thing I ask: if by our goodness
We have deserved it, grant your aid, confirm this omen!
   The old man had hardly spoken when from our left hand came
A sudden crash of thunder, and a shooting star slid down
   [*Lines 656–693*]

43

The sky's dark face, drawing a trail of light behind it.
We watched that star as it glided high over the palace roof,
And blazing a path, buried its brightness deep in the woods of
Ida; when it was gone, it left in its wake a long furrow
Of light, and a sulphurous smoke spread widely over the terrain.
That did convince my father. He drew himself upright,
Addressed the gods above, and worshipped the heaven-sent star:—
    No more, no more lingering! I follow, I'm there, where you guide
                                                                    me!

Gods of our fathers, guard this family, guard my grandson!
This sign is yours, and Troy is still in your heavenly keeping.
Yea, I consent. I refuse no longer, my son, to go with you.
    He had spoken; and now more clearly over the town the fire's roar
Was heard, and nearer rolled the tide of its conflagration.
Quick, then, dear father, I said, climb onto my back, and I will
Carry you on my shoulders—that's a burden will not be burdensome.
However things turn out, at least we shall share one danger,
One way of safety, both of us. Let little Ascanius walk
Beside me, and Creusa follow my steps at a distance.
And you, servants, pay careful attention to what I shall tell you.
As you go out of the city, you come to a mound with an ancient
Temple of Ceres upon it, secluded; nearby, an old cypress
Stands, which for many years our fathers preserved in reverence.
Let this be our rendezvous: we'll get there by different routes.
Do you, my father, carry the sacred relics and home-gods:
Sinful for me to touch them, when I have just withdrawn
From battle, with blood on my hands, until in running water
I am purified.
    With these words, I laid the pelt of a tawny lion
For covering over my broad shoulders and bowed neck;
Then stooped to lift my burden: Ascanius twined his fingers
In mine, hurrying to keep up with his father's longer stride.
My wife came on behind. We fared on, hugging the shadows.
I, who just now had faced the enemy volleys, the Greeks'
Concentrated attack, without turning a hair—I was scared by
Every breeze, alarmed by every sound, so strung up
Was I with anxiety for my burden and my companion.
    And now I was nearing the gates and thinking that we had made it,
When on a sudden there came to my ears the sound of many

[*Lines 694–731*]

44

Footsteps—or so it seemed. Then, peering into the gloom,
My father exclaimed:—
                    Run! They're upon us! Run, Aeneas!
I can see the shine of their shields and the bronze accoutrements
                                              winking.
    Well, I panicked. My wits were fuddled, were snatched away
By some malignant prompting. For even as I darted off
Into byways, off my course among streets I knew not—O god,
The anguish of it!—my wife Creusa, fate took her—did she
Stop there? or lose her way? Did she sink down in exhaustion?
We never knew. We never set eyes on her again.
I did not look back for the lost one, I did not give her a thought
Until we had reached the mound, the ancient, hallowed place
Of Ceres. Here at last, when all were assembled, one was
Missing, one had denied husband and son her company.
I was out of my mind. What mortal, what god did I not curse?
In all the city's ruin what bitterer thing did I see?
Commending Ascanius, Anchises and the Teucrian home-gods
To my friends' care, and hiding them deep in the hollow vale,
I put on my shining armour, I made for the city once more.
To reconstruct those events, to retrace our path through Troy
And expose my life to its perils again—that was my purpose.

    For a start, I returned to the shadowed gate in the city wall
By which I had sallied forth, noting my tracks and following them
Back through the night, straining my eyes to scan them. Everywhere
Dread and the sheer silence reduced my courage to nothing.
Next, I went home, in case—just on the chance that she might have
Gone there. The Greeks had broken in, the whole house was occupied.
That instant, gluttonous fire was fanned by the draught right up to
The roof top; flames burst out there, the blast of the heat roared
                                              skywards.
I went on, to revisit Priam's house and the citadel.
Here, in the empty colonnades of Juno's sanctuary,
Phoenix and fell Ulysses were engaged on the duty allotted them,
Guarding the loot. To this point from all over Troy had plunder,
Salvaged from burning shrines, been brought: tables of gods,
Solid gold bowls and looted vestments were being piled up here
In heaps. Children and frightened mothers were standing about
In a long queue.
    [*Lines 732–767*]

45

I dared (you will hardly believe it) to call out loud through the gloom
And fill the streets with shouting: sadly I cried "Creusa!"—
Called to her over and over again, but it was no good.
As I roamed on that endless, frenzied search through the city buildings,
There appeared before my eyes a piteous phantom, yes,
The very ghost of Creusa—a figure larger than life.
I was appalled: my hair stood on end, and my voice stuck
In my throat. It was she who spoke then, and thus relieved my pain:—
    Darling husband, it's madness of you to indulge your grief
Like this. These happenings are part of the divine
Purpose. It was not written that you should bring Creusa
Away with you; the great ruler of heaven does not allow it.
For you, long exile is destined, broad tracts of sea to be furrowed;
Then you will reach Hesperia, where Lydian Tiber flows
Gently through a land in good heart, and good men live.
There, your affairs will prosper; a kingdom, a royal bride
Await you. No more tears now for your heart's love, Creusa:
I shall not see the proud halls of the Myrmidons or Dolopes,
Nor work as a slave for Greek women—I, who am Dardan
And daughter-in-law to the goddess Venus.
No, the great Mother of the gods is going to keep me here.
Good-bye, Aeneas. Cherish our love in the son it gave us.
    With these words, though I wept and had so much to say
To her, she left me, fading out into thin air.
Three times I tried to put my arms round her neck, and three times
The phantom slipped my hands, my vain embrace: it was like
Grasping a wisp of wind or the wings of a fleeting dream.
So in the end I went back to my friends, the night being over.
I was astonished to find, when I got there, a great number
Of new arrivals come in, both women and men, a sorry
Concourse of refugees assembled for exile. From all sides
They'd come together, their minds made up, their belongings ready
For me to lead them wherever I wished across the sea.
And now was the dawn star rising over the ridges of Ida,
Bringing another day. The Greeks were holding the gates of
The city in force. Troy was beyond all hope of aid.
I accepted defeat, picked up my father and made for the mountains.

[*Lines 768–804*]

BOOK III

After the gods had seen fit to destroy our Asian empire
And Priam's innocent people, after proud Ilium's fall,
When Neptune's Troy was an area of flattened, fuming rubble,
We were impelled by signs from heaven to go into exile
In some far-off and virgin land. Hard by Antandros
At the foot of Phrygian Ida we laboured to build a fleet,
Not knowing where destiny would lead us or let us settle,
And mustered our company. In the first days of summer
Father Anchises bade us hoist our sails to fate.
I was in tears as I left my country's coast, the harbour,
The plain where Troy had stood. Homeless, I took to the deep sea—
I, with my friends, my son, my home-gods and the great gods.
    Yonder there lay a land of broad plains, tilled by the Thracians,
A land protected by Mars, ruled once by hot-tempered Lycurgus,
Allied with Troy from of old through friendly relations and marriage,
While fortune smiled on us. Thither I went, and began to
Build a town by its shore (an enterprise which fate
Was biassed against), and made up its name from my own, Aenea.
I was sacrificing to Venus, my mother, and to the rest of
The gods, that they should bless our project—was sacrificing
A sleek bull on the shore to the king of the heaven-dwellers.
There was a dune nearby, as it chanced, topped by brushwood
Of cornel and of myrtle sprouted with thickset shafts.
I approached it, wanting some foliage to festoon over the altar,
And tried to root up its dense greenery: as I did so
I saw an uncanny thing, which horrifies me to speak of.
From the first sapling that I tore up, its roots dissevered,
There oozed out, drop by drop, a flow of black blood
Fouling the earth with its stains. My whole frame shook in a palsy
Of chilly fear, and my veins were ice-bound. Well, I proceeded
To pluck out the whippy shaft of another sapling; I wanted
To investigate the mystery and get at the reason for it.
From the bark of this one too there issued the black blood.
    [Lines 1–33]

Pondering much, I prayed to the deities of the woodland
And Gradivus who looks after the Thracian fields, that they should
Take the sting out of the omen and turn it to our advantage.
But when, with my knees deep in the sand to get a purchase,
I was putting forth a still greater effort upon a third shaft—
Shall I say it aloud, or be silent?—then, a pathetic moan
Came from the depth of the dune, a voice was saying to me:—
     Aeneas, you're tearing me! I am buried here. Don't hurt me!
Don't dishonour your guiltless hands. I am a Trojan,
No foreigner. That blood is drawn not from the wood.
Get away from this cruel land, from these hard-fisted shores!
I am Polydorus. The spears that nailed me down here have sprouted
An iron crop above me, a thicket of javelin wood.
     Then an acute conflict appalled my mind. I stood there
Dazed: my hair was on end and my voice stuck in my throat.
This Polydorus had been unluckily sent by Priam
With store of gold, in secret, to lodge with the Thracian king,
At a time when Priam began to have doubts about the resistance
Of Troy, perceiving how the blockade of the city was tightening.
That king, when the Trojan fortunes ebbed and our power was crushed,
Went over to Agamemnon, tagged on to the winning side,
Breaking all laws of good faith. He murdered Polydorus
And seized the gold. What lengths is the heart of man driven to
By this cursed craving for gold! When I'd got over my panic,
I referred the supernatural affair to our chosen counsellors,
My father foremost, and asked them to give their views upon it.
They were unanimous for leaving this guilty land
Where guest-laws had been thus outraged, and setting sail again.
So we hold a funeral service for Polydorus: we pile up
Earth on the dune, make an altar for the departed spirit,
Drape it with mourning bands and melancholy cypress;
Our women stand round it, hair unbound as the rites require;
Vessels foaming with fresh milk and bowls of victims' blood
We ceremonially offer: we lay the ghost in its tomb,
And call aloud on the spirit—a last hail and farewell.
     As soon as we dared launch forth, the winds granting a calm sea,
A gently-rustling breeze inviting the voyage, my comrades
Swarmed on the beach and warped our ships down into the water.
We glide out of the roadstead: cities and land grow distant.

[*Lines 34–72*]

There is a holy island, sea-girt, in the good graces
Of the Nereids' mother and of Aegean Neptune:
A floating island, it used to rove the archipelago,
Till Apollo moored it for men's use to Myconus and Gyarus,
Stationary now, no more at the beck and call of the winds.
Hither I came. That peacefullest place—how securely it havened
Us weary folk. Disembarking, we worshipped Apollo's city.
King Anius, who held both temporal and spiritual power there,
Came to meet us, wearing the sacred laurels and chaplet
Of Phoebus: he recognised Anchises as an old friend:
Host and guests clasped hands; then we went into the temple.

    I worshipped the god's dwelling of antique stone, and besought
him:—

Grant us a walled home of our own, a place for tired men,
A future, and a continuing city! Ensure for us few,
Left by the Greeks and relentless Achilles, a second Troy!
Who guides us? Where do you bid us go? Where shall we settle?
Give us a sign, O Lord, and inspire our minds with your wisdom!

    The words were hardly out when a sudden tremor visibly
Quaked the god's house and his laurel; the mountain shook all over,
The doors of the shrine flew open, and the sacred cauldron boomed.
We prostrated ourselves on the earth. An utterance came to our ears:—

    O long-enduring Trojans, the land which first produced
The stock from which you come, that same will take you back
To her abundant breast. Seek out, then, your first mother.
Here shall your house hold sway over earth, from shore to shore—
You and your children's children and the generations after them.

    Phoebus had spoken. A great babble of joy broke out:
Everyone was asking, where is that promised land
The god bids us return to out of our wanderings?
Then my father, pondering our people's traditions, said:—

    Give ear, O chieftains, and understand where your hopes are centred!
There is a sea-girt island called Crete, Juppiter's birthplace:
Here a Mount Ida stands, here was our race cradled.
A hundred inhabited cities that prosperous kingdom owns.
Thence, if I recollect the story aright, did Teucer,
Our famous ancestor, migrate once to the Troad,
Choosing a place for a kingdom. This was before Ilium
And Troy's towers had been built: men lived in the valley bottoms.

    [*Lines 73–110*]

From Crete are derived the Great Mother, the patron of Cybele, the
cymbals

Of the Corybantes, the grove of Ida, the hush of the faithful
Which belong to Cybele's cult and the lions yoked for her chariot.
Come then and let us follow where the gods' guidance leads:
Let us appease the weather and sail for the land of Crete.
It is not far away: if Juppiter favours us
Our ships should reach the Cretan shore three days from now.

Those were his words. Then he made due sacrifice at the altars—
For Neptune a bull, and a bull for you, beauteous Apollo,
A black lamb to the Storm-god, a white to the genial Zephyrs.

A report went round that king Idomeneus had been exiled
From his ancestral realm, that the coast of Crete and its dwellings
Being emptied of our foe, we'd find homes ready and waiting.
So we left the port of Delos, and skimming the deep we coasted
Naxos, the hilly haunt of Bacchantes, and green Donysa,
Olearos, and marble-white Paros, the Cyclades dotted
Over the sea, through straits that blossomed with many an island.
The boatswains are calling the stroke, the oarsmen straining in rivalry;
Crews shout one to another, Roll on, Crete and our home-land!
A following breeze gets up, giving us speedy passage,
Until at last we glide to the ancient shores of Crete.
Eagerly setting to work on the walls of my chosen city,
I name it Pergamea; I encourage my folk, who delight in
That name, to love it as home and make the town-centre imposing.

Our ships had not been beached long, our men were just engaged in
Breaking the soil and taking wives, while I was busy
On laws and housing, when a blight spread over the sky,
A wasting epidemic attacked our bodies, there fell
On trees and crops a hideous plague, a season of death.
Some gave up the ghost, some dragged out life in sickness;
The dog-days seared the fields with a heat-wave till they were barren;
Grass died of thirst, the diseased crops denied us nourishment.
My father now advised we should sail back again
To the oracle of Delos, that the god might graciously tell us
What end was assigned to these crippling mischances, where we
should look to

For help out of our troubles, and whither should steer our course.
It was night, and sleep enfolded all denizens of earth:

[*Lines 111–147*]

50

The sacred images of the gods, the Trojan home-gods
Which I had carried with me from out the blazing heart
Of Troy—as I lay asleep now, their presences appeared
Before my eyes, revealed in a fulness of light, where the full moon's
Radiance was flooding through the windows of my room.
They spoke to me, and their words relieved my anxious heart:—
    That which Apollo would say if you went up to Delos
He utters here. Aye, look! He sends us to you of his own grace.
We, when Ilium burned, followed you and your cause,
We went with you on shipboard over the surging sea;
Even so shall we exalt your seed to heaven,
And make their city an empress. Do you seek out a great place
For great ones, and never give up, though long and hard your exile.
You must change homes. This is not the land which Delian Apollo
Oracled for you; it was not in Crete he bade you settle.
There is a place—the Greeks call it Hesperia—
An antique land, well warded, possessed of a rich soil.
Oenotrians colonised it; whose heirs, so rumour says now,
Have named it, after their first founder, Italy.
There is our real home: there was Dardanus born,
And old Iasius; there did our line begin.
Rise up then, with a cheerful mind repeat to your father
These sure and certain sayings: let Corythus be his bourne
And Italy, for Jove forbids you to colonise Crete.
    I was amazed by that vision and voice of the deities—
This was not sleep; I seemed to recognise in the room there,
The aspect, the garlanded hair, the very face of my home-gods;
And a cold sweat was trickling over my body then.
I was out of bed in a moment, lifting the palms of my hands
To heaven, putting up a prayer, pouring upon the hearth
A libation of wine unwatered. When the rite was done, I felt better
And told Anchises exactly what I had experienced.
He saw that he'd confused two branches of our family
And made a novel mistake in the old topographical lore.
Now he is saying:—
                    My son, much wrought by the doom of Ilium,
You must know that Cassandra alone prophesied me such happenings.
I recollect now her predicting these things as our people's destiny—
Hesperia and Italy were often upon her tongue.
    [*Lines 148–185*]

51

But who could have thought that Trojans would ever come to the
                                                            shores of
Hesperia? Whom could Cassandra's presages influence then?
Let us bow to Apollo's warnings and take the better way.

  He spoke. We agreed with his words. All were enthusiastic.
So this place too we abandoned, leaving a few behind us,
And spreading sail we drove our hulls through the vasty sea.

  When we were well away, in deep water, out of sight now
Of land, with nothing but sea and sky wherever we looked,
An indigo-coloured rain cloud stood overhead, the precursor
Of gloom and storm, and the sea's face darkened with shuddering
                                                            catspaws.

Winds billowed the sea at once, the seas were running high,
And we were hurled in a tossing waste, all contact gone.
Rain-storms muffled the daylight, a streaming night inked out
The sky, flash upon flash of lightning shattered the clouds.
Thrown off our course, we blindly groped about on the waters.
Palinurus himself, our steersman, could not tell day from night,
Confessed he had lost his way in the wilderness of water.
Three days, three days befogged and unsighted by that darkness,
We wandered upon the sea, three starless nights we wandered.
At last, on the fourth day, we sighted land in the offing—
A view of faraway mountains and smoke spiralling up.
We struck our sails, we strained at the oars; our mariners quickly
Made the foam fly with their hard stroke, sweeping the dark-blue sea.

  It was the coast of the Strophades which rose to welcome me
Preserved from the waves—Strophades being the Greek name for
Those islands in the broad Ionian Sea where dreadful
Celaeno and her coven of Harpies dwell, now the house of
Phineus is barred and in fear they have left their pristine banquets.
No viler monstrosity than they, no pest more atrocious
Did ever the wrath of god conjure up out of Hell's swamp.
Bird-bodied, girl-faced things they are; abominable
Their droppings, their hands are talons, their faces haggard with hunger
Insatiable.
When we had made our landfall and entered port, we observed
Abundant herds of cattle dotted over the vale
And goat flocks browsing there without any goat-herd by them.
We slaughtered some; we invited Jove and the other gods
                                              [*Lines 186–222*]

52

To take their share of the spoil. Then by the winding shore
Seated on makeshift benches, we are most richly feasting.
But, the next moment, we hear a hoarse vibration of wing-beats—
The Harpies are on us, horribly swooping down from the mountains.
They tear the banquet to pieces, filthying all with their bestial
Touch. Hideous the sounds, nauseous the stench about us.
We choose a secluded spot under an overhanging
Crag, enclosed by trees and their shifting shadows, to set up
Our tables again and light a fire on a new altar.
Again from their hidden lairs, flying in from different angles,
That noisy coven claws at the feast, hovering around it,
Their mouths tainting the meat. So then I order my friends,
Stand to arms, for we must fight this damnable brood.
They did as they were ordered: they hid their swords in the grass
Ready to hand, and put their shields out of sight beside them.
So when the creatures again came screeching round the bay,
Misenus, from an observation-post above us,
Blew the alarum. My friends went in to an unfamiliar
Combat, trying their steel on sinister birds of the sea.
But blows did not make them turn a feather, their bodies would not
Be wounded—they simply flew off at high speed into the blue,
Leaving a half-devoured feast and their own disgusting traces.
Celaeno alone, perching upon a rock pinnacle, stayed
Behind, and broke into speech, a fortune-teller of evil:—

So you're willing to go to war—to war, sons of Laomedon,
Over the cattle you slaughtered, over slain bullocks? prepared
To drive us innocent Harpies out of our rightful domain?
Very well: take these words to heart, and never forget them.
What the Father almighty foreshowed to Phoebus Apollo
And he to me, will I, the chief of the Furies, reveal you.
You are making all speed for Italy, and the winds won over,
To Italy you shall go, even enter port you may:
But, before you can wall your promised city, outrageous
Famine shall fasten upon you, in return for trying to kill us,
And force you to chew your tables—yes, gnaw at them and devour
them.

She spoke: she winged away into the sheltering forest.
As for my friends, their blood went cold with the shock of panic
And curdled; their hearts sank: no more fighting, they said—

[*Lines 223–260*]

53

Through vows and prayers alone we must seek security, whether
Those creatures are of heaven or uncanny birds of ill omen.
Anchises stretched out his hands from the shore in supplication
To the powers above, appointing due sacrifice in their honour.

Ye gods, prevent these threats! Ye gods, avert this calamity!
Incline your hearts to the faithful! Oh, save us!
                                                    Then he gave orders
To cast off the moorings, to free the sheets and pay them out.
A South wind filled the sails; we flew before it over
The white-capped waves whither the breeze and our helmsman took us.
Presently hove in sight the sea-girt, woody Zacynthos,
Dulichium and Samé and the sheer cliffs of Néritos.
We ran past the promontories of Ithaca, Laertes'
Kingdom, cursing the land that bred cruel Ulysses.
Later we opened the cloudy peaks of Mount Leucata,
Then the temple of Apollo—a warning land-mark to mariners.
Here we put in, exhausted, near to the little town:
Bow anchors were thrown out, the ships were beached by the stern.

So at last, hoping against hope, we'd come to land: we performed
Purification rites to Jove, we made burnt offerings,
And on the shores of Actium we held the Trojan Games.
Stripping and oiling their bodies, my comrades practised our old
Traditional wrestling bouts. Light-hearted they were to have won past
So many Greek cities, made good their escape through the enemy.
The sun went rolling on through the circuit of a whole year,
Freezing winter roughened the sea with northerly gales.
A rounded shield of bronze, borne once by the warrior Abas,
I nailed to a door, and wrote this line in dedication—
THESE ARMS AENEAS FROM THE VICTORIOUS DANAI.
Then I gave orders to man the ships and clear from harbour.
Eagerly rowed my comrades, sweeping the sea with long strokes.
Soon were the lofty peaks of Corcyra lost to view;
We coasted along Epirus, and coming to the Chaonian
Harbour, we drew near Buthrotum, that hill city.

Here we heard a rumour of quite extraordinary doings—
That Helenus, son of Priam, was king over Greek cities,
Having acquired Pyrrhus' sceptre and wife, Andromache,
Who thus had passed again to a man of her own people.
I was astonished: I felt a wonderful strong desire

[*Lines 261–298*]

54

To talk with Helenus and learn how it all happened.
I set forth from the harbour, leaving our fleet on the shore;
Just then, as it chanced, in a grove near the city, where flowed a
                                           make-believe
Simois, was Andromache performing the sad and solemn
Rites of the Dead, with wine for the ashes and invocations
To the spirit, at Hector's cenotaph—an empty mound of green turf
And twin altars the widow had consecrated to grief.
When she caught sight of me coming and saw the Trojan accoutrements,
She was frightened out of her wits by the marvel of it—her body
Went rigid as she gazed, and the warmth ebbed from her bones.
She fainted; after a long while she just managed to speak:—
    Are you real—this shape I see? Can you really bring me news,
O goddess-born? Are you living? Or, if your day is done,
Tell me, where's Hector?
                      With these words, she burst into tears; one could hear
Only her sobs. I can hardly get in a brief answer, she's so
Upset; my own voice is broken and incoherent with feeling:—
I'm alive, to be sure—living on through every kind of adversity;
Doubt not that what you see is real.
But oh, how have you fared since of so great a husband
You were deprived? What fortune, worthy of Hector's Andromache,
Has smiled on you? Or are you still united to Pyrrhus?
    With eyes downcast, and speaking in a low voice, she said:—
    Oh, luckiest of us all, that maiden daughter of Priam
Who was appointed to die on an enemy's tomb beneath
The walls of Troy—the one whom no man drew lots for, the one
Who never knew captivity or the bed of a conqueror!
But I, when our home lay in ashes, was carried off overseas,
Endured the contemptuous treatment of Achilles' insolent son,
And bore his children in slavery. Afterwards, when he wanted
A Greek wife, Leda's Hermione, he passed me on
To Helenus and made me the slave wife of a slave.
But Orestes then, consumed with violent love for his stolen
Bride, and driven mad by the Furies which punish crime,
Took Pyrrhus off guard and murdered him at his father's altar:
On whose decease, a part of his kingdom was restored
To Helenus, who christened these the Chaonian plains,
Named the whole of the country after Chaon of Troy and

[*Lines 299–335*]

55

Rebuilt Troy's very keep upon our foothills here.
But you—what made you come? Was it weather or Providence
brought you?
Which of the gods impelled you towards this land you knew not?
What of your boy, Ascanius? Is he still in the land of the living?
He was your son, in the old days, at Troy.
Does he still think about the mother whom he lost?
Does the example of Aeneas and his uncle, Hector,
Awake in him the old-time virtues, the hero spirit?

   The words poured out. She was weeping—a long-drawn fit of fruitless
Weeping, when from the city, with a great retinue round him,
Approached the son of Priam, the hero Helenus.
He recognised his kin, and took us back to the palace
Talking to us, interspersing his words with tears of happiness.
As we went, I saw the town was a miniature Troy, a model
Of mighty Pergamum; saw a dry watercourse named for
The Xanthus, and a Scaean gate whose threshold I kissed.
My Trojans enjoyed with me the city's hospitality.
The king was entertaining them in his great hall surrounded
By colonnades; they were drinking from cups of wine, each man
Goblet in hand, with a feast on golden plates before them.

   One day passed, and another; and now the breezes wooed
Our sails impatiently, and the canvas swelled in a South wind.
So then I approached the seer, making request of him:—
Scion of Troy, and heaven's mouthpiece, you that vibrate to
Apollo's presence, the tripod, the laurels, you the diviner
Of what the stars portend and the songs and flights of birds,
O tell me—since I have had divine sanction for all my
Journey, and all the gods have expressed their will that I
Should make for Italy, should try for that faraway land;
Only the Harpy, Celaeno, prophesies an uncanny
New horror, threatening us with malevolent wrath and a gruesome
Famine—tell me what dangers I am first to avoid,
Or in what way I can overcome these numerous troubles.

   Helenus sacrificed some bullocks, as is the custom,
Beseeching heavenly grace, unbound the head-dress from
His reverend head, and took me by the hand into Apollo's
Temple (how awed I was by the sense of immanent deity!)
Then was the priestly king inspired to utter these words:—

[*Lines 336–373*]

Goddess-born, it is beyond question true that your voyage
Has higher sanction: the Father of heaven predestines it,
And spinning the wheel of chance, ordains for you such fortunes.
Therefore, that you may safelier travel the unfamiliar
Seas, and winning to port, establish yourself in Italy,
A few things out of many will I reveal. The Fates
Deny me further knowledge and Juno forbids me to say more.
First, then, the Italy you imagine so close that you're ready,
Mistakenly, to enter her ports any day now, in fact is
A very long way from here, and the way is far from easy.
You will have to strain at the oars in the Sicilian waters,
Voyage the whole length of the Ausonian sea,
And pass the infernal lakes and the Tyrrhene island of Circe,
Before you can establish your town in a land safe for you.
These signs will I declare you. Store them up in your memory.
When, anxious of heart, you shall come to a lonely river and find there
Under the ilex trees lining its bank, a sow—
A great white sow, with a litter of thirty new-born piglets,
White as she, clustered at the teats of their sprawling mother—
There is the site for your city, the terminus of your travails.
And do not let the threat about biting the tables intimidate you:
Fate will find out a way, Apollo will come to your call.
What you must shun is that part of Italy yonder, the coast
Nearest to ours and washed by the tides of our own sea,
For ill-disposed Greeks are settled in all the townships there.
In one place the Narycian Locri have built battlements,
And Lyctian Idomeneus has garrisoned the plains of
The Sallentines: elsewhere, you'd find little Petelia squat on
Its walls, the town of the Meliboean chief, Philoctetes.
Another thing—when your ships have crossed the seas and are anchored,
When you perform your vows at the altar set up ashore,
Remember to veil your head with a purple covering, lest,
As you worship the gods amid the altar fires, some enemy
Visage should meet your gaze and turn the omens awry.
This ceremonial you and your friends must always adhere to:
By this observance your heirs may stand firm in the faith.
Now when you have left that first landfall and sail to Sicily,
At the point where Pelorus begins to reveal a narrow opening
Steer for the land on your port bow, the seas to port, and make

[*Lines 374–412*]

A detour giving a wide berth to shore and breakers a'starboard.
Once on a time, they say, these two lands were a single
Country; then there came a convulsion of nature which tore them
Hugely asunder—the ages can bring such immense geological
Change—and the sea rushed violently in between them, dividing
Italy from Sicily, severing their coasts and washing
Cities and fields on either side with a narrow strait.
Scylla guards the right shore, insatiable Charybdis
The left. Three times a day the latter, down in the depths of
A whirlpool, gulps whole tons of wave into her maw,
Then spews them up again, flailing the heavens with spray.
But Scylla lurks unseen in a cavernous lair, from which
She pushes out her lips to drag ships on to the rocks.
Her upper part is human—a girl's beautiful body
Down to the privates; below, she is a weird sea-monster
With dolphin's tail and a belly of wolverine sort. It's advisable
To fetch a long compass, although it protracts the voyage, and sail
Right round the Sicilian cape of Pachynum, a southernmost mark,
Rather than to set eyes on that freakish Scylla within
Her cavern vast or the rocks where her sea-blue hounds are baying.
Finally, if I have any foresight, if you can trust
My divinings at all, if Apollo inspires my soul to truth,
This one thing, Aeneas, I solemnly tell you—one thing
Which sums up all—and I cannot repeat the warning too often:—
It's paramount that Juno should have your prayers and homage;
Be zealous in making your vows to Juno and wooing her powerful
Partisanship with a suppliant's gifts. Do this, and at last
You will obtain a fair passage from Sicily to Italy.
Now when you are safely there, close to the city of Cumae
And the haunted lake Avernus deep in a soughing wood,
You will find an ecstatic, a seeress, who in her antre communicates
Destiny, committing to leaves the mystic messages.
Whatever runes that virgin has written upon the leaves
She files away in her cave, arranged in the right order.
There they remain untouched, just as she put them away:
But suppose that the hinge turns and a light draught blows through
the door,
Stirs the frail leaves and shuffles them, never thereafter cares she
To catch them, as they flutter about the cave, to restore

[*Lines 413–450*]

Their positions or reassemble the runes: so men who have come to
Consult the sibyl depart no wiser, hating the place.
Here you must not grudge time spent, although it delays you—
However impatient your friends may grow, however fine
The weather for sailing, however strongly the sea calls you—
Time spent in approaching the sibyl, asking an oracle of her,
Praying that she will graciously open her mouth and prophesy.
Then will she tell you of wars to come with the tribes of Italy,
How to evade, or endure, each crisis upon your way;
And if you pay reverence to her, she will give you a favourable passage.
Such are the counsels I am permitted to offer you.
Go your way, then, exalting great Troy with famous deeds.

   After the prophet had spoken thus, in friendly wise,
He gave instructions for presents to be carried down to the ships,
Presents of solid gold, objects inlaid with ivory;
He cargoed us with silver and cauldrons from Dodona,
A cuirass made of golden chain-mail, triple-meshed,
And a helmet fine with plumes on its tapering crest, which had once
Belonged to Pyrrhus. Besides, there were personal gifts for my father.
He furnished, as well, horses and guides,
Brought the crews up to strength and fully equipped my friends.
Now was Anchises urgent for the sails of our fleet to be rigged,
So that a favouring wind should find us not unready.
Whereupon the prophet of Phoebus respectfully addressed him:—

   Anchises, once thought worthy of divine marriage by Venus,
Close to the heart of the gods, twice saved from Troy's destruction,
Look yonder! There is Italy. Make sail for that land with all speed!
Yet is it written that you shall drift past yonder shore.
Far is the region of Italy revealed for you by Apollo.
Fare forth, Anchises, blest in the love of your son! The winds
Are rising. No more words from me, no more delaying.

   Andromache too, saddened by this long last farewell,
Brings Ascanius presents—a robe patterned with gold thread
And an embroidered cloak: she is not backward in courtesy,
But loads him with the work of her loom, and says to him:—

   Take these things too, dear lad, as keepsakes to remind you
Of her who made them, tokens of the abiding love of Andromache,
Hector's wife. Yes, take these gifts from your kin, these last gifts.
You are the image of my son, Astyanax; in eyes
   [Lines 451–489]

And hands and mien the picture of him, the one picture left me:
He would have been your age now, like you growing to manhood.

Tears came to my eyes as I spoke these parting words:—
Long may you live and lucky, you who have now accomplished
Your destiny! We are bandied from one vicissitude
To another. For you no ploughing the prairies of sea, no endless
Chasing after the ever-receding fields of Italy:
Peace, for you, is born. You behold a Xanthus in replica,
A Troy your hands have built—under better omens, I pray,
Than the old Troy, and further out of the way of the Greeks.
If ever I get to Tiber and the lands adjacent to Tiber,
If ever I set eyes on the place marked out for my people,
One day, from those sister cities, those neighbouring tribes in Epirus
And in Hesperia, which share the same ancestor, Dardanus,
And the same tale of disaster, we'll make one single-hearted
Troy. Let that be a charge we leave to our posterity.

Forth we went on the sea, the Ceraunian cliffs being close in
The offing, for that course gave the shortest passage to Italy.
Now the sun went down and the mountains were veiled in shadow.
Putting ashore, we shipped the oars, then gratefully sinking
Down on the bosom of earth, we lay scattered about on the dry beach
Restoring our strength, while sleep flowed over our spent bodies.
Night, driven on by the hours, was not yet in mid-career,
When Palinurus alertly rose from his bed and tested
The weather, pricking his ears for any breath of a breeze;
All the stars he scanned as they slid through the quiet sky,
Arcturus and the rainy Hyades and the Twin Bears;
Orion he observed with its golden sword and sword-belt.
Noting that all was set fair in the calm sky, he blew
A clear trumpet-call from the poop: we left that bivouac,
And spreading the sails' pinions went forth upon our way.
And now, the stars dispersed by the first flush of dawn,
We sighted, far away, dim hills and a low coast-line,
Italy. Achates was the first to hail, "Italy!"
"Italy!" my comrades echoed in cheerful greeting.
Then did my father, Anchises, garland a mighty bowl
And fill it with wine, and taking his stand high up on the stern
Above us, invoked the gods:—

You deities who control the sea, the earth and the weather,

[*Lines 490–528*]

60

Grant us fair winds and an easy passage! Breathe kindly upon us!
    A freshening breeze answered his prayer: getting nearer, we opened
A harbour mouth, and saw on Minerva's Height a temple.
Furling the sails, my comrades changed course direct for the land.
That harbour was hollowed out by the action of heavy seas
In east winds: at its entrance are reefs that smoke in a smother
Of spray, concealing the harbour: turreted cliffs slope down
Two arms to form its walls, and the temple lies back from the foreshore.
Here, an initial omen, I espied four horses freely
Grazing the deep-grassed vale, four horses white as snow.
Then pronounced Anchises:—

                  War is your word, O strange land.
For war are horses needed; and those steeds there mean war.
Nevertheless, in time can these same cattle be trained for
The shafts and learn to bear in amity yoke and bridle:
So there are hopes for peace, too.

                       Then we prayed to the power divine
Of Athene, the clasher of arms, who received our first thanksgiving,
Veiling our heads at the altar with wraps of embroidered stuff,
And following the instructions which Helenus had most emphasised,
Duly offered to Argive Juno a burnt sacrifice.
At once, as soon as our vows had been properly performed,
Trimming our yards to the wind, under a press of canvas
We left that abode of Greeks, that unreassuring district.
Next we raised the gulf of Tarentum—Hercules' town,
If the legend is true; and opposite, the temple of the Lacinian
Goddess, Caulonia's heights and shipwrecking Scylacéum.
Then we made out Trinacrian Aetna on the horizon,
And from afar we heard a thunder of waves throbbing
On rocks, and inshore noises broke fitfully on our ears;
The race was dancing with fury, the shoal-water boiling with sand.
Anchises cried:—

               That must be the infamous Charybdis!
Those are the reefs, the terrible rocks that Helenus told of!
Row for your lives, my comrades! Pull together! Pull!
    Yarely they all obeyed my father's command. Palinurus
Turned away first to port, the bows of his vessel creaking;
Then the whole convoy, with oars and sails, clawed off to port.
We were tossed up high on an arching surge, then down we went
[*Lines 529–564*]

In the trough as the wave fell away, down to the very Pit.
Thrice roared aloud the reefs and the caverns of rock beneath us,
Thrice we beheld the sky through a spattering flounce of spindrift.
Time passed. The wind went down with the sun. Utterly spent,
Not knowing where we were, we crept to the shores of the Cyclops.
    There lies a haven, sheltered from all four winds; it is calm
And roomy too; but, nearby, Aetna thunderously erupts.
Ever and anon it discharges at heaven a mirky cloud,
A swirl of pitch-black smoke lurid with white-hot cinders,
And volleys huge balls of flame, singeing the very stars.
Ever and anon, as if the mountain's guts were being coughed up,
It belches rock, and groaning, vomits out thick streams
Of lava, seething up from its roots. The story goes
That Enceladus, charred by Jove's lightning, is crushed beneath
This mountain mass—that Aetna was dumped down bodily on him,
And like a leaky furnace jets out the fire which consumes him;
So, every time he turns over to rest one aching side,
Sicily quakes and rumbles, smoke hangs above like an awning.
That night we hid in the woods, enduring these gigantic
Phenomena, and unable to see what caused the din;
For the lights of the stars were out, there was no shine on the face of
Heaven from the constellations, only a fog which bandaged
Its eyes, and clouds which muffled the moon at this dead of night.
    And now to-morrow was here, with the first star of the morning,
And sunrise had uncurtained the dark dew-dropping sky,
When suddenly there stepped out of the woods a strange individual,
A man unknown to us, in rags and a state of extreme
Emaciation, who stretched imploring hands to us
On the shore. We looked round. Appallingly dirty, his beard overgrown,
His rags held together with thorns, in all else he was a Greek,
A man who had gone to Troy once in the Greek expeditionary force.
He, when from a distance he saw our Trojan dress
And equipment, stood stock still for a little, scared at the sight,
Unable to move. But soon he was frantically running down to
The beach, sobbing out entreaties:—

                              By the heavens above, Trojans,
By the gods in heaven, by the breath and light of life, I beseech you
Rescue me! Get me away! to whatever land, I care not.
That's all I ask. I know I was one of the Greek invaders,

[*Lines 565–602*]

62

I own that I helped to make war against your Trojan homes.
If you feel what I did was so dreadful a crime, then punish me—
Tear me limb from limb and sink my remains in the broad sea.
If I must die, at least I'll have died at the hands of humans.
    He spoke: he clasped our knees and clung, writhing about them.
So we encouraged him to tell us his name and his family,
Tell us what fate had brought him to this. My father, Anchises,
After a brief hesitation offered the man his hand—
A gesture of immediate good-faith to reassure him.
He, at last throwing off his apprehensions, spoke out:—
    I am of Ithaca, a comrade of luckless Ulysses,
Achemenides by name: my father Adamastus
Being poor (would that we'd stayed as we were!), I went to Troy.
Here, in the Cyclops' cave, my companions left me behind,
Forgetting me in their panicky haste to quit the ogre's
Demesne. A house of blood and bloody feasts that cave is,
Gloomy within, immense. So tall is its master, he knocks
His head on the stars (ye gods, rid the earth of such cankers!).
He is not easy on the eye, not one you can cosily talk to.
He fancies the flesh and dark blood of wretched human victims.
I saw him myself seize two of our company with his huge hand,
Then, lolling back in the cave, smash their bodies against
A rock, until the whole place was spattered and swimming with gore:
And then I saw him munching my friends' blood-boultered bodies,
Saw the still-warm limbs quivering under his teeth.
Ulysses did not let the Cyclops go unpunished:
Dire was the extremity, but Ulysses kept his head.
For when, gorged on the meal and sodden with wine, the Cyclops
Bowed his neck, lay down, stretched himself the whole
Length of the cave, and was belching blood and human fragments
Mingled with bloody wine in his sleep, we then, after praying
The gods for strength and drawing by lot our places, hemmed
The ogre round, bored into his eye with a sharp stake—
That single, gigantic eye deep-set in his savage brow,
That eye as huge as an Argive shield or the sun itself.
So, with fierce joy, we avenged our comrades in the end.
But you must get out of here. Quick! Cut the cables, or else
You'll rue it!
That Polyphemus, folding his woolly flocks in the cave
    [*Lines 603–641*]

And milking them—he is not unique. There are a hundred
Other Cyclops, as big and fierce as he, at large
Over these winding shores and these high hills, the monsters.
Three times now have the horns of the moon filled up with light
Since I began to lead this life in the woods, among dens
And uninhabited haunts of wild beasts, on crags looking out for
The one-eyed giants, trembling at the sound of their voice and tread.
A starveling diet of berries and stone-hard cornels was all
The woods supplied, with roots of herbs I plucked to feed on.
Though long and everywhere I gazed, I saw no help
Till your ships hove in sight. To you, however it turned out,
I committed myself: anything to have escaped that brood of
Abomination. At your hands would any death be preferable.

 Scarce had he finished speaking when, moving down from the
mountain
Towards the well-known shore, mammoth in bulk, his sheep flock
Round him, we saw that same shepherd, that Polyphemus—
A monster, grisly, misshapen, titanic, his eye gone.
He carries the trunk of a pine tree to guide and support him walking:
The fleecy sheep go with him—they are his only pleasure
And consolation in woe.
When he had come to the sea's edge and touched the surging deep,
He washed the socket of his eye, which oozed blood, with sea-water,
Gritting his teeth and groaning; then waded into the deep sea,
Yet even there the water did not come up to his waist.
Frightened, we hurried to get far away, taking on board
That Greek who so merited mercy, and stealthily cutting the cables:
Frantically we tugged at the oars, we swept the sea's face.
He sensed us, veered his steps towards the noise of our passage.
But when he found there was no way of laying his hands upon us
And he was falling behind in his race with the waves which carried us,
Then he let out a stupendous bellow, shivering the whole
Expanse of the sea, shaking Italy to its core
With fright, and reverberating through Aetna's anfractuous caves.
Whereupon the Cyclops people were roused; from hill and forest
They ran down towards the roadstead and swarmed upon the beach.
There they stood, the fraternity of Aetna, impotent,
With baleful eyes and their sky-scraping heads—we saw them—
A terrifying assembly: so on some mountain top

[*Lines 642–679*]

64

Head-in-air oaks are massed, or cone-bearing cypresses—
Juppiter's own tall wood, or a grove sacred to Diana.
Our panic prompted us to pay out the sheets and run for it,
Whatever the course might be, scudding before the wind.
Yet Helenus had warned not to attempt the passage
Between Scylla and Charybdis, there being on either side
So narrow a margin of safety. Well, in the end we resolved
To put about. But just then we caught a northerly wind
Slanting from Cape Pelorus; so on we went past the rocks at
Pantagias' mouth, the Megarian bay, and low-lying Thapsus.
Such places along the coast Achemenides pointed out to us,
Retracing now the route he had come with unlucky Ulysses.

   Over against wave-worn Plemyrium there's an island
Athwart the gulf of Syracuse, an isle the ancients named
Ortygia. According to legend, Alpheus, the river of Elis,
Once drove a secret passage hither, beneath the sea-bed,
To mingle at Arethusa's fount with waters of Sicily.
As instructed, we worship the patron spirits of the place; then on past
The marshy mouth of Helorus with its most fertile soil.
Next, we skirt Pachynus—a place of high rocks and jutting
Reefs; and now, far off, is Camarina, which fate said
Must never be reclaimed, and the Geloan plains,
And Gela, which is named after its own wild river.
Then Acragas on its crag shows from afar its great walls—
A town renowned one time for its mettlesome breed of horses.
The wind blows fair, and we leave palm-fringed Selinus behind
To skirt Lilybaeum's waters, tricky with reefs submerged.
After which, we put in at port Drepanum, a landfall
Of little joy; for here, after so many storms weathered,
I lost, alas, my father, him who had lightened my cares
And troubles—lost Anchises. Oh, best of fathers, to leave me
Here, sick-hearted, when you had survived—yet all for nothing—
Such dangers! The seer, Helenus, though many horrors he warned of,
Never predicted this grief, nor did the sinister Celaeno.
This was the last agony, the turning-point of my long course.
From there Providence took me and drove me upon your coasts.

   So, while all the others intently listened, Aeneas
Recounted his heaven-sent trials and told about his wanderings.
Now he stops talking and falls silent, his story done.
   [Lines 680–718]

BOOK IV

But now for some while the queen had been growing more
                                grievously love-sick,
Feeding the wound with her life-blood, the fire biting within her.
Much did she muse on the hero's nobility, and much
On his family's fame. His look, his words had gone to her heart
And lodged there: she could get no peace from love's disquiet.
   The morrow's morn had chased from heaven the dewy darkness,
Was carrying the sun's torch far and wide over earth,
When, almost beside herself, she spoke to her sister, her confidante:—
   Anna, sister, why do these nerve-racking dreams haunt me?
This man, this stranger I've welcomed into my house—what of him?
How gallantly he looks, how powerful in chest and shoulders!
I really do think, and have reason to think, that he is heaven-born.
Mean souls convict themselves by cowardice. Oh, imagine
The fates that have harried him, the fight to a finish he told of!
Were it not that my purpose is fixed irrevocably
Never to tie myself in wedlock again to anyone,
Since that first love of mine proved false and let death cheat me;
Had I not taken a loathing for the idea of marriage,
For him, for this one man, I could perhaps have weakened.
Anna, I will confess it, since poor Sychaeus, my husband,
Was killed and our home broken up by my brother's murderous act,
This man is the only one who has stirred my senses and sapped
My will. I feel once more the scars of the old flame.
But no, I would rather the earth should open and swallow me
Or the Father of heaven strike me with lightning down to the shades—
The pale shades and deep night of the Underworld—before
I violate or deny pure widowhood's claim upon me.
He who first wedded me took with him, when he died,
My right to love: let him keep it, there, in the tomb, for ever.
   So Dido spoke, and the rising tears flooded her bosom.
Anna replied:—
            You are dearer to me than the light of day.
                             [*Lines 1–31*]

Must you go on wasting your youth in mourning and solitude,
Never to know the blessings of love, the delight of children?
Do you think that ashes, or ghosts underground, can mind about
such things?
I know that in Libya, yes, and in Tyre before it, no wooers
Could touch your atrophied heart: Iarbas was rejected
And other lords of Africa, the breeding-ground of the great.
Very well: but when love comes, and pleases, why fight against it?
Besides, you should think of the nations whose land you have settled
in—
Threatening encirclement are the Gaetuli, indomitable
In war, the Numidians (no bridle for them), the unfriendly Syrtes;
On your other frontier, a waterless desert and the far-raging
Barcaei: I need not mention the prospect of Tyrian aggression,
Your brother's menacing attitude.
I hold it was providential indeed, and Juno willed it,
That hither the Trojan fleet should have made their way. Oh, sister,
Married to such a man, what a city you'll see, what a kingdom
Established here! With the Trojans as our comrades in arms,
What heights of glory will not we Carthaginians soar to!
Only solicit the gods' favour, perform the due rites,
And plying our guest with attentions, spin a web to delay him,
While out at sea the winter runs wild and Orion is stormy,
While his ships are in bad repair, while the weather is unacquiescent.
    These words blew to a blaze the spark of love in the queen's heart,
Set hope to her wavering will and melted her modesty's rigour.
So first they went to the shrines, beseeching at every altar
For grace: as religion requires, they sacrificed chosen sheep to
Ceres, giver of increase, to Phoebus, and to the Wine-god;
To Juno, chief of all, for the marriage-bond is her business.
Dido herself, most beautiful, chalice in hand, would pour
Libations between the horns of a milk-white heifer, and slowly
Would pace by the dripping altars, with the gods looking on,
And daily renew her sacrifice, poring over the victims'
Opened bodies to see what their pulsing entrails signified.
Ah, little the soothsayers know! What value have vows or shrines
For a woman wild with passion, the while love's flame eats into
Her gentle flesh and love's wound works silently in her breast?
So burns the ill-starred Dido, wandering at large through the town
    [*Lines 32–68*]

In a rage of desire, like a doe pierced by an arrow—a doe which
Some hunting shepherd has hit with a long shot while unwary
She stepped through the Cretan woods, and all unknowing has left his
Winged weapon within her: the doe runs fleetly around the Dictaean
Woods and clearings, the deathly shaft stuck deep in her flank.
Now she conducts Aeneas on a tour of her city, and shows him
The vast resources of Carthage, the home there ready and waiting;
Begins to speak, then breaks off, leaving a sentence unfinished.
Now, as the day draws out, she wants to renew that first feast,
In fond distraction begs to hear once again the Trojan
Story, and hangs on his words as once again he tells it.
Then, when the company's broken up, when the moon is dimming
Her beams in turn and the dipping stars invite to sleep,
Alone she frets in the lonely house, lies down on her bed,
Then leaves it again: he's not there, not there, but she hears him and
                                                    sees him.

Or charmed by his likeness to his father, she keeps Ascanius
Long in her lap to assuage the passion she must not utter.
Work on the half-built towers is closed down meanwhile; the men
Of Carthage have laid off drilling, or building the wharves and vital
Defences of their town; the unfinished works are idle—
Great frowning walls, head-in-air cranes, all at a standstill.
  Now as soon as Juppiter's consort perceived that Dido was mad
With love and quite beyond caring about her reputation,
She, Juno, approached Venus, making these overtures:—
  A praiseworthy feat, I must say, a fine achievement you've brought
                                                       off,
You and your boy; it should make a great, a lasting name for you—
One woman mastered by the arts of two immortals!
It has not entirely escaped me that you were afraid of my city
And keenly suspicious of towering Carthage's hospitality.
But how will it all end? Where is our rivalry taking us?
Would it not be far better, by arranging a marriage, to seal
A lasting peace? You have got the thing you had set your heart on:
Dido's afire with love, wholly infatuated.
Well then, let us unite these nations and rule them with equal
Authority. Let Dido slave for a Trojan husband,
And let the Tyrians pass into your hand as her dowry.
  Venus, aware that this was double-talk by which

                                 [*Lines 69–105*]

69

Juno aimed at basing the future Italian empire
On Africa, countered with these words:—

                                     Senseless indeed to reject
Such terms and prefer to settle the matter with you by hostilities,
Provided fortune favour the plan which you propose.
But I'm in two minds about destiny, I am not sure if Juppiter
Wishes one city formed of Tyrians and Trojan exiles,
Or would approve a pact or miscegenation between them.
You are his wife: you may ask him to make his policy clearer.
Proceed. I will support you.

                               Queen Juno replied thus:—
That shall be my task. Now, to solve our immediate problem,
I will briefly put forward a scheme—pray give me your attention.
Aeneas and his unfortunate Dido plan to go
A-hunting in the woods to-morrow, as soon as the sun
Has risen and unshrouded the world below with his rays.
On these two, while the beaters are scurrying about and stopping
The coverts with cordon of nets, I shall pour down a darkling

                                             rain-storm
And hail as well, and send thunder hallooing all over the sky.
Dispersing for shelter, the rest of the hunt will be cloaked in the mirk:
But Dido and lord Aeneas, finding their way to the same cave,
Shall meet. I'll be there: and if I may rely on your goodwill,
There I shall join them in lasting marriage, and seal her his,
With Hymen present in person.

                               Venus made no opposition
To Juno's request, though she smiled at the ingenuity of it.
So now, as Aurora was rising out of her ocean bed
And the day-beam lofted, there sallied forth the élite of Carthage:
With fine-meshed nets and snares and the broad hunting lances
Massylian riders galloped behind a keen-nosed pack.
The queen dallies: the foremost Carthaginians await her
By the palace door, where stands her horse, caparisoned
In purple and gold, high-spirited, champing the foam-flecked bit.
At last she comes, with many courtiers in attendance:
She wears a Phoenician habit, piped with bright-coloured braid:
Her quiver is gold, her hair bound up with a golden clasp,
A brooch of gold fastens the waist of her brilliant dress.
Her Trojan friends were there too, and young Ascanius

  [*Lines 106–140*]

70

In high glee. But by far the handsomest of them all
Was Aeneas, who came to her side now and joined forces with hers.
It was like when Apollo leaves Lycia, his winter palace,
And Xanthus river to visit Delos, his mother's home,
And renew the dances, while round his altar Cretans and Dryopes
And the tattooed Agathyrsi are raising a polyglot din:
The god himself steps out on the Cynthian range, a circlet
Of gold and a wreath of pliant bay on his flowing hair,
The jangling weapons slung from his shoulder. Nimble as he,
Aeneas moved, with the same fine glow on his handsome face.
When they had reached the mountains, the trackless haunt of game,
Wild goats—picture the scene!—started from crags up above there,
Ran down the slopes: from another direction stags were galloping
Over the open ground of a glen, deserting the heights—
A whole herd jostling together in flight, with a dust-cloud above it.
But young Ascanius, proud of his mettlesome horse, was riding
Along the vale, outstripping group after group of hunters,
And praying hard that, instead of such tame quarry, a frothing
Boar might come his way or a sand-coloured mountain lion.
    At this stage a murmur, a growling began to be heard
In the sky: soon followed a deluge of rain and hail together.
The Trojan sportsmen, their Carthaginian friends and the grandson
Of Venus, in some alarm, scattered over the terrain
Looking for shelter. Torrents roared down from the mountain-tops.
Now Dido and the prince Aeneas found themselves
In the same cave. Primordial Earth and presiding Juno
Gave the signal. The firmament flickered with fire, a witness
Of wedding. Somewhere above, the Nymphs cried out in pleasure.
That day was doom's first birthday and that first day was the cause of
Evils: Dido recked nothing for appearance or reputation:
The love she brooded on now was a secret love no longer;
Marriage, she called it, drawing the word to veil her sin.
    Straight away went Rumour through the great cities of Libya—
Rumour, the swiftest traveller of all the ills on earth,
Thriving on movement, gathering strength as it goes; at the start
A small and cowardly thing, it soon puffs itself up,
And walking upon the ground, buries its head in the cloud-base.
The legend is that, enraged with the gods, Mother Earth produced
This creature, her last child, as a sister to Enceladus

[*Lines 141–179*]

And Coeus—a swift-footed creature, a winged angel of ruin,
A terrible, grotesque monster, each feather upon whose body—
Incredible though it sounds—has a sleepless eye beneath it,
And for every eye she has also a tongue, a voice and a pricked ear.
At night she flits midway between earth and sky, through the gloom
Screeching, and never closes her eyelids in sweet slumber:
By day she is perched like a look-out either upon a roof-top
Or some high turret; so she terrorises whole cities,
Loud-speaker of truth, hoarder of mischievous falsehood, equally.
This creature was now regaling the people with various scandal
In great glee, announcing fact and fiction indiscriminately:
Item, Aeneas has come here, a prince of Trojan blood,
And the beauteous Dido deigns to have her name linked with his;
The couple are spending the winter in debauchery, the whole long
Winter, forgetting their kingdoms, rapt in a trance of lust.
Such gossip did vile Rumour pepper on every mouth.
Not long before she came to the ears of king Iarbas,
Whispering inflammatory words and heaping up his resentment.

He, the son of Ammon by a ravished African nymph,
Had established a hundred shrines to Jove in his ample realm,
A hundred altars, and consecrated their quenchless flames
And vigils unceasing there; the ground was richly steeped in
Victims' blood, and bouquets of flowers adorned the portals.
He now, driven out of his mind by that bitter blast of rumour,
There at the altar, among the presences of the gods,
Prayed, it is said, to Jove, with importunate, humble entreaty:—

Almighty Jove, whom now for the first time the Moorish people
Pledge with wine as they banquet on ornamental couches,
Do you observe these things? Or are we foolish to shudder
When you shoot fire, O Father, foolish to be dismayed
By lightning which is quite aimless and thunder which growls
without meaning?
That woman who, wandering within our frontiers, paid to establish
Her insignificant township, permitted by us to plough up
A piece of the coast and be queen of it—that woman, rejecting my
offer
Of marriage, has taken Aeneas as lord and master there.
And now that philanderer, with his effeminate following—
His chin and oil-sleeked hair set off by a Phrygian bonnet—

[Lines 180–216]

That fellow is in possession; while we bring gifts to your shrine,
If indeed you are there and we do not worship a vain myth.

    Thus did Iarbas pray, with his hands on the altar; and Jove
Omnipotent, hearing him, bent down his gaze upon Dido's
City and on those lovers lost to their higher fame.
Then he addressed Mercury, entrusting to him this errand:—

    Go quick, my son, whistle up the Zephyrs and wing your way
Down to the Trojan leader, who is dallying now in Carthage
Without one thought for the city which fate has assigned to be his.
Carry my dictate along the hastening winds and tell him,
Not for such ways did his matchless mother guarantee him
To us, nor for such ends rescue him twice from the Greeks;
Rather, that he should rule an Italy fertile in leadership
And loud with war, should hand on a line which sprang from the noble
Teucer and bring the whole world under a system of law.
If the glory of such great exploits no longer fires his heart
And for his own renown he will make no effort at all,
Does he grudge his son, Ascanius, the glory of Rome to be?
What aim, what hope does he cherish, delaying there in a hostile
Land, with no thought for posterity or his Italian kingdom?
Let him sail. That is the gist. Give him that message from me.

    Jove spake. Mercury now got ready to obey
His father's command. So first he bound on his feet the sandals,
The golden sandals whose wings waft him aloft over sea
And land alike with the hurrying breath of the breezes. Then
He took up his magic wand (with this he summons wan ghosts
From Orcus and consigns others to dreary Tartarus,
Gives sleep or takes it away, seals up the eyes of dead men).
Now, with that trusty wand, he drove the winds and threshed through
The cloud-wrack; descried as he flew the peak and precipitous flanks
of

Atlas, that dour mountain which props the sky with his summit—
Atlas, his pine-bristled head for ever enwrapped in a bandeau
Of glooming cloud, for ever beaten by wind and rain;
Snow lies deep on his shoulders, and watercourses plunge down
That ancient's chin, while his shaggy beard is stiff with ice.
Here first did Mercury pause, hovering on beautifully-balanced
Wings; then stooped, dived bodily down to the sea below,
Like a bird which along the shore and around the promontories

[Lines 217–254]

Goes fishing, flying low, wave-hopping over the water.
Even so did Mercury skim between earth and sky
Towards the Libyan coast, cutting his path through the winds,
On his way from that mountain giant, Atlas, his mother's sire.
As soon as his winged feet had carried him to the shacks there,
He noticed Aeneas superintending the work on towers
And new buildings: he wore a sword studded with yellow
Jaspers, and a fine cloak of glowing Tyrian purple
Hung from his shoulders—the wealthy Dido had fashioned it,
Interweaving the fabric with threads of gold, as a present for him.
Mercury went for him at once:—

                So now you are laying
Foundations for lofty Carthage, building a beautiful city
To please a woman, lost to the interests of your own realm?
The king of the gods, who directs heaven and earth with his deity,
Sends me to you from bright Olympus: the king of the gods
Gave me this message to carry express through the air:—What do you
Aim at or hope for, idling and fiddling here in Libya?
If you're indifferent to your own high destiny
And for your own renown you will make no effort at all,
Think of your young hopeful, Ascanius, growing to manhood,
The inheritance which you owe him—an Italian kingdom, the soil of
Rome.

    Such were the words which Mercury delivered;
And breaking off abruptly, was manifest no more,
But vanished into thin air, far beyond human ken.

  Dazed indeed by that vision was Aeneas, and dumbfounded:
His hair stood on end with terror, the voice stuck in his throat.
Awed by this admonition from the great throne above,
He desired to fly the country, dear though it was to him.
But oh, what was he to do? What words could he find to get round
The temperamental queen? How broach the matter to her?
His mind was in feverish conflict, tossed from one side to the other,
Twisting and turning all ways to find a way past his dilemma.
So vacillating, at last he felt this the better decision:—
Sending for Mnestheus, Sergestus and brave Serestus, he bade them
Secretly get the ships ready, muster their friends on the beach,
Be prepared to fight: the cause of so drastic a change of plan
They must keep dark: in the meanwhile, assuming that generous Dido

[*Lines 255–291*]

74

Knew nothing and could not imagine the end of so great a love,
Aeneas would try for a way to approach her, the kindest moment
For speaking, the best way to deal with this delicate matter. His
comrades
Obeyed the command and did as he told them with cheerful alacrity.
But who can ever hoodwink a woman in love? The queen,
Apprehensive even when things went well, now sensed his deception,
Got wind of what was going to happen. That mischievous Rumour,
Whispering the fleet was preparing to sail, put her in a frenzy.
Distraught, she witlessly wandered about the city, raving
Like some Bacchante driven wild, when the emblems of sanctity
Stir, by the shouts of "Hail, Bacchus!", and drawn to Cithaeron
At night by the din of revellers, at the triennial orgies.
Finding Aeneas at last, she cried, before he could speak:—
Unfaithful man, did you think you could do such a dreadful thing
And keep it dark? yes, skulk from my land without one word?
Our love, the vows you made me—do these not give you pause,
Nor even the thought of Dido meeting a painful death?
Now, in the dead of winter, to be getting your ships ready
And hurrying to set sail when northerly gales are blowing,
You heartless one! Suppose the fields were not foreign, the home was
Not strange that you are bound for, suppose Troy stood as of old,
Would you be sailing for Troy, now, in this stormy weather?
Am I your reason for going? By these tears, by the hand you gave
me—
They are all I have left, to-day, in my misery—I implore you,
And by our union of hearts, by our marriage hardly begun,
If I have ever helped you at all, if anything
About me pleased you, be sad for our broken home, forgo
Your purpose, I beg you, unless it's too late for prayers of mine!
Because of you, the Libyan tribes and the Nomad chieftains
Hate me, the Tyrians are hostile: because of you I have lost
My old reputation for faithfulness—the one thing that could have
made me
Immortal. Oh, I am dying! To what, my guest, are you leaving me?
"Guest"—that is all I may call you now, who have called you
husband.
Why do I linger here? Shall I wait till my brother, Pygmalion,
Destroys this place, or Iarbas leads me away captive?

[*Lines 292–326*]

If even I might have conceived a child by you before
You went away, a little Aeneas to play in the palace
And, in spite of all this, to remind me of you by his looks, oh then
I should not feel so utterly finished and desolate.

She had spoken. Aeneas, mindful of Jove's words, kept his eyes
Unyielding, and with a great effort repressed his feeling for her.
In the end he managed to answer:—

Dido, I'll never pretend
You have not been good to me, deserving of everything
You can claim. I shall not regret my memories of Elissa
As long as I breathe, as long as I remember my own self.
For my conduct—this, briefly: I did not look to make off from here
In secret—do not suppose it; nor did I offer you marriage
At any time or consent to be bound by a marriage contract.
If fate allowed me to be my own master, and gave me
Free will to choose my way of life, to solve my problems,
Old Troy would be my first choice: I would restore it, and honour
My people's relics—the high halls of Priam perpetuated,
Troy given back to its conquered sons, a renaissant city,
Had been my task. But now Apollo and the Lycian
Oracle have told me that Italy is our bourne.
There lies my heart, my homeland. You, a Phoenician, are held by
These Carthaginian towers, by the charm of your Libyan city:
So can you grudge us Trojans our vision of settling down
In Italy? We too may seek a kingdom abroad.
Often as night envelops the earth in dewy darkness,
Often as star-rise, the troubled ghost of my father, Anchises,
Comes to me in my dreams, warns me and frightens me.
I am disturbed no less by the wrong I am doing Ascanius,
Defrauding him of his destined realm in Hesperia.
What's more, just now the courier of heaven, sent by Juppiter—
I swear it on your life and mine—conveyed to me, swiftly flying,
His orders: I saw the god, as clear as day, with my own eyes,
Entering the city, and these ears drank in the words he uttered.
No more reproaches, then—they only torture us both.
God's will, not mine, says "Italy".

All the while he was speaking she gazed at him askance,
Her glances flickering over him, eyes exploring the whole man
In deadly silence. Now, furiously, she burst out:—

[*Lines 327–364*]

Faithless and false! No goddess mothered you, no Dardanus
Your ancestor! I believe harsh Caucasus begat you
On a flint-hearted rock and Hyrcanian tigers suckled you.
Why should I hide my feelings? What worse can there be to keep
them for?
Not one sigh from him when I wept! Not a softer glance!
Did he yield an inch, or a tear, in pity for her who loves him?
I don't know what to say first. It has come to this,—not Juno,
Not Jove himself can view my plight with the eye of justice.
Nowhere is it safe to be trustful. I took him, a castaway,
A pauper, and shared my kingdom with him—I must have been mad—
Rescued his lost fleet, rescued his friends from death.
Oh, I'm on fire and drifting! And now Apollo's prophecies,
Lycian oracles, couriers of heaven sent by Juppiter
With stern commands—all these order you to betray me.
Oh, of course this is just the sort of transaction that troubles the calm of
The gods. I'll not keep you, nor probe the dishonesty of your words.
Chase your Italy, then! Go, sail to your realm overseas!
I only hope that, if the just spirits have any power,
Marooned on some mid-sea rock you may drink the full cup of agony
And often cry out for Dido. I'll dog you, from far, with the
death-fires;
And when cold death has parted my soul from my body, my spectre
Will be wherever you are. You shall pay for the evil you've done me.
The tale of your punishment will come to me down in the shades.

   With these words Dido suddenly ended, and sick at heart
Turned from him, tore herself away from his eyes, ran indoors,
While he hung back in dread of a still worse scene, although
He had much to say. Her maids bore up the fainting queen
Into her marble chamber and laid her down on the bed.

   But the god-fearing Aeneas, much as he longed to soothe
Her anguish with consolation, with words that would end her troubles,
Heavily sighing, his heart melting from love of her,
Nevertheless obeyed the gods and went off to his fleet.
Whereupon the Trojans redoubled their efforts, all along
The beach dragging down the tall ships, launching the well-tarred
bottoms,
Fetching green wood to make oars, and baulks of unfashioned timber
From the forest, so eager they were to be gone.

[*Lines 365–400*]

You could see them on the move, hurrying out of the city.
It looked like an army of ants when, provident for winter,
They're looting a great big corn-heap and storing it up in their own
                                                            house;
Over a field the black file goes, as they carry the loot
On a narrow track through the grass; some are strenuously pushing
The enormous grains of corn with their shoulders, while others marshal
The traffic and keep it moving: their whole road seethes with activity.
Ah, Dido, what did you feel when you saw these things going forward?
What moans you gave when, looking forth from your high roof-top,
You beheld the whole length of the beach aswarm with men, and the
                                                            sea's face
Alive with the sound and fury of preparations for sailing!
Excess of love, to what lengths you drive our human hearts!
Once again she was driven to try what tears and entreaties
Could do, and let love beggar her pride—she would leave no appeal
Untried, lest, for want of it, she should all needlessly die.

    Anna, you see the bustle down there on the beach; from all sides
They have assembled; their canvas is stretched to the winds already,
And the elated mariners have garlanded their ships.
If I was able to anticipate this deep anguish,
I shall be able to bear it. But do this one thing, Anna,
For your poor sister. You were the only confidante
Of that faithless man: he told you even his secret thoughts:
You alone know the most tactful way, the best time to approach him.
Go, sister, and make this appeal to my disdainful enemy:—
Say that I never conspired with the Greeks at Aulis to ruin
The Trojan people, nor sent squadrons of ships against Troy;
I never desecrated the ashes of dead Anchises
So why must Aeneas be deaf and obdurate to my pleading?
Why off so fast? Will he grant a last wish to her who unhappily
Loves him, and wait for a favouring wind, an easier voyage?
Not for our marriage that was do I plead now—he has forsworn it,
Nor that he go without his dear Latium and give up his kingdom.
I ask a mere nothing—just time to give rein to despair and thus calm it,
To learn from ill luck how to grieve for what I have lost, and to
                                                            bear it.

This last favour I beg—oh, pity your sister!—and if he
Grants it, I will repay him; my death shall be his interest.
    [*Lines 401–436*]

Such were her prayers, and such the tearful entreaties her agonised
Sister conveyed to Aeneas again and again. But unmoved by
Tearful entreaties he was, adamant against all pleadings:
Fate blocked them, heaven stopped his ears lest he turn complaisant.
As when some stalwart oak-tree, some veteran of the Alps,
Is assailed by a wintry wind whose veering gusts tear at it,
Trying to root it up; wildly whistle the branches,
The leaves come flocking down from aloft as the bole is battered;
But the tree stands firm on its crag, for high as its head is carried
Into the sky, so deep do its roots go down towards Hades:
Even thus was the hero belaboured for long with every kind of
Pleading, and his great heart thrilled through and through with the
pain of it;
Resolute, though, was his mind; unavailingly rolled her tears.
    But hapless Dido, frightened out of her wits by her destiny,
Prayed for death: she would gaze no more on the dome of daylight.
And now, strengthening her resolve to act and to leave this world,
She saw, as she laid gifts on the incense-burning altars—
Horrible to relate—the holy water turn black
And the wine she poured changing uncannily to blood.
She told noone, not even her sister, of this phenomenon.
Again, she had dedicated a chantry of marble within
The palace to her first husband; held it in highest reverence;
Hung it with snow-white fleeces and with festoons of greenery:
Well, from this shrine, when night covered the earth, she seemed
To be hearing words—the voice of that husband calling upon her.
There was something dirge-like, too, in the tones of the owl on the
roof-top
Whose lonely, repeated cries were drawn out to a long keening.
Besides, she recalled with horror presages, dread forewarnings
Of the prophets of old. Aeneas himself pursued her remorselessly
In dreams, driving her mad; or else she dreamed of unending
Solitude and desertion, of walking alone and eternally
Down a long road, through an empty land, in search of her Tyrians.
Just so does the raving Pentheus see covens of Furies and has the
Delusion of seeing two suns in the sky and a double Thebes:
Just so on the stage does Orestes, the son of Agamemnon,
Move wildly about while his mother pursues him with torches and
black snakes,

[*Lines 437–472*]

79

And at the door the avenging Furies cut off his retreat.

   So when, overmastered by grief, she conceived a criminal madness
And doomed herself to death, she worked out the time and method
In secret; then, putting on an expression of calm hopefulness
To hide her resolve, she approached her sorrowing sister with these
words:—

   I have found out a way, Anna—oh, wish me joy of it—
To get him back or else get free of my love for him.
Near Ocean's furthest bound and the sunset is Aethiopia,
The very last place on earth, where giant Atlas pivots
The wheeling sky, embossed with fiery stars, on his shoulders.
I have been in touch with a priestess from there, a Massylian, who once,
As warden of the Hesperides' sacred close, was used to
Feed the dragon which guarded their orchard of golden apples,
Sprinkling its food with moist honey and sedative poppy-seeds.
Now this enchantress claims that her spells can liberate
One's heart, or can inject love-pangs, just as she wishes;
Can stop the flow of rivers, send the stars flying backwards,
Conjure ghosts in the night: she can make the earth cry out
Under one's feet, and elm trees come trooping down from the
mountains.

Dear sister, I solemnly call to witness the gods and you whom
I love, that I do not willingly resort to her magic arts.
You must build up a funeral pyre high in the inner courtyard,
And keep it dark: lay on it the arms which that godless man
Has left on the pegs in our bedroom, all relics of him, and the
marriage-bed

That was the ruin of me. To blot out all that reminds me
Of that vile man is my pleasure and what the enchantress directs.

   So Dido spoke, and fell silent, her face going deadly white.
Yet Anna never suspected that Dido was planning her own death
Through these queer rites, nor imagined how frantic a madness
possessed her,

Nor feared any worse would happen than when Sychaeus had died.
So she made the arrangements required of her.

   When in the innermost court of the palace the pyre had been built up
To a great height with pinewood and logs of ilex, the queen
Festooned the place with garlands and wreathed it with funereal
Foliage: then she laid on it the clothes, the sword which Aeneas

   [*Lines 473–507*]

Had left, and an effigy of him; she well knew what was to happen.
Altars were set up all round. Her hair unloosed, the enchantress
Loudly invoked three hundred deities—Erebus, Chaos,
Hecate, three in one, and three-faced Diana, the virgin.
She had sprinkled water which came, she pretended, from Lake
Avernus;
Herbs she had gathered, cut by moonlight with a bronze knife—
Poisonous herbs all rank with juices of black venom;
She had found a love charm, a gland torn from the forehead of a
new-born
Foal before its mother could get it.
Dido, the sacramental grain in her purified hands,
One foot unsandalled, her dress uncinctured, stood by the altars
Calling upon the gods and the stars that know fate's secrets,
Death at her heart, and prayed to whatever power it is
Holds unrequited lovers in its fair, faithful keeping.

Was night. All over the earth, creatures were plucking the flower
Of soothing sleep, the woods and the wild seas fallen quiet—
A time when constellations have reached their mid-career,
When the countryside is all still, the beasts and the brilliant birds
That haunt the lakes' wide waters or the tangled undergrowth
Of the champain, stilled in sleep under the quiet night—
Cares are lulled and hearts can forget for a while their travails.
Not so the Phoenician queen: death at her heart, she could not
Ever relax in sleep, let the night in to her eyes
Or mind: her agonies mounted, her love reared up again
And savaged her, till she writhed in a boiling sea of passion.
So thus she began, her thoughts whirled round in a vicious circle:—

What shall I do? Shall I, who've been jilted, return to my former
Suitors? go down on my knees for marriage to one of the Nomads
Although, time and again, I once rejected their offers?
Well then, am I to follow the Trojan's fleet and bow to
Their lightest word? I helped them once. Will that help me now?
Dare I think they remember with gratitude my old kindness?
But even if I wished it, who would suffer me, welcome me
Aboard those arrogant ships? They hate me. Ah, duped and ruined!—
Surely by now I should know the ill faith of Laomedon's people?
So then? Shall I sail, by myself, with those exulting mariners,
Or sail against them with all my Tyrian folk about me—

[*Lines 508–544*]

My people, whom once I could hardly persuade to depart from Sidon—
Bidding them man their ships and driving them out to sea again?
Better die—I deserve it—end my pain with the sword.
Sister, you started it all: overborne by my tears, you laid up
These evils to drive me mad, put me at the mercy of a foe.
Oh, that I could have been some child of nature and lived
An innocent life, untouched by marriage and all its troubles!
I have broken the faith I vowed to the memory of Sichaeus.

    Such were the reproaches she could not refrain from uttering.
High on the poop of his ship, resolute now for departure,
Aeneas slept; preparations for sailing were fully completed.
To him in a dream there appeared the shape of the god, returning
Just as he'd looked before, as if giving the same admonitions—
Mercury's very image, the voice, the complexion, the yellow
Hair and the handsome youthful body identical:—

    Goddess-born, can you go on sleeping at such a crisis?
Are you out of your mind, not to see what dangers are brewing up
Around you, and not to hear the favouring breath of the West wind?
Being set upon death, her heart is aswirl with conflicting passions,
Aye, she is brooding now some trick, some desperate deed.
Why are you not going, all speed, while the going is good?
If dawn finds you still here, delaying by these shores,
You'll have the whole sea swarming with hostile ships, there will be
Firebrands coming against you, you'll see this beach ablaze.
Up and away, then! No more lingering! Woman was ever
A veering, weathercock creature.

                      He spoke, and vanished in the darkness.
Then, startled by the shock of the apparition, Aeneas
Snatched himself out of sleep and urgently stirred up his comrades:—

    Jump to it, men! To your watch! Get to the rowing benches!
Smartly! Hoist the sails! A god from heaven above
Spurs me to cut the cables, make off and lose not a moment:
This was his second warning. O blessed god, we follow you,
God indeed, and once more we obey the command joyfully!
Be with us! Look kindly upon us! Grant us good sailing weather!

    Thus did Aeneas cry, and flashing his sword from its scabbard,
With the drawn blade he severed the moorings. The same sense of
Urgency fired his comrades all; they cut and ran for it.
The shore lay empty. The ships covered the open sea.

    [*Lines 545–582*]

The oarsmen swept the blue and sent the foam flying with hard strokes.
    And now was Aurora, leaving the saffron bed of Tithonus,
Beginning to shower upon earth the light of another day.
The queen, looking forth from her roof-top, as soon as she saw the sky
Grow pale and the Trojan fleet running before the wind,
Aware that the beach and the roadstead were empty, the sailors gone,
Struck herself three times, four times, upon her lovely breast,
Tore at her yellow hair, and exclaimed:—

                              In god's name! shall that foreigner
Scuttle away and make a laughing-stock of my country?
Will not my people stand to arms for a mass pursuit?
Will some not rush the warships out of the docks? Move, then!
Bring firebrands apace, issue the weapons, pull on the oars!
What am I saying? Where am I? What madness veers my mind?
Poor Dido, the wrong you have done—is it only now coming home
                                              to you?
You should have thought of that when you gave him your sceptre.
                                              So this is
The word of honour of one who, men say, totes round his home-gods
Everywhere, and bore on his back a doddering father!
Why could I not have seized him, torn up his body and littered
The sea with it? finished his friends with the sword, finished his own
Ascanius and served him up for his father to banquet on?
The outcome of battle had been uncertain?—Let it have been so:
Since I was to die, whom had I to fear? I should have stormed
Their bulwarks with fire, set alight their gangways, gutted the whole
                                              lot—
Folk, father and child—then flung myself on the conflagration.
O sun, with your beams surveying all that is done on earth!
Juno, the mediator and witness of my tragedy!
Hecate, whose name is howled by night at the city crossroads!
Avenging Furies, and you, the patrons of dying Elissa!—
Hear me! Incline your godheads to note this wickedness
So worthy of your wrath! And hear my prayer! If he,
That damned soul, must make port and get to land, if thus
Jove destines it, if that bourne is fixed for him irrevocably,
May he be harried in war by adventurous tribes, and exiled
From his own land; may Ascanius be torn from his arms; may he
                                              have to
[*Lines 583–616*]

Sue for aid, and see his own friends squalidly dying.
Yes, and when he's accepted the terms of a harsh peace,
Let him never enjoy his realm or the allotted span,
But fall before his time and lie on the sands, unburied.
That is my last prayer. I pour it out, with my lifeblood.
Let you, my Tyrians, sharpen your hatred upon his children
And all their seed for ever: send this as a present to
My ghost. Between my people and his, no love, no alliance!
Rise up from my dead bones, avenger! Rise up, one
To hound the Trojan settlers with fire and steel remorselessly,
Now, some day, whenever the strength for it shall be granted!
Shore to shore, sea to sea, weapon to weapon opposed—
I call down a feud between them and us to the last generation!
　These things she said; then tried to think of every expedient,
Seeking the quickest way out of the life she hated.
Briefly now she addressed Barce, the nurse of Sychaeus,
Her own being dust and ashes, interred in her native land:—
　Dear nurse, please will you get my sister, Anna. She must
Hasten to purify herself with living water, and fetch
The cattle, tell her—the atonement offerings, as directed;
Then let her come. And do you go and put on the holy head-band.
These rites to Jove of the Underworld, duly made ready and started,
I mean to go through with now, and put an end to my troubles,
Committing to the flames the funeral pyre of that Trojan.
　She spoke. The nurse hurried off with senile officiousness.
But Dido, trembling, distraught by the terrible thing she was doing,
Her bloodshot eyes all restless, with hectic blotches upon
Her quivering cheeks, yet pale with the shade of advancing death,
Ran to the innermost court of the palace, climbed the lofty
Pyre, frantic at heart, and drew Aeneas' sword—
Her present to him, procured once for a far different purpose.
Then, after eyeing the clothes he had left behind, and the memoried
Bed, pausing to weep and brood on him for a little,
She lay down on the bed and spoke her very last words:—
　O relics of him, things dear to me while fate, while heaven allowed,
Receive this life of mine, release me from my troubles!
I have lived, I have run to the finish the course which fortune gave me:
And now, a queenly shade, I shall pass to the world below.
　[*Lines 617–654*]

I built a famous city, saw my own place established,
Avenged a husband, exacted a price for a brother's enmity.
Happy I would have been, ah, beyond words happy,
If only the Trojan ships had never come to my shore!
    These words; then, burying her face in the bed:—

                                        Shall I die unavenged?
At least, let me die. Thus, thus! I go to the dark, go gladly.
May he look long, from out there on the deep, at my flaming pyre,
The heartless! And may my death-fires signal bad luck for his voyage!
    She had spoken; and with these words, her attendants saw her falling
Upon the sword, they could see the blood spouting up over
The blade, and her hands spattered. Their screams rang to the roofs of
The palace; then rumour ran amok through the shocked city.
All was weeping and wailing, the streets were filled with a keening
Of women, the air resounded with terrible lamentations.
It was as if Carthage or ancient Tyre should be falling,
With enemy troops breaking into the town and a conflagration
Furiously sweeping over the abodes of men and of gods.
Anna heard it: half dead from extreme fear, she ran through
The crowd, tearing her cheeks with her nails, beating her breast
With her fists, and called aloud by name on the dying woman:—
    So this was your purpose, Dido? You were making a dupe of me?
That pyre, those lighted altars—for me, they were leading to this?
How shall I chide you for leaving me? Were you too proud to let your
Sister die with you? You should have called me to share your end:
One hour, one pang of the sword could have carried us both away.
Did I build this pyre with my own hands, invoking our family gods,
So that you might lie on it, and I, the cause of your troubles, not be

                                                  there?
You have destroyed more than your self—me, and the lords
And commons and city of Sidon. Quick! Water for her wounds!
Let me bathe them, and if any last breath is fluttering from her mouth,
Catch it in mine!
                So saying, she had scaled the towering pyre,
Taken the dying woman into her lap, was caressing her,
Sobbing, trying to staunch the dark blood with her own dress.
Dido made an effort to raise her heavy eyes,
Then gave it up: the sword-blade grated against her breast bone.
Three times she struggled to rise, to lift herself on an elbow,

                                    [*Lines 655–690*]

Three times rolled back on the bed. Her wandering gaze went up
To the sky, looking for light: she gave a moan when she saw it.

Then did almighty Juno take pity on her long-drawn-out
Sufferings and hard going, sent Iris down from Olympus
To part the agonised soul from the body that still clung to it.
Since she was dying neither a natural death nor from others'
Violence, but desperate and untimely, driven to it
By a crazed impulse, not yet had Proserpine clipped from her head
The golden tress, or consigned her soul to the Underworld.
So now, all dewy, her pinions the colour of yellow crocus,
Her wake a thousand rainbow hues refracting the sunlight,
Iris flew down, and over Dido hovering, said:—

As I was bidden, I take this sacred thing, the Death-god's
Due: and you I release from your body.

                                She snipped the tress.
Then all warmth went at once, the life was lost in air.

   [*Lines 691–705*]

BOOK V

Meanwhile Aeneas held his fleet on its course through the deepsea
Undeviating, and clove the waves that were gloomed by a North wind.
He looked back at Carthage's walls; they were lit up now by the
death-fires

Of tragic Dido. Why so big a fire should be burning
Was a mystery: but knowing what a woman is capable of
When insane with the grief of having her love cruelly dishonoured,
Started a train of uneasy conjecture in the Trojans' minds.
    The ships being now well out to sea, no further sight of
Land in the offing, nothing but sea and sky all round them,
An indigo-coloured rain cloud stood overhead, the precursor
Of gloom and storm, and the sea's face darkened with shuddering
catspaws.

Palinurus, the steersman, high on the afterdeck, exclaimed:—
    My god! What does this pack of cloud in the sky portend?
Father Neptune, what have you in store for us?
                                        Then he ordered
His comrades to make all fast and strain at the stalwart oars,
And sailing his ship closer-hauled to the wind, he spoke again:—
    Great-hearted Aeneas, not even if Juppiter guarantees it,
Have I any hope of making Italy in such weather.
The wind has changed, and is blowing abeam: the West looks black—
A gale is getting up there, clouds are gathering densely.
I am certain we cannot sail in the teeth of that storm, or make
Enough way against it. Since fortune's too strong for us, we should
give in,

Change course at her direction. The coasts of your brother Eryx
Are safe, and not far off, I think, and the harbours of Sicily,
Let me but remember the stars I steered by, last time we sailed there.
    Aeneas the true replied:—
                            I agree. I have seen for some time that
The wind so requires and you have been making no headway against it.
Pay off on this other course, then. What land could be more welcome,
                                        [Lines 1–28]

Where would I rather get these battered ships to port,
Than the place where my Trojan friend, Acestes, is still living
And the bones of my father, Anchises, lie in the lap of earth.

When he had spoken, they turned for port; the sails drew well
In the West wind from astern and the fleet raced over the rough sea,
Until, elated, they brought up on the sandy beach they knew.

Afar, from a high hilltop, Acestes marvelled to see
His friends' ships bearing toward his coast: he went to meet them,
A rough-looking man with his javelins and the pelt of the Libyan
she-bear

He wore—Acestes, son of a Trojan dame and the river
Crimisus. Thinking now of the Trojan blood in his veins
He congratulates them on their return, genially plies them
With rustic plenty, comforts the tired travellers with good cheer.

On the morrow, at early dawn, when the bright day had sent
The stars packing, Aeneas summoned his men from their bivouacs
Along the shore to a meeting, stood on a dune and addressed them:—

Proud Dardans, you who trace your lineage from the high gods,
Twelve months have passed, a year has almost come full circle
Since we interred the remains, the bones of my own sainted
Father, and consecrated an altar to him in sorrow.
And now, unless I'm mistaken, the day is near which will always
Be bitter and sacred to me—such was your will, you gods.
Were I spending it as an exile among the Gaetulian Syrtes,
If it came upon me in mid-Aegean or in Mycenae,
I would keep that day with anniversary vows and solemn
Cortege, loading the altars with the gifts that are proper to them.
But now—and I'm quite sure it's with the design and approval of
heaven—
We're actually close to the spot where my father's ashes and bones
Are buried, we have been brought to enter this friendly harbour.
Come then, let us all with cheerful hearts honour the festival:
Pray we for favourable winds: may he grant me, my city founded,
Yearly to hold these rites at a shrine dedicated to him.
Like a good son of Troy, Acestes is contributing
Two head of oxen for every ship. Invite to the feast
Our own home-gods and the ones whom our host, Acestes, worships!
What's more, if the ninth dawn from now, with her rays unshrouding
The earth below her, should bring a fine day for us to enjoy,

[Lines 29–65]

I shall hold a Trojan Games: a regatta, first, for the ships;
Then let the champion runners, and those who take the arena
Confident in their skill at throwing the javelin or archery;
Those, too, that boldly challenge with the rawhide boxing gloves—
Let them all come forward, eager to win the palm of the victor.
Now silence, all, for the rites, and garland your heads with greenery!

So saying, Aeneas put on a wreath of his mother's myrtle.
Helymus did the same, and the ripe-aged Acestes
And young Ascanius; the rest of the men there followed suit.
Then from the place of meeting, with a great crowd about him,
Thousands of them, Aeneas moved on to the burial mound.
Here, in a ceremonial libation, he poured on the earth
Two goblets of wine unwatered, two of fresh milk, and two
Of victims' blood; and scattering bright-coloured blossoms, he spoke:—

I greet you again, my hallowed sire! Greetings, ye ashes,
Spirit and shade of the father I rescued from Troy in vain!
It was not allowed I should have you with me upon my quest for
Italy, our destined home, and that mysterious Tiber.

So much he had said, when a giant snake came slithering out from
Under the shrine. It had seven great rolling coils. Inoffensive,
It now encircled the barrow, sliding between the altars:
Upon its back was a sheen, a dapple of blueish markings
And of gold-glinting scales, like the shimmer of many colours
A rainbow lays on the dark cloud, refractions from the sunlight.
Aeneas was awed by the sight. The snake now, dragging its gradual
Length among the bowls and polished wine-cups, tasted
The sacramental meats, then harmlessly went back under
The burial mound again, leaving the altars he'd fed from:
Heartened by this, Aeneas resumed the rites he'd begun
In Anchises' honour, not sure if that snake should be deemed his father's
Familiar or the genius of the place: as the rites require,
He sacrificed two sheep, two swine and two black heifers;
Poured out wine from the bowls, invoked the spirit of noble
Anchises, invoked his phantom, a revenant from death's domain.
His comrades too—each man as his means permitted—with high hearts
Brought offerings, made sacrifice of bullocks, loaded the altars;
While others in turn set up cauldrons and, stretched at their ease,
Roasted the meat upon spits over the charcoal embers.

The day was come they had so looked forward to—the ninth day,

[*Lines 66–104*]

Dawning fine and calm, brought on by the Sun-god's horses.
Attracted by the name and prestige of famous Acestes,
Crowds of people were coming in holiday spirits from all round,
To stare at Aeneas' men, and some to take part in the Games.
First were the prizes displayed, for all to see, in the middle
Of the arena—tripods for sacrifice, green garlands,
Palm-wreaths, the winners' awards, with pieces of armour, and clothing
Purple-dyed, and gold and silver weighed out in talents.
A fanfare, blown from a mound at the centre, opened the Games.
The first event was a rowing race, for which four galleys
Equally matched, and chosen from the whole fleet, were entered.
The speedy *Whale*, with its lively crew, was commanded by

Mnestheus—

Soon to be Mnestheus of Italy and found the Memmian clan:
Gyas was skipper of the *Chimaera*, a huge vessel,
Big as a town, which its Dardan crew propelled with triple-banked
Oars—three tiers of them, one staggered over another:
Sergestus, from whom the Sergian family gets its name,
Shipped in the great *Centaur*: Cloanthus had the sea-blue
Scylla—from him is descended your family, Roman Cluentius.
    Well out at sea, right opposite this spindrift-tossing shore,
There is a rock, submerged and thumped by a heavy swell
At times when the wintry nor'-westers blot out the stars from the sky:
In a calm, it's a quiet place, lifting above still water
A flat top, where the gulls love to perch and bask in the sunshine.
Here Aeneas erected an ilex, leaves and all,
As a seamark for the mariners, to show them where they must turn,
And rounding it, row back the length of the course again.
Then they drew lots for position: the masters, up on the afterdecks,
Noticeable from afar in their gold and purple finery;
The rest of the crews wearing garlands of poplar leaves,
Their shoulders bare and shining with the oil they had applied.
They get to the rowing thwarts, their arms are braced on the oars;
Tensely they wait the starting signal, hearts drained of blood,
Leaping and pounding with nervousness and the lust for victory.
Then a clear trumpet-call was given. In a flash, the four ships
Were over the starting-line. The bosuns' calls beat out,
White with foam is the water churned up by those strong arms pulling.
Side by side they furrow the sea, whose face is all
    [*Lines 105–142*]

90

Convulsed and troughed by the oars and the trident-like bows of the
galleys.

Not at such headlong speed, in a race for two-horse chariots,
Do the cars leap forth from the starting-box and burn up the track,
when wildly
The charioteers have shaken their rippling reins hard over
The necks of the bolting horses and are leaning right forward to lash
them.

Now the woods all resound with applause, with the shindy of backers
Yelling their favourites on, and the shouting is bandied around
The hills that shut in the shore as it strikes them and echoes back.
Amidst that hurly-burly, Gyas gets out in front
Of the ruck and leads the others: Cloanthus is lying second—
His crew are better together, but the weight of their pine-built ship
Handicaps them. At an equal distance behind these two,
The *Whale* and the *Centaur* struggle, jockeying for a lead;
Now the *Whale* has it, now the big *Centaur* spurts and passes her,
Now, neck and neck they are rowing, both, their bows dead level
And their long keels together cutting the briny deep.
When they were nearing the rock and close to the turning-point,
Gyas, who at the halfway mark was still ahead,
Loudly hailed Menoetes, the coxswain of his galley:—
    Why are you keeping so far out to starboard? Steer in! Port rudder!
Hug the rock's edge! I want the port-side oarblades to graze it!
Let the rest of them keep to deep water!
He spoke: but Menoetes, fearing
Some hidden reef, turned further away to the open sea.
    Where are you wandering? I've told you, make for the rock,
Menoetes!
Gyas shouted him back on his course. But that moment he saw
Over his shoulder Cloanthus in the inside berth and closing him.
He, to port of Gyas, scrapes through between Gyas' ship
And the surf-roaring rock-face; and all at once he has passed
The leader, rounded the sea-mark, and won into safe water.
Then was young Gyas pierced to the quick by extreme chagrin,
And tears rolled down his cheeks: forgetting decorum, blind to
His crew's safety, he seized the unenterprising Menoetes
And heaved him bodily overboard from the afterdeck,
Then taking the tiller himself, as master and coxswain both,

[Lines 143–176]

Cheered on his men and ruddered the galley closer inshore.
But heavy with age, his soaked clothes weighing him down, Menoetes
Struggled at last to the surface from the bottom of the sea, and dripping
Clambered up the rock and sat down on its dry top.
The Trojans laughed at the sight of him going overboard, swimming,
And now they laugh to see him spew up the brine from his stomach.
This event cheered the two last captains, Sergestus and Mnestheus:
They had a possible hope now to catch up with Gyas and pass him.
Nearing the rock, Sergestus draws just ahead; but there is no
Daylight yet between his ship and Mnestheus'—he only leads
By half a length, the *Whale's* bows are pressing him hard amidships.
Mnestheus, moving among his crew, in the waist of the galley,
Encourages them:—

        Now for a spurt! Quicken the stroke now!
You fought at Hector's side. I chose you to be my comrades
In the last days of Troy. Now let us see the strength,
The valour of heart you showed among the Gaetulian quicksands,
In the Ionian sea and the hard-running waves off Malea.
I do not aim at the first place now, or strive to be winner,
Although—— But let victory go to the crew for whom Neptune
                        intends it!

To come in last *would* be a disgrace: don't fail so badly,
My friends! Avoid such a scandal!
             So, with the utmost exertion
They pulled; and the bronze poop throbbed at their tremendous strokes,
And the sea whisked by beneath them: their bodies, their bone-dry
                        mouths
Shook as their breath came faster: they ran rivers of sweat.
An accident, pure chance gave Mnestheus the honour he wanted:
For, while Sergestus edges his prow towards the rock
In a frantic attempt to get through on the inside, the space there being
Too narrow, his ship unluckily grounds on a jutting reef.
The rock was jarred, the oars smashed on its jagged edge
As they struck it; the impact lifted the bows and wedged them fast.
The crew, cursing aloud this hold-up, leapt to their feet,
With iron-tipped poles and sharp-pointed quants struggling to push off
The galley, and salvaging the splintered oars from the sea.
But Mnestheus, heartened and braced in nerve by this bit of luck,
At a high rate of striking, the wind at his back, made for

[*Lines 177–211*]

92

The sea that sloped before him, raced on through the open water.
Just as a pigeon, startled and suddenly flushed from the cave
Where her home, her darling nest is hidden deep in the rock,
Goes flying over the fields—first a loud, terrified clapping
Of wings as she breaks from cover, then through the noiseless air
She fluently skims her way, gliding without a wing-beat:
So Mnestheus went, so the *Whale* ran rapidly over the last lap
Of the course, so was she carried on by her own momentum.
First she leaves Sergestus behind, high and dry on the reef,
In the shoal water, struggling to back off, vainly shouting
For help, and taking a lesson in rowing with broken oars.
Next, she is after Gyas and his huge, ponderous ship,
Chimaera, which falls away, through lack of her proper helmsman.
And now, as they near the finish, Cloanthus alone is left:
In chase of him, Mnestheus goes all out—a tremendous spurt.
Then was the din redoubled; the spectators all to a man
Cheered on the pursuer; crash after crash of applause thundered.
One crew was impelled by the shame of losing a prize they had all but
Gained for their own, and would give their lives for its glory; the other
Was fired by success—they could do it because they believed they
                                                        could do it.
And now they had drawn level and well might win the prize,
But that Cloanthus, stretching his palms out to the sea,
Poured forth a prayer and invited the gods to strike a bargain:—

  You gods, you emperors of the sea, whose waters I race on,
Gladly upon this shore will I offer up at your altars
A sleek white bull, in discharge of my vow, presenting its entrails
To the salt waves and making libation of wine as well.

  He spoke; and from deep under water was heard by the whole
                                                        company
Of Nereids and of Phorcus and by the sea-nymph Panopea;
And father Portunus himself pushed the ship on its way
With a huge hand, so that it sped to the shore swifter than wind
Or a flying arrow, and buried itself deep in the harbour.
Now the son of Anchises, calling them all around him
In the usual way, proclaimed, through a loud-voiced herald, Cloanthus
The winner, and placed on his head a garland of green bay leaves;
Then gave him first choice of the prizes presented for each of the
                                                        crews—
                    [*Lines 212–247*]

Namely, three bullocks, with wine, and a heavy talent of silver.
Special awards were made to the actual captains next:
The victor received a cloak wrought of gold thread, with a double
Key-patterned border of rich Meliboean purple around it;
Woven upon it was Ganymede, hunting on leafy Ida
With his javelin, hunting down swift stags—you could almost see him
Panting, the nimble boy; he was pictured, too, being snatched up
Aloft from Ida in the claws of Juppiter's fast-flying eagle—
His aged guardians are raising their impotent hands to heaven,
His dogs are furiously barking up at the sky above them.
Next, the captain whose stout heart had won him the second place
Was given for his own—a handsome thing and a safeguard in battle—
A corselet made of smooth gold chain mail, triple-meshed,
That Aeneas himself had stripped from the corpse of Demoleos,
vanquished
In combat beneath the walls of Ilium, near Simois' torrent.
The servants, Phegeus and Sagaris, were staggering under the weight of
Its intricate mesh, could hardly shoulder it; yet Demoleos,
Wearing it, used to pursue at a run the Trojans he'd routed.
For third prize, Aeneas put up a pair of copper cauldrons
And two bowls, fashioned of silver, with designs in high relief.
Now all the recipients were moving away, showing off their prizes,
With purple ribbon strung through the garlands upon their temples,
When Sergestus, who'd worked himself off that cruel rock with great
skill
And trouble, oars lost, one tier of them quite disabled, was bringing
His vessel ingloriously to port, amid general laughter.
As often occurs when a snake has been caught on the hump of a
high road,
A bronze wheel running across it, or a wayfarer smashing it hard with
A stone and leaving it there, crushed and half dead, the serpent
Makes futile attempts to escape, wriggling its long body—
Part of it still defiant, eyes blazing, the neck reared upright
And hissing; while part of it, crippled by injury, drags,
Lashing itself into knots and writhing back on its own coils.
Something like this was the oarage working that sluggish vessel:
However, she made sail too and fetched into port under full sail.
Aeneas, pleased that the ship was not wrecked and his friends had got
back

[*Lines 248–282*]

Safely, presented Sergestus with the reward he had promised.
His personal prize was a slave girl, skilled in Minerva's tasks—
Pholoë, of Cretan stock, with twin sons at her breast.

This event being decided, true-hearted Aeneas now
Moved off to a grassy plain which lay with wooded hills
All round it—the valley forming a natural amphitheatre
And race-track. Hither, a great throng about him, repaired the hero
And sat down on a dais amid the assembled crowds.
Here, for whoever might wish to compete in a running race,
He set up prizes—awards to stimulate their rivalry.
Competitors came flocking, Sicilians and Trojans together:
Nisus and Euryalus were first—
Euryalus outstanding in beauty and bloom of youth,
Nisus renowned for his pure love of his friend: they were followed
By prince Diores, a young man of Priam's noble stock;
After him, side by side, Salius and Patron, the one
Acarnanian, the other Arcadian, of a Tegaean family:
Next were two young Sicilians, Helymus and Panopes,
Expert foresters both, attendants on old Acestes;
And many besides, less known to fame, their names not mentioned.
Aeneas gathered them round him, and spoke to them now like this:—

Give me your cheerful attention, take to heart what I'm saying.
None of you will depart without a present from me.
I shall give to every man, as a token of honour, a pair of
Gnossian arrowheads, made of bright-polished steel, and an axe
Chased with silver, to carry away. The first three to finish
Get prizes as well, and a garland of pale-green olive to wear.
For the winner there is a horse, finely caparisoned:
For second place, an Amazon's quiver filled with Thracian
Arrows, slung upon a broad belt gold-embossed,
And fastened by a buckle set with a polished gem:
He who comes third may be pleased to take this Argive helmet.

After this speech, they took up position. The starting signal
Was given. In a flash they are off and sprinting along the track,
Like a ragged rain-cloud, keeping their eyes fixed on the finish.
Now Nisus, going faster than wind or a winged thunderbolt,
Shoots to the lead and draws right away from the ruck of the runners.
Next to him, but next with a long distance between them,
There follows Salius; and then, some way behind him,

[*Lines 283–321*]

Euryalus lies third.
Euryalus is being chased by Helymus: but Diores
Is right at Helymus' shoulder, running there stride for stride
And grazing his heel—if only the course were a little longer,
He'd get ahead and leave him fighting for a place.
Now the race was almost over; the spent runners
Were nearing the tape, when Nisus had the misfortune to slip
In a greasy patch of blood which lay on the course and made its
Grass surface slippery (bullocks, it chanced, had been slaughtered there).
Here the young man, already flushed with victory, could not
Keep his footing on the ground; he teetered, and fell headlong
Face down in the filthy slime and the blood of the sacrificed animals.
Yet, even so, he remembered Euryalus, his dear friend;
Rose from the slippery mess, got in the way of Salius
And sent him spinning, tumbling down on the clotted earth.
Euryalus now darted by, and thanks to his friend's act,
Ran in first, and flew on to wild cheering, a popular winner.
Helymus came in next: Diores took the third place.
Salius at once, before the whole crowd in the huge amphitheatre
And the elders who sat in the best seats, loudly objected, claiming
He'd been done out of the prize by foul play, and ought to be given it.
Popular feeling sided with Euryalus—there was also
His manly distress, and that worth which is made the more winning
                                                              by good looks.
Diores backed him too, with appeals to the public: Diores
Had got a place, but in vain—there would be no third prize
For him, if the first prize were handed over to Salius.
Then father Aeneas proclaimed:—
                              Your prizes, my lads, are assured you:
Noone is changing the order of the first three who finished.
But I may show my regret for an innocent friend's downfall.
    So saying, he gave Salius the skin of a great Gaetulian
Lion—a weighty thing with its shock of hair and its gilt claws.
Now Nisus remarked:—
                              If you give such rewards to losers and feel
So sorry for those who have come a cropper, what suitable prize
Have you got for me? After all, I'd have won the victor's crown
If I had not been baulked by the same bad luck as Salius.
    While he was speaking, Nisus displayed his face and limbs
[*Lines 322–357*]

96

Fouled with the slimy filth. Then good Aeneas laughed at him
And ordering a shield to be brought (Didymaon's work, it had hung
once
By the gateway of Neptune's temple and been torn down by the
Greeks),
Presented it to the excellent youth, a prize of value.
   Later, the races finished and the prizes all distributed,
Now, said Aeneas, if any has courage and speed of reaction,
Let him step forward and put on the gloves for a boxing match.
For this contest Aeneas set up a couple of prizes:
The winner would get a garlanded bullock with gilded horns,
The loser console himself with a sword and a fine-looking helmet.
They didn't wait long, for at once Dares stood forth in all his
Powerful bulk; a deep murmur came from the crowd as he rose:
He—no others dared—used to take Paris on;
He it was, at the tomb where mighty Hector sleeps,
Who met the champion Butes, a mountain of a man, when he came
To Troy (Butes was of the Bebrycian clan of Amycus),
Knocked him out, laid him dying upon the tawny sand.
Such was the Dares who now put himself in a challenging posture,
Exhibiting his broad shoulders, leading with left and right
As he pounded the air and indulged in a bout of shadow-boxing.
An opponent for him was sought: but, from that whole gathering,
Not one man had the nerve to come forward and put on the gloves.
So, thinking he'd get the prize by default, Dares exultantly
Stepped right up to Aeneas and, without further preamble
Seizing the bullock by a horn with his left hand, spoke as follows:—
   Goddess-born, if noone dares enter the ring against me,
What am I waiting for? How long am I to be kept here?
Let me take my award!
                    Then all the Trojans unanimously
Called out, saying the man should be given the guaranteed stake.
But at this point Acestes sternly reproved Entellus,
Who happened to be sitting next him upon the grassy mound:—
   Entellus, you were once the bravest of heroes: but now!—
Are you going to sit there tamely and let such a prize be won
Without a blow? Where now is Eryx, your heaven-born instructor?—
We are foolish, it seems, to take pride in him. And what of your own
Sicily-wide reputation? the trophies that hang in your house?
[Lines 358–393]

97

Entellus replied:—

                It is not that my love of fame, of glory,
Has yielded to cowardice. No, but I'm getting old and sluggish;
My reactions are slower, my blood runs cooler, my strength is burnt out.
If I had now what I once had—what that exhibitionist yonder
So brashly relies on—if only I had my youth again,
By god, I'd need no inducement, no prizes of beautiful bullocks,
To enter the ring! But to hell with prizes!

                           Entellus spoke;
Then hurled into the ring a pair of enormously heavy
Boxing gloves, which the fast-footed Eryx was used to wear
When he was fighting, their tough hide laced tight over his forearms.
Petrified were the spectators; for seven huge ox-hides had gone to
Those terrible gloves, lead and iron had been sewn in to harden them.
Dares himself, above all, stood aghast, shrank back and refused
To fight. Great-hearted Aeneas was turning this way and that
The gloves, testing their weight and the numerous layers of their
                                     bindings.
Then did Entellus, the veteran, utter these words from his heart:—
  What would you say if you'd seen the gloves which great Hercules
                                     used
In the ring, or the fatal bout that took place on this very shore?
These are the ones which belonged to Eryx, your own brother:
Look, you can still see the marks of blood and of brains upon them!
With these he stood up to great Hercules. I too have often worn them
In my best days, when the blood ran strong in my veins, before
Envious age began to sprinkle my head with grey hair.
But if Dares the Trojan refuses to meet these weapons,
If that is Aeneas' ruling, approved by my backer, Acestes,
Let's fight upon level terms. I'll forgo the gloves of Eryx;
So don't be frightened, Dares—just take off those Trojan gloves!

  So saying, he doffed the double-folded cloak from his shoulders;
The mighty joints of his limbs, the mighty bones and thews were
Revealed, and he took up his stand, a giant, in the arena.
Then the son of Anchises, presiding, had gloves of equal weight
Brought out, so the combatants' fists were bound with identical
                                    weapons.
Now straight away they both went into their fighting positions,
  [*Lines 394–426*]

Up on their toes, up with their fists, cool and undaunted.
Heads held high and well back, to keep out of reach of a punch,
Hand to hand they were sparring, and warming up to the business.
Dares relied upon his youth and his faster footwork;
Entellus' strength was his massive physique, but his legs were slow
And shaky, and soon he was breathing heavily, out of condition.
Many punches are thrown by both of them, missing their target;
Many get home on the hollow ribs or beat a tattoo on
The mighty chests: against ear and temple their fists go flickering
Constantly out, and their cheek-bones are rattled by heavy punches.
Entellus stands solidly rooted, not changing his stance, avoiding
Blows by weaving and carefully watching his enemy's movements.
Dares, like one who assaults with siege-works a towering city
Or skirmishes round some mountain redoubt he is blockading,
Tries here and there for an opening, reconnoitres with expert skill,
And launches attacks from every angle, but all to no purpose.
Now, rising to his full height, Entellus signalled and swung
An overarm hook with his right; his nimble opponent saw it
Coming all the way, and quickly side-stepped out of trouble.
The force of the blow was spent on thin air—and worse, Entellus,
Losing his balance, with all his heavyweight bulk went crashing
Heavily to earth; so a pine tree, eaten out by age,
Might have fallen, its roots wrenched up, on Ida or Erymanthus.
Trojans and Sicilians leapt to their feet in solicitude:
Amid the hubbub, Acestes got to Entellus first
And with compassion helped his veteran friend to rise.
But the hero, far from being slowed or unnerved by his fall,
Went back to the fight more aggressively, more violent now because
He was seeing red. The humiliation, and with it the sense that
His courage was unimpaired, kindled his strength: impetuously,
Battering Dares with lefts and rights, he sent him reeling
All round the ring. No pause, no respite: thick as a hail-storm
Rattling on roofs, came the punches Entellus threw, as he pounded
Dares and spun him about with a two-fisted attack.
Aeneas refused to let the murderous fray go on—
Entellus was blind with rage, like a killer, and must be stopped;
So he called an end to the bout, saving the punch-drunk Dares
From further punishment, and spoke a few words to console him:—
Poor chap, can you not see that to go on now would be madness?

[*Lines 427–465*]

That you have lost the ascendancy, and how the gods have turned
Against you? Give in to their will.
                              At his word, the contest is over.
Dares is led away to the ships by his loyal friends,
All groggy, knees sagging, legs trailing behind him, his head lolling
From side to side, and spitting teeth and clotted blood
Out of his mouth. Then they're called up to take the sword and helmet
On his behalf, leaving the bullock and palm for Entellus.
The victor, in highest spirits, overjoyed with his bullock, exclaims:—
    O goddess-born, and all you Trojans, let this inform you
What strength of body I had in my young days, and also
From what a fate you have rescued and are preserving Dares.

    With these words, Entellus placed himself in front of the bullock,
His prize for the bout, which was standing nearby, drew back his
                                                      right fist
And brought it hard down from full height just between the horns
Of the beast: that blow smashed into its skull and dashed the brains
                                                              out.
Sprawling, quivering, lifeless, down on the ground the brute fell.
Over its corpse Entellus spoke, and with great emotion:—
    Eryx, this better life instead of the death of Dares
I give you; and now, a champion lays down his gloves, his science.

    Immediately after this, Aeneas called upon those who
Wished to compete at archery, announced the prizes; and then
He had a mast unshipped from Serestus' great galley
And erected. A dove was tied, fluttering, with cord passed through
A hole in the high masthead, as a target for the arrows.
The competitors gathered, and tossed their lots into a helmet
Of bronze. Hippocöon's number was drawn out first, amid cheers
From his fanciers—Hippocöon, son of Hyrtacus: next
In the order of shooting was Mnestheus—he who had just now won
A prize in the rowing race, and wore a green garland of olive.
Eurytion drew third turn; a brother he was of the famous
Pandarus who, on a day long ago, being bidden to break
The truce, had shot the first arrow into the Grecian ranks.
Last, from the bottom of the helmet, Acestes' lot came up—
Yes, he would have a go at this strenuous, young man's sport.
Then, putting forth their strength, each in his own measure,
They bent and strung their bows, and drew shafts from the quivers.
    [*Lines 466–501*]

The son of Hyrtacus shot the first arrow, his bowstring twanging;
It sped through the air with a sound like the whine of a whip-lash, then
It was home, stuck fair and square in the tough wood of the mast.
The mast quivered, the dove was all one terrified flurry
Of wings, and a roar of applause broke out across the arena.
Now Mnestheus took up position eagerly, drew back the bowstring
For a high shot, then aimed the arrow and sighted along it.
He was unlucky, failing to hit the bird itself
With his shaft, but cutting in two the knotted, hempen cord
Which had tied its foot and held it dangling down from the masthead;
The dove sped off to the fleecy clouds in the sky. Quickly
Eurytion, who'd been ready, bow bent and arrow nocked,
For some time, breathed a vow to his brother Pandarus,
And marking the dove up there in the blue, exultantly clapping
Its wings, he shot, and transfixed it before it could reach cloud cover.
Stone-dead the dove came down, leaving its life in the regions
Of air—came tumbling down with the arrow still stuck through it.
Acestes alone was left, and the prize already won:
However, he aimed his arrow up at the sky, so that all could
Witness a veteran's skill and hear the strong tone of his bow.
A startling phenomenon was seen now—one of the utmost
Significance for the future: huge events were to show
Its meaning, and frightening seers one day would declare what it
                                                        omened.

The shaft, as it sped among the streaming clouds, took fire,
Blazing a trail in the sky, then burnt itself out and vanished
Into thin air: thus, often, a star dislodges itself
From heaven and shoots across it, trailing a long-haired flame.
Sicilians and Trojans alike were amazed, and in two minds about it:
They prayed to the Powers above: Aeneas himself accepted
The omen favourably, put his arms round the elated
Acestes, loaded him with a splendid present, and spoke:—

    Sire, take this. The great lord of Olympus has given clear signs
That he wishes you to receive an extra-special award.
You shall have this prize, as it were from old Anchises in person—
This bowl, engraved with figures: it was originally
Presented to my father by Thracian Cisseus, a notably
Fine present, for a keepsake and token of deep friendship.

                                        [*Lines 502–538*]

When he had spoken, Aeneas put on Acestes' head
The wreath of green laurel, and publicly named him the first prize-
                                                              winner.
Good-natured Eurytion grudged him not the premier
Award, although it was he himself who had shot the bird down.
Next after him for a prize was the man who had severed the cord;
And last, the one who had pierced the mast with his flying arrow.
But father Aeneas, before the archery match was over,
Called Epytus' son to his side, the guardian and chief attendant
Of young Ascanius, and confidentially whispered these words:—
    Off you go, and tell Ascanius, if he is ready
With the boys' squadron now and the riders are all in formation,
To lead them on and give us his martial display, in honour
Of his grandfather.
                    Aeneas ordered the crowd, which had been
Encroaching upon the arena, to move back and leave it empty.
Now the boys ride in, before the eyes of their fathers,
In perfect dressing, a brilliant sight on their bridled horses—
Sicilians and Trojans greet them with murmurs of admiration.
They wear on their hair ceremonial garlands of leaves, well trimmed,
And each of them carries a couple of steel-tipped, cornel-wood lances;
Some have a polished quiver slung over the shoulder; high up on
The breast and round the neck lies the flexible golden torque.
Three troops compose the squadron, and three troop-majors ride
In front, each of them followed by a detachment of twelve boys:
The three troops, each with its leader, make a most gallant show.
The first was led, on this ceremonial parade, by a little
Priam, named after his grandsire, the noble son of Polites,
Destined to breed Italians: he rode on a Thracian horse—
An animal with white markings, the pasterns showing white
As it paced, and white the forehead it carried high. Next came
Atys, from whom the Latin Atii trace their descent—
Young Atys, who was a special friend of Ascanius.
Ascanius himself, the best-looking of all of them, led the third troop,
Riding upon the Tyrian horse that Dido had trustingly
Given him, as a token of love, to remind him of her.
The rest of the boys were mounted upon Sicilian horses
Lent by Acestes.
As they rode shyly on, the Trojans clapped, in delight at
    [*Lines 539–575*]

102

The spectacle, tracing family likenesses in the boys' features.
When they had proudly passed in review before the eyes of
Their relatives and the rest, and were drawn up ready, the signal
Was given by Epytides from a distance—a shout and a whip-crack.
The three troops now broke up, each into its two detachments,
Which wheeled apart and then, at the word of command, again
Came galloping back and charged one another with lances levelled.
Next, they staged a new set of manoeuvres and counter-manoeuvres,
Keeping their relative positions, each group, while performing their
                                                        maze of
Evolutions—a mimic engagement of mounted troops:
Now they turn their backs in flight, now wheel and charge
With lance in rest, and now ride peacefully, file by file.
It was like the fabled Labyrinth constructed in mountainous Crete—
A maze of unbroken walls, with thousands of blind alleys
To keep the venturer guessing and trick him, so that the right path
Into the heart of the maze was a puzzle to find or retrace.
Just like this were the tracks made by the complex manoeuvres
Of the boys, as they wove their patterns of sham flight or sham
                                                        encounter,
Moving as dolphins move when they gambol among the waves,
Through the Carpathian and Libyan seas sportively swimming.
This kind of cavalry tournament Ascanius, when he was building
The walled town of Alba Longa, first introduced to the early
Latins, and taught them to follow its ceremonial routine
Just as he'd done when a boy, with the Trojan boys of his squadron.
The Albans taught their children; and finally Rome herself
Received the tradition and kept it to honour her ancestors.
We call it "the Trojan Game", and the squadrons are named after
                                                        Troy.
Thus far, the Sports in honour of the sainted Anchises.

   At this point, fickle Fortune changed sides and turned against them.
For, while they perform the rites at the tomb with various contests,
Iris has been despatched from heaven by Saturnian Juno,
On the wings of a favouring wind, to the Trojan fleet: the goddess
Has certain designs; unappeased as yet is her old resentment.
Unseen by any, the virginal Iris speeds to earth,
Sliding along the curve of a rainbow of many colours.
She observes the vast assembly, and then, scanning the shore,
                                [*Lines 576–611*]

103

Sees the deserted harbour, the ships left unattended.
But, by themselves, at a distance, upon a lonely beach
The Trojan women lamented Anchises' death, and weeping
Gazed out on the deep together. Alas, such a wearisome waste of
Water still to be travelled—that was the cry of them all.
They yearn for a home; they are sick of the sea and endless voyaging.
Iris, who was an expert at trouble-making, put off now
Her heavenly mien and raiment, went quickly amongst them and joined
The group of Trojan matrons, transformed into the likeness
Of Beroe, the aged wife of Tmarian Doryclus,
A dame of good family who had once had position and children:—
    Pity it is that we were not dragged by the Greek soldiers
To death under our own walls during the war! Unlucky
People, for what catastrophe is fortune saving you up?
Now wanes the seventh summer since the destruction of Troy,
And still over land and water we roam, over a world of
Unharbouring rocks, as we steer by the stars and around the wide seas
From wave to wave chase after that will-o'-the-wisp, Italy.
Here's the land of a brother, Eryx. Here's hospitable Acestes.
Who stops us laying our walls here, giving our people a home?
Dear Troy! Dear home-gods, why were you rescued from the foe,
If Troy-town's walls are to be for ever a dream? if nowhere
I am to see a Xanthus, a Simois, rivers of Hector?
Quick! Help me then to burn these ships that bring no luck!
There came to me, as I slept, the phantom of our prophetic
Cassandra: she gave me a burning torch, it seemed, and said,
Here find your Troy. Here is your home. It is time for action—
Such prodigies brook no delay. Look at these four altars
To Neptune! He furnishes us with fire and the will to use it.
    So saying, as ring-leader, Iris violently snatched up a dangerous
Firebrand, swung back with her right hand strongly, waved it aloft,
                                                                    then
Hurled it. The Trojan women lost their good sense, and awoke to
A phantasy world. One of their number, the oldest, Pyrgo,
The nurse of so many royal children of Priam, called out:— .
    Ladies, this is not Beroe! This is not the Trojan wife of
Doryclus, I tell you! Look at the signs of heavenly
Grace that she bears! the fire in her eyes! Mark well her spirit,
Her countenance, the timbre of her voice, and the way she walks!

[*Lines 612–649*]

104

Why, it was only just now that I left Beroe behind,
Ailing, and fretting because she alone could take no part in
The ceremonies nor bring the offerings due to Anchises.
   Thus Pyrgo spoke.
The ladies were in two minds at first, eyeing the ships
With malicious glances, torn between their piteous craving
For the land they were in and the call of the land promised by destiny.
But now, spreading her wings, the goddess took off from earth,
Describing a rainbow arc under the clouds as she flew.
Then indeed, amazed at the miracle, driven by a frenzy,
All crying out, they ransack the nearby houses for flame:
Some strip the altars, to hurl greenery, twigs, torches
Onto the ships. The Fire-god gallops in full career
Over the thwarts, the oars, the poops of painted pinewood.
Now to Anchises' tomb and the crowded stands of the sports ground
Eumelus brought the news that the fleet was on fire: the spectators
Could see for themselves the black ashes eddying up in a smoke cloud.
At once Ascanius, just as he was when blithely commanding
The mounted display, galloped off with great presence of mind to
                                                    the riotous

Ship-stead, leaving his breathless trainers far behind.
   What weird madness is this? My poor good Trojan ladies,
What, oh what were you after? No enemy, no Greek camp
But your own future goes up in smoke. Look, it is I, your
Ascanius!
              he said, and threw down at their feet the clattering helmet
Which he had worn when leading his boys in the sham fight.
Aeneas hurried up now, and with him the mass of the Trojans.
But the scared women broke and fled in every direction
Over the shore, running for woods or caves—anywhere
To hide, ashamed to be seen after what they had done, themselves
Again and knowing their kin, now Juno's spell was broken.
Not in the least though, for that, did the flames of the conflagration
Slacken their unquenched violence: between the wet planks, the
                                                    caulking

Smouldered and gave off greasy smoke; and the heat slowly
Ate its way down through the hulls, consuming them like a cancer,
So that all efforts to put out the fire with water were useless.
Then god-fearing Aeneas rent his garments and called

                              [*Lines 650–685*]

105

Aloud on the gods for help, stretching his palms out to heaven:—
  Almighty Jove, if you do not yet abhor each one of
Us Trojans, if as of old in your loving-kindness you have some
Regard for men's sufferings, grant that our fleet may escape this fire

now,

And save, O Father, save our frail hopes from destruction!
Or else, if there's nothing left for it and this is what I deserve,
Let your lightning send us straight to perdition here and now!
  Scarce were the words out when the sky grew dark and there came
A cloudburst, a storm of unparalleled violence: hill and dale
Were rocked by thunderclaps; all the firmament was one avalanche
Of driving rain, one blackness of cloud piled up by the South wind.
The hulls were brimmed by that downpour, the half-burnt timbers

soaked,

Until the fires were all extinguished, and the ships—
All but four of them—had been saved from complete destruction.
  But lord Aeneas, hard hit by this most cruel disaster,
Was full of anxiety, and his mind kept oscillating
Between two thoughts—should he settle down in Sicily here
And forget his destiny, or struggle on towards Italy?
Then did the aged Nautes—he whom Pallas Athene
Had singled out as a pupil to learn her lore and be famed for it
(Him she favoured with explanations of what a god's
Great wrath should mean, and what the scheme of the fates

demanded)—

He now addressed to Aeneas these words of consolation:—
  Goddess-born, let us follow our destiny, ebb or flow.
Whatever may happen, we master fortune by fully accepting it.
Acestes now—he's a Dardan, and of divine lineage:
Make him a partner in your plans; I think he'll agree.
Detail to him the crews of the burnt-out ships, and any
Who have lost heart in your great enterprise and your fortunes:
Let the oldest men fall out, the women who are sick of voyaging,
And any weaker vessels you have, ones daunted by danger—
Weed them out, they are spent, let them make a walled home here;
If he permits the name, they shall call their city Acesta.
  Aeneas was much disturbed by the words of his aged friend;
All the more he was pulled this way and that by his worries.
And when dark night, upwheeling, possessed the sky, there came
  [*Lines 686–721*]

To him in a vision, gliding down through the gloom, his father
Anchises' figure, which at once urgently spoke:—
    My son, dearer to me than life when life was mine,
My son, much wrought upon by the fate of Ilium,
At Jove's command I am come here—Jove who repulsed the fire
From your ships, and showered down pity from heaven in the nick
                                                        of time.
Follow the excellent advice which aged Nautes
Gives you. Choose out warriors, the bravest of heart, and lead them
To Italy: for tough and primitive are the people
That you will have to subdue in Latium. First, however,
Death's kingdom you must enter, and traversing the vale of
Avernus, come to meet me, my son. I dwell not with
The damned in Tartarus or the purgatorial spirits,
But with the happy throngs of the Blessed in Elysium.
Here, when you've sacrificed many black sheep, the chaste Sibyl shall
                                                        bring you.
Then shall you learn where your home is to be, and your people's
                                                        destiny.
Farewell now. Dewy night drives on at mid-career,
And close I feel the breath of dawn's coursers, come to part us.
    These words: then he vanished, like a wisp of smoke, into thin air.
So quickly gone? Aeneas cried: gone from me whither?
Whom do you flee? Who fences you off from my embrace?
So saying, Aeneas stoked up the fire, the sleepy embers,
Paid reverence to Troy's patron spirit, and to Vesta
Time-hallowed, with offerings of ritual corn and clouds of incense.
    Immediately then he summoned his friends, Acestes first,
To inform them of Jove's command, his own dear father's injunctions,
And of the firm decision which now at last he had come to.
No time was lost in debating it. Acestes gave his consent.
They enrolled the women for the colony, off-loaded the men who
                                                        wanted
To stay there—persons with no great hankering after glory.
The remainder renewed the thwarts, made good the timbers charred
By fire on the ships, and fitted them out with new oars and rigging—
Few in number they were, but in high heart for warfare.
Meanwhile Aeneas traced with a plough the city's circumference,
Allotted the sites, and named one quarter of the town "Ilium",
                                    [*Lines 722–756*]

107

Another "Troy". The Trojan Acestes was glad to be king of it,
Appointed a court, gave laws to an assembled parliament.
Then, on the skyey peak of Mount Eryx, was founded a shrine
To Idalian Venus, while for the sepulchre of Anchises
A priest was ordained and a sacred grove planted all round it.

Nine days now the whole people have spent in feasting and paying
Sacrifice on the altars: the waves are lulled by gentle
Breezes; a South wind, steadily blowing, invites them to sea again.
Over the salient shore goes up a great noise of weeping:
Embracing each other, they try to make night and day last longer.
Those women, those very men who, before, had shrunk from the
venomous
Face of the sea and could not abide even the thought of it
Wanted to go now, were willing to bear every ordeal of travelling.
These did the good Aeneas console with kindly words,
And weeping, gave them into the care of their cousin, Acestes.
Then he had three bull-calves sacrificed to Eryx
With a lamb to the Storm-gods, and ordered the ships to weigh
anchor in turn.
Himself, a garland of well-trimmed olive about his temples,
He stood high up in the bows, holding a bowl from which he
Cast wine over the salt waves, and with it the votive entrails.
A freshening off-shore wind drove them upon their course.
Eagerly rowed the mariners, sweeping the sea with long strokes.

While this was doing, Venus, anxious of heart, approached
Neptune and unburdened herself of a grievance, thus:—

The heavy wrath of Juno, the grudge she implacably cherishes,
Force me to have recourse to every kind of entreaty.
She is softened neither by time nor by any propitiations,
Unswayed by the ruling of Jove or by fate, still active against us.
It is not enough for her infamous hatred to have devoured
The heart of the Phrygians, Troy, and made its survivors run
A whole gamut of retribution: she hunts down the very ashes
Of the dead city. She'd best have good reason for such vindictiveness.
You are my witness, Neptune, what a wild riot of waters
She raised but now in the Libyan sea, what a hell she brewed up
Employing the storm-winds of Aeolus. She failed in her purpose.
But this
She actually dared to do in your province.

[*Lines 757–792*]

108

Then, just think, she wickedly worked on the Trojan women
To burn the ships, a foul deed! And thus she has forced Aeneas,
Fleet gone, to leave his friends behind in a foreign country.
All I ask now is that you should give the remnant a safe
Sea passage up to Laurentine Tiber—if indeed
What I ask is lawful, and there is the home which the Fates have
                                                    granted them.
   Then spoke Saturn's son, the emperor of the deep:—
Every right you have to rely on me, the ruler
Of ocean, where you were born. I have earned your confidence, too,
For often have I quelled the mad fury of wind and sea.
Also on land—I call to witness Xanthus and Simois—
I have looked after your Aeneas. When Achilles
Pursued the panicking Trojans and crushed them against their walls,
When he dealt death to thousands till the choked rivers groaned with
Corpses, and Xanthus could not find or wind his way
To the sea, even then I carried off in a hollow cloud
Aeneas, who faced Achilles in a combat where neither the gods
Nor the combatants were equally matched—I did it, though
My will was to root up the perjured Troy I had built with my own
                                                    hands.
So fear no more: as then, my attitude is unaltered.
He shall get safe to the harbour of Cumae: you have your wish.
One only shall you miss, one shall be lost at sea,
One life must be surrendered for many lives.
   When he had gladdened the goddess' heart with these comforting
                                                    words,
Her father put the gold yoke on his horses, fastened the foaming
Bridles on the spirited creatures and freely shook out the reins.
Lightly skims the dark-blue chariot over the sea's face:
The waves go down, beneath those roaring wheels the steep swell
Turns to a calm, the storm-clouds fleet from the wastes of the sky.
Then come his retainers, diverse in appearance—prodigious whales,
The antique school of Glaucus, Palaemon the son of Ino,
With the fast-swimming Tritons and all the flotilla of Phorcus;
On the left are Thetis and Melite and maiden Panopea,
Nesaea, too, and Spio, Thalia and Cymodoce.
   Aeneas had been in suspense; but his mood changed now, and a
                                                    calm joy
                        [*Lines 793–827*]

109

Thrilled through his heart. He gave orders that all the masts should
at once
Be stepped and the sails broken out from the yards. The crews all set
Their mainsheets, and all together slanted the lofty yard-arms
This way or that, to keep the sails filled, as the breeze shifted
To port or starboard quarter. A fair wind bore them on.
They were sailing in close column, with Palinurus ahead
In the lead, the rest being ordered to shape their course by his.
And now the dewy night had nearly come to its halfway
Mark in the heavens: the mariners, sprawled on the hard benches
Beside their oars, were all relaxed in solacing quiet.
Just then did Sleep come feathering down from the stars above,
Lightly displacing the shadowy air, parting the darkness,
In search of you, Palinurus, carrying death in a dream
To your staunch heart. Now, taking the shape of Phorbas, the
Sleep-god
Perched up there in the stern-sheets and rapidly spoke these words:—
    Palinurus, son of Iasus, the seas are bearing the ships on,
Steadily blows the breeze, and you have a chance to rest.
Lay your head down, and take a nap; your eyes are tired with
Watching. I will stand your trick at the helm for a little.
    Palinurus could hardly raise his heavy eyes, but he answered:—
    Are you asking me to forget what lies behind the pacific
Face of the sea and its sleeping waves? to trust this devil?
What? Shall I leave Aeneas to the mercy of tricky winds—
I who, time and again, have been taken in by a clear sky?
    While he spoke, Palinurus kept a good grip on the tiller—
By no means would he release it—and a steadfast gaze on the stars.
But look! over his temples the god is shaking a bough
That drips with the dew of Lethe, the drowsy spell of Stygian
Waters. And now, though he struggles, his swimming eyes are closing.
As soon as, taken off guard, he was relaxed in unconsciousness,
The god, leaning down over him, hurled him into the sea
Still gripping the tiller; a part of the taffrail was torn away:
As he fell, he kept calling out to his friends, but they did not hear him.
Up and away skywards the Sleep-god now went winging.
Safe as before, the fleet was scudding upon its course—
Nothing to fear, for Neptune had guaranteed a safe passage.
And now, racing on, they were near the rocky place of the Sirens,
    [*Lines 828–864*]

110

Dangerous once for mariners, white with the bones of many;
From afar the rasp of the ceaseless surf on those rocks could be heard.
Just then Aeneas became aware that his ship was yawing
Badly, her helmsman missing; he brought her back on to course
In the night sea, and deeply sighing, stunned by the loss of his friend,
said:—

O Palinurus, too easily trusting clear sky and calm sea,
You will lie on a foreign strand, mere jetsam, none to bury you.

[*Lines 865–871*]

BOOK VI

Thus spoke Aeneas, in tears, then gave the ships their head,
And at long last they slid to the shores of Euboean Cumae.
The bows are swung round to face the sea, the vessels made fast with
The biting hook of their anchors, and the sheer sterns are lining
The beach. Now, full of excitement, the heroes tumble out
On the Hesperian shore: some look for the seeds of fire
Hidden in veins of flint, some scour the woods, the tangled
Haunts of wild beasts, for fuel, and point to the springs they have
found.
But the god-fearing Aeneas made for the shrine where Apollo
Sits throned on high, and that vasty cave—the deeply-recessed
Crypt of the awe-inspiring Sibyl, to whom the god gives
The power to see deep and prophesy what's to come.
Now they passed into Diana's grove and the gold-roofed temple.
    The story is that Daedalus, when he escaped from Minos,
Boldly trusting himself to the air on urgent wings,
An unprecedented mode of travel, went floating northwards
Until he was lightly hovering above the Cumaean hilltop.
Here he came first to earth, hung up his apparatus
Of flight as a thanks-offering to Phoebus, and built a great temple.
On its door was depicted the death of Androgeos; also the legend
Of how the Athenians, poor souls, were forced to pay yearly tribute
With seven of their sons—the scene when the lots had just been drawn.
Facing this, there's a bas-relief; with Crete rising out of the waves;
Pasiphae, cruelly fated to lust after a bull,
And privily covered; the hybrid fruit of that monstrous union—
The Minotaur, a memento of her unnatural love:
Here's the insoluble maze constructed by Daedalus;
Yet, sympathising with Ariadne in her great passion,
He gives her himself the clue to the maze's deceptive windings,
And guides with a thread the blind steps of Theseus. In the artifact
Icarus too would have had a prominent place, if his father's
Grief had allowed: but twice, trying to work the boy's fall
    [Lines 1–32]

In gold, did Daedalus' hands fail him. They'd have perused
The sculptured tale right through, but that Achates, who had
Been sent ahead, turned up with the priestess of Phoebus and Trivia,
Deiphobe, daughter of Glaucus. She now addressed Aeneas:—

This is no time for poring over those works of art.
Just now you would do best to sacrifice seven bullocks
That have not been yoked, and as many properly chosen sheep.

She addressed Aeneas; and he promptly performing the rites she
Requested, the priestess summoned them into the lofty temple.

There's a huge cave hollowed out from the flank of Cumae's hill;
A hundred wide approaches it has, a hundred mouths
From which there issue a hundred voices, the Sibyl's answers.
They had reached its threshold when "Time it is to ask your destiny"
The Sibyl cried, "for lo! the god is with me." And speaking,
There by the threshold, her features, her colour were all at once
Different, her hair flew wildly about; her breast was heaving,
Her fey heart swelled in ecstasy; larger than life she seemed,
More than mortal her utterance: the god was close and breathing
His inspiration through her:—
                                        What? Slow to pay your vows
And say your prayers, Aeneas of Troy? Yet only then
Will the spell work and the doors open,
                                        she cried, and again
Fell silent. An icy shudder ran through their very bones
And Aeneas poured out a prayer from the bottom of his heart:—

O Phoebus, often you pitied the load Troy had to bear;
You it was who guided the hand and the Trojan arrow
Of Paris against Achilles; you were the guide I followed
Into so many seas, lapping great lands, and through
Remote Massylian peoples, the fields the Syrtes fringe:
And now, at long last, we have caught the elusive shores of Italy.
Let Troy's ill luck, that has dogged us so far, follow no further.
Ye too, gods and goddesses all, who could not bear
Ilium and the great fame of the Dardans, it is all right now
For you to spare the Trojans. And, O most holy Sibyl,
Foreseer of future things, grant—I but ask for the kingdom
Owed by my destiny—grant that we Trojans may settle in Latium,
We and our wandering gods, the hard-driven deities of Troy.
Then will I found a temple of solid marble to Phoebus

[*Lines 33–69*]

114

And Trivia, appointing festival days in Phoebus' honour.
You too shall have your holy place in the realm to be,
Where I shall deposit the oracles, the mystic runes you utter
For my own people, ordaining a priesthood to their service,
O gracious one. But do not commit your sayings to leaves,
Lest they become the sport of whisking winds and are scattered:
Speak them aloud, I pray.

       Aeneas made an end now.
But the Sibyl, not yet submissive to Phoebus, there in her cavern
Prodigiously struggled, still trying to shake from her brain the powerful
God who rode her: but all the more he exhausted her foaming
Mouth and mastered her wild heart, breaking her in with a firm hand.
And now the hundred immense doors of the place flew open
Of their own accord, letting out the Sibyl's inspired responses:—

 O you that at last have done with the dangers of the deep
(Yet graver ones await you on land), the Trojans shall come
To power in Lavinium—be troubled no more about this—
But shall not also be glad that they did. Wars, dreadful wars
I see, and Tiber foaming with torrents of human blood.
You will not escape a Simois, a Xanthus there, a Greek
Encampment; Latium has a new Achilles in store for you,
He too a goddess' son: nor yet shall the Trojans anywhere
Be rid of Juno's vendetta. Ah then, in your extremity,
What tribes, what townships of Italy shall you not sue for aid!
Once more it's an alien bride, a foreign marriage that's destined
To cause such terrible harm to the Trojans.
But never give way to those evils: face them all the more boldly,
Using what methods your luck allows you. The way of salvation
Begins where you'd least expect it, stems from a Greek city.

 Thus from her sanctum spoke the Cumaean ·Sibyl, pronouncing
Riddles that awed them; her voice came booming out of the cavern,
Wrapping truth in enigma: she was possessed; Apollo
Controlled her, shaking the reins and twisting the goad in her bosom.
As soon as her ecstasy ebbed and her raving mouth was silent,
The hero Aeneas began to speak:—

       Maiden, there's nothing
New or unexpected to me in such trials you prophesy.
All of them I have forecast, worked out in my mind already.
I have one request: since here is reputed to be the gateway

[*Lines 70–106*]

Of the Underworld and the dusky marsh from Acheron's overflow,
May it befall me to go into my dear father's
Presence—open the hallowed gates and show me the way!
Him through the flames, through a thousand pursuing missiles I rescued
Out of the enemy's midst and bore him away on these shoulders:
He voyaged with me, enduring sea after sea, enduring
All menace of sea and storm, weak as he was—great ordeals
Beyond his strength, exceeding the normal lot of old age.
Yes, and he himself most earnestly bade me, more than once,
To come to you here and make this appeal. I pray you, kind one,
Take pity on father and son. You have the power: it was not
For nothing that Hecate put you in charge of the grove of Avernus.
Orpheus, with only the tuneful strings of a Thracian lyre
To aid him, could conjure forth the ghost of his wife; Pollux,
Who, turn about, shares life and death with his mortal brother,
Constantly comes and goes this way; I need not mention
Theseus or Hercules; I too am descended from great Jove.
      Thus he was making petition, his hands upon the altar,
When the Sibyl began to speak:—
                                    O child of a goddess' womb,
Trojan son of Anchises, the way to Avernus is easy;
Night and day lie open the gates of death's dark kingdom:
But to retrace your steps, to find the way back to daylight—
That is the task, the hard thing. A few, because of Jove's
Just love, or exalted to heaven by their own flame of goodness,
Men born from gods, have done it. Between, there lies a forest,
And darkly winds the river Cocytus round the place.
But if so great your love is, so great your passion to cross
The Stygian waters twice and twice behold black Tartarus,
If your heart is set on this fantastic project,
Here's what you must do first. Concealed in a tree's thick shade
There is a golden bough—gold the leaves and the tough stem—
Held sacred to Proserpine: the whole wood hides this bough
And a dell walls it round as it were in a vault of shadow.
Yet none is allowed to enter the land which earth conceals
Save and until he has plucked that gold-foil bough from the tree.
Fair Proserpine ordains that it should be brought to her
As tribute. When a bough is torn away, another
Gold one grows in its place with leaves of the same metal.

[*Lines 107–144*]

So keep your eyes roving above you, and when you have found the
                                                              bough
Just pull it out: that branch will come away quite easily
If destiny means you to go; otherwise no amount of
Brute force will get it, nor hard steel avail to hew it away.
Also—and this you know not—the lifeless corpse of a friend
Is lying unburied, a dead thing polluting your whole expedition,
While you are lingering here to inquire about fate's decrees.
Before anything else, you must give it proper burial and make
Sacrifice of black sheep: only when you are thus
Purified, shall you see the Stygian groves and the regions
Untreadable by the living.
                            She spoke, then closed her lips.
Aeneas, eyes downcast, countenance full of sorrow,
Moved off, leaving the cave, pondering much in his heart
On the cryptic issues the Sibyl had raised. Loyal Achates
Walked with him, his gait heavy beneath the same load of trouble.
Many were the conjectures they threw out, one to the other,
As to which of their dead friends the Sibyl had meant, and whose
                                                              body
Must be interred. Now when they drew near the beach, they saw there
The body of Misenus, cut off by cruel death—
Misenus, son of Aeolus, whom none had excelled in firing
The warrior passions of men with thrilling trumpet calls.
He had been a comrade of mighty Hector, at Hector's side
Had fought and won great fame as a trumpeter and a spearman.
After Achilles had defeated Hector and killed him,
This valiant hero, Misenus, attached himself to Dardan
Aeneas' company, following now no lesser a man.
But to-day, as he sent his horn's notes ringing over the sea,
Mostly rashly challenging the gods to a musical contest,
Jealous Triton caught him off guard—if we may credit
The story—and plunged him down in the surf among those rocks.
Now they were all standing around him, lamenting loudly,
Not least the good-hearted Aeneas. And now at once they hasten
Weeping to carry out the Sibyl's instructions, piling
Timber up with a will for a towering funeral altar.
Into the age-old forest, where only wild things lurk,
They go: spruces are felled, the holm oak rings with axe blows,
  [*Lines 145–180*]

117

Wedges are used to split ash logs and the cleavable wood
Of oaks, immense rowans are rolled down from the heights.
Aeneas himself, in the middle of these activities,
Carrying the same tools as they, encouraged his friends.
But also, sad at heart, gazing up at the huge forest,
He brooded; and then he uttered his thoughts aloud in a prayer:—
    If only I might glimpse that golden bough on its tree
In the great wood this very moment! for all that the Sibyl
Said about you, Misenus, was true, too sadly true.
    The words were hardly out when it befell that two doves
Came planing down from above before his very eyes
And alighted upon the green turf. The hero recognised
His mother's birds. His heart leapt up and he said a prayer:—
    Show me the way, if way there is! Oh, wing your flight
To that part of the forest where the precious bough overshadows
The fruitful soil. Do not forsake me, heavenly mother,
At this most crucial hour!
                            He spoke; stopped in his tracks
To note what signs they gave and in what direction they'd move.
Now the doves, as they fed, flitted on from spot to spot, but never
So far ahead that one who followed lost sight of them.
Then, when they came to the mouth of foul-breathing Avernus,
Swiftly they soared, went gliding through the soft air and settled,
The pair of them, on a tree, the wished-for place, a tree
Amid whose branches there gleamed a bright haze, a different colour—
Gold. Just as in depth of winter the mistletoe blooms
In the woods with its strange leafage, a parasite on the tree,
Hanging its yellow-green berries about the smooth round boles:
So looked the bough of gold leaves upon that ilex dark,
And in a gentle breeze the gold-foil foliage rustled.
Aeneas at once took hold of the bough, and eagerly breaking
It off with one pull, he bore it into the shrine of the Sibyl.
Meantime upon the shore the Trojans were still lamenting
Misenus, and paying the last rites to his oblivious dust.
First they laid resinous wood, and upon it sections of oak trees
To build the pyre up high; the sides of the pyre were wattled
With sombre-foliaged boughs; in front they planted funereal
Cypresses, and his shining arms adorned its top.
Some lit fires beneath the cauldrons, and boiled water;

                                            [*Lines 181–218*]

118

They washed and anointed the corpse of their friend, so cold in death.
All were lamenting. When they had wept him, they laid on the bier
His body, covering it with purple drapes and the dead man's
Own clothing. The bearers lifted the bier onto the pyre,
A melancholy office, and in the traditional manner
Averting their eyes, applied the lighted torches. The pile of
Offerings burned—the incense, the meat, the libations of oil.
Now when the ashes had fallen in and the flames died down,
They quenched the remains, the thirsty embers, with wine; and
collecting
The bones, Corynaeus put them away in a casket of bronze.
He then moved round his comrades three times, bearing pure water;
Aspersing them with drops he shook from a branch of fruitful
Olive, he purified them, and spoke the farewell words.
Aeneas the true now raised over his friend a massive
Tomb, laying on it the man's own arms, his oar and his trumpet,
Beneath that high headland which takes its name from him,
Misenum, and preserves his fame unto all ages.
   This done, Aeneas hastened to follow the Sibyl's directions.
A deep, deep cave there was, its mouth enormously gaping,
Shingly, protected by the dark lake and the forest gloom:
Above it, no winged creatures could ever wing their way
With impunity, so lethal was the miasma which
Went fuming up from its black throat to the vault of heaven:
Wherefore the Greeks called it Avernus, the Birdless Place.
Here the Sibyl first lined up four black-skinned bullocks,
Poured a libation of wine upon their foreheads, and then,
Plucking the topmost hairs from between their brows, she placed
These on the altar fires as an initial offering,
Calling aloud upon Hecate, powerful in heaven and hell.
While others laid their knives to these victims' throats, and caught
The fresh warm blood in bowls, Aeneas sacrificed
A black-fleeced lamb to Night, the mother of the Furies,
And her great sister, Earth, and a barren heifer to Proserpine.
Then he set up altars by night to the god of the Underworld,
Laying upon the flames whole carcases of bulls
And pouring out rich oil over the burning entrails.
But listen!—at the very first crack of dawn, the ground
Underfoot began to mutter, the woody ridges to quake,

[*Lines 219–256*]

119

And a baying of hounds was heard through the half-light: the
goddess was coming,
Hecate. The Sibyl cried:—
Away! Now stand away,
You uninitiated ones, and clear the whole grove!
But you, Aeneas, draw your sword from the scabbard and fare forth!
Now you need all your courage, your steadfastness of heart.
So much she said and, ecstatic, plunged into the opened cave mouth:
Unshrinking went Aeneas step for step with his guide.

You gods who rule the kingdom of souls! You soundless shades!
Chaos, and Phlegethon! O mute wide leagues of Nightland!—
Grant me to tell what I have heard! With your assent
May I reveal what lies deep in the gloom of the Underworld!

Dimly through the shadows and dark solitudes they wended,
Through the void domiciles of Dis, the bodiless regions:
Just as, through fitful moonbeams, under the moon's thin light,
A path lies in a forest, when Jove has palled the sky
With gloom, and the night's blackness has bled the world of colour.
See! At the very porch and entrance way to Orcus
Grief and ever-haunting Anxiety make their bed:
Here dwell pallid Diseases, here morose Old Age,
With Fear, ill-prompting Hunger, and squalid Indigence,
Shapes horrible to look at, Death and Agony;
Sleep, too, which is the cousin of Death; and Guilty Joys,
And there, against the threshold, War, the bringer of Death:
Here are the iron cells of the Furies, and lunatic Strife
Whose viperine hair is caught up with a headband soaked in blood.

In the open a huge dark elm tree spreads wide its immemorial
Branches like arms, whereon, according to old wives' tales,
Roost the unsolid Dreams, clinging everywhere under its foliage.
Besides, many varieties of monsters can be found
Stabled here at the doors—Centaurs and freakish Scyllas,
Briareus with his hundred hands, the Lernaean Hydra
That hisses terribly and the flame-throwing Chimaera,
Gorgons and Harpies, and the ghost of three-bodied Geryon.
Now did Aeneas shake with a spasm of fear, and drawing
His sword, offered its edge against the creatures' onset:
Had not his learned guide assured him they were but incorporeal
Existences floating there, forms with no substance behind them,

[*Lines 257–293*]

120

He'd have attacked them, and wildly winnowed with steel mere
                                                         shadows.
  From here is the road that leads to the dismal waters of Acheron.
Here a whirlpool boils with mud and immense swirlings
Of water, spouting up all the slimy sand of Cocytus.
A dreadful ferryman looks after the river crossing,
Charon: appallingly filthy he is, with a bush of unkempt
White beard upon his chin, with eyes like jets of fire;
And a dirty cloak draggles down, knotted about his shoulders.
He poles the boat, he looks after the sails, he is all the crew
Of that rust-coloured wherry which takes the dead across—
An ancient now, but a god's old age is green and sappy.
This way came fast and streaming up to the bank the whole throng:
Matrons and men were there, and there were great-heart heroes
Finished with earthly life, boys and unmarried maidens,
Young men laid on the pyre before their parents' eyes;
Multitudinous as the leaves that fall in a forest
At the first frost of autumn, or the birds that out of the deepsea
Fly to land in migrant flocks, when the cold of the year
Has sent them overseas in search of a warmer climate.
So they all stood, each begging to be ferried across first,
Their hands stretched out in longing for the shore beyond the river.
But the surly ferryman embarks now this, now that group,
While others he keeps away at a distance from the shingle.
Aeneas, being astonished and moved by the great stir, said:—
  Tell me, O Sibyl, what means this mustering at the river?
What purpose have these souls? By what distinction are some
Turned back, while other souls sweep over the wan water?
  To which the long-lived Sibyl uttered this brief reply:—
  O son of Anchises' loins and true-born offspring of heaven,
What you see is the mere of Cocytus, the Stygian marsh
By whose mystery even the gods, having sworn, are afraid to be
                                                         forsworn.

All this crowd you see are the helpless ones, the unburied:
That ferryman is Charon: the ones he conveys have had burial.
None may be taken across from bank to awesome bank of
That harsh-voiced river until his bones are laid to rest.
Otherwise, he must haunt this place for a hundred years
Before he's allowed to revisit the longed-for stream at last.
  [*Lines 294–330*]

121

The son of Anchises paused and stood stock still, in deep
Meditation, pierced to the heart by pity for their hard fortune.
He saw there, sorrowing because deprived of death's fulfilment,
Leucaspis and Orontes, the commodore of the Lycian
Squadron, who had gone down, their ship being lost with all hands
In a squall, sailing with him the stormy seas from Troy.

And look! yonder was roaming the helmsman, Palinurus,
Who, on their recent voyage, while watching the stars, had fallen
From the afterdeck, thrown off the ship there in mid-passage.
A sombre form in the deep shadows, Aeneas barely
Recognised him; then accosted:—

                         Which of the gods, Palinurus,
Snatched you away from us and made you drown in the mid-sea?
Oh, tell me! For Apollo, whom never before had I found
Untruthful, did delude my mind with this one answer,
Foretelling that you would make your passage to Italy
Unharmed by sea. Is it thus he fulfils a sacred promise?

  Palinurus replied:—

                      The oracle of Phoebus has not tricked you,
My captain, son of Anchises; nor was I drowned by a god.
It was an accident: I slipped, and the violent shock
Of my fall broke off the tiller to which I was holding firmly
As helmsman, and steering the ship. By the wild seas I swear
That not on my own account was I frightened nearly so much as
Lest your ship, thus crippled, its helmsman overboard,
Lose steerage-way and founder amid the mountainous waves.
Three stormy nights did the South wind furiously drive me along
Over the limitless waters: on the fourth day I just
Caught sight of Italy, being lifted high on a wave crest.
Little by little I swam to the shore. I was all but safe,
When, as I clung to the rough-edged cliff top, my fingers crooked
And my soaking garments weighing me down, some barbarous natives
Attacked me with swords, in their ignorance thinking that I was a
                                    rich prize.
Now the waves have me, the winds keep tossing me up on the shore
                                     again.
So now, by the sweet light and breath of heaven above
I implore you, and by your father, by your hopes for growing Ascanius
Redeem me from this doom, unconquered one! Please sprinkle

                         [*Lines 331–365*]

Dust on my corpse—you can do it and quickly get back to port Velia:
Or else, if way there is, some way that your heavenly mother
Is showing you (not, for sure, without the assent of deity
Would you be going to cross the swampy Stygian stream),
Give poor Palinurus your hand, take me with you across the water
So that at least I may rest in the quiet place, in death.

    Thus did the phantom speak, and the Sibyl began to speak thus:—

    This longing of yours, Palinurus, has carried you quite away.
Shall you, unburied, view the Styx, the austere river
Of the Infernal gods, or come to its bank unbidden?
Give up this hope that the course of fate can be swerved by prayer.
But hear and remember my words, to console you in your hard
                                          fortune.
I say that the neighbouring peoples, compelled by portents from heaven
Occurring in every township, shall expiate your death,
Shall give you burial and offer the solemn dues to your grave,
And the place shall keep the name of Palinurus for ever.

    Her sayings eased for a while the anguish of his sad heart;
He forgot his cares in the joy of giving his name to a region.

    So they resumed their interrupted journey, and drew near
The river. Now when the ferryman, from out on the Styx, espied them
Threading the soundless wood and making fast for the bank,
He hailed them, aggressively shouting at them before they could
                                        speak:—

    Whoever you are that approaches my river, carrying a weapon,
Halt there! Keep your distance, and tell me why you are come!
This is the land of ghosts, of sleep and somnolent night:
The living are not permitted to use the Stygian ferry.
Not with impunity did I take Hercules,
When he came, upon this water, nor Theseus, nor Pirithous,
Though their stock was divine and their powers were irresistible.
Hercules wished to drag off on a leash the watch-dog of Hades,
Even from our monarch's throne, and dragged it away trembling:
The others essayed to kidnap our queen from her lord's bedchamber.

    The priestess of Apollo answered him shortly, thus:—

    There is no such duplicity here, so set your mind at rest;
These weapons offer no violence: the huge watch-dog in his kennel
May go on barking for ever and scaring the bloodless dead,
Proserpine keep her uncle's house, unthreatened in chastity.

    [*Lines 366–402*]

123

Trojan Aeneas, renowned for war and a duteous heart,
Comes down to meet his father in the shades of the Underworld.
If you are quite unmoved by the spectacle of such great faith,
This you must recognise——
                              And here she disclosed the golden
Bough which was hid in her robe. His angry mood calms down.
No more is said. Charon is struck with awe to see
After so long that magic gift, the bough fate-given;
He turns his sombre boat and poles it towards the bank.
Then, displacing the souls who were seated along its benches
And clearing the gangways, to make room for the big frame of Aeneas,
He takes him on board. The ramshackle craft creaked under his weight
And let in through its seams great swashes of muddy water.
At last, getting the Sibyl and the hero safe across,
He landed them amidst wan reeds on a dreary mud flat.

   Huge Cerberus, monstrously couched in a cave confronting them,
Made the whole region echo with his three-throated barking.
The Sibyl, seeing the snakes bristling upon his neck now,
Threw him for bait a cake of honey and wheat infused with
Sedative drugs. The creature, crazy with hunger, opened
Its three mouths, gobbled the bait; then its huge body relaxed
And lay, sprawled out on the ground, the whole length of its cave
                                                              kennel.
Aeneas, passing its entrance, the watch-dog neutralised,
Strode rapidly from the bank of that river of no return.

   At once were voices heard, a sound of mewling and wailing,
Ghosts of infants sobbing there at the threshold, infants
From whom a dark day stole their share of delicious life,
Snatched them away from the breast, gave them sour death to drink.
Next to them were those condemned to death on a false charge.
Yet every place is duly allotted and judgment is given.
Minos, as president, summons a jury of the dead: he hears
Every charge, examines the record of each; he shakes the urn.
Next again are located the sorrowful ones who killed
Themselves, throwing their lives away, not driven by guilt
But because they loathed living: how they would like to be
In the world above now, enduring poverty and hard trials!
God's law forbids: that unlovely fen with its glooming water
Corrals them there, the nine rings of Styx corral them in.

[*Lines 403–439*]

Not far from here can be seen, extending in all directions,
The vale of mourning—such is the name it bears: a region
Where those consumed by the wasting torments of merciless love
Haunt the sequestered alleys and myrtle groves that give them
Cover; death itself cannot cure them of love's disease.
Here Aeneas descried Phaedra and Procris, sad
Eriphyle showing the wounds her heartless son once dealt her
Evadne and Pasiphae; with them goes Laodamia;
Here too is Caeneus, once a young man, but next a woman
And now changed back by fate to his original sex.
Amongst them, with her death-wound still bleeding, through the
                                                    deep wood
Was straying Phoenician Dido. Now when the Trojan leader
Found himself near her and knew that the form he glimpsed through
                                                    the shadows
Was hers—as early in the month one sees, or imagines he sees,
Through a wrack of cloud the new moon rising and glimmering—
He shed some tears, and addressed her in tender, loving tones:—
    Poor, unhappy Dido, so the message was true that came to me
Saying you'd put an end to your life with the sword and were dead?
Oh god! was it death I brought you, then? I swear by the stars,
By the powers above, by whatever is sacred in the Underworld,
It was not of my own will, Dido, I left your land.
Heaven's commands, which now force me to traverse the shades,
This sour and derelict region, this pit of darkness, drove me
Imperiously from your side. I did not, could not imagine
My going would ever bring such terrible agony on you.
Don't move away! Oh, let me see you a little longer!
To fly from me, when this is the last word fate allows us!
    Thus did Aeneas speak, trying to soften the wild-eyed,
Passionate-hearted ghost, and brought the tears to his own eyes.
She would not turn to him; she kept her gaze on the ground,
And her countenance remained as stubborn to his appeal
As if it were carved from recalcitrant flint or a crag of marble.
At last she flung away, hating him still, and vanished
Into the shadowy wood where her first husband, Sychaeus,
Understands her unhappiness and gives her an equal love.
None the less did Aeneas, hard hit by her piteous fate,
Weep after her from afar, as she went, with tears of compassion.

[*Lines 440–476*]

125

Then he passed on the appointed way. They came to the last part
Of Limbo, the place set apart for men famous in war.
Here Tydeus met him, here that warrior of high renown
Parthenopaeus, here the pale spectre of Adrastus;
Then those for whom lamentation had risen on earth—the fallen
Fighters of Troy; Aeneas groaned aloud when he saw those
Long ranks of death—Glaucus, Medon, Thersilochus,
The three sons of Antenor, Polyphoetes the priest of Ceres,
Idaeus, still with the arms he bore, the chariot he drove once.
To right and left the spirits press thickly around Aeneas.
Not enough just to have seen him once—they want to detain him,
To pace along beside him and find out why he has come there.
But the Greek generals and the regiments of Agamemnon,
When they beheld his armour glinting through the gloom,
Were seized with fear and trembling; some turned tail, even as
In the old days they had run for their ships; some uttered a wraith of
A war cry—they tried to shout, but their wide mouths only
whimpered.

Just then Aeneas caught sight of Deiphobus, his whole body
A mass of wounds, most horribly mangled about the face—
The face and both the hands, head mutilated with ears
Torn off, and the nose lopped—a barbarous disfigurement.
The moment he'd recognised that shrinking creature who covered
His ghastly wounds, Aeneas burst out in familiar tones:—

Deiphobus, great fighter, descended from high-born Teucer,
Who was it chose to inflict such atrocious punishment on you?
Who could go to such lengths against you? On Troy's last night
I heard a rumour that, worn out with killing and killing Greeks,
You had sunk down on a huge indiscriminate heap of dead bodies.
Then, myself, I erected by the Rhoetean shore
A cenotaph for you, and thrice invoked your spirit aloud.
Your name and a trophy mark the spot; yourself I could not
Find to inter in your native soil before I departed.

The son of Priam replied:—

Dear friend, you neglected nothing;
All that was needed you've done for Deiphobus and his shade.
My destiny and the destructive nature of that Lacaenian
Woman brought me to this: it was she who gave me these souvenirs.
You remember how we spent that last night in rejoicings,

[*Lines 477–513*]

126

In a fools' paradise; too well, no doubt, you remember it.
When the horse of doom had cleared at a bound the battlements
Of Troy, bearing an armed detachment within its belly,
That woman faked a dance, led the Trojan women around,
Yelling in Bacchanal orgy; under cover of which herself
With a blazing torch in her hand signalled the Greeks from our citadel.
I, worn out by our ordeals and leaden with sleep, was lying
In my unlucky bedroom under a coverlet
Of deep, delicious rest, very like the peace of death.
Meantime that nonpareil wife of mine removed all the arms from
Our house, yes, even my trusty sword from beneath my pillow;
Then called Menelaus inside, opened the door to him, hoping—
Vile thing—to make a wonderful present of me to her lover
And thus erase the stigma of her old wicked doings.
No more of this: they burst into the bedroom; Ulysses was with them,
Promoter and compère of crimes. Ye gods, may such deeds recoil
On the Greeks, if my prayer for revenge is made with a clear
                                                        conscience.
But tell me now, in turn, what chance has brought you here
Alive. Were you compelled by your wanderings on the ocean,
Or a command from heaven? Or what fate irks you, that you should
Enter this joyless, sunless abode, these vague, vexed regions?

    So they conversed, till Aurora, driving her rosy chariot,
Had passed the midway point of the sky in her flying course;
And indeed they might have used up all the allotted time thus,
Had not his guide, the Sibyl, spoken a few words of warning:—

    Night comes apace, Aeneas; yet we spend the hours in grieving.
Here is the spot where the way forks, going in two directions;
The right-hand leads beneath the battlements of great Dis,
And is our route to Elysium; the left-hand takes the wicked
To Tartarus, their own place, and punishment condign.

    Deiphobus said:—

                    Great Sibyl, do not be angry with me.
I will leave you, return to the shades and make their number complete.
Fare on, Aeneas, our pride, and with better luck than mine!

    Thus he spoke, and speaking, turned on his heel and went.

    Aeneas looked back on a sudden: he saw to his left a cliff
Overhanging a spread of battlements, a threefold wall about them,
Girdled too by a swift-running stream, a flaming torrent—

[*Lines 514–550*]

Hell's river of fire, whose current rolls clashing rocks along.
In front, an enormous portal, the door-posts columns of adamant,
So strong that no mortal violence nor even the heaven-dwellers
Could broach it: an iron tower stands sheer and soaring above it,
Whereon Tisiphone sits, wrapped in a bloodstained robe,
Sleeplessly, day-long, night-long, guarding the forecourt there.
From within can be heard the sounds of groaning and brutal lashing,
Sounds of clanking iron, of chains being dragged along.
Scared by the din, Aeneas halted; he could not move:—
    What kinds of criminals are these? Speak, lady! What punishments
Afflict them, that such agonised sounds rise up from there?
    Then the Sibyl began:—
                        O famous lord of the Trojans,
No righteous soul may tread that threshold of the damned:
But, when Hecate appointed me to the Avernian grove,
She instructed me in heaven's punishments, showed me all.
Here Rhadamanthus rules, and most severe his rule is,
Trying and chastising wrongdoers, forcing confessions
From any who, on earth, went gleefully undetected—
But uselessly, since they have only postponed till death their atonement.
At once Tisiphone, the avenger, scourge in hand,
Pounces upon the guilty, lashing them, threatening them
With the angry snakes in her left hand, and calls up her bloodthirsty
                                          sisters.

Then at last the hinges screech, the infernal gates
Grind open. Do you see the sentry, who she is,
Posted over the forecourt? the shape that guards the threshold?
Within, there dwells a thing more fierce—the fifty-headed
Hydra, with all its black throats agape. Then Tartarus
Goes sheer down under the shades, an abyss double in depth
The height that Olympus stands above a man gazing skyward.
Here Earth's primaeval offspring, the breed of Titans, who
Were hurled down by Jove's lightning, writhe in the bottomless pit.
Here have I seen the twin sons of Aloeus, the gigantic
Creatures who sought to pull down heaven itself with their own
Bare hands, and to unseat Jove from his throne above.
Salmoneus too have I seen undergoing the rigorous sentence
Imposed when he mimicked the thunder and lightning of Jove
                                    almighty:
                         [*Lines 551–586*]

Drawn by a four-horse team and shaking a lighted torch,
He would go through Greece exulting, even through the middle of Elis
City, claiming the homage due to the gods alone—
Madman, to copy the nonpareil lightning, the thunderstorm
With a rumble of bronze wheels and a clatter of hard-hoofed horses!
But the Father almighty, among his serried storm clouds, launched
A weapon—no torches, no smoky light of farthing dips
Was this—and hurled the blasphemer down with the wind of its

passage.

Tityos too, the nursling of Earth who mothers all,
Was to be seen, his body pegged out over a full nine
Acres, a huge vulture with hooked beak gnawing for ever
His inexhaustible liver, the guts that are rich in torment,
Pecking away for its food, burrowing deep through the body
It lives in, and giving no rest to the always-replenished vitals.
Need I mention the Lapithae, Ixion or Pirithous?
Over them, always about to fall and looking as if it were
Falling, a black crag hangs: banqueting couches gleam with
Golden legs, raised high, and feasts of regal opulence
Are set before damned eyes; but the chief of the Furies, reclining
Nearby, forbids them to stretch out their hands for the food; she

leaps up,

Menacing them with her lifted torch, and shouts like thunder.
Here are those who in life hated their own brothers,
Or struck their parents; those who entangled their dependants
In fraudulent dealing; and those who sat tight on the wealth they had

won,

Setting none aside for their own kin—most numerous of all are these;
Then such as were killed for adultery, took part in militant treason,
Men who made bold to break faith with their masters:—all such await
Punishment, mewed up here. And seek not to know what punishment,
What kind of destined torment awaits each one in the Pit.
Some have to roll huge rocks; some whirl round, spreadeagled
On spokes of wheels: the tragic Theseus sits, condemned to
Spend eternity in that chair: the poor wretch, Phlegyas,
Admonishes all, crying out through the mirk in solemn avowal,
Be warned by me! Learn justice, and not to belittle the gods!
One sold his country for gold, putting her under the yoke of
Dictatorship, and corruptly made and unmade her laws;

[*Lines 587–622*]

129

One entered the bed of his daughter, forced an unholy mating:
All dared some abominable thing, and what they dared they did.
No, not if I had a hundred tongues, a hundred mouths
And a voice of iron, could I describe all the shapes of wickedness,
Catalogue all the retributions inflicted here.

Thus spoke the long-lived priestess of Phoebus, then added this:—
But come, resume your journey, finish the task in hand!
Let us go quickly on. I can see the bastions, forged in
The Cyclops' furnaces, and the arch of the gateway yonder,
Where we are bidden to put down your passport, the golden bough.

She had spoken. Side by side they went the twilight way,
Rapidly covering the space between, and approached the gateway.
Aeneas stopped at the entrance, sprinkled himself with holy
Water, and placed the bough right at the doorway there.

Now this was done at last, and Proserpine had her offering,
They went on into the Happy Place, the green and genial
Glades where the fortunate live, the home of the blessed spirits.
What largesse of bright air, clothing the vales in dazzling
Light, is here! This land has a sun and stars of its own.
Some exercise upon the grassy playing-fields
Or wrestle on the yellow sands in rivalry of sport;
Some foot the rhythmic dances and chant poems aloud.
Orpheus, the Thracian bard, is there in his long robe,
To accompany their measures upon the seven-stringed lyre
Which he plucks, now with his fingers, now with an ivory plectrum.
Here is the ancient line of Teucer, a breed most handsome,
Great-hearted heroes born in the happier days of old,
Ilus, Assaracus, and Dardanus, founder of Troy.
From afar Aeneas marvelled at the arms, the phantom chariots.
Spears stood fixed in the ground, everywhere over the plain
Grazed the unharnessed horses. The pleasure those heroes had felt,
When alive, in their arms and chariots, the care they had taken to
pasture
Their sleek horses—all was the same beyond the tomb.
Aeneas noticed others to left and right on the greensward
Feasting and singing a jovial paean in unison
Amidst a fragrant grove of bay trees, whence the river
Eridanus springs, to roll grandly through woods of the world above.
Here were assembled those who had suffered wounds in defence of

[*Lines 623–660*]

Their country; those who had lived pure lives as priests; and poets
Who had not disgraced Apollo, poets of true integrity;
Men who civilised life by the skills they discovered, and men whose
Kindness to other people has kept their memory green—
All these upon their temples wore headbands white as snow.
Now the Sibyl addressed the company dotted about there,
And specially Musaeus, for round him a large group
Gazed up at him as he towered head and shoulders above them:—
    Tell me, you blessed spirits, and you, most honoured poet,
Whereabouts can we find Anchises? We have come here,
Crossing the great rivers of the Underworld, to see him.
    So did Musaeus make reply with these few words:—
    None of us has a fixed abode: we dwell in shady
Groves, we make our beds on river-banks, reside in
Watersweet meadows. But if your heart's desire is such,
Then climb this rise and I'll set your feet on an easy path.
    He spoke, and leading the way, showed them the luminous plains
Extending below them. Now they went down from the uplands.
    Deep in a green valley stood father Anchises, surveying
The spirits there confined before they went up to the light of
The world above: he was musing seriously, and reviewing
His folk's full tally, it happened, the line of his loved children,
Their destinies and fortunes, their characters and their deeds.
Now, when he saw Aeneas coming in his direction
Over the grass, he stretched out both hands, all eagerness,
And tears poured down his cheeks, and the words were tumbling

out:—
    So you have come at last? The love that your father relied on
Has won through the hard journey? And I may gaze, my son,
Upon your face, and exchange the old homely talk with you?
Thus indeed I surmised it would be, believed it must happen,
Counting the days till you came: I was not deceived in my hopes, then.
Over what lands, what wide, wide seas you have made your journey!
What dangers have beset you! And now you are here with me.
How I dreaded lest you should come to some harm at Carthage!
    Aeneas replied:—
                    Your image it was, your troubled phantom

[*Lines 661–695*]

131

That, often rising before me, has brought me to this place.
Our ships are riding at anchor in the Tyrrhene sea. Oh, let me
Take your hand and embrace you, father! Let me! Withdraw not!
  Even as he spoke, his cheeks grew wet with a flood of tears.
Three times he tried to put his arms round his father's neck,
Three times the phantom slipped his vain embrace—it was like
Grasping a wisp of wind or the wings of a fleeting dream.
  Now did Aeneas descry, deep in a valley retiring,
A wood, a secluded copse whose branches soughed in the wind,
And Lethe river drifting past the tranquil places.
Hereabouts were flitting a multitude without number,
Just as, amid the meadows on a fine summer day,
The bees alight on flowers of every hue, and brim the
Shining lilies, and all the lea is humming with them.
Aeneas, moved by the sudden sight, asked in his ignorance
What it might mean, what was that river over there
And all that crowd of people swarming along its banks.
Then his father, Anchises, said:—
                                They are souls who are destined for
Reincarnation; and now at Lethe's stream they are drinking
The waters that quench man's troubles, the deep draught of oblivion.
Long, long have I wanted to tell you of these and reveal them
Before your eyes, to count them over, the seed of my seed,
That you might the more rejoice with me in the finding of Italy.
  But, father, must it be deemed that some souls ascend from here
To our earthly scene? re-enter our dull corporeal existence?
Why ever should so perverse a craving for earth possess them?
  I will tell you, my son, certainly; I will not keep you in doubt,
Answered Anchises, and then enlarged on each point successively:—
  First, you must know that the heavens, the earth, the watery plains
Of the sea, the moon's bright globe, the sun and the stars are all
Sustained by a spirit within; for immanent Mind, flowing
Through all its parts and leavening its mass, makes the universe work.
This union produced mankind, the beasts, the birds of the air,
And the strange creatures that live under the sea's smooth face.
The life-force of those seeds is fire, their source celestial,
But they are deadened and dimmed by the sinful bodies they live in—
The flesh that is laden with death, the anatomy of clay:
Whence these souls of ours feel fear, desire, grief, joy,

[*Lines 696–733*]

132

But encased in their blind, dark prison discern not the heaven-light
above.
Yes, not even when the last flicker of life has left us,
Does evil, or the ills that flesh is heir to, quite
Relinquish our souls; it must be that many a taint grows deeply,
Mysteriously grained in their being from long contact with the body.
Therefore the dead are disciplined in purgatory, and pay
The penalty of old evil: some hang, stretched to the blast of
Vacuum winds; for others, the stain of sin is washed
Away in a vast whirlpool or cauterised with fire.
Each of us finds in the next world his own level: a few of us
Are later released to wander at will through broad Elysium,
The Happy Fields; until, in the fullness of time, the ages
Have purged that ingrown stain, and nothing is left but pure
Ethereal sentience and the spirit's essential flame.
All these souls, when they have finished their thousand-year cycle,
God sends for, and they come in crowds to the river of Lethe,
So that, you see, with memory washed out, they may revisit
The earth above and begin to wish to be born again.
    When Anchises had finished, he drew his son and the Sibyl
Into the thick of the murmuring concourse assembled there
And took his stand on an eminence from which he could scan the
long files
Over against him, and mark the features of those who passed.
    Listen, for I will show you your destiny, setting forth
The fame that from now shall attend the seed of Dardanus,
The posterity that awaits you from an Italian marriage—
Illustrious souls, one day to inherit our Trojan name.
That young man there—do you see him? —who leans on an untipped
spear,
Has been allotted the next passage to life, and first of
All these will ascend to earth, with Italian blood in his veins;
He is Silvius, an Alban name, and destined to be your last child,
The child of your late old age by a wife, Lavinia, who shall
Bear him in sylvan surroundings, a king and the father of kings
Through whom our lineage shall rule in Alba Longa.
Next to him stands Procas, a glory to the Trojan line;
Then Capys and Numitor, and one who'll revive your own name—
Silvius Aeneas, outstanding alike for moral rectitude
    [*Lines 734–769*]

And prowess in war, if ever he comes to the Alban throne.
What fine young men they are! Look at their stalwart bearing,
The oak leaves that shade their brows—decorations for saving life!
These shall found your Nomentum, Gabii and Fidenae,
These shall rear on the hills Collatia's citadel,
Pometii, and the Fort of Inuus, Bola and Cora—
All nameless sites at present, but then they shall have these names.
Further, a child of Mars shall go to join his grandsire—
Romulus, born of the stock of Assaracus by his mother,
Ilia. Look at the twin plumes upon his helmet's crest,
Mars' cognisance, which marks him out for the world of earth!
His are the auguries, my son, whereby great Rome
Shall rule to the ends of the earth, shall aspire to the highest
                                               achievement,
Shall ring the seven hills with a wall to make one city,
Blessed in her breed of men: as Cybele, wearing her turreted
Crown, is charioted round the Phrygian cities, proud of
Her brood of gods, embracing a hundred of her children's children—
Heaven-dwellers all, all tenants of the realm above.
Now bend your gaze this way, look at that people there!
They are *your* Romans. Caesar is there and all Ascanius'
Posterity, who shall pass beneath the arch of day.
And here, here is the man, the promised one you know of—
Caesar Augustus, son of a god, destined to rule
Where Saturn ruled of old in Latium, and there
Bring back the age of gold: his empire shall expand
Past Garamants and Indians to a land beyond the zodiac
And the sun's yearly path, where Atlas the sky-bearer pivots
The wheeling heavens, embossed with fiery stars, on his shoulder.
Even now the Caspian realm, the Crimean country
Tremble at oracles of the gods predicting his advent,
And the seven mouths of the Nile are in a sweat of fear.
Not even Hercules roved so far and wide over earth,
Although he shot the bronze-footed deer, brought peace to the
                                               woods of
Erymanthus, subdued Lerna with the terror of his bow;
Nor Bacchus, triumphantly driving his team with vines for reins,
His team of tigers down from Mount Nysa, travelled so far.
Do we still hesitate, then, to enlarge our courage by action?
                                          [Lines 770–806]

Shrink from occupying the territory of Ausonia?
Who is that in the distance, bearing the hallows, crowned with
A wreath of olive? I recognise—grey hair and hoary chin—
That Roman king who, called to high power from humble Cures,
A town in a poor area, shall found our system of law
And thus refound our city. The successor of Numa, destined
To shake our land out of its indolence, stirring men up to fight
Who have grown unadventurous and lost the habit of victory,
Is Tullus. After him shall reign the too boastful Ancus,
Already over-fond of the breath of popular favour.
Would you see the Tarquin kings, and arrogant as they, Brutus
The avenger, with the symbols of civic freedom he won back?
He shall be first to receive consular rank and its power of
Life and death: when his sons awake the dormant conflict,
Their father, a tragic figure, shall call them to pay the extreme
Penalty, for fair freedom's sake. However posterity
Look on that deed, patriotism shall prevail and love of
Honour. See over there the Decii, the Drusi, Torquatus
With merciless axe, Camillus with the standards he recovered.
See those twin souls, resplendent in duplicate armour: now
They're of one mind, and shall be as long as the Underworld holds
them;
But oh, if ever they reach the world above, what warfare,
What battles and what carnage will they create between them—
Caesar descending from Alpine strongholds, the fort of Monoecus,
His son-in-law Pompey lined up with an Eastern army against him.
Lads, do not harden yourselves to face such terrible wars!
Turn not your country's hand against your country's heart!
You, be the first to renounce it, my son of heavenly lineage,
You be the first to bury the hatchet! . . .
That one shall ride in triumph to the lofty Capitol,
The conqueror of Corinth, renowned for the Greeks he has slain.
That one shall wipe out Argos and Agamemnon's Mycenae,
Destroying an heir of Aeacus, the seed of warrior Achilles,
Avenging his Trojan sires and the sacrilege done to Minerva.
Who could leave unnoticed the glorious Cato, Cossus,
The family of the Gracchi, the two Scipios—thunderbolts
In war and death to Libya; Fabricius, who had plenty
In poverty; Serranus, sowing his furrowed fields?
[*Lines 807–844*]

135

Fabii, where do you lead my lagging steps? O Fabius,
The greatest, you the preserver of Rome by delaying tactics!
Let others fashion from bronze more lifelike, breathing images—
For so they shall—and evoke living faces from marble;
Others excel as orators, others track with their instruments
The planets circling in heaven and predict when stars will appear.
But, Romans, never forget that government is your medium!
Be this your art:—to practise men in the habit of peace,
Generosity to the conquered, and firmness against aggressors.

    They marvelled at Anchises' words, and he went on:—
    Look how Marcellus comes all glorious with the highest
Of trophies, a victor over-topping all other men!
He shall buttress the Roman cause when a great war shakes it,
Shatter the Carthaginian and rebel Gaul with his cavalry,
Give to Quirinus the third set of arms won in single combat.

    Aeneas interposed, seeing beside Marcellus
A youth of fine appearance, in glittering accoutrements,
But his face was far from cheerful and downcast were his eyes:—
    Father, who is he that walks with Marcellus there?
His son? Or one of the noble line of his children's children?
How the retinue murmurs around him! How fine is the young man's
                                       presence!
Yet is his head haloed by sombre shade of night.
    Then father Anchises began, tears welling up in his eyes:—
    My son, do not probe into the sorrows of your kin.
Fate shall allow the earth one glimpse of this young man—
One glimpse, no more. Too puissant had been Rome's stock, ye gods,
In your sight, had such gifts been granted it to keep.
What lamentations of men shall the Campus Martius echo
To Mars' great city! O Tiber, what obsequies you shall see
One day as you glide past the new-built mausoleum!
No lad of the Trojan line shall with such hopeful promise
Exalt his Latin forebears, nor shall the land of Romulus
Ever again be so proud of one she has given birth to.
Alas for the sense of duty, the old-time honour! Alas for
The hand unvanquished in war! Him would no foe have met
In battle and not rued it, whether he charged on foot
Or drove his lathering steed with spurs against the enemy.
Alas, poor youth! If only you could escape your harsh fate!

                       [*Lines 845–882*]

136

Marcellus you shall be. Give me armfuls of lilies
That I may scatter their shining blooms and shower these gifts
At least upon the dear soul, all to no purpose though
Such kindness be.
                    So far and wide, surveying all,
They wandered through that region, those broad and hazy plains.
After Anchises had shown his son over the whole place
And fired his heart with passion for the great things to come,
He told the hero of wars he would have to fight one day,
Told of the Laurentines and the city of Latinus,
And how to evade, or endure, each crisis upon his way.
    There are two gates of Sleep: the one is made of horn,
They say, and affords the outlet for genuine apparitions:
The other's a gate of brightly-shining ivory; this way
The Shades send up to earth false dreams that impose upon us.
Talking, then, of such matters, Anchises escorted his son
And the Sibyl as far as the ivory gate and sent them through it.
Aeneas made his way back to the ships and his friends with all speed,
Then coasted along direct to the harbour of Caieta.
Bow-anchors out, the ships are lining the shore with their sterns.
    [*Lines 883–901*]

BOOK VII

Caieta too, who was nurse to Aeneas, when she died
Gave Italy's coast undying fame: for even now
The place where she rests is preserved by her legend, she has an epitaph
In a place-name of great Hesperia—no small glory.
When the ever-faithful Aeneas has paid her the last rites
And heaped a burial mound above her, the deepsea now
Being calm, he weighed from harbour and set course under sail.
The wind blew steadily on into the night, a bright moon
Favoured their voyage, its radiance dancing upon the water.
Soon they were skirting close by the shore of Circe's land
Where that luxurious daughter of the Sun, her song for ever
Thrilling through spell-protected groves, in her proud palace
Burns fragrant cedarwood during the night to see by,
While the rattling shuttle runs through the gossamer warp.
From this place could be heard through the small hours the groaning
Roars of angry lions resentful at their captivity;
Bristly boars and bears were heard from the enclosures
Furiously raging, and wolf-like creatures howling—
Men they had once been, but the terrible goddess had turned them
Into beast faces, things on all fours, with her magic herbs.
So, lest the god-fearing Trojans touched at that fiendish coast,
And putting in there, suffered the same weird transformation,
Neptune, filling their sails with a wind from the right quarter,
Got them away and past the surf that boils inshore.
Now was the sea's face blushing with dawn rays, and in heaven
Rosily charioted shone crocus-yellow Aurora,
When the wind dropped—all of a sudden not one breath
Was blowing—and the oars toiled in water slow as syrup.
Now, looking forth from the deep, Aeneas sighted a big wood:
Through this wood the genial stream of Tiber flowing,
Yellow with racing eddies that stir up sand galore,
Debouches into the sea. Around and above, bright-plumaged
Birds whose habitat is the river banks and channel

[*Lines 1–33*]

139

Charmed the air with their song, flitted about the wood.
Aeneas ordered his squadron to change course towards the land.
Soon in high spirits he entered the shady mouth of the river.

Come, Muse of Love, let me rehearse the kings, the phase of
History, and the conditions that reigned in antique Latium
When first that expedition arrived upon the beaches
Of Italy: I'll recall what first led to the war there.
Speak through me, then, Spirit of Song! Grim wars I'll tell of,
And battlefronts, and princes courageous unto death,
The levies of the Etruscans, aye, all Hesperia mustered
In arms. A grander train of events is now before me,
A grander theme I open. An old man now, Latinus
Was king of the towns and country, his reign being long and peaceful.
He was the son, we are told, of Faunus and the Laurentian
Nymph, Marica: Faunus was son of Picus, who called
Saturn his father—yes, Saturn originated their line.
Latinus, by fate's decree, had no son now; his male
Succession was no more, cut off in the bloom of first youth.
One daughter he had, sole prop of his house and heir of his ample
Estate, a girl fully budded now and ripe for marriage.
Many sought her hand, from all over Latium, from all
Italy: the handsomest by far of these wooers was Turnus—
He had the prestige of a splendid pedigree and the backing
Of the queen, who had set her heart on getting him as a son-in-law:
But various alarming portents from heaven were proving an obstacle.
There grew in the central court of the palace a laurel tree,
Its leafage holy and held in reverence for many years,
Which king Latinus was said to have found there, when he first
Established the city, and dedicated the tree to Phoebus,
Using its name to christen his colonists the Laurentes.
A strange thing happened now: a tight-packed swarm of bees
Came loudly humming through the limpid air, and settling
Upon the top of that tree, they interlocked their feet;
Next moment a swarm was hanging down from the green bough.
At once the soothsayer cried:—

                    I see a stranger coming.
Men are coming from where the bees came—coming to settle
Where the bees have settled, this fortress their seat of empire.

Apart from this, while the maiden Lavinia stood beside
[*Lines 34–71*]

140

Her father, who with ritual taper was lighting the altar—
Sinister thing—they beheld her long hair set on fire
And all her head-dress burning with crackling flames; they saw
Those queenly tresses ablaze, ablaze her coronet
Of precious stones: before long, enshrouded in golden-glowering
Smoky flame, she was fountaining sparks all over the palace.
It was counted, of course, as a dreadful, miraculous manifestation:
The maiden herself, they foretold, was singled out for a famous
Destiny, but for the people it meant a widespread war.

The king, greatly disturbed by this portent, goes to visit
The oracle of Faunus, his prophet father, and questions
The grove where Albunea towers over the forest, resounding
With hallowed cascade and darkly exhaling a deadly vapour.
Here the Italian tribes, all the Oenotrians, go for
Advice in times of perplexity: hither the priestess brings
The offerings, and couched at dead of night on the fleeces
Of the sheep sacrificed there, she woos slumber; and then
Visions appear to her, shapes are floating strangely about her,
And in her ears are many voices—she is conversing
With deity, addressing the powers of the nether regions.
This was where Latinus now went to consult the oracle;
After the ritual sacrifice of a hundred wool-bearing sheep
He lay down and reclined upon the hides, the outspread
Fleeces: and at once from the depths of the wood a voice came:—

Seek not, my son, to marry your daughter to a man of
The Latin race. Embark not upon a native alliance.
From abroad shall sons-in-law come, to wed our women and make
Our name illustrious: to their descendants the whole
Spinning globe shall be a footstool and an empire—
All that the sun looks down on, even to the ends of the earth.

The oracle of his father, Faunus, the counsel given
Thus in the stilly night, Latinus kept not secret;
But rumour had already flown it far and wide
Throughout the towns of Ausonia, when the Trojan expedition
Lay with their vessels moored to the grassy bank of the Tiber.

Aeneas, his lieutenants and fair Ascanius
Sat themselves down beneath the boughs of a tall tree
To have a meal. Now it happened—Juppiter prompted the action—
They laid the viands on flat cakes of meal about the grass,

[*Lines 72–110*]

141

Using those cereal mats to heap the fruits of the earth on.
Well, when they'd eaten all the rest, being still hungry,
It befell that they turned their attention to the slender cakes of meal:
With hands and teeth they were broaching incontinent those round
cakes
(Symbol of destiny) and devouring their broad sections,
When "Goodness, we're eating our tables too!" Ascanius cried
Joking. Just that. But that was enough; for his words proclaimed
The beginning of the end of their trials: as such, his father at once
Seized upon them, and struck by their god-sent meaning, would
have no more said,
But cried himself on the instant:—
O promised land of my destiny,
All hail! And all hail to you, ye gods of Troy, for you spoke truth!
Here is our home, this is our country. I recall now
My father Anchises bequeathed me this secret of fate, saying,
When you are come to a strange shore and compelled by hunger,
Food running short, to devour your tables, that is the time
To look for a home in your weariness, that is the place—mark well—
To choose a site and begin to work hard on a fortified settlement.
This was the hunger he spoke of, this the last ordeal awaiting us,
Putting a term to our deadly perils.
Come therefore, at sunrise in high heart let us spread out all ways
From the harbour, let us explore the interior and investigate
What manner of men live here and where their cities are sited.
Now offer libations from bowls to Juppiter, offer a prayer to
My father Anchises, and set forth a good supply of wine.
After these words Aeneas, twining about his temples
A leafy bough, invoked the genius of the place, and Earth,
First of deities; called on the Nymphs and the still unknown
Rivers; then called on Night and the rising Stars of Night,
Juppiter, patron of Ida, the Phrygian Mother next;
Called on his parents, one in heaven, one in the Underworld.
Now from a clear sky did the Father almighty thunder
Three times, and his own hand showed forth a cloud from heaven,
A cloud that blazed and quivered with dartings of golden light.
A rumour spread like magic among the rank and file,
That the day had come at last to found their promised city.
Exhilarated by so splendid an omen, they eagerly
  [*Lines 111–146*]

142

Started the feast again, set wine and crowned the bowl.

When the next day had dawned and its early beams were lighting
The earth, they went out in parties to reconnoitre the land,
Its city, shores and frontiers. Here, they found, was the pool of
Numicius' spring, here Tiber, here dwelt the stalwart Latins.
Then did Aeneas send out to the stately town of the king
A hundred ambassadors, chosen from every rank in his company,
Garlanded all with olive branches, Athene's emblem,
Bidden to take the king presents and to ask peace for the Trojans.
At once they set off on their mission, hastening towards the palace.
Aeneas himself traced out the walls with a shallow trench,
And breaking the ground, threw up a rampart and battlements, as for
A military encampment, round his first home there on the coast.
Now, their journey accomplished, his emissaries drew near
The walls and could see the towers and high roofs of the Latins.
In front of the town were boys, and youths in their first flower,
practising
Horsemanship and training chariot teams on the campus,
Or bending the lively bow, or the tough javelin hurling
Strenuously, and challenging one another at running or boxing.
Just then a rider brought to the ears of the long-lived king
A message that some mighty men, in unfamiliar
Livery, had arrived. He orders them to be summoned
To the great hall, and awaits them there on the throne of his fathers.
A stately hall there was on the city's heights, a huge place
Of a hundred soaring columns, the palace once of Laurentian
Picus: it stood in a grove dark with ancestral dread.
Here, to have fortunate reigns, their kings must be crowned and
display first
The symbols of office: this temple was senate house and scene of
Religious banquets alike; here, when a ram had been sacrificed,
Elders were used to sit down at the long, refectory tables.
Here too, in a row, were standing the statues of their forefathers,
Carved from old cedarwood—Italus; father Sabinus,
The planter of vines, with a pruning-knife held in his carven hand;
Ancient Saturn, and Janus facing-both-ways—all stood
Near to the entrance, with other kings from the earliest days
And heroes who had suffered wounds in defence of their country.
Numerous trophies, too, were displayed on the sacred portals—
[Lines 147–183]

Chariots captured in war, battle-axes with curving blades,
Helmet crests, huge bars from the gates of ransacked cities,
Javelins and shields, and beaks removed from warships.
There, holding the augur's staff, arrayed in a short toga
Purple-striped, the holy shield on his left arm, sat
Picus, tamer of horses: vainly lusting to bed with him,
Golden Circe had used her wand and her magic potions,
And turned him into a bird, into a pied woodpecker.
Such was the holy shrine, the ancestral hall within which
Latinus sat enthroned and summoned the Trojans to him.
When they had entered his presence, he began, and peaceably spoke:—
    Trojans—oh yes, your city and line are not unknown to us,
We'd heard of you before you sailed this way—pray tell me
What you would have. What motive, what need has brought your
                                                              ships
So many leagues of blue sea to these Ausonian shores?
Did you mistake your course, or were you driven off it
By gales—for such things often happen to men on the high seas—
That you have sailed into the estuary and lie at anchor here?
Anyway, feel you are welcome; and know that we, the Latins,
Are children of Saturn, depend on no penal system for equity,
Keeping from wrong of our own free will in the time-honoured,
                                                              golden
Rule of that god. I indeed remember, though time has dimmed
The legend, Auruncan elders telling how Dardanus
Was born here, and hence migrated to the towns of Phrygian Ida
And into Thracian Samos, which men call Samothrace now.
His beginnings were here, in the Tuscan home of Corythus: now
He has his throne in the golden palace of the star-glistering
Heavens, and adds one more to the altars of the gods.
    Latinus had spoken: Ilioneus then made reply as follows:—
    O king, illustrious son of Faunus, no black storm,
No heavy seas it was that drove us to your country,
Nor did we err in our course through misreading the stars or the
                                                              landmarks.
By common consent, of our own volition, have we come to
Your city, being cast out from our empire, once the greatest
The sun could see as it travelled from the very east of the sky.
Jove was the first of our line: the Dardan people boasts of

[*Lines 184–219*]

Jove as their ancestor: our king, Trojan Aeneas,
Who sent us to you, was born of the most high stock of Jove.
How terrible a storm, unleashed from cruel Mycenae,
Burst over the plains of Ida; how destiny compelled
A war between East and West, the collision of Europe and Asia:—
All have heard this: it is known in remotest lands where Ocean
Breaks on the earth's rim, known where the tyrant sun cuts off
From us the dwellers in tropical countries about the equator.
That storm swept Troy away. We voyaged on sea after sea:
Now we but ask a small, inoffensive plot for our home-gods
Here on the coast, with water and air that are free to all men.
We shall not disgrace your kingdom; to receive us will bring you
                                                    great honour
Amongst mankind and win undying gratitude from us;
Ausonia will never regret having taken Troy to her bosom.
By the destiny of Aeneas I swear it, and his strong right arm
Trusty alike in friendship or war to whoever has tried it,
Many the peoples, the nations have willingly sought for alliance
And union with us; so do not look down on us because now
It is we who make the petition and offer the olive branch.
At heaven's express command, fate's bidding, we sought out
Your land. From here Dardanus took his origin: hither
Apollo recalls us, strictly enjoining that we come back
To Tuscan Tiber and the sacred pools of Numicius' spring.
Aeneas offers you, too, these gifts—small tokens of
Our old prosperity, relics we saved from burning Troy:
A chalice of gold which his father, Anchises, used for libations;
And these, Priam's regalia when he gave laws in the old way
To his assembled peoples—a sceptre, a royal diadem,
And vestments wrought by the ladies of Ilium.

   Latinus received this speech of Ilioneus with a gaze
Steadily fixed on the ground; he remained motionless, thinking
Hard, his eyes restive. It was not so much that the royal purple-
Embroidered robe and the sceptre of Priam influenced the king,
As that his mind was absorbed by the thought of his daughter's
                                                    marriage
And deeply pondering the oracle Faunus had given him.
This, he reflected, must be the man from abroad who is meant
By the fates to become my son-in-law and to be partner in
                              [*Lines 220–256*]

My sovereignty: from him shall stem that future breed,
Excelling in courage, whose might is to master the whole world.
At last, much elated, he said:—
                                        May the gods forward our project
And fulfil their revelation! You shall have what you ask for, Trojan.
Nor do I slight these presents. As long as I'm king, you shall not
Be lacking in fertile land, and Troy as of old shall be prosperous.
Let but Aeneas come here in person; if such is his need
For us, if he's eager to join us in amity and be called
Our ally, he must not be shy of meeting friends face to face.
For me, a part of the bargain it is to shake hands with your sovereign.
Do you take back, in reply, this commission of mine to Aeneas.
I have a daughter, whom neither my sire's most arcane oracle
Nor heaven's will, expressed in many portents, permits to marry
A man of her own people: rather, they presage, for Latium
Is destined a prince consort from overseas, and his blood shall
Exalt our name to the skies. I believe it's Aeneas that fate means,
And if there's any truth in my intuition, accept him.

   Thus spoke the king; and then chose out from the three hundred
Beautifully-groomed horses which stood in his lofty stables.
For each of the envoys, there and then, he bade to be brought
A courser caparisoned in crimson-embroidered trappings:
Their chests were hung with parures of gold, and gold-embroidered
Their housings were, and red-gold the bits they champed in their
                                                                    mouths.

To the absent Aeneas he sent a chariot and two horses
Of pedigree divine, breathing fire from their nostrils;
They came of that mixed breed which the sorceress, Circe, had raised
To her father, the Sun, when she stole his stallions and put them to a
                                                                    mare.

Now, with these words and gifts from Latinus, did the Trojan
Envoys return, proudly mounted, bearers of peace.

   But look! from Argos, city of Inachus, now returning
And well on her way through the sky, the vindictive consort of
                                                                    Juppiter

Saw from the air above Pachynus in Sicily,
At a great distance, Aeneas triumphant, his fleet all there.
She notes they have disembarked from their ships and are busily
                                                                    building

[*Lines 257–290*]

146

Habitations already, feeling quite safe in that land.
Bitter resentment checked her. Shaking her head, she burst out:—
    Ah, those obnoxious Trojans, whose destiny so conflicts with
The destinies of my peoples! Could they perish on Ilium's plains?
Be kept in captivity when they'd been captured? be burnt to ashes
In blazing Troy? Not they! Through fire and steel they found
A way of escape. I think my deity must be spent
And supine, or else my rancour is sleeping from sheer satiety.
Yet, when they'd been hurled out of their country, I was not slow to
Persecute them in their exile and oppose every stage of their voyage.
Against the Trojans I spent all the might of sea and sky.
What use to me were the Syrtes, Scylla, engulfing Charybdis?
The Trojans are snug in Tiber's channel, their hoped-for haven,
Snapping their fingers at ocean and me. Yet Mars had the power to
Destroy the giant brood of the Lapithae; Jove himself
Gave over to the wrath of Diana time-honoured Calydon.
What had the Lapithae done, or Calydon, to deserve it?
Yet I, the great consort of Jove, who have left nothing untried,
Who have stooped to every expedient against him, am a failure—
Beaten by Aeneas. Well, if my powers are not great enough,
I shall not hesitate—that's sure—to ask help wherever
Help may be found. If the gods above are no use to me, then I'll
Move all hell. From his Latin kingship I may not bar him;
The fates are firm that he shall marry Lavinia: so be it.
What I can do is to postpone these great events, to delay them,
And to wreak havoc upon the peoples of both the kings.
They shall pay with their lieges' lives the price for becoming related;
And you, Lavinia—Italian and Trojan blood shall be your
Marriage portion, and War your bridesmaid. Not only Hecuba
Shall have conceived a firebrand, brought forth a fire-raising
                                                    bridegroom:
No, Venus' son is the same—a second Paris, whose wedding-
Taper shall be a funeral torch to resurgent Troy.
    When she had spoken, Juno came down to earth, horrific,
And haled forth from the infernal regions, the home of the terrible
Deities, Allecto, maker of grief, who revels
In war, in open and underhand violence, in damaging quarrels.
Even her father, Pluto, and her hellish sisters loathe
That fiend, Allecto, so manifold her aspects and so ferocious

                                              [*Lines 291–328*]

147

Each form she takes, such a nest of vipers swarms in her black hair.
Now Juno began to speak, whetting this creature's appetite:—
    Maiden, daughter of Night, do me this favour—it's your kind—
This service, so that our honour and reputation may not be
Diminished, so that the Trojans fail to wheedle Latinus
By means of this marriage or to take possession of Italy.
You can set brothers of one mind at one another's throats,
Torment a home with hatred, bringing your whips and destructive
Firebrands to lash a house: you have a thousand titles,
A thousand tricks for making mischief. Stir up your teeming
Ideas! Disrupt the peace they have made! Sow seeds of war!
Let them wish for weapons, demand them and use them, all in an
                                                            instant.

    At once Allecto went, steeped in her viperish venom,
And sought out first the high walls of the Laurentine monarch
In Latium. There she pickets Amata's quiet threshold—
The queen, whose motherly heart is seething with grief and chagrin
Over the Trojans' coming and the marriage with Turnus cancelled.
On her the fiend now casts a serpent, one of her snake-blue
Tresses, and thrusts it into her bosom, deep into her heart,
So that the queen may discharge through the household its maniac
                                                            infection.

Gliding between her dress and her smooth breasts, that serpent
Coils—she feels not its touch nor notices it in her madness—
Breathing its morbid breath into her: swelling, it turns
Into a golden necklace, into the head-dress binding
Her hair, and its pendant ribbon, and slithers over her body.
Now, while that moist and magic contagion was but beginning
To work upon her mind and twine her bones with fire,
The queen, whose thoughts were not yet wholly possessed by the
                                                            flame in

Her breast, quite gently spoke, as soft-hearted mothers do,
Greatly distressed by the thought of her daughter wedding a Trojan:—
    Father, must our Lavinia be wed to a Trojan, an outcast?
Have you no feeling for her? no sense of your own interests?
No pity for her mother?—that false-hearted pirate will leave me
As soon as a fair wind blows, and sail away with my daughter.
It's Paris all over again—just so did Paris steal into
Sparta, then carried Ledaean Helen away to Troy.

    [*Lines 329–364*]

148

What of your solemn pledge? the love you had in the old days
For your own people? the promise given so often to Turnus,
Your kinsman? If it is settled our son-in-law must be
Of foreign extraction—if thus your father, Faunus, enjoins you—
I say that any land which is separate from ours and autonomous
Is in fact foreign, and this was what the oracle meant.
Now Turnus, if we go back to the origin of his family,
Is Mycenaean, descended from Inachus and Acrisius.

But when she saw these arguments had no effect on Latinus
And he was firmly opposed; when the serpent's frenzying poison
Had worked its way into her marrow and spread all over her being;
Then, overwrought by monstrous hallucinations, the poor queen
Went uncontrollably raving, beside herself, round the city.
Just so it is that a top goes spinning under the whip lash—
A top that boys, absorbed in their play, whip round an empty
Court in a great circle: driven by the lash, it moves
Round and round, gyrating: puzzled, in childish amazement
The boys hang over it there and gape at the top's revolutions,
Livelier at every blow. So fast and furious the queen was
Driven right through the city among the inflammable populace.
What's more, pretending to hear the call of Bacchus (a greater
Evil this, and launched her forth on a wilder madness),
She flew to the woods, hid her daughter among the forested hills,
To cheat of his bride the Trojan, or at least delay the marriage.
Hail, Bacchus! she shrieked: you alone are worthy of the maid,
She kept shouting·   for you she takes up the soft-leafed thryrsus, and you
She follows in the dance, and to you is vowed the tress she is growing!
The rumour flew fast: a mass hysteria swept the housewives,
A burning compulsion to go and find new dwellings somewhere.
They have left their homes, they are baring neck and hair to the breeze;
Some of them fill the air with whimpering cries, dress up in
Fawn-skins, and carry staves all twined about with vine-shoots.
Amongst them, holding aloft a blazing torch, the hectic
Queen is chanting a marriage song for her daughter and Turnus:
Her bloodshot eyes are rolling: harshly all of a sudden
She cries:—

   Mothers of Latium, listen, wherever you are!
Do you feel in your duteous hearts any kindness for poor Amata?
             [*Lines 365–401*]

Does any care for a mother's rights still prick your conscience?
Then loose your hair from the headband and join the revels with me!
   So with the scourge of Bacchus Allecto, who was everywhere
Among the trees, in the wild-beast coverts, chivvied the queen.
   When it was clear that the queen's first injection of madness was
                                                      strong enough,
And that Latinus' purpose and household were thoroughly shaken,
The louring Allecto mounted at once on her sombre wings
And made for the walls of hot-headed Turnus—the city which men say
Danae founded and colonised with her Acrisians, when she
Was driven that way by the South wind. Our ancestors called the place
Ardea; though it retains the great name of Ardea still,
Its best days are far behind it. Here, in the lofty palace,
Turnus was taking his rest at the mid-hour of night.
Allecto now sloughed off her grim looks and diabolical
Form, changing herself to the likeness of an old crone,
Uncannily furrowing her brow with wrinkles; she assumed
White hair and a headband, wreathed her head with a chaplet of olive:
So, as the aged priestess of Juno's temple, Calybe,
Coming before the young man's eyes, she spoke as follows:—
   Turnus, will you tolerate that all your efforts should run
To waste, the dominion you've worked for pass into the hands of
                                                      foreigners?
The king denies you your bride and the marriage-portion you've
                                                      bought with
Bloodshed: an alien now is called in to be his successor.
Go then, you laughing-stock, face dangers, mow down the Tuscans,
Ensure peace for the Latins!—this is the thanks you get.
Indeed, almighty Juno appeared in person and bade me
Speak to you even thus, while you lay in the quiet of night.
Up, then! Take heart of grace! Mobilise the army! March
Out of the gates to war! Those Trojan ships and leaders
That occupy our beautiful river—burn them to ashes!
These are orders from the heavenly powers. Let king Latinus,
Unless he agree to stand by his word and allow your marriage,
Suffer for it, and discover what Turnus is like as an enemy.
   Here the young man in his turn began to speak, deriding
Her prophecy:—
                    I am not, as you seem to think, unaware that
   [*Lines 402–436*]

150

A fleet has sailed into the Tiber; the news did come to my ears.
Do not be such an alarmist, I beg you. Queen Juno is not
Indifferent to me and mine.
As for you, mother—it's old age, clogging the mind and impairing its
Sense of reality, that haunts you with bogey-man worries,
And scares your prophetic soul with delusions of civil war.
Your job's to look after the temple and the images of the gods:
Leave making of war and peace to men, whose business is warfare.
    These words of Turnus made Allecto explode into anger.
As the young prince still spoke, a sudden palsy shook him,
And his eyes went stiff with fear; for the Fury, hissing-snake-tressed,
Was hideously revealed at her full height. She rolled
Her flaming eyes, she flung him back as he tried to falter
A few more words; two snakes stood up like horns on her head,
And she cracked her whip, and spoke again, her mouth like a mad
                                                            dog's:—
    So! My mind is clogged? Old age, impairing my sense of
Reality, scares me with delusions of civil war?
Look at me, then! I am come from the place where the Furies are.
War and death I bear in this hand.
So saying, she hurled an incendiary brand at Turnus, which buried
Itself deep in his heart, blazing and pitchily smoking.
Extreme terror awoke him from sleep; a sweat broke out
All over the young man's body, soaked him from head to foot.
Madly yelling for arms, by his bed, through his house he hunts for
                                                            them;
Crazy with bloodlust he is, with the criminal mania for fighting,
Still more, with resentment. So, when a fire of wood, loud crackling,
Is stoked up high beneath the belly of a boiling cauldron,
The water dances in the heat; within the cauldron the water
Seethes and fumes, bubbling, spitting up foam, till it cannot
Contain itself any more and a cloud of dense steam rises.
Breaking the peace, then, Turnus ordered his army commanders
To get on a war footing and march against king Latinus:
Italy must be protected, the foe thrown back from its frontiers;
He would be more than a match for Trojans and Latins together.
So Turnus proclaimed, and called the gods to witness his vow.
The Rutuli egg one another on to war with enthusiasm,
Some being stirred by the youthful, handsome presence of Turnus,

[*Lines 437–473*]

151

Some by his royal lineage, some by his notable deeds.
   While Turnus inspired his people with the spirit of aggression,
Allecto sped to the Trojans upon her hellish wings,
Hatching a new scheme, spying out the place where handsome
Ascanius, with snares and hounds, was hunting near the seashore.
Here, the devilish hag cast a sudden frenzy upon
Those hounds, touching their nostrils with a familiar scent,
So that they ran in full cry after a stag: the beginning
Of trouble this was, for it kindled to war the hearts of the countryfolk.
There was a stag, a most noble creature, with high-branched antlers,
Which had been taken away from its mother, when young, and kept
As a pet by the boys of Tyrrheus and Tyrrheus himself, the warden
Of the royal herds, who had charge of the pastures throughout the
                                                                  kingdom.
Silvia, the boys' sister, had taught the beast to obey her,
Looked after it, used to adorn it with soft-leafed garlands wreathed
About its antlers, and groom it, and bathe it in fresh spring water.
The stag was meek to her touch and trained to its master's table:
It used to rove the woods; but at night, however late it was,
Always could find its own way home to the well-known door.
This creature the hot-foot hounds of Ascanius now started
While it was far from home—by turns, so it happened, floating
Down a river and cooling itself on the verdurous bank.
Ascanius, too, was immensely keen to get so glorious
A prize. He bent his bow and shot an arrow. Luck
Was with him, his aim was true. The shaft streaked from the
                                                                  bowstring,
Viciously whirring, to pierce the stag through flank and belly.
Wounded, the animal ran to hide in the well-known homestead,
Crept sobbing into its stall there, covered with blood, and filled
The place with pathetic cries like some beseeching creature.
Silvia, the sister, striking her arms in grief, was the first
To call for help, and her call brought the tough countrymen round her.
They—for that virulent Fury lurked in the quiet woods—
Were with her quicker than thought, brandishing fire-hardened stakes
Or bludgeons of knotty wood; whatever came first to hand
As they angrily groped for a weapon, served them as such. Now
                                                                  Tyrrheus,
Panting with rage, snatched up an axe—just then, so it happened,
   [*Lines 474–509*]

152

He was splitting an oak into four with wedges—and mustered his men.
From aloft the fell Fury could see that this was the moment for
mischief:
She flew to the steep-pitched roof of the shippon, and perching upon it
Blew the rustic alarum, a blast on a crooked horn,
With the full force of her demon lungs; the sound rang on,
Shaking the woods to their roots, through the deep forest baying:
The lake of Diana heard it afar, the Nar heard it—
That sallow, sulphurous river, the springs of Velinus heard it;
Terrified mothers clutched their babies to their breasts.
Then, ah then, how swift to answer the summoning call
Of that sinister horn, snatching up their arms, the hardy countrymen
Gathered from far and wide. The warriors of Troy at the same time
Poured through the gates of their camp and hurried to help Ascanius.
The two sides face each other. This is no village brawl now
To be fought out with rugged shillelaghs and fire-toughened stakes:
With steel, with two-edged steel they join issue; all over the field
Darkly bristles a crop of drawn swords; their bronze accoutrements
Fling the sun's challenge back, send flashes of light upwards.
So, in a rising wind, white horses begin to appear
On the sea's face; then little by little the sea gets rougher,
The waves steeper, until the sea is all mountains and valleys.
Now in the front rank Almo, he who had been the eldest
Of Tyrrheus' sons, was laid low, hit by a whirring arrow:
Deep in his throat was the wound; the arrow stuck there and choked
With blood the fluent passageway of the voice, the frail life.
Around him were many corpses, old Galaesus amongst them,
Most upright of men and the biggest landowner once in Ausonia,
Killed while trying to mediate between the combatants:
Five flocks of bleating sheep he had owned, five herds of cattle
He pastured, and a hundred ploughs worked on his land.

While they fought over the plain there, with neither side prevailing,
Allecto, her promise fulfilled now she had given the war
Its baptism of blood and opened its first encounter with killings,
Took leave of Hesperia; wheeling up and away through the airs of
Heaven, she addressed queen Juno in tones of insolent triumph:—
See, discord has been brought to fruition in stern war!
Try telling them to be friends and to make a pact of peace!
Now that I've splashed the Trojans with blood of Ausonian men,

[Lines 510–547]

153

This too will I add to my feats, if I am assured of your backing—
I'll drag the neighbouring peoples into the war by spreading
Rumours, and kindle their passions with the mad lust for battle,
So that they all come in and the whole country's at war.
Juno replied:—
                    We have plenty enough of alarm and aggression.
A reason for war is established; already they're fighting bitterly.
An accident started the quarrel, but bloodshed now has confirmed it.
Let that so wonderful son of Venus, let king Latinus
Celebrate thus the marriage they have arranged between them!
The Father, supreme lord of Olympus, would not be pleased
To find you trespassing too freely here on high.
Away, then! Whatever else may befall in this conflict, I
Myself will deal with it.
                            Thus the daughter of Saturn spoke.
And Allecto, the Fury, spreading her wings that hissed with serpents,
Made for her home in the Underworld, leaving the height of heaven.
There is a place in the heart of Italy, under the mountains,
A well-known spot whose fame is told of in many countries—
The Vale of Amsanctus. On either side, steep, wooded slopes
Darken this vale with dense foliage, and down its middle
A watercourse rumbles, eddying and clucking among the rocks.
Here can be seen an awesome cave and the vents of the dreadful
Underworld; a great chasm formed by the upthrust of Acheron
Yawns, emitting a plague-breath: into it now disappeared
The hateful Fury, relieving earth and sky of her presence.
But the royal daughter of Saturn was still giving the war
Its finishing touches. The shepherds all broke from the field of battle
And hurried into the city, bearing their dead with them—
Young Almo and Galaesus, who was horribly disfigured.
There they supplicated the gods and appealed to Latinus.
Turnus was present, amid their angry complaints at the bloodshed
Redoubling his threats: The Trojans are called in to rule us, he
                                                    shouted;
Our blood's to be mingled with Phrygian; I am debarred from the
                                                    palace.
Next they whose womenfolk, possessed by Bacchus, were roving
The trackless woods in their coven (great too was Amata's influence)
Gathered together and clamoured importunately for war.

[*Lines 548–582*]

154

Accursed war they will have, at once, flying in the face of
Omens and oracles, impelled by a power malign.
A belligerent mob surrounds the palace of Latinus:
He like a sea-cliff stands, resistant, inexpugnable;
Like a sea-cliff that, when a comber comes crashing against it,
Stands in its massive bulk unmoved, with the wave-pack yelping
Below it; about the reefs and the foaming rocks the sea howls
Impotent; seaweed is dashed on its flanks, flung streaming back again.
But when he saw he had no power to quell their purblind
Demand and all was going merciless Juno's way,
Latinus made many appeals to the gods, to the deaf, blind heavens:—
    Oh! We are pounded by doom, adrift at the storm's mercy!
It is you, poor souls, who will pay in your own blood for this sacrilege.
Yours is the guilt, Turnus; punishment most severe is
In store for you: too late shall you turn to the gods with prayer.
My rest is assured; I am right at the mouth of the haven, with nothing
To lose but a peaceful death.
                              Latinus said no more,
But shutting himself in his palace, relinquished the reins of government.
    There was a custom of old in Latium, religiously
Kept up by the Alban townships, and now a tradition observed by
Rome, mistress of empire, when first she prepares for battle,
Whether she goes to make war, with all its tears, on the Getae,
The Arabs or the Hyrcanians; or to march further east
Against the Indians, or get back her standards from the Parthians.
There are twin gates of War—that is their name; the religion
And terrible indwelling presence of Mars have sanctified them.
A hundred bronzen bolts and bars of durable iron
Secure them: Janus keeps his perpetual watch by the entrance.
When the Senate has made a final decision for war,
The Consul, grand in Quirinal robe caught up with the Gabine
Cincture, himself opens these gates on their grinding hinges,
In person proclaims war; the soldiers take up his cry
And the bronze trumpets blare together in hoarse accord.
After this manner Latinus was now told to declare
War on Aeneas' people and open the joyless gates.
But the good old king would not touch them: turning away in
                                                        revulsion
From such a shocking duty, he buried himself from sight.

                              [*Lines 583–619*]

155

Then did the queen of heaven glide down, and with her own hand
Roughly push open those resisting doors, dash wide
Upon their turning hinges the iron gates of war.
Indifferent before and lethargic, Ausonia now caught fire.
Some ready themselves to march as infantry; others are mounted
On tall steeds and kick up a galloping dust: all clamour to fight.
What burnishing now of shields and javelin points with rich fat
Until they shine again! What whetting of battle-axes!
Their hearts are stirred to hear the trumpets and troop the colours.
Five great towns establish workshops for the production
Of new armaments—powerful Atina, haughty Tibur,
Ardea, Crustumerium, and turreted Antemnae.
Here they are fashioning helms to protect the head, manufacturing
Wicker frames for shields, hammering out bronze breastplates,
And working polished leg-guards from malleable silver.
To this has come their pride in share and sickle, to this
The plough's prestige. In the furnace they temper their father's swords
                                                                again.

Now the trumpets sound; the word goes out for war.
One man hurriedly takes his helmet from store; another
Yokes his neighing horses, slips on the shield, the cuirass
Of triple-meshed gold chainmail, and straps his trusty sword on.
    Muses, throw Helicon wide now! Inspire me to tell the tale,
To sing of the chieftains aroused to war, the ranks that followed
Each chieftain, packing the plains, the manhood that even in those days
Our bountiful Italy bloomed with, the martial array that blazed there!
For you are divine, you remember it all, you can recount it—
All that for me has become the faint whisper of antique story.
    The first to arm his men and enter the war was Mezentius,
A Tuscan exile, a man embittered and irreligious.
Beside him marched his son, Lausus, who far excelled
All others in personal beauty except for Laurentine Turnus.
Lausus, the tamer of steeds, the mighty hunter, was leading
A thousand men from the town of Agylla—an enterprise
Doomed to disaster. Well he deserved to live under a better
Regime and to have a better father than Mezentius.
    After these came the handsome son of handsome Hercules,
Aventinus: on the greensward he showed off his prize-winning horses
And chariot bearing the victor's palm; he wore on his shield
    [Lines 620–657]

156

His father's blazon—the snake-clad Hydra, and a hundred serpents.
Him upon the woody Aventine hill a priestess,
Rhea, brought privily forth to the light of day, when she
A mortal had lain with a demigod, the champion from Tiryns,
                                                    Hercules,
Who, after killing Geryon, came to the Laurentine land
And dipped his Iberian cattle in the waters of Tuscany's Tiber.
His men bore javelins and stabbing-spears into battle,
For they fought with the tapering spearhead and the short Sabine blade.
Aventinus himself, on foot, swathed in a great big
Lion-skin, shaggy and terribly bristling its hair, the white fangs
Grinning above his head, entered the royal palace
Like that, all hairy, the garment of Hercules over his shoulders.

   Next, twin brothers marched from the walled city of Tibur
Where lived a people named after their brother, Tiburtus—
Catillus and mettlesome Coras they were, warriors born in
Argos, and moving now in the van where the fire is hottest:
Even as when two Centaurs, born of the clouds, descend
From some high mountain-top, galloping rapidly down from
Homole or snow-capped Othrys, and the great forest yields to
Their passage as they career and crash through the undergrowth.

   Caeculus too was there, the founder of Praeneste,
The king who men throughout the ages have believed
Was son of Vulcan, born among flocks and herds, and found
On the hearth. A yeoman regiment came straggling on behind him—
Warriors who dwelt in high Praeneste, or the Gabine district
Where Juno is worshipped, or by the cold Anio, or in the stony
Hernican brooklands; men whom fertile Anagnia reared
Or the river Amasenus. Not all of them had armour,
Shields or clattering chariots: most of them used slings
With bullets of light-grey lead, while some carried a pair of
Javelins: they wore brown-coloured caps of wolf-skin
As covering for their heads; the left foot, taking the weight of
The slinger's stance, was naked, the right being shod with rawhide.

   Messapus, tamer of horses, the seed of Neptune—he
Whom no man might lay low with fire or steel—now calling
All of a sudden to arms his tribes that had long been torpid
And lost the habit of fighting, took up the sword again.
They lived on Fescennae's jagged skyline, at Falerii

[*Lines 658–695*]

157

The just, in the fields of Flavinium, or the hill-country of Soracte,
By the lake and mountain of Ciminus, in the woodland of Capena.
Evenly dressed they marched, singing their chieftain's glory:
So it is when snow-white swans come winging away
From their feeding ground through a whey of cloud, their necks
                                                    strain forward
Uttering rhythmic cries, and the watermeads of Caÿster
Sound and resound.
Noone would ever have thought it a multitude all made up
Of armoured files, but rather a cloud of birds overhead
Driving to land from over the deepsea with husky cries.

  See next how Clausus comes, of the old pure Sabine blood,
Leading a mighty host, and he a host in himself—
Clausus from whom are descended the Claudian clan and family,
Widespread in Latium now since Rome was shared with the Sabines.
With him, a big Amiternian detachment, and men from historic
Cures, and all from Eretum and olive-growing Mutusca;
Citizens of Nomentum, dwellers in the Rosean district
Around Velinum, in craggy Tetrica, Mount Severus,
Casperia, Foruli, and by the river Himella;
Those who drink from Tiber and Fabaris, those whom frigid
Nursia sent, with Ortine hordes and tribes of Latium;
Men whom the flood of Allia (ill-omened name!) sequesters:
In multitude like the waves that sweep the Libyan sea
When raging Orion sinks down below the wintry waters,
Thick as the ears of corn that bake in the orient sunshine
Over the plain of Hermus or the yellow prairies of Lycia.
Shields clang, and the earth trembles with men marching in step.

  Next, Agamemnon's son, Halaesus, who hated everything
Trojan, harnessed his chariot team and brought to Turnus
Post-haste a thousand warlike clans—hoers of the wine-rich
Massic country, men whom their fathers had sent from the hills
Of Aurunca, men who had come from the nearby Sidicine plains,
Men who hailed from Cales, men who lived by the shallow
Volturnus river; and with them, Oscan levies and warlike
Saticulans. Their weapons were missiles with rounded handles
Which they were used to throw with whippy thongs attached:
A targe protected their left side; a scimitar was carried for close work.

  Then Oebalus must not go unhonoured and unsung—
  [*Lines 696–733*]

158

Oebalus whom, it is said, Telon begat on the nymph
Sebethis, when he was king of Teleboean Capreae,
Advanced now in years. But his son, not content with his father's
frontiers,
Even at this time held sway, further afield, over
Sarrastian tribes and the plains which the river Sarnus irrigates,
Over the dwellers in Rufrae, Batulum, rural Celemna,
And the dwellers below the town of apple-growing Abella,
Whose practice it was to hurl boomerangs, Celtic-fashion:
Their head-pieces were made of bark stripped from the cork tree;
Their light shields plated with bronze glittered, their bronze swords
glittered.

The mountainy district of Nursae sent forth to the war Ufens,
Who had a high reputation as a successful fighter:
His clan, the Aequi, living on a thin soil and hardened
By constant hunting over the woodlands, excelled in toughness.
Armed to the teeth they are when they till the ground, and they never
Tire of carrying off new plunder, living on loot.

Again, from the Marruvian tribe there came a priest,
His helmet adorned with a favour of fruitful olive leaf,
Sent by his chieftain, Archippus: this hero's name was Umbro:
He had a remarkable talent for hypnotising by spell
And touch the serpent kind, all evilly-breathing snakes;
He was able to charm their anger and cure their bites with his skill.
But his art was powerless to heal the wound he got from a Trojan
Spearpoint; neither his soporific spells nor the simples
He'd gathered on Marsian hills availed him when he was wounded.
The grove of Angitia wept him; Fucinus, glassy-watered,
All limpid lakes lamented him.

The son of Hippolytus, too, most beautiful, went to the wars—
Virbius, a fine young man, sent by his mother, Aricia,
Who'd brought him up near the shore of the lake in Egeria's wood
Where stands an altar to Diana, rich and reverenced.
The legend is that Hippolytus, after he'd been laid low
By his stepmother's plotting and, torn to bits by bolting horses,
Had slaked with blood his father's vengeance, rose to the starry
Firmament and breathed the air of heaven, brought back
To life by Diana's love and the herbs of Aesculapius.
But then the Father almighty, wroth that a mortal being
[*Lines 734–770*]

Should rise to light and life from the shades of underground,
Hurled down to hell with a levin-stroke from his hand this son
Of Phoebus, who had discovered so potent an art of healing.
But Diana was kind and hid Hippolytus in a secret
Place, removing him to the grove of the nymph Egeria,
Where he should live out his days a solitary, unknown,
In Italian woods, having changed his name and become Virbius.
Wherefore to this day horses are not allowed near Diana's
Temple or sacred wood, because horses, scared by a sea beast,
Had spilt Hippolytus once and his chariot on the shore.
His son, for all that, was now driving fiery horses
Upon the level plain and racing to war in a chariot.

  Turnus himself, of magnificent build, bearing his weapons
Moved amongst the leaders, a head higher than they.
Upon his triple-crested, tall helmet a Chimaera
Was rampant, breathing out volcanic fire from its jaws;
The bloodier waxed the battle, the more did that creature appear to
Roar and rage, to go berserk and shoot forth glowering flames.
But on his polished shield was blazoned in gold the image
Of Io, now changed to a heifer, with horns uplifted, and

                                             rough-haired—
A potent symbol; also her guardian, Argus, and Inachus
Her father, pouring out his stream from a graven pitcher.
At Turnus' heels there followed a cloud of infantry, packing
The plain with their armoured columns—Argive warriors marching,
Auruncan levies, Rutuli, old-established Sicani,
Sacranian files and the painted bucklers of the Labicans;
Men who ploughed Tiber's vales, and the sacred coastland about the
Numicius; men who worked with the plough the Rutulian hills
And the promontory of Circe; men from the parts round Anxur
Where Jove is patron, men from the greenwoods of Feronia,
The fenlands dark of Satura, and the deep combes where Ufens
Cold-running winds its way down and plunges into the sea.

  Beside all these there came from the Volscian nation Camilla
Leading a cavalry column, squadrons petalled with bronze:
A warrior maid, her woman's hand unaccustomed to womanly
Tasks—to the distaff, the basket of wool; a girl, but hardy
To face the horrors of battle and to catch up with the winds.
She could have skimmed along the blades of an unmown corn-crop
  [*Lines 771–808*]

160

Without so much as bruising their tender ears as she ran:
She could have flitted over the waves of a swelling sea
Without so much as wetting the quicksilver soles of her feet.
From field and cottage the young came running, the housewives
gathered

To stare at this Camilla and marvel as she went by,
Gaping, struck with amazement to see how nobly sat
The cloak of royal crimson on her smooth shoulders—see
The gold clasp in her hair, the Lycian quiver she carried
And the spear-shaft of country myrtle with its warhead.

[*Lines 809–817*]

BOOK VIII

When Turnus hoisted the ensign of war from the Laurentine
Citadel, and the trumpets blared out their husky calls;
When Turnus lashed his mettlesome horses and clashed his weapons,
Instantly men were excited: the alarm brought about a feverish
Uprising and leaguing-together in Latium: war hysteria
Gripped the youth. Now first their commanders, Messapus and Ufens
And the god-mocker, Mezentius, combed the country all round
For troops, so that the fields were stripped of labourers everywhere.
Next was Venulus sent to the city of great Diomedes
To ask his aid and tell him that Trojans had planted themselves
In Latium, Aeneas had come with a fleet, bringing in Troy's vanquished
Home-gods, claiming that destiny demanded he should be king there;
Many tribes, what's more, were joining the cause of the Dardan
Hero, whose reputation was spreading all over the country:
What purpose lay behind this undertaking, or what
Aeneas hoped would result from a war, if fortune blessed him,
Would be clearer to Diomed than it was to Latinus or Turnus.
   So things went in Latium. Aeneas, seed of Laomedon,
Seeing them so, was much agitated by surging worries,
His mind in feverish conflict, tossed from one side to the other,
Twisting and turning all ways to find a way past his dilemma;
As when, in a bronze basin, the quivering water reflects
A sunbeam or the round of the radiant moon, a light
Goes glancing hither and thither, now shooting up from the water
And jigging upon the fretted ceiling over your head.
It was night, and throughout the earth deep slumber lay upon
All weary creatures, lay on bird and beast alike.
Bedded upon the river-bank under the chilly vault
Of heaven, his heart much exercised by sombre thoughts
About war, Aeneas at last yielded himself to sleep.
Before his face there appeared now, rising amidst the leaves of
The poplars out of that pleasant river, its deity, old
Tiberinus: a veil of grey and gauzy stuff was draped
   [*Lines 1–33*]

163

About him, a coronal of reeds shadowed his brow.
He spoke to Aeneas, relieving his troubled heart like this:—

O prince of divine lineage, who out of the enemy's clutches
Bring Troy town back to us, preserving it for all time;
O long-awaited in the Laurentine land, in Latium,
Here your appointed home is, the resting place for your gods.
Do not give up, or be frightened by threats of war. The swelling
Anger of heaven has abated.
Even now, lest you think all this but a baseless fiction of sleep,
You shall find lying beneath the oaks on the river-bank
A great white sow, with a litter of thirty new-born piglets
White as she, clustered at the teats of their sprawling mother.
Here is the site for your city, sure terminus of your travails.
And this is the sign that, when thirty years roll by, Ascanius
Shall found the white town, Alba, the city of shining name.
I prophesy certainties. Now pay heed while I tell you briefly
How you may best unravel the urgent problem before you.
Arcadians, a people descended from Pallas, followers now
Of king Evander in peace and war, having chosen a site
Within this country, have built a township on the hills
And named it Pallanteum after their ancestor, Pallas.
This people wages war persistently with the Latins:
Make a treaty with them, and get them onto your side.
I for my part will conduct you straight up my waterway
That, rowing against the current, you may achieve a passage.
Rise up then, goddess-born, and with the waning stars
Make solemn prayer to Juno, avert her menacing wrath
By vows and supplication. To me you may do honour
When you're successful. I, whom you see with ample stream
Lipping these banks and flowing through these rich farmlands—I am
Caerulean Tiber, the river most beloved by the gods.
Here's my broad home; my source emerges among tall cities.

Thus the River-god spoke, then sank out of sight deep into
His watery home. Aeneas awoke from night and dreaming,
Rose up, beheld the light of the orient sun in the sky,
Held out in solemn oblation his hands which cupped some water
Scooped from the stream, and uttered these heartfelt words to
heaven:—

Nymphs, Laurentine nymphs, you fountain-heads of rivers,

[*Lines 34–71*]

164

And you, O father Tiber, you and your hallowed stream,
Bless Aeneas, keep him from harm at this long last!
Wherever the secret springs of your being, and wherever
You issue forth in majesty, since you have shown compassion
For my hard trials, you shall be always graced with homage
And offerings from me, horned River, king of Italian waters.
Only be with me, confirm your revelation directly!

Such were Aeneas' words: then he chose a couple of galleys
Out of his fleet, manned them and issued the crews weapons.

But look!—a prodigy startling, amazing for them to view—
Among the trees there, shining, the same white hue as her litter,
Sprawled on the verdant bank, for all to behold, a sow.
To Juno, mightiest Juno, god-fearing Aeneas then
Led mother and young to stand at the altar, and sacrificed them.
All that night the Tiber smoothed down its popply stream
And the current beneath its quietened surface came to a standstill,
So that the face of the waters was flat as a gentle pool
Or a calm mere, and rowing cost no strenuous effort.
So with the river helping they sped on the trip they had started.
The well-tarred ships glide on; waters and woods admire
A spectacle new to them—shields of warriors shining
Afar down the river and painted hulls floating upon it.
All night and the following day the Trojans rowed without respite,
Up the long loops of the river, under the shade of diverse
Trees, through the green reflection of woods in the glass-calm water.
The blazing sun had climbed to the midway of heaven
When they saw in the distance walls, a citadel, and a few
Scattered roofs: Rome's dominion has since exalted that place
To the skies; but then Evander was lord of a meagre realm.
Quickly the Trojans steered to the bank and approached the settlement.

It happened that day the Arcadian king was holding a festival
Honouring Hercules, heir of Amphitryon, and the gods
In a grove outside the city. With him his son, Pallas,
The younger notables all and the plain-living senators
Burnt incense, while the warm blood of victims steamed at the altars.
Now when they saw the tall ships come gliding up amid
The trees, through the wood's dim vistas, and the oars quietly moving,
Alarmed by so unexpected a sight, they started up from
The banquet as one man. But Pallas, undaunted, forbade them

[*Lines 72–110*]

165

To leave the rites unfinished; seizing a weapon, he hurried
Towards the Trojans and hailed them from a vantage-point at a
distance:—
    Strangers, whither away, taking a route so strange to you?
Who are you? Where do you come from? Do you bring peace or war?
    Then, where he stood high up on the poop, Aeneas answered,
Holding out in his hand an olive branch, emblem of peace:—
    We are sons of Troy that you see here, and no friends to the Latins
Who have driven us out of their land by a cynical act of aggression.
We're looking for king Evander. Tell him a deputation
Of Trojan leaders has come to plead for his alliance.
    Pallas, struck with awe by so famous a name, called out:—
    Come ashore, whoever you are, sir. Come, and talk to my father
Yourself. Do us the honour of being a guest in our house.
    He extended a welcoming hand and clasped Aeneas' right hand.
Leaving the river-bank they went forward into the wood.
Before long, Aeneas was making a friendly speech to the king:—
    Best of the sons of Greece, it is fortune's will that to you
I should come for a favour, extending the formal olive branch.
I do so without misgivings, although you are an Arcadian,
A leader of Greeks, and related by blood to the twin Atridae.
My own merit, the sacred oracles of the gods,
The kinship between our fathers, your own far-reaching fame
Have bound me to you, and I follow the bidding of fate most gladly.
Dardanus, the progenitor and founder of Ilium's city,
Born, as the Greeks maintain, of Electra, daughter of Atlas,
Sailed to our Teucrian land: yes, Electra's father was mighty
Atlas, who holds aloft on his shoulders the heavenly firmament.
Now Mercury is your father—Mercury whom fair Maia
Conceived and bore upon the snowy peak of Cyllene.
But Maia, if we believe at all the tales we have heard,
Was begotten by Atlas, the Atlas who props the starry sky.
So both of our families stem from the same original source.
Relying on this, I launched no professional-diplomatic
Overtures, to make a compact with you: I have come
In person to ask your aid and have put my life in your hands.
We are bitterly menaced in war by that same Daunian people
Which persecutes you: they believe they have only to drive us out
And nothing will stop them from subjugating the whole of Hesperia
[*Lines 111–148*]

166

And getting control of the Adriatic and Tuscan seaboards.
Let us exchange guarantees. My men are stout-hearted fighters,
And their morale is high; as soldiers, their deeds speak for them.
   Thus spoke Aeneas. The king for some time had been watching
                                                         intently
His face and eyes, scrutinising the whole man while he talked.
Now he replied briefly:—
                        Most glad am I, bravest of Trojans,
To welcome and get to know you. How vividly you remind me
Of your great father Anchises in speech, in accent and feature!
For I remember how Priam, Laomedon's son, when he travelled
To visit his sister Hesione's kingdom, *en route* for Salamis,
Came on from there and crossed the borders of cold Arcadia.
I was a young man then, in the first flush of youth:
I used to hero-worship your Trojan chiefs and their prince,
The son of Laomedon; but taller than any, strode
Anchises. I recollect in boyish enthusiasm
Longing to speak to the hero and shake him by the hand.
I went up to him, eagerly brought him into the city of Pheneus.
He gave me, when he left, a very fine quiver containing
Lycian arrows, a gold-embroidered scarf, and a pair of
Golden bridles which now are owned by my son, Pallas.
And so, the hand you ask for in friendship—here, it is yours!
To-morrow, as soon as the earth grows light, I will send you away
With an escort to gladden your heart, and will aid you from my
                                                       resources.
Meantime, this annual feast which we cannot rightly defer—
Since you have come here as friends, do us the kindness of sharing it
With us, begin straight away to get used to the board of your comrades.
   So saying, he has the dishes and wine cups put back, which had been
Removed, and himself arranges the Trojans on grassy seats,
Inviting Aeneas, as guest of honour, to take his place on
A maple chair which is draped with the shaggy pelt of a lion.
Then picked young men and the priest of the altar, promptly attentive,
Bring on the roast meat   bulls, and baskets loaded high with
Cereal food expertly prepared, and serve the wine.
Aeneas and his Trojan comrades all are feeding
On a whole chine of beef, and the meat left from the sacrifice.
   Hunger being satisfied, the desire for eating checked now,
   [*Lines 149–184*]

167

King Evander began:—
                              These solemn ceremonies,
This ritual feast, this altar hallowed by deity were not
Imposed on us by some fanciful heresy regardless
Of older gods. We keep up these rites, Aeneas, in honour
Of one who saved us from cruel danger and well deserves them.
Look at that scarp up there, that overhanging rock face!
See the wide scatter of boulders! How desolate stands the mountain
Abode, with the crags that have toppled down, gigantic debris!
Once a cavern was there, deeply recessed in the hillside,
Impervious to the sun's rays: its occupant was a half-human,
Horrible creature, Cacus; its floor was for ever warm with
New-spilt blood, and nailed to its insolent doors you could see
Men's heads hung up, their faces pallid, ghastly, decaying.
This ogre was the son of Vulcan; as he moved
In titan bulk, he breathed out his father's deadly flame.
But to us too, in our longing that help would some day come,
Time brought deliverance, aid divine. For the great avenger
Hercules came, in the glory of having slain and despoiled
Triform Geryon; victorious, he drove this way
His great bulls, and his herds were thronged by our marshy river.
Cacus, beside himself with lunatic greed, so that nothing
Crooked or criminal should remain undared, unattempted,
Rustled four bulls of surpassing build out of the steadings,
And with them as many heifers, very fine creatures. These,
To ensure that they left no tracks pointing the way they had gone,
He dragged by their tails backwards into his cave, reversing
The trail, and hid his plunder deep in the sunless rock there.
A searcher would find no clues leading him to the cave.
Well, when the time had come for Hercules to move on
His herds from the pasturage they had cropped down, as he was going,
His oxen plaintively mooed at leaving the place, our hills
And woods all rang with the lowings of the departing herd.
Just then one of the heifers, corralled within that desolate
Cavern, bellowed in answer, betraying Cacus' plot.
Then, bitterly galled, the son of Alcides erupted in furious
Anger: seizing his weapons, his heavily-knotted club,
He made hot-foot for the top of that mountain, right up there.
Then did our folk for the first time see Cacus thoroughly frightened,
                              [*Lines 185–222*]

168

With panic in his eyes: he was off in a flash and running
Towards his cave like the wind; fear gave wings to his feet.
Now he had shut himself in there by breaking the iron chains,
His father's handiwork, which held a huge rock poised,
So that it fell, blocking and reinforcing the entrance
Like a portcullis: next moment Hercules, wild with rage,
Was there, looking this way and that to find a possible way in,
Grinding his teeth. Three times all over Mount Aventine
He scoured in furious anger; three times he vainly went for
That rock barricade; three times sank down in the valley, exhausted.
There stood a tapering needle of flint, sheer upon all sides,
Which soared up out of the cave's roof, dizzily high to view—
A convenient place for carrion birds to lodge their nests in.
This pinnacle leaned from the ridge at an angle over the stream
To its left: Hercules threw his whole weight against its right side,
Shook it, wrenching it loose from its deep-rooted base; then suddenly
Pushed: at that push a crack like thunder rang through the wide sky,
The river-banks leapt apart, the river recoiled in terror.
But the den of Cacus, his whole great castle, unroofed, was now
Visible, the dark cavern revealed to its inmost depths.
It was as if the earth, violently fissured and yawning
Right to its depths, should uncover the regions of hell, the spectral
Domain unloved by the gods, and you could peer into the abyss
From above and see the ghosts there flinch at the gush of daylight.
As Cacus, caught in his rocky chamber, startled and shocked
By the unexpected torrent of light, was uncouthly roaring,
Hercules showered down arrows upon him, then anything
That would do to pelt him with—boughs and immense boulders.
Cacus, seeing no other escape from his predicament,
Belched a great cloud of smoke (you may well be amazed at this part of
The story), so that a smoke-screen went rolling over his lair,
Blotting out everything from sight, and the cave was all one
Thick, black, fog-bound night, shot through with glares of flame.
Hercules lost all restraint, in his fury at this: he hurled himself
Down through the fire with a headlong leap, to the point where the
smoke
Rolled thickest and billowed about the huge cave in eddying black
clouds.
He laid hands on the ogre, who vainly was vomiting flame
  [*Lines 223–259*]

169

Through the mirk, got a quick hold, knotted him double, and
throttled him
So that his eyes started, a haemorrhage came in his dry throat.
At once the doors were torn open and the dark den exposed,
Bringing to light the cattle which Cacus had stolen, the loot
He'd had to disgorge, while his own grotesque carcase was dragged
Out by the heels. Our people could never be done with gazing
At the bestial creature—his terrible eyes, his face, the bristling
Hair on his breast, the extinct volcano of his gullet.
Since then these rites have been practised, this day kept holy by grateful
Posterity, headed by its founder, Potitius, and by
The Pinarian family, wardens of the worship of Hercules.
This altar, which he himself set up in the grove here, always
Shall be for us, in name and in truth, the Ara Maxima.
Come then, my friends, do honour to such heroic feats!
Garland your hair with leaves, solemnly raise the wine cups,
Call on the gods we share now, and freely offer libation!

Evander had spoken: the shade of silver-green poplar, an emblem
Of Hercules, twined his hair—a circlet of leaves with a pendant;
The consecrated chalice was in his right hand. At once
With a will they all made libation and put up a prayer to the gods.

Evening the while drew nearer, hastening down the sky:
So now the priests went forth, Potitius at their head,
Robed in hides, their traditional vestment, and carrying torches.
Renewing the feast, they brought on welcome offerings to furnish
A second banquet, and piled the altars with loaded dishes.
The Salii too, their temples enwreathed with poplar leaves,
Stood by at the kindled altars, ready to sing—one choir
Of young men, one of older; who now rehearsed in song
The feats and fame of Hercules:—how as a babe he strangled
Two snakes, the first of the monsters raised up in his path by his
stepmother;
How he tore, stone from stone, two cities renowned in war,
Troy and Oechalia; how, at the will of that same stepmother,
Hostile Juno, he went through a thousand heavy labours
For king Eurystheus. Invincible hero, you killed the cloud-born
Centaurs, Hylaeus and Pholus, you killed the monster of Crete,
You killed the huge great lion in the Nemaean den.
You daunted the river Styx, and the watch-dog of Hell couched on
[*Lines 260-296*]

A pile of half-gnawed bones within its blood-stained cave.
Nothing you saw could affright you, not even Typhoeus himself—
That towering, armoured Titan. You did not lose your nerve when
The heads of the Lernaean dragon encircled you like a mob.
All hail, true son of Jove, new splendour in the pantheon!
Graciously grant your favouring presence to us, your worshippers!
Such was the paean they sang in his honour, crowning it with
A passage about fire-breathing Cacus himself and his cavern.
The woods all rang with their singing, the hills echoed it back.

    As soon as the sacred rites had been completed, they went
Home to the town in a body. The aged king, as he walked,
Kept his son and Aeneas beside him for company,
Whiling away the road in talk on various subjects.
Aeneas was looking around him with unforced admiration,
Enthralled by the scenes they passed through, eagerly asking questions
And hearing the stories behind those monuments of past ages.
Then king Evander, the founder of Rome's citadel, said:—

    These woods were once the home of indigenous fauns and nymphs,
And of men who had sprung from hard-wood oaks, who had no settled
Way of life, no civilisation: ploughing, the forming of
Communal reserves, and economy were unknown then.
They lived on the produce of trees and the hard-won fare of the hunter.
The first thing was that Saturn came hither from Olympus,
An exile deprived of his kingdom, fleeing the power of Jove.
He made a united nation of this intractable folk
Scattered among the hills, gave laws to them, chose the name of
Latium—a word suggesting the safe refuge he had found here.
His reign was the period called in legend the Golden Age,
So peacefully serene were the lives of his subjects. It lasted
Till, little by little, the time grew tarnished, an age of baser
Metal came in, of mad aggression and lust for gain.
Ausonian hordes and tribesmen from Sicily arrived then,
And more than once the land of Saturn resigned its name.
Tyrants arose, for example the harsh, huge-bodied Thybris
From whom, in later days, our Italian river was called
The Tiber, and lost its original name, which used to be Albula.
I myself, an exile seeking the ocean's uttermost
Verge, at the will of all-powerful Fortune and inescapable
Destiny settled here: I had followed the solemn warnings

    [*Lines 297–335*]

171

My mother, the nymph Carmentis, gave me, inspired by Apollo.
  He finished; and going a little way onward, was able to point out
The altar and the Carmental gate, as Romans call it,
Which were set up of yore to honour the nymph, Carmentis,
Prophetic seeress, the first to foretell how great would be
Aeneas' line, how glorious the town of Pallanteum.
Next he showed a large grove, which later the active Romulus
Called a Retreat, and a cave on the cold hillside—the Lupercal,
Named in Arcadian fashion after Lycaean Pan.
He pointed out also the sacred wood of Argiletum,
Explained how his guest, Argos, had died, showing the very
Spot. From here he took them along to the Tarpeian site
And the Capitol, golden to-day, but then a tangle of thicket.
Even at that time the timorous countrymen went in awe of
The god-haunted feel of the place, trembled at wood and rock.
Evander remarked:—
                    This wood, this hill with its leafy crest
Some god inhabits; though which, we cannot be sure. The Arcadians
Believe they have witnessed great Jove himself, seen him repeatedly
Shaking his dark aegis and summoning up the storm clouds.
Now look at those ruined walls: there used to be two towns there,
And what you see are the relics, the monuments of a past age.
Janus built a citadel here, there Saturn built one;
This was called the Janiculum, that other the Saturnian.
  Conversing thus together, they approached the unpretentious
Dwelling of Evander: cattle were everywhere, lowing
In what is now the Forum of Rome and the elegant Ship-Place.
Arrived at the palace, the king said:—
                                      Hercules stooped to enter
This door: this humble palace received the conquering hero.
Have the courage, my guest, to despise possessions: train yourself,
As he, to be worthy of godhead: don't be intolerant of poverty.
  Evander, with these words, led tall Aeneas beneath
The roof of his simple dwelling, and gave him a couch of leaves
With a coverlet made from the skin of a Libyan bear, to sleep in.
  Night came down, enfolding the earth in her dusky wings.
Venus, her mother's heart alarmed, as well it might be,
Perturbed by the threats and the fierce uprising of the Laurentines,
Spoke to her husband, Vulcan, as they lay in their gold bedchamber,
                                              [*Lines 336–372*]

Breathing into the words all her divine allurement:—
    While Argive kings assaulted in war the foredoomed stronghold
Of Pergamum, the towers destined to fall in flames,
I asked no help of you for my unhappy people,
Made no demands on your skill and resource as a forger of weapons:
I did not care to put you to work that was bound to be wasted,
Dearest husband, although I owed a great debt to the sons of
Priam, and often had grieved at the ordeal Aeneas was suffering.
Now, at the will of Jove, he has set foot in Italy:
Yet it is now that I'm asking a deity whom I reverence
For arms, appealing to you on my son's behalf. You were moved by
The tears of Thetis once, and the tears of the wife of Tithonus.
See, what peoples are mustering, what cities have barred their gates
And are sharpening weapons against me, to exterminate those I love!
    Since Vulcan complied not at once, the goddess softly embraced him
In snowdrift arms, caressing him here and there. Of a sudden
He caught the familiar spark and felt the old warmth darting
Into his marrow, coursing right through his body, melting him;
Just as it often happens a thunderclap starts a flaming
Rent which ladders the dark cloud, a quivering streak of fire.
Pleased with her wiles and aware of her beauty, Venus could feel them
Taking effect. Vulcan, in love's undying thrall, said:—
    You need not delve in the past for persuasions. What has become of
Your trust in me, my goddess? If you had brought me your troubles
That other time, then too I could rightfully have armed the Trojans;
For neither the Father almighty nor fate's decrees forbade
That Troy should stand or Priam survive another ten years.
And now, if your purpose is to make all ready for warfare,
Any effort that's mine to give in the exercise of my craft,
Whatever can be done with iron and molten alloys,
All work of furnace and bellows—nay, plead no more; why need you
Cast doubt upon your influence over me?
                                        Thus saying,
He gave his wife the love he was aching to give her; then he
Sank into soothing sleep, relaxed upon her breast.
    As soon as he'd woken, rested, requiring to sleep no longer,
In the small hours when night was waning (the time when the
                                                    housewife,
Who must eke out a slender livelihood with her loom
    [*Lines 373–409*]

173

And distaff, pokes the drowsy embers upon the hearth,
Making night too a work-time and keeping her maids employed
At the long shift by lamp-light, so that her married life
And the bringing up of her little sons be not endangered),
Just so, and active as she at that very hour, did the Fire-lord
Rise from his downy bed and go to his ironworks.
Between the Sicilian coast and Aeolian Lipare there's an
Island, whose cliffs, sheer-rising, jet out smoke from their crannies:
Deep within it are vaults, a rumbling volcanic cavern
Scooped out by the action of the Cyclops' fires; you can hear
The clang of hard blows on the anvils, the roaring when masses of ore
Are smelted within, and a throbbing blast of flame from the furnaces.
Here is Vulcan's place; the island is called Vulcania.
Hither now the Fire-god repaired from heaven above.
The Cyclops were hard at work in this underground iron-foundry—
Brontes and Steropes, Pyracmon stripped to the buff.
They manufactured a thunderbolt, such as the Father of heaven
Shoots down in such great numbers at earth from all over the sky:
Part of it was already streamlined, part unfinished.
They had given it three fins of twirling sleet, and three
Of cloudburst, three of russet fire and three of stormwind.
Now they were putting in as components frightening flashes,
The noise that creates panic, the piercing flames of wrath.
Elsewhere, a job was being hurried on for Mars—a chariot
With swift wheels, such as he rides in to rouse up men and nations.
Some busily burnished the aegis Athene wears in her angry
Moods—a fearsome thing with a surface of gold like scaly
Snake-skin, and the linked serpents and the Gorgon herself upon
The goddess' breast—a severed head rolling its eyes.

   Put all that work aside, pack up the jobs you're engaged on,
You Cyclops of Mount Aetna, and turn your attention to this—
The making of arms for a hot-blooded hero! Now there is need for
Your strength, your speediest work and your master-craftsmanship.
Get bustling on it at once!
                              That was all Vulcan said:
Quickly they set to the business, shared out the tasks among them
Equally. Rivers of molten bronze and gold are flowing;
The deadly steel is smelted in an immense furnace.
They fashion a shield of heroic size, to withstand by itself

[*Lines 410–447*]

174

Every missile the Latins can use, welding seven rounds of metal
One on another to make it. Some pump away at the bellows,
Drawing in air and expelling it; some dip the hissing metal
In troughs. The cavern groans under the stress of anvils.
They raise their arms with the powerful alternate rhythm of cranks,
They keep the iron-ore turning in the close grip of their tongs.
    While on Aeolian shores the lord of Lemnos was hurrying
Forward this work, Evander was roused from his humble dwelling
By the genial light and the dawn song of birds beneath his eaves.
The old man got out of bed, clothed himself in a tunic,
And laced the Tyrrhene clogs on his feet; then shouldered a baldric
So that his sword of Tegea could hang at his side, and threw
A panther-skin over his left shoulder to dangle behind him.
Two dogs, his bodyguard, preceded him as he stepped
Through the doorway, and went with their master on his errand.
He made for the private room where his guest, Aeneas, was lodged,
For he'd not forgotten their talk, the old hero, or what he had
                                                        promised.
Aeneas too was up and about that early morning:
Achates walked at his side; at Evander's, his son Pallas.
The four of them met, shook hands, then retired to an inner room
Where they could sit and at last converse together freely.
The king began:—
    Great captain of the Teucrians—believe me, I'll never admit
The cause of Troy is lost, or its hope of dominion, while you
Are alive—though our reputation is high, we are short in the sinews
Of war to aid you, confined as we are on this side by the Tiber,
Hard pressed on that by the Rutuli, whose arms clang round our walls.
But I propose to bring to your side a confederation
Of rich and numerous peoples: an unforeseen chance has offered
This reinforcement. It must have been fate that brought you here.
Not far away lies Caere, a populous city, founded
On ancient rock: a tribe from Lydia, renowned in war,
Settled it long ago upon a hill of Etruria.
For many years they flourished; but there rose a king, Mezentius,
Who with insolent tyranny and cruel force oppressed them.
I will not enlarge on that despot's brutish acts or his damnable
Massacres—may the gods keep such things for himself and his breed!
Why, he would even have live men bound to dead bodies,
    [*Lines 448–485*]

175

Clamping them hand to hand and face to face—a horrible
Method of torture—so that they died a lingering death
Infected with putrefaction in that most vile embrace.
At last the townsfolk could stand it no more: they rose in arms
Against the criminal maniac, besieged him in his palace,
Put his friends to the sword and set the place alight.
But Mezentius somehow escaped through the slaughter into Rutulian
Territory, and asked his guest-friend, Turnus, for protection.
So all Etruria has risen in righteous anger, demanding
His extradition for punishment, or else they'll make war at once.
Thousands they are, Aeneas, and I'll put you at their head:
You see, their invasion fleet is serried along the shore
And they're clamouring to advance, but an aged seer restrains them,
Uttering fate's decree:— You crack troops of the Etruscans,
You flower and chivalry of an ancient people, your honest
Indignation, your just wrath at Mezentius spur you against
The foe: but no Italian may lead a team of such fighters
As you. You must find a foreign commander. At this, the Etruscan
Army, awed by the warning of heaven, settled back on the plain there.
Tarchon himself has sent me ambassadors with the royal
Crown and sceptre, offering the insignia of his power
If I will go to their camp and take over command of the Etruscans.
But I cannot accept it; for I am outworn with years, old age
Has chilled my blood and withered my aptitude for adventure.
I'd encourage my son to go, were it not that he inherits
Italian blood from his mother, a Sabine. But you are the right man
In age and race, fate's chosen, the one the divine Will calls for:
Go then, most valiant leader of Trojans and of Italians.
Besides, you shall have my son here, my hope and consolation,
Pallas, that under your tuition he may be trained
In soldiering, the rough work of war—to endure its rigours,
And watching your deeds, to model himself on you from the start.
Him will I give two hundred Arcadian horsemen, the flower of
Our youth, and Pallas shall give you two hundred in his own name.

He had barely finished speaking. Aeneas, son of Anchises,
And his confidant, Achates, their eyes downcast, were reflecting
Sadly on the hard trials before them, and long would have done so
But that Venus sent them a sign out of the clear sky.
All of a sudden the heavens shook with a flash of lightning

[*Lines 486–524*]

176

And thunder pealed: it seemed as if the whole universe suddenly
Tottered and Etruscan trumpets were bawling above them.
They looked up: again and again a terrific crash resounded.
Up there among the fleecy clouds in the fair-weather sky
Were arms, red-glinting and thunderously clashing through the clear
air.
The rest were stunned with amazement: but the Trojan hero heard
In the sound his divine mother keeping a promise she'd given.
So then he exclaimed:—
My friend, do not, oh, do not ask
What issue these portents may bring! They're a call from above,
and the call is
For me. My goddess mother foretold she would send this sign
If war was looming close, and would come to my help through the air
With arms of Vulcan's making.
Ah, what terrible slaughter awaits the Laurentines now!
What a price you will pay me, Turnus! How many shields and helmets
And corpses of gallant men shall the Tiber roll beneath
Its waves! Now let them clamour for war and break their treaties.
    When he'd said this, Aeneas got up from where he was sitting,
And at once rekindling the drowsy fire on the altar of Hercules,
Cheerfully paid his respects to the guardian angel of the house
And its humble gods, as he'd done on the previous day. Evander
Sacrificed duly chosen sheep, and the Trojans likewise.
Then Aeneas returned to the ships, where the rest of his comrades were,
And selected the bravest of them to accompany him upon
His military mission; while the remainder floated
Effortlessly down the glass-calm river, borne by
Its current, to tell Ascanius how it fared with his father and the rest.
The Trojans on their way to the Etruscan camp were furnished
With horses; for Aeneas a specially fine one, housed in
The tawny skin of a lion with glittering, gilded claws.
    The news was quickly spread abroad through the little township
That men were riding post-haste to the Etruscan king.
In apprehension, the mothers pray harder; fear walks closer
In peril's train, and the spectre of war looms larger now
Then did Evander, weeping uncontrollably, cling to
The hand of his departing son, Pallas, and say:—
    If Juppiter would only restore those bygone years
    [*Lines 525–560*]

177

And the man I was when under Praeneste's walls I laid
The front rank low and triumphantly burnt the piled-up shields!
Yes, and with this right hand I despatched to Hades king Erulus—
He whom his mother, Feronia, had given at birth three lives
(Frightening it is to relate), and three sets of equipment;
Thrice over he had to be slain, yet on that day my strong hand
Took all his lives away and thrice despoiled him of armour.
The man I was then would not have been torn from you now, my
dear son,
That's sure; nor would Mezentius ever have heaped such insults
On me, his neighbour, with all those killings he ruthlessly
Has perpetrated, depriving my town of so many citizens.
Ye heaven-dwellers, and you, great ruler of the gods,
Juppiter, have compassion for an Arcadian king
And hear a father's prayer, I implore you: if your will
And fate's it is to keep my Pallas safe and sound for me,
If I am living to see him again, again to be with him,
Then let me live; for that, I can bear any burden. But if
Fortune means something I dare not speak of to happen to him,
Let me be rid of my bitter existence this very moment
Before anxiety becomes certainty, and hope dies
In the known event—yes now, as I hold you, dear lad, my last
Lone joy, or ever some terrible tidings should hurt my ears.
     So, at their final parting, the old man spoke from his heart;
Then he collapsed, and his servants carried him into the house.
     And now the gates had been opened and the horsemen had sallied
forth,
Aeneas with his close friend, Achates, among the leaders;
Next, other Trojan princes; Pallas himself was riding
In the middle of the column, his tunic and blazoned armour
conspicuous—
Just like the Morning Star, beloved by Venus above all
The stars of heaven, when it rises from bathing in ocean deeps, and
Puts forth its holy light from the sky and melts the darkness.
On the city wall stand the mothers, trembling; their eyes follow
Those squadrons—flashes of bronze and a dust cloud rolling about
them.
The armoured horsemen, taking a short cut, pick their way
Through brushwood; then loud shouts are heard as, all in a body,
[Lines 561–595]

178

With clatter of hammering hooves they go galloping over the dry flats.
There's an extensive woodland near the cool stream of Caere,
Reverenced by all around in the faith of their fathers: encircled
By hills, that wood of dark green fir-trees lay in a hollow.
The legend is that the ancient Pelasgians, the first settlers
Of Latium in the old days, had dedicated the wood
And a festival day to Silvanus, the god of fields and cattle.
Not far from here were Tarchon and his Etruscans, camped in
A good defensive position; and now from the hills above
They could see the whole of his army, their tents all over the plain.
Aeneas, leading his chosen combat brigade, soon entered
The camp: his tired men saw to their horses and then their own
comfort.

Venus, divinely shining among the dark clouds, descended
Bringing her presents: when she had seen from afar Aeneas
On the other side of a cool stream in a secluded dell,
She offered herself to his view quite unexpectedly, saying:—
Look! Here are the presents my consort promised. All his science
Has gone to their making. Now you need not shrink from challenging
Haughty Laurentines and hot-headed Turnus to battle, my son.
With these words, the Cytherean went into her son's embrace:
The radiant arms she had propped up against an oak, before him.
Aeneas, overjoyed by her gifts and the glory of them,
Eyed each piece, couldn't have enough of gazing: in wonder
He took them up with his hands, in his arms, examining each—
The formidable helmet with plumes like fountains of fire,
The sword that would deal out doom, the breastplate of hard bronze,
Massive and ruddy-coloured, like to some louring cloud
When it catches fire from the rays of the sun and glows afar;
Then the burnished greaves of gold-alloy inlaid with high-carat
Gold, and the spear, and the shield's miraculous workmanship.
Upon this shield the Fire-god, with knowledge of things to come,
Being versed in the prophets, had wrought events from Italian history
And Roman triumphs; upon it appeared the whole line that would
spring from
Ascanius' stock, and the wars they would fight in, one by one.
He had depicted the mother wolf as she lay full length in
The green-swarded cave of Mars, with the twin boy babies fondling
And suckling at her udders, fearlessly nuzzling their dam;

[*Lines 596–632*]

She, her graceful neck bent sideways and back, is caressing
Each child in turn with her tongue, licking them into shape.
Nearby he had pictured the Sabine women so unceremoniously
Snatched from among the crowds around the arena at Rome
During the Great Games; then the war that immediately came,
Between Romulus' people and Tatius' hard-living Sabines.
Next, these same two kings, their quarrel laid aside,
Are standing at Jove's altar, armed, with bowls in their hands,
Ratifying a treaty by the sacrifice of a sow.
Near this was the scene where chariots, driven apart, had torn
Mettus to pieces (but you should have kept to your word, Alban!)—
Tullus is dragging away the remains of that false-tongued man
Through a wood, and the brambles there are drenched with a bloody
dew.
Again, you could see Porsenna telling the Romans to take back
The banished Tarquin, and laying strenuous siege to Rome,
While the sons of Aeneas took up the sword for freedom's sake:
He was pictured there to the life, pouring out threats and wild with
Chagrin, seeing that Cocles dared to break down the bridge
And Cloelia had slipped her fetters and was swimming across the river.
At the top of the shield, Manlius, warden of the Tarpeian
Fortress, stood before the temple, guarding the Capitol—
The palace, just built by Romulus, being shown with a rough
thatched roof.
Here too a silvery goose went fluttering through a golden
Colonnade, honking out an alarum, that the Gauls are on us:
Under the cover of a dark night, lucky for them, the Gauls
Creep closer through the brushwood, some have already scaled
The citadel's heights: their clothing and hair were done in gold;
The stripes on their cloaks are gleaming; about their fair-skinned throats
Are necklaces fastened; each of them brandishes two Alpine
Spears in his hand, and carries a tall, narrow shield for protection.
Vulcan had also embossed the dancing Salii and naked
Luperci, their head-dresses bound with wool, and the shields that fell
from
Heaven: a solemn procession of virtuous ladies was moving
In cushioned carriages through the city. Elsewhere the deep gates
Of hell were represented, the domicile of the damned
And the torments they suffer—Catiline hangs from the edge of a terrible
[*Lines 633-668*]

180

Precipice, shrinking away from the faces of Furies above him:
But the righteous are set apart, with Cato as their law-giver.
Among these subjects extended a wide and swelling sea;
It was done in gold, yet it looked like the blue sea foaming with
                                                        white-caps:
Dolphins, picked out in silver, were cart-wheeling all around,
Lashing the face of the deep with their tails and cleaving the water.
Centrally were displayed two fleets of bronze, engaged in
The battle of Actium; all about Cape Leucas you saw
Brisk movement of naval formations; the sea was a blaze of gold.
On one side Augustus Caesar, high up on the poop, is leading
The Italians into battle, the Senate and People with him,
His home-gods and the great gods: two flames shoot up from his
                                                        helmet
In jubilant light, and his father's star dawns over its crest.
Elsewhere in the scene is Agrippa—the gods and the winds fight for
                                                        him—
Prominent, leading his column: the naval crown with its miniature
Ships' beaks, a proud decoration of war, shines on his head.
On the other side, with barbaric wealth and motley equipment,
Is Anthony, fresh from his triumphs in the East, by the shores of the
                                                        Indian
Ocean; Egypt, the powers of the Orient and uttermost Bactra
Sail with him; also—a shameful thing—his Egyptian wife.
The fleets are converging at full speed, the sea is all churned and
                                                        foaming
As the oarsmen take their long strokes and the trident bows drive on.
They manoeuvre for sea-room: you'd think the Cyclades isles were
                                                        unmoored
And afloat, or mountains were charging at mountains, to see those
                                                        massive
Galleys on one side attacking the turreted ships of the other.
Volleys of flaming material and iron missiles fly thick
And fast; a strange new slaughter reddens the plains of Neptune.
In the midst, Cleopatra rallies her fleet with Egyptian timbrel,
For she cannot yet see the two serpents of death behind her.
Barking Anubis, a whole progeny of grotesque
Deities are embattled against Neptune and Minerva
And Venus. Mars is raging in the thick of the fight, his figure
  [*Lines 669–700*]

181

Wrought from iron, and ominous Furies look on from above;
Here Discord strides exulting in her torn mantle, and she is
Followed by Bellona wielding a bloodstained scourge.
Viewing this, Apollo of Actium draws his bow
From aloft: it creates a panic; all the Egyptians, all
The Indians, Arabians and Sabaeans now turn tail.
You could see the queen Cleopatra praying a fair wind, making
All sail, in the very act of paying the sheets out and running.
The Fire-god had rendered her, pale with the shadow of her own
death,
Amid the carnage, borne on by the waves and the westerly gale;
And, over against her, the Nile, sorrowing in all its length,
Throws wide the folds of its watery garment, inviting the conquered
To sail for refuge into that blue, protective bosom.
But Caesar has entered the walls of Rome in triumphal procession,
Three times a victor; he dedicates now a thanks-offering immortal
To Italy's gods—three hundred great shrines all over the city.
The streets resound with cheering, rejoicing and merrymaking:
In all the temples women are chanting, altars are lit up;
At the foot of the altars lie the bodies of sacrificed bullocks.
Caesar, enthroned in the marble-white temple of dazzling Apollo,
Inspects the gifts from the nations and hangs them up on the splendid
Portals: subjected tribes pass by in a long procession—
A diversity of tongues, of national dress and equipment.
Here Vulcan had represented the Nomads, the flowing robes of
Africans, here the Leleges, Carians, Gelonian bowmen;
Some carry a picture of Euphrates, its waters pacified;
There go the Morini, furthest of men, the branching Rhine,
The Scythians untamed, the Araxes fretting about its bridge.

Such were the scenes that Aeneas admired on the shield of Vulcan
His mother gave him. Elated by its portrayal of things
Beyond his ken, he shouldered his people's glorious future.

[*Lines 701–731*]

BOOK IX

Now while Aeneas was thus engaged in a far-distant
Part of the country, Saturnian Juno sent down Iris
From heaven to the fiery Turnus. He, as it happened, was then
Taking his ease in the hallowed vale of Pilumnus, his forefather.
Rose-lipped Iris, daughter of Thaumas, thus addressed him:—
Turnus, what none of the gods would dare to promise, however
You prayed, has been brought about by the mere passage of time.
Aeneas, leaving his fleet, his friends and his settlement,
Has gone afar to the Palatine kingdom, the home of Evander;
Nay more, he has made his way to remote Etruscan cities,
Is gathering armed levies among the Lydian yeomen.
Why hesitate? Now is the time to call for horses and chariots.
Move fast! Make a surprise attack on his camp and capture it!
So she said; then soaring to heaven on balanced wings,
Blazed a rainbow trail beneath the clouds as she flew.
Turnus recognised her divinity, raised his two hands
Heavenwards, and sent these words after the fleeting goddess:—
Iris, glory of the sky, who was it conveyed you, cloud-borne,
Down to me here on earth? How came this sudden brightness
Up there? For I can see the firmament roll apart
And the vagrant stars unveiled. I acknowledge the sign, whoever
You are that call me to battle.
                                        Turnus, with these words, went to
The waterside, scooped up water out of the brimming stream,
And offered many prayers and vows to the gods above.
Soon his whole army was marching across the open plains,
A mass of chargers, a mass of gold-embroidered apparel:
Messapus is marshalling the advance guard, Tyrrhus' sons
The rear, while the main body is under the command of Turnus,
Who rides there fully armed, a head higher than all;
Even as Ganges or Nile, all seven tranquil branches,
Silently rise in flood, and then withdrawing from the low lands
Their fertilising water, return to their channels again.

[*Lines 1–32*]

Now did the Trojans see, as they looked forth, a dust cloud
Suddenly formed, a darkness mounting above the plain.
Caicus was first to spy it from the rampart and raise the alarum:—
   Hey there! What is that body looms up in a gloom of dust?
To arms! Jump to it! Issue the weapons! Man the walls!
The enemy is upon us!
                            There were loud shouts as the Trojans
Came hurrying in through all the gates and lined the battlements.
Aeneas, that excellent soldier, had instructed them so to do,
Before he left: if such an emergency should arise
In his absence, they must not risk deploying to fight in the open,
Only defend the camp from behind the ramparts' protection.
So now, though rage and humiliation tempt them to mix it,
They secure the gates, just as Aeneas had told them, take cover
Inside the turrets; ready their weapons and wait the foe.
Turnus, who'd shot ahead of his cumbrously-moving column
With a bodyguard of twenty picked horsemen, got to the camp
Unexpectedly soon: the Thracian charger he rode had markings
Of white, and he wore a helmet of gold with blood-red plume.
Will any of you be the first, lads, with me against the foe to—
Watch me! he cried; and hurled a javelin into the blue,
A prelude of battle, then stately advanced out on the field.
His companions acclaimed it with cheers and followed him with
                                                    bloodcurdling
War-cries: they were amazed at the Trojans' inactivity,
Amazed that such warriors did not come out on the open plain
And there oppose them, but huddled in the camp. Impatiently Turnus
Rode this way and that round the walls, seeking a way in where
                                                    none was.
Just as a wolf that lurks near to some crowded sheepfold,
Howling around the pens, with rainstorms driving upon him,
And late at night—meanwhile the lambs safe under their mothers
Bleat and bleat—the wolf in a fury of exasperation
Snarls at the prey he cannot reach, for long-sharpening, grinding
Hunger has driven him wild and his throat is parched for blood:—
Just so did Turnus gaze at the camp's fortifications
With mounting rage: his chagrin burned him right to the bone
As he cast about for some way to get at the Trojans, dislodge them
From their besieged emplacements and tumble them out in the open.
                                            [*Lines 33–68*]

Their fleet, which lay concealed close to one flank of the camp,
Protected all round by earth-works and the river itself, he now
Moved against; told his exulting men to bring incendiaries;
Snatched up a blazing pine-torch himself in his hot excitement.
How they went to it then! The presence of Turnus inspired them.
Soon the hearths had been stripped, and every soldier was armed with
A smoking firebrand: the resinous torches were spouting up
To the sky a mirky glare which gave off volleys of sparks.

What deity was it, O Muses, averted that merciless blaze
From the Trojans? Who drove away so fierce a fire from their ships?
Tell me! The proofs are deep-buried in the past, but the tale is undying.
At the time when, in Phrygian Ida, Aeneas was beginning
To build a fleet and preparing to venture forth on the deepsea,
Cybele herself, mother of the gods, is said to have made
This appeal to mighty Juppiter:—

Grant me, my son, what I ask—
What your dear mother asks who helped you to power in Olympus.
I had a forest of pine trees, cherished for many a year,
A plantation high up on the mountain, dusky with glooming spruces
And maple wood: men used to bring me offerings there.
This did I gladly give to the Dardan prince, when he needed
A fleet; but now a dreadful anxiety gnaws and troubles me.
Banish my fears: let a mother's prayer be so far efficacious
That neither hurricanes nor any other stress of voyaging
Vanquish those ships; may they find it a blessing they came from my
                                                                mountain.

Her son, who turns the heavenly constellations, replied:—
What would you bend the fates to? What is this you are asking,
                                                                my mother,
For those ships? May vessels built by mortal hands have immortals'
Privilege? or Aeneas go, sure of immunity,
Through hazards whose issue is unsure? No god has the power to
                                                                grant that.
No, when they've accomplished their task and lie at journey's end
One day in Italian harbour, such ships as escape the sea
And carry the Dardan hero to the Laurentine land
I shall relieve of their mortal shape, and command they become
Goddesses of the great deep, like Doto, Nereus' child,
And Galatea, who cleave the foaming sea with their breasts.

[*Lines 69–103*]

185

So Juppiter spoke; and then by the stream of his Stygian brother,
The banks where boiling pitch flows in a black maelstrom, he nodded,
Confirming his promise: the nod caused all Olympus to tremble.

So now that promised day was here, the allotted time
Fulfilled by the Fate-spinners. Cybele now was warned, by the outrage
Turnus intended, to ward off the fire from her sacred ships.
First did a strange light blaze upon their eyes, and a huge cloud
Was seen to career across the sky from the eastwards, loud with
The crashing of Cybele's cymbals: a voice that awed them broke
From the cloud and fell about the ears of Trojans and Rutuli:—

Teucrians, do not trouble yourselves to defend my ships!
Put by your weapons! For Turnus shall sooner burn up the sea
Than those blessed ships of mine. Go forth, enfranchised barques,
As goddesses of the sea. The Mother bids you.

At once
Each vessel snapped the moorings that held her stern to the bank,
And all, burying their beaks in the water, plunged deep down
Like dolphins. Soon they surfaced again, but—wonder of wonders—
Each was a maiden now as they coursed over the sea—
Each ship that had been lying, bronze-beaked, along the shore.

The Rutuli were dumbfounded: Messapus himself was terrified;
His horses reared in panic; the river, harshly growling,
Checked its flow—yes, Tiber recoiled from the deepsea then.
But the fiery Turnus did not lose confidence—far from it,
He spoke to raise their spirits, he even rebuked his men:—

This portent is pointed *against* the Trojans. Jove himself
Has removed their usual stand-by: their ships are not staying to face
Rutulian fire and steel. Well, the seaways are closed to the Teucrians,
And that was their only escape route; one half of the world is lost them,
While we have command of the land, since in their thousands the

tribes of
Italy have flocked to arms. I am not in the least dismayed by
This or that god-given ruling of destiny they may boast of:
The Fates and Venus have had their pay-off, in that the Trojans
Have reached our fertile land of Ausonia. I too have oracles
Backing me; I am to root out this damnable race with the sword
In revenge for their stealing my bride—a resentment not only the

sons of
Atreus can feel; others may take up arms for the same cause.

[*Lines 104–139*]

186

Let the Trojans say,   It's enough to have once been ruined : I say
It should be enough to have sinned once and then to loathe well

nigh all

The feminine sex. It's quaint how a rampart between, a delaying
System of trenches—frail barricades against death—have given them
Courage and confidence! Have they not seen Troy's battlements,
Built by the hand of Neptune, collapse into the flames?
But you, my storm troops, which of you is ready to hack his way
At my side through the rampart and break into their flustered defences?
I don't need arms from Vulcan, or a thousand ships, before
I'll fight the Trojans. Let all the Etruscans flock to their side
This very minute. The foe need fear no cowardly theft
Of Athene's image, in darkness, with the sentries up on the citadel
Murdered: nor are we going to hide in a horse's dark paunch.
By day, from the open, I mean to fire their walls' perimeter.
I'll make them realise they're not dealing with Danaans or with
Pelasgian troops, such as Hector fought off till the tenth year.
For the present, since the better part of to-day is over,
You shall have the rest to recuperate, set up by the knowledge that

so far

You have done well, the assurance that I am preparing for battle.
   Messapus was given charge now of watching the enemy's gates
With pickets and lighting a ring of fires around the perimeter.
Fourteen Rutulian officers were picked for the duty—to keep
Watch on the camp; each led a detachment, a hundred strong,
In golden glittering accoutrements with red plumes on their helmets.
Briskly they pass to and fro, relieved and relievers; they sprawl on
The grass to take their wine, tilting the bowls of bronze.
Brightly shine the watch-fires; the watchers keep awake
By gaming through the night.
   The Trojans, standing to arms on the ramparts above, looked

down at

These operations. In a bustle of alarm they tested the bars of
Their gates, and laid out gangways communicating between
The strongpoints, carrying arms as they did so. Mnestheus and gallant
Serestus urged on this work—the two whom Aeneas had chosen
To be field commanders and civil governors in case of emergency.
Their whole force manned the walls, drawing lots for the points of

danger,

[*Lines 140–174*]

187

And mounted guard in turn, each at his post as ordered.

One gate was held by Nisus, that most aggressive of fighters:
He was Hyrtacus' son, and had come from the hunting grounds of Ida
To follow Aeneas; a lightning shot with arrow or javelin.
Euryalus was beside him, his friend; no man of Aeneas,
No wearer of Trojan arms was handsomer than he—
That lad with the bloom of youth on his unshaven cheeks.
These two were one in love; they would charge into battle together:
To-night they were doing sentry-duty at the same gate.
Nisus said:—

Is it God that makes one burn to do brave things,
Or does each of us make a god of his own fierce passion to do them?
For long I've been itching to hurl myself into a fight, or venture
Some notable deed; inaction and calm do not appeal to me.
Look at the confidence the Rutuli have in their fortunes:
Far apart glimmer their watch-fires; unstrung by wine and sleep
They are prostrate; all is silence down there. Well, listen to what I'm
Debating in my mind, the idea that comes to me now.
Everyone, commons and councillors alike, has been saying that we must
Send for Aeneas, send men with official news of what's happened.
If they promise you the reward I shall ask (for myself the glory
Of the deed is enough), I believe, under cover of yonder high ground,
I can find a way through to the fortified town of Pallanteum.

Euryalus was dazed, struck by the same great zest
For glory: at once he spoke to his eager friend, like this:—

Nisus, you wouldn't fight shy of having me as your comrade
In such an adventure? Could I let you go into danger without me?
Not so did my father, the veteran soldier Opheltes, teach me,
Who brought me up in the midst of the Argive terror, the ordeal
Of Troy: nor, during our friendship, have I done aught to make you
                                                            doubt me,
As I followed great-heart Aeneas wherever his destiny led us.
I am no clinger to life, not I, but rather one
Who believes it were well exchanged for the renown you aim at.

Nisus replied:—

I had no such fears about you, I swear it:
That would be wrong indeed. May Jove (or however we should
                                                        name him
Who looks on these things with favour) restore me to you triumphant.

[*Lines 175–209*]

But if, as so often happens in desperate affairs like this,
Some accident or god should send my plans awry,
I would like you to survive me; you're young, with your life before
                                                    you.
May there be one to rescue my corpse from the fray, or ransom it,
And, in our fashion, inter it—or, if some chance should prevent that,
To build a handsome cenotaph and to bring offerings there.
Nor do I want to cause your poor mother such terrible anguish,
Dear lad, who alone of Troy's elderly women would have no
Truck with Acestes' city but bravely came on with you here.
    But Euryalus made answer:—
                              It's no use your bringing out all these
Arguments, for my mind is made up and you cannot shift me.
Let us get down to it quickly.
                              At once he awoke the guard, who
Relieved them and took their watch. Leaving his post, he walked
At the side of Nisus, his friend, and they went to look for the prince.
    All other living creatures on earth were asleep, their worries
Dissolved in sleep, their minds oblivious of toil and trouble:
But the high command of the Trojans, the flower of the people,
                                                    were holding
A conference on the critical state of affairs, discussing
What they should do and whom they should send to report to Aeneas.
Leaning upon their long spears, with shields on their arms, they stand
In the centre of the camp's parade-ground. Euryalus and Nisus
Come hurrying up and eagerly beg an immediate audience:
An important matter, they say—well worth the interruption.
Ascanius greeted the impatient pair, told Nisus to speak.
He began like this:—
                              Gentlemen, please give a kindly hearing
To what we propose, and do not dismiss it as coming from men
So junior to you. Relaxed by drinking and sleep, the Rutuli
Are silent all. We have noticed a possible place for a stealthy
Break-out: it lies by the seaward gate where two ways fork.
The ring of watch-fires is broken there, some being extinguished,
Others all smoke. If you'll let us make use of this bit of luck
To go in quest of Aeneas to fortified Pallanteum,
You'll soon see us back again—and laden with spoils, having done
Great execution on the foe. We shall not mistake our way, either;

[*Lines 210–243*]

189

For we have sighted that town from below in the valley coverts
Where often we go hunting, and have got to know the whole river.

Then spoke the aged Aletes, a man of mature judgment:—

Gods of our fathers, beneath whose protection Troy remains always,
You cannot, for all that has happened, intend to destroy us completely
When you have brought us young men of such spirit and such a

resolute

Character—

Even as he spoke, he put his arms round their shoulders
And gripped their hands, with the tears rivering down his cheeks:—

My lads, what recompense can I think of for you, that's at all
Worthy of an enterprise so glorious? The first and fairest
Reward will come from heaven and your own virtue: in addition,
Aeneas the true will repay you promptly, and also Ascanius
Whose life is before him, who's never forgetful of noble service.

Ascanius at once took it up:—

Why, yes! I adjure you—I whose
Salvation lies in my father's return—adjure by the great gods
Of home, the first family god of Assaracus and the shrine of
Revered Vesta: my fortunes, my every hope for the future,
I lay in your hands, Nisus. Bring back my father, oh, let me
See him again! If he comes, all our dejection goes.
I will give two goblets made of silver and richly encrusted
With figures—my father took them as spoils at the sack of Arisba,
Also a pair of tripods, two full talents of gold,
And an antique bowl—a present from Carthaginian Dido.
But if it befalls that we win the war and become masters
Of a conquered Italy, so that I portion out the spoils— ·
You saw the horse which Turnus was riding, and his golden
Armour—that same horse, that shield and the red-plumed helmet
I shall set aside; consider them yours, my reward to you, Nisus.
Besides, my father shall give you twelve women of choicest beauty
And as many male captives, too, each with his own equipment;
In addition to these, you shall have the private estates of Latinus.
Now, Euryalus, for you: I admire you greatly, and I am
Not far behind you in age; so I take you now to my heart—
You shall be my friend and share my fortunes, whatever they are.
I shall never seek renown for myself without you beside me:
Whether in peace or war, I shall put the utmost reliance

[*Lines 244–279*]

On you for word and deed.
                    Euryalus made answer:—
    You shall never be disillusioned by my falling away from
So brave a beginning as this: let only my luck stay good
And not turn sour on me. But, apart from what you have given,
I beg one boon: my mother, a lady of Priam's ancient
Lineage, would not remain behind in the land of Ilium
Or settle in Acestes' township, poor soul, but has travelled with me.
I am leaving her now—she knows naught of these dangers I have to
                                                                    face,
Whatever they are—without saying good-bye, because (I swear it
By Night and your own right hand) her tears would be sure to
                                                            unman me.
Helpless she'll be, and lonely; I implore you, befriend and console her.
If I know I can count on you for this, I shall go the more bravely
To meet what I have to meet.
                            Deeply touched by his words,
The Trojans shed some tears; especially fair Ascanius,
At the image of filial love thus printed upon his mind.
Then he began, like this:—
    All shall be done as befits your great enterprise, I assure you.
Indeed I will be a son to your mother, and she shall become
Creusa in all but name; much kindness is coming to her
Who bore such a son. Whatever the consequences of your action—
By my own head, which my father was wont to swear by, I swear it—
All that I've promised to give you if you return successful,
The same shall hold good for your mother and for your kin always.
    So Ascanius spoke, in tears. Then he unslung from his shoulder
The gold-hilted sword which Lycaon of Gnossos had fashioned with
                                                            wonderful
Workmanship and had fitted with an ivory sheath for carrying.
Mnestheus presented to Nisus the shaggy skin of a lion,
While good Aletes exchanged his own helm for the helmet of Nisus.
At once, full-armed, the pair moved off: the Trojan leaders
Escorted them to the gate, old and young in a body,
With prayers for their safety. Ascanius, who had a grown man's sense
Of responsibility and an old head on young shoulders,
Gave them many commissions to take to his father. But all was
Whirled aloft by the winds, atomised, went for nothing.
    [Lines 280–313]

191

Sallying out, they crossed the earthworks and made through the
dark night
Towards the fatal camp—fatal for them, though first
They would be death to many. All over the grass they see
Bodies asprawl in drunken sleep, chariots parked by
The shore, men lying amidst the harness and wheels, a litter
Of weapons and wine-cups together. Nisus began to say:—
    Euryalus, we must risk it. Now is our opportunity.
Here lies our route. You must guard me and keep a look-out all
behind us,
On the alert for any who tries to attack from the rear.
I'm going to make havoc here, and hack a broad path for your feet.
    These words he whispered, no more; and at once he thrust with
his sword at
The haughty Rhamnes, who chanced to be lying nearby on a great
heap
Of rugs, his broad chest heaving in slumber—he was a king
Himself, but also the prophet most favoured by king Turnus:
Now, his prophetic gifts could not avert his doom.
Then Nisus killed three attendants who lay, off guard, at his side
Among their weapons, with Remus' squire and his charioteer
Whom he found at the horses' feet, and severed their lolling heads:
Next he beheaded their master, Remus, and left his trunk
Throbbing out jets of blood like sobs; the warm, wet blood
Darkened his couch and the ground. Lamyrus, Lamus he slew,
And young Serranus—a man of exceptional looks, who'd begun
The night with an orgy of gaming and now was lying completely
Insensible from wine; well for him, if he'd gone on
Gambling all night, protracted his play into the morning.
So does a famishing lion, driven by insensate hunger,
Run amok through the crowded sheepfolds, mauling and dragging
The meek sheep, mute with terror, and roars from his bloodstained
mouth.

No less was the damage done by Euryalus; unlagging
In fury, he surprised and killed Fadus, Herbesus, Rhoetus,
Abaris, and many others who lay in his path unconscious.
Rhoetus was actually awake, a witness of all this,
But in extreme terror was crouching behind a big wine-jar;
His enemy got him full in the breast at close quarters, just as

[*Lines 314–347*]

192

He rose, drove the sword right through him, withdrew it in spouts
                                                        of blood.
Rhoetus poured out his life, all crimson; dying, he coughed up
Blood and wine: the other pressed on with his stealthy killing.
Now he was nearing the lines of Messapus, where he could see
The watch-fire burning low and the horses, properly tethered,
Browsing upon the grass. At this moment Nisus, aware that
His friend was being carried too far by bloodlust, called out to him:—
    Let's stop! It will be light soon, and light is no friend to us.
We have taken toll enough, we have cut a swathe through the enemy.
    They had to leave behind a wealth of solid silver
Accoutrements, of drinking bowls and magnificent carpets.
The ornaments Rhamnes had worn on his breast, and his gold-
                                                        studded baldric—
They were presents, originally, sent to Remulus of Tibur
By the rich Caedicus, to obtain his friendship, in absence;
Remulus on his death-bed bequeathed them to his grandson,
Then they became the battle spoils of the Rutuli—these did
Euryalus whip off and put over his own strong shoulders,
A short-lived prize: he donned Messapus' well-fitting helmet
With its gay plume. Then they left the camp and made for safety.
Meanwhile a cavalry force sent ahead from the Latin city,
While the rest of the army remained, in formation, upon the plain,
Were on their way, carrying despatches to king Turnus—
Three hundred, with modern equipment, under command of Volscens.
Now they were nearing the camp, almost beneath its ramparts,
When they saw at a distance the pair turning off by a path to their
                                                        left hand,
Euryalus being betrayed by the helmet he'd thoughtlessly clapped on
Reflecting the moonbeams among the glimmering shades of night.
That sight was not lost on them. From the head of the column cried
                                                        Volscens:—
    Halt, there! What is your business? Who are you that carry arms,
And where are you off to?
                        The pair made no reply to this challenge
But hurried on into the wood, hoping the darkness would save them.
The horsemen, knowing the place well, stationed themselves at the
                                                        crossways
On either hand, and cordoned the wood to stop each exit.
    [*Lines 348–380*]

193

That wood was an unkempt tangle of bushes and black holm-oaks
Right through, and everywhere thickly overgrown with brambles:
Here and there showed their path among a confusion of dim tracks.
Euryalus, who was hampered by the weight of his spoils, unsighted
And hindered by the branches, in fright lost his direction.
Nisus got clear away; forgetting his friend, he had slipped
The foe and reached the place which later was called Alba,
After Albanus, but then housed the royal herds of Latinus,
When, halting, he looked back—in vain, for his comrade was not
                                        behind him:—
    Euryalus, my poor dear friend, where did I leave you?
Where shall I look for you, should I retrace all my ravelled path
Through that bewildering wood?
                        At once he turns back; and carefully
Following the trail he'd made, roves through the hushed thickets.
Soon he can hear horses and the din that means a pursuit.
Not long now before a loud cry comes to his ears,
And he sees his friend whom, tricked by the mazy wood and the
                                        darkness,
Bemused by their sudden attack, the whole mob has pounced on and
                                        now
Is dragging away, overpowered, frantically, vainly struggling.
What can Nisus do? What weapons or strength can avail him
To rescue the lad? Or shall he just hurl himself to destruction
Upon their swords, to die quickly and honourably of his wounds?
On the instant he draws back his arm, with spear poised ready to throw,
And looking up at the moon above, he says this prayer:—
    Goddess, be with me and help me in what I have to do,
Latona's child, supremest of stars and warden of woodlands!
If ever my father Hyrtacus brought offerings to your altar
On my behalf; if I've honoured you with the spoils of the chase,
Hung them within your dome or on your hallowed roof-top—
Grant me to rout this mob, and speed my weapons unerringly!
    Then, putting all his body into the throw, he hurled
The spear. It flew with a swish through the shadowy night and struck
Sulmo, whose back was turned, from behind: the shaft broke there,
But the splintered wood drove on, piercing the wall of the heart.
Spouting warm blood from his breast, Sulmo went rolling; the
                                        chill of
[*Lines 381–414*]

194

Death came upon him; his flanks heaved with long-drawn gaspings.
His comrades looked round them everywhere. Nisus, the more

aggressive

For this, was poising another weapon above his ear-tip.
With the foe quite at a loss, it went right through both temples
Of Tagus, and warmly weltering stuck in the brain it transfixed.
Volscens, unable to see the assailant anywhere,
Or what direction to charge in, was bloody-hearted with rage:—
     All right! In the meantime *you* shall pay the account for these two
With your own life-blood,

he cried; and instantly, drawing his sword,
He went for Euryalus. Then, frightened out of his wits,
Nisus gave a yell—he could not any longer
Remain concealed by the darkness or stand such terrible anguish:—
     Here! I am standing here! I did it! Oh, Rutuli, turn your
Weapons on me! It was all my doing. He couldn't have harmed you
Or tried to. I swear it by heaven and the all-seeing stars.
Only he loved too well a friend who has brought him bad luck.
     So Nisus spoke. But the sword, violently thrust, had passed through
The ribs, and while he yet spoke, was boring a hole in the white breast.
Euryalus rolled over, dying: the blood ran down
His beautiful limbs, and his neck dropped feebly onto one shoulder.
So, when its stalk is cut by the ploughshare, a shining flower
Grows limp and dies, or poppies droop down their heads upon
The languid stems when the weight of a shower is too much for them.
But Nisus went straight in at the foe: he was after Volscens
And nobody else; nothing would stop him getting at Volscens.
Closely hemming him round on this side and that, they struggle
To fight him off: but he presses forward all the more furiously,
Whirling his sword in arcs of lightning, until he has slashed it
Full in the screaming face of Volscens, and dying, slain him.
Then, riddled with wounds, he throws himself down over his lifeless
Friend, and there at last grows still in the calm of death.
Ah, fortunate pair! if my poetry has any influence,
Time in its passing shall never obliterate your memory,
As long as the house of Aeneas dwell by the Capitol's moveless
Rock, and the head of the Roman family keeps his power.
     Now the victorious Rutuli stripped the spoils from the bodies
And weeping carried the lifeless Volscens into their camp.

[*Lines 415–451*]

195

Lamentation waxed there when they found Rhamnes dead
And so many of their best men, like Numa and Serranus,
Killed in the same massacre. A crowd collected around
The dead and dying, the spot where the ground was warm and reeking
With the late slaughter, and blood ran like rivers foaming in spate.
The spoils were identified—Messapus' glittering helmet
And the breast adornments of Rhamnes, recovered with so much effort.

   And now was Aurora, leaving the saffron bed of Tithonus,
Beginning to shower upon earth the light of another day.
As soon as the sun was risen and there was light to see by,
Turnus, in full armour, whipped up his men to fight:
Each captain mustered for battle his bronze-accoutred company,
All with their anger whetted by tales of the night's doings.
What's more—a shocking sight—impaled on spears, uplifted,
And followed by the shouting Rutuli were the heads of
Euryalus and Nisus.
On the left flank of their ramparts, the right being well protected
By the river, the tough troops of Aeneas took up position;
They man the system of trenches or stand on the turrets above,
In low spirits and shocked to see the impaled heads—
Those too familiar faces, alas, dripping with black gore.

   Meantime winged Rumour, flitting over the shaken encampment,
Came with post-haste news and swooped to the ears of the mother
Of Euryalus. Poor woman, her bones suddenly turned
To ice, the shuttle was dashed from her hands, the thread unwound.
A pathetic figure, she darted out, wailing and keening,
Tearing her hair, and frantically made for the walls, the front line of
Defenders; she was regardless of the men stationed there
Or the danger of flying missiles. Loudly now she lamented:—

   Oh, Euryalus, to see you like this! How could you leave me
Desolate—oh, heartless—you, the solace of my sere
Old age? And to think that you went on so dangerous a mission
Without your poor mother being allowed to say farewell to you!
O god! you are lying, a prey to the dogs and birds of Latium,
On alien soil! And I, your mother, have not brought you—
Your body—to burial, not closed the eyes nor washed
The wounds, nor wrapped you in the robe I had been busily working
For you, by day and night, to distract my old mind from its troubles.
Where shall I seek you? In what place are lying your mutilated

[*Lines 452–490*]

196

Body, your severed limbs? Is this all of yourself you bring me
Back—this head? Was it this I journeyed by land and sea for?
Rutuli, if you have any human feelings, oh, kill me!
Turn all your weapons upon me! Let me be the first to die!
Or else may the Father of heaven take pity on me, and finish
This life I hate, striking me down with his fire to Hades,
Since I've no other way to end my cruel existence.

    Her wailing shook their hearts: a general groan of sorrow
Went up: they were benumbed, and had lost all spirit for fighting.
As she was fanning their grief, by the orders of Ilioneus
And the bitterly weeping Ascanius, Idaeus and Actor lifted
Her up in their arms and carried her back into her dwelling.

    Then did the brazen tongue of the trumpet utter afar
Its terrible call: war-cries went up, and the whole sky bellowed.
Under a driving, tight-fitting roof of shields the Italians
Charged, essaying to fill in the trenches and break through the
                                            breastwork.
Some of them tried to get in by scaling the walls on ladders
At a point where the ring of defenders was thinnest and daylight showed
Between their spaced-out bodies. In reply, the Trojans rained
All kinds of missile and thrust down with tough poles at the attackers,
Being trained by long experience of siege to defend their battlements.
Ponderous, deadly rocks they pitched down, too, in an effort
To shatter that armoured column; but these, beneath their compact
Casemate of shields, were in good shape to take whatever might come
                                                down.
But now they failed: for where the great press of assailants threatened,
The Trojans rolled up an enormous boulder and tipped it over,
Which falling burst through the casemate of shields, knocked down
                                          the Rutuli
Like ninepins. The latter, though brave men, were now less keen to
                                          engage in
Such a blind, head-on assault; so they tried to drive the defenders
Off the ramparts by sniping.
On another sector Mezentius, ferocious of aspect, brandished
Etruscan torches, attacked with smoking incendiaries;
While Messapus, tamer of horses, a son of Neptune, hacked through
The palisade and shouted for ladders to scale the battlements.

    Calliope, I pray that the Muses inspire my song,
    [*Lines 491–525*]

197

To tell what execution the sword of Turnus now wrought there,
What deaths; what men each fighting-man despatched to Hades.
I pray you unroll with me the spacious map of the battle.
For you are divine, you remember it all, and can recount it.

There stood, in a key position, a turret tall and sheer,
And linked with gangways aloft. This the Italians were struggling
With all their might to storm, putting all their skill to its overthrow;
While for their part the Trojans fought back, volleying stones,
Keeping up a heavy fire of arrows through its embrasures.
At the head of his men, Turnus now hurled a lighted fire-dart
Which stuck in the tower's side, blazing: fanned by the wind, it rapidly
Spread fire all over the planking, consumed the door it was lodged in.
Alarm and confusion seized the defenders within; they sought to
Escape their doom, but in vain. Jammed together, they pressed back
To the side of the tower that was free from fire: but suddenly, bodily
The tower collapsed and fell with a crash that resounded to heaven.
Half dead they were pitched to the ground, the huge mass of the
                                                    tower avalanching
Upon them, impaled by their own weapons, with splinters of tough
                                                    wood
Spitting their bodies through. Helenor and Lycus alone
Just managed to scramble clear: Helenor, a man in the prime of
Youth, was the natural son of the Lydian king by a slave from
Licymna, who'd sent him to fight at Troy, though forbidden—a
                                                    light-armed
Swordsman, with no reputation in war, no device on his shield.
As soon as he saw that he was hemmed in by the hordes of Turnus—
A ring of Latin troops, rank upon rank, around him—
Like some wild beast, walled in by a thick cordon of hunters,
Which furiously snarls at their weapons, and knowing she's doomed,
                                                    with a great spring
Hurls herself to her death upon the hunting spears,
Even so did the young man charge right into the press of the foe,
Where he saw their weapons were thickest, as one who was bound to
                                                    die.

But Lycus, being much swifter a runner, made good his escape
Through all the hostile arms as far as the rampart; and now
He was struggling to grip its parapet and clutch the hands of his
                                                    comrades.

[*Lines 526–558*]

But Turnus, who'd been in hot pursuit and had hurled a weapon,
Triumphantly taunted him thus:—
                              You half-wit, did you really
Think you could give us the slip?
                              Then he seized the man as he clung there
And tore him off; a large piece of the wall came away with him.
It was like when the war-bird of Jove has seized a hare or a snow-white
Swan in its crooked talons and soars aloft to its eyrie;
Or the wolf of Mars has snatched from the fold a lamb which its
                                                                    mother
Looks for with long-drawn bleatings. On the whole front the din
Crescendoed, the foe running in and bridging the trenches with rubble,
While some of them tossed incendiaries up at the wall-tops above.
With a rock as big as a chunk of mountain, Ilioneus
Now felled Lucetius, who was close to the gate with a firebrand:
Emathion was killed by Liger, Corynaeus by Asilas—
Liger good with his spear, Asilas at long-range bowshots:
Ortygius went down to Caeneus, who then was killed by Turnus;
Turnus as well slew Itys, Clonius, Dioxippus, Promulus,
Sagaris, and Idas who stood in defence of a turret.
Capys killed Privernus, who had just received a flesh wound
From the spear of Themilla: he foolishly let go his shield and clapped
His hand to the wound; so now the flighted arrow of Capys
Pinned his hand to his left side, and deeply penetrating
Buried its point in his lungs and gave him a mortal wound.
The son of Arcens stood, conspicuous in his armour
And finely-embroidered tunic of a bright Spanish rust-red:
A handsome fellow he was—had grown up in the woods of his mother
About Symaethus river, where stands the Palici's rich
And reverenced altar: him, then, his father Arcens had sent.
Downing his spears, Mezentius now whirled his buzzing sling
Three times around his head on a tense thong, then shot;
And the scorching bullet struck that warrior clean in the forehead,
Splitting it open, and laying him out full length on the ground.
    This, so legend tells, was the first time that Ascanius
Fired in war the arrows with which he'd been used to terrorise
Swift-running game: a shot of his struck down the gallant Numanus,
Whose surname was Remulus; this man had recently taken
In marriage the younger sister of Turnus. To-day he was strutting
    [Lines 559-594]

199

In front of the Latin lines, yelling out remarks—some proper,
Some not, to record; his royal alliance had given him
A swelled head—showing off his giant physique, and shouting:—
    You men of twice-captured Troy, aren't you ashamed to be once
                                                                    more
Besieged and cooped up in your ramparts? skulking from death
                                                behind battlements?
Look at the heroes who make war to win them brides from our people!
What god—or what lunatic impulse—has dragged you to Italy?
You'll find no Atridae here, no double-talking Ulysses.
We are brought up hard from birth; we take our children young to
The river and harden them in the painful, ice-cold water.
Our boys go hunting all night and tirelessly rove the forests:
The taming of horses, and archery practice, to them are pastimes.
Our young men, inured to hard work and an austere way of living,
Tame the soil with hoes or rock cities in battle.
We live with steel in our hands; reversing the spear, we use it
To belabour the backs of our oxen. Not even old age, that cramps
                                                                    others,
Weakens our mental powers or impairs our physical vigour:
Though our hair be grey, we put on the helmet, and never lose
Our gusto for carrying off fresh plunder and living upon it.
But you, in your dresses embroidered with yellow and loud purple,
You with the hearts of loafers, you devotees of dancing,
With frilly sleeves to your tunics, and bonnets kept on by ribbons!—
You Phrygian women (for Phrygian men you are not), run away
To mount Dindymus, where the double-mouthed pipe tweedles for
                                                                    addicts!
The timbrels and Berecynthian fife of Cybele call you.
Leave fighting to men, I advise you; relinquish sword-play to others.
    Ascanius found this fellow's bragging and loud-mouthed frightfulness
Intolerable. So, drawing back his bowstring of horse-gut
With arrow nocked, he took up his stance, with his arms extended
Wide, having first uttered a prayer and a vow to Jove:—
    Almighty Jove, grant me success in this brave venture!
I in return will bring to your temple a yearly offering
And set up at your altar a bullock with gilded horns—
A snow-white bullock standing as many hands high as its mother,
One old enough to butt with its horns and paw the ground.

                                            [*Lines 595–629*]

                                200

The Father heard his prayer: from a clear tract of sky
He thundered upon the left: simultaneously twanged the fatal
Bow, and the arrow sped from the string with a terrible whirr
To pass through the head of Remulus, its point transfixing the hollow
Temples:—
        Now go and mock good men with insolent words!
The men of twice-captured Troy send this reply to the Rutuli.
  No more did Ascanius say. The Trojans hailed his feat
With a cheer, and shouted for joy; their morale was raised sky-high.
Now it happened that long-haired Apollo, throned on a cloud, was
                                   looking
Down from the regions of air at the Italian lines
And the settlement; then he spoke to the triumphant Ascanius:—
  More power to your young valour, my son! You're going the right
                                    way
To starry fame, O god-born and sire of gods to be!
Rightly all destined foes shall be quelled by the house of Assaracus.
Troy is not big enough for you.
                       Thus did he say; then launched
Himself from the heights of heaven, and brushing aside the breezes,
Made his way to Ascanius. He now took on the appearance
Of aged Butes—a man who had formerly been the squire
And trusted household guard of Trojan Anchises; later
Aeneas made him Ascanius' personal aide. Apollo
Came as the living image of this old man—the same voice,
Complexion and white hair, the same fierce-clashing accoutrements—
And to the fiery-spirited prince addressed these words:—
  Son of Aeneas, let it suffice to have killed Numanus
And come off scot-free yourself. Great Apollo has granted you this first
Distinction, and is not jealous you've won it with his own weapon.
But take no more part in the fighting, young prince.
                       So Apollo began;
But while he was yet speaking, he went from the sight of men,
Vanishing into the distance before their eyes, into thin air.
The Trojan commanders recognised him for a god, and his arms
Divine, catching the noise of his quiver which rattled as he flew.
So they used the god's authority to deter Ascanius
From further fighting, keen though he was, and themselves returned
To the combat, risking their lives at the deadly breach of danger.
  [*Lines 630–663*]

Now the din rises along the walls, over all the defences:
They are aiming the vicious bows, and spinning the spears. The
ground
Is one great litter of missiles: the shields and the rounded helmets
Ring with their blows: the fray swells to a bitter climax.
It was wild as the storm that comes from the West, at the time of the
rainy
Goat-stars, flailing the earth; or the gales that go racing seawards
Pelting with hail, when Juppiter, terrible in the South wind,
Bursting the clouds above us, unleashes tornadoes of water.
    Pandarus and Bitias, sprung from Alcanor of Ida,
Reared by the dryad Iaera in Juppiter's sacred wood—
Young men as tall as their native pine trees and mountains—these two,
Confident in their weapons, threw open the gate which their general
Had given them to guard, positively inviting the foe to enter
The ramparts; while they, swords drawn, flaunting the plumes on
their tall heads,
Stood just inside, to left and right, in front of a turret.
So by some flowing river—by the banks of the Po, it might be,
Or Athesis' genial waters—twin oaks stand, head in air,
Soaring up side by side, raising their leafy crowns
Into the sky, their tops dizzily nodding. The Rutuli,
Seeing a gateway open, made a concerted rush for it.
But, the next minute, Quercens, handsomely-armed Aquicolus,
Tmarus the impetuous and Haemon the scion of Mars,
With all their detachment, were either routed and running away
Or had laid down their lives right in that very entrance.
Then did the hearts of the combatants kindle to fiercer rage;
The Trojans, rallying, concentrated at that point, willing
To mix it and make extensive sallies beyond their walls.
    Now Turnus, who was fighting ferociously and creating
Havoc elsewhere on the field, received a despatch—the Trojans,
Flushed with the losses they'd just inflicted, had thrown a gate open.
He left the work in hand, and moved by prodigious anger,
Charged at the Trojan gate and those insolent brothers who fought
there.

Antiphates first (for he was there in the forefront) Turnus
Felled with a javelin-throw—Antiphates, bastard son of
Sarpedon by a woman of Thebes: the cornel-wood lance
[*Lines 664–698*]

Flew through the soft air, went home in the stomach just under his tall
Chest; the darkly-gaping wound spouted a torrent
Of blood, and the lung it was lodged in warmed its iron point.
Then Turnus slew Meropes and Erymas, then Aphidnus;
Then Bitias, whose eyes were blazing, whose mind was berserk—
But not with a javelin—no javelin would have killed him.
A heavy projectile came catapulted and screeching at him,
Travelling like a meteor: the reinforced, bull's-hide shield,
The trusty cuirass and its two layers of golden chainmail, could not
Withstand that weapon; Bitias' giant frame fell crashing.
Earth groaned, and his mighty shield came clattering down upon him.
That fall was like when a stone pier, constructed from huge, shaped
                                                                    blocks
Of masonry and built out into the sea in the bay of
Baiae, near Cumae, collapses: the wall of it falls away, dragging
A mass of rubble behind, slaps the water and sinks to the bottom;
The sea is all in a welter, black sludge oozes up to the surface:
That impact shakes to the core Prochyta and the bedrock
Of Inarime beneath which, at Jove's bidding, Typhoeus was buried.
   At this, the War-god Mars lent extra courage and strength
To the Latins, applying his sharpest stimulus to their hearts,
But loosing the spirit of Flight and Panic among the Trojans.
The Latins gather their forces, for now they can get to grips with
The foe, and the god of battle possesses them.
Pandarus, when he saw his brother laid low, and realised
How the engagement was going, the momentous turn it had taken,
Putting his broad shoulders to the gate, with a convulsive
Effort swung it shut upon its hinges, leaving
Many of his comrades in desperate action outside the battlements.
Others he locked in with him as they came streaming back,
But fatally failed to notice the Rutulian leader amongst them,
Yes, breaking into the settlement: he'd actually locked him in there—
As bad as putting a tiger in with a helpless flock.
At once a new light blazed from the eyes of Turnus, and dreadfully
Clashed his armour; the blood-red plumes on his helmet quivered;
His shield gave off bright shimmers, like lightning. Aeneas' men
In sudden consternation recognise that detested
Visage, those giant limbs. Now the immense Pandarus,
Burning with vengefulness for his brother's death, leaps forward
   [*Lines 699–736*]

203

And cries:—

        This is not the palace that goes with Amata's daughter
As dowry. Nor is it Ardea, your native town, you're shut up in.
This is an enemy camp, and you'll never get out of it, Turnus.

  But Turnus, quite unflustered, smiling a little, replied:—

  Come on, then, if you've courage enough! Come on and fight!
You can tell Priam later you met a second Achilles.

  He spoke. Pandarus summoned all his strength and hurled
A spear, its shaft rugged with knots and the unpeeled bark.
The winds received it: Saturnian Juno was there to deflect it
From Turnus' body: the weapon stuck harmlessly in the door:—

  But you'll not escape this weapon I wield in my strong right hand.
I'm not a man who misses or leaves his opponent a whole skin,

  Said Turnus; then, rising on tiptoe, he whirled his sword aloft, and
Brought the blade down between his enemy's temples, splitting
The young man's forehead and face in half, a hideous gash.
There was a crash as the young giant came to the ground:
Dying, he lay stretched out, his limbs unstrung and his armour
Spattered with blood and brains from the head that was slashed in two
And sagging away to left and right over each shoulder.
The Trojans, panicking wildly, turned, scattered and ran.
And if only the conquering Turnus had had the presence of mind
To break open the bars of the gate and let his own comrades in,
That day would have been the end of the war and the Trojan nation.
But he was fighting-mad; the blood lust drove him on
Against his adversaries.
First he caught Phaleris, and Gyges whom he had hamstrung;
Then, snatching up their spears, he hurled them at the backs of
The fleeing enemy: Juno supplied him with strength and courage.
Now he killed Halys too, and Phegeus, whose shield he pierced;
And while the defenders fought on the walls, unaware of his presence,
He killed Alcander, Halius, Noemon and Prytanis.
Lynceus came at him next, calling up his comrades; but Turnus,
The rampart on his right, lashed out with his flickering sword
And got him; his head, swept off by that one short-arm blow,
Tumbled and lay at a distance, still helmeted. Amycus next,
That mighty hunter, was slain—none was so adept as he
In the business of impregnating the tips of weapons with poison;
Then Clytius, son of Aeolus, and Cretheus, beloved by the Muses—

                      [*Lines 737–774*]

Cretheus, the Muses' darling, whose heart was given for ever
To song and the lyre, to plucking the tuneful strings, who sang
For ever about war-horses, battles, heroic deeds.

When news of the losses their men were suffering came at last to
The Trojan generals, Mnestheus and fiery Serestus arrived,
To see their people scattered and the foe within the gates.
So Mnestheus shouted:—

                     Where do you think you're running away to?
What other refuge have you? What battlements but these?
My lads, is one man going to make such a killing all over
The settlement—one man who is trapped in our ramparts—and get
Away with it? one who has sent so many of our best to perdition?
You cowards, aren't you ashamed? Have you no pride, no feeling
For our distressful country, our ancient gods, and Aeneas?

Stung by his words, the Trojans closed up their ranks and stiffened
Resistance. Little by little Turnus gave back from the onslaught
Towards the river, that part of the wall which the Tiber bounded.
Made more aggressive by this, the Trojans pressed in on him, shouting
And concentrating their forces; so will a crowd of men harry
A savage lion with spears levelled; the brute, in alarm,
Backs away, murderous-minded, viciously glaring; his rage
And his courage forbid him to turn tail; but equally, much as
He'd like to, he cannot drive a path through those men with their
                                    weapons.
Just so did Turnus give ground. He was in a fix, but his movements
Were quite unflurried; his fighting blood was on the boil still.
Yes, even then he had twice gone in at the thick of the foe,
Driven them twice in headlong confusion all round the ramparts.
But the whole garrison came running to form up against him.
Saturnian Juno dared not lend him the strength to oppose them,
Not now, for Juppiter sent Iris flying down
From on high with a very brusque command to his sister and consort—
There will be trouble if Turnus leaves not the Trojans' encampment.
And so that warrior found his shield less sure to protect him,
His sword-arm flagging: volleys of missiles from every angle
Were snowing him under. The helmet upon his temples rang with
Incessant blows, its strong bronze cracked open by fusillades of
Stones, and the plumes torn away from its crest: his shield's boss
                                    could not

[*Lines 775–810*]

Stand up to the battering: led by Mnestheus, who fought like a fury,
The Trojans redoubled their fire. Then Turnus was bathed in sweat
Which ran—he had not a moment's breathing-space—dirty and sticky
All over him, and he panted heavily, sick with exhaustion.
At last he hurled himself, full-armed as he was, at one leap
Into the river below. Its yellow tide received him
As he plunged in, and bearing him up on its gentle waters,
Washed the blood off and restored him in high heart to his friends.

[*Lines 811–818*]

BOOK X

Now a new day threw open the halls of almighty Olympus,
And a council was called by the Father of heaven, the ruler of mankind,
To meet in his sky palace where, from the heights, he surveyed
All earth, the Trojan encampment and the peoples of Latium.
They passed to their seats in the great hall, and Jove it was who
                                                    spoke:—
  Great heaven-dwellers, why have you reversed the decision
Agreed on? What is the meaning of such unruly contentiousness?
I had forbidden that Italy should meet the Trojans in war.
Do you brawl in spite of my veto? What agency has frightened
This side or that into taking up arms and provoking a conflict?
A time will come when it's right to fight—do not be premature—
One day when barbarous Carthage shall open a way through the Alps
And roll a tide of disaster up to Rome's very towers.
Then will strife and hatred, then will all violence be lawful.
Have done now! Give your whole-hearted assent to the pact I've
                                                    decreed.
  So Juppiter briefly declared. But golden Venus in answer
Spoke at some length:—
  Father, eternal Power over men and men's affairs—
What other power is there which I can now entreat?—
Do you mark how the Rutuli are exulting? how Turnus goes
Through the fray, charioted and conspicuous? how he speeds,
Puffed up with triumph? The ring of their ramparts no longer protects
The Trojans: no, they are battling within the gates, on the high-built
Parapets of the earthworks, and flooding the moat with blood.
Aeneas is far away, and knows nothing of this. Will you never
Allow the siege to be lifted? Once more an enemy threatens
Troy town—this baby Troy—and a second army assails us:
Once more from Aetolian Arpi is Diomed moving against
The Trojans. I well believe I too am not done with being wounded—
Your child—and till then this war of mortals will not be over.
If it's without your leave and against your will that the Trojans
  [*Lines 1–31*]

207

Made for Italy, let them expiate their sins, and withhold
Your succour from them: but if they were following out the solemn
Commands of the gods and the dead, why is anyone now permitted
To cancel what you have ordered and to re-write their destiny?
Need I bring up again the burning of their fleet on the shore
Of Eryx? or the suborning against them of the Storm-king
And his wild winds from Aeolia? or the mission that Iris was sent on?
Now Juno is dredging up the Underworld—a province
Hitherto unexplored—and has suddenly loosed Allecto
On the earth, to spread delirium through the Italian towns.
Empire means nothing to me now: that was something we hoped for
While luck was with us. Let them you prefer to win be the winners.
If there's no place on earth which your hard-hearted wife
Will ever concede to the Trojans, I implore you, sire, by the smoking
Ruins of fallen Troy, let Ascanius be released
Unharmed from the battlefield, O let my grandson survive it.
Aeneas may be tossed on unknown waters—so be it—
Pursuing whatever path Fortune has found for him:
I ask but to preserve, to withdraw his son from the fatal
Fight. I possess Amathus, Mount Paphus, and Cythera,
And a shrine in Idalia: here let him live out his days, unknown
To fame, laying down his arms. Command, if you will, that Carthage
Crush Italy, hold her down with supreme power: there shall be no
Opposition from Ascanius. What was the use in escaping
The horrors of war, slipping out between the Argive fires,
Running the gamut of peril through seas and desolate lands,
When the Trojans are still in search of a second Troy in Latium?
Better, I think, to have settled amongst his own country's expiring
Ashes, upon the soil where Troy stood. Father, I beg you,
Give Xanthus and Simois back to my piteous Trojans, grant them
To tread out the doom of Troy a second time!

                                        Then queen Juno,
Inspired by strong passion, spoke up:—

                                    Why do you force me to break
My profound silence, to tear the skin from my grief and expose it?
Has any mortal man or any god compelled
Aeneas to be the aggressor and attack the ruler of Latium?
"At the bidding of fate he came to Italy": very well—
Though Cassandra's ravings it was that moved him. But did *I*

                                        [*Lines 32–68*]

Ask him to quit the settlement or trust his life to the winds?
To leave his camp and the focal point of the war in a boy's charge?
Undermine the Etruscans' loyalty? make trouble among peaceful tribes?
Was he driven to this treacherous policy by a god, or some ruthless
                                                    compulsion
Of mine? How does Juno, or Iris' mission, come into it?
Shocking, you say, that Italians should ring your baby Troy
With fire, and Turnus should set foot on his own native soil—
Turnus, grandson of Pilumnus, son of the nymph Venilia.
Well, what of the Trojans spreading fire and havoc in Latium?
Oppressing a land not theirs and driving off plunder? choosing
Whom they shall wed, and abducting betrothed girls from their lovers?
Pretending to offer peace while their ships bristle with weapons?
You may filch your Aeneas out of the grip of the Greeks,
Stretching a veil of cloud, thin air, in defence of your hero.
You may transform his vessels into as many sea-nymphs:
But if I help the Italians at all, that is a crime.
"Aeneas is far away, unknowing of this": let him stay so.
You possess Paphos, Idalium, lofty Cythera: well then,
Why then do you meddle with hot-tempered folk who are spoiling
                                                    for battle?
Are you saying it's I who am trying to capsize the leaky cause
Of Troyland? I? Not the one who threw the pitiable Trojans
To the Greeks? What started Europe and Asia rising in arms
Against each other? Whose thieving hand broke down their peace?
Was I responsible for the Dardan philanderer ransacking
Sparta? Did I give him weapons, or kindle a war with his lust?
Then was the time to have feared for your people: too late now you
                                                    rise with
Unjustified grievances, spattering futile insults upon me.
    Such was Juno's plea; it got a mixed reception
From the heaven-dwellers, who raised a buzz like the sound in a forest
When a wind's getting up among the branches, gustily,
Sulkily murmuring, warning sailors of gales to come.
Then the almighty Father, the first lord of the universe,
Uttered; and as he spoke, the high places of heaven fell silent,
Earth shook to its foundations, and the firmament was still;
The West winds held their breath, the sea smoothed out its face:—
    Now take my words to heart, and let them not be forgotten.
[*Lines 69–104*]

209

Since it was not permitted that the Italians should come to
Terms with the Teucrians, and your dispute allows of no ending,
This day, whatever the fortune each warrior has and the hope
He pursues, be he Trojan or Rutulian, I shall make no distinction—
Whether the camp is besieged through the destiny of the Italians,
Or a fault inherent in Troy, or the taking of bad advice.
I do not exempt the Rutuli. The selfhood of each shall determine
His effort and how it fares. I am king to all, and impartial.
Fate will settle the issue.
                                        By the stream of his Stygian brother,
The banks where boiling pitch flows in a black maelstrom, he nodded,
Confirming his promise: the nod caused all Olympus to tremble.
That was the end of the conference. Juppiter rose from his golden
Throne, and the heaven-dwellers escorted him to his own place.
    Meantime the Rutuli pressed hard on the gates all round,
Doing great execution, encircling the walls with fire,
While Aeneas' men were hemmed in behind their ramparts and had
No hope of getting away. They stood, dispirited, helpless,
In the turrets, and manned the ring of their walls with thinning forces.
Asius, son of Imbrasus, Thymoetes, son of Hicetaon,
The two Assaraci, with Castor and aged Thymbris,
Were in the forefront: beside them stood Clarus and Themon, the two
Brothers of Sarpedon, who came from mountainous Lycia.
There, lifting a huge boulder, a sizeable chunk of mountain,
With a superhuman effort, is Acmon of Lyrnesus—
A giant like Clytius, his father, and his brother Menestheus.
With javelins and stones the defenders are fighting bitterly,
Shooting incendiaries and fitting arrow to bowstring.
Among them, see! the Dardan lad, special favourite of Venus
And looking it too, his noble head uncovered, Ascanius
Glows like some jewel set in yellow gold, which graces
The wearer's neck or hair; like ivory which an artist
Has inlaid upon boxwood or terebinth-wood from Oricum
He shines: his hair is falling loose about his milk-white
Neck, and is gathered above by a circlet of pliant gold.
Ismarus, you too your great-hearted clansmen saw
As you steeped arrows in poison and fired with unerring aim—
High-born Ismarus from Maeonia, where they till
Fertile fields irrigated by the gold-bearing river Pactolus.

[*Lines 105–142*]

Mnestheus was there as well, raised to the heights by the glory
Of beating Turnus off just now from the high-built ramparts;
And Capys, from whom the town in Campania gets its name.
    So they were all engaged in the exacting struggle
Of war. And now, at midnight, Aeneas was ploughing the seas.
On leaving Evander and entering the Etruscan camp, he presented
Himself before their king, told him his name and nation,
The aid he sought and the offer he brought; acquainted him
Of the forces Mezentius had won to his side, and the violent reactions
Of Turnus; warned him what need there was for reciprocal trust
If the king's own affairs were to prosper, and added a plea. Tarchon
Struck a treaty at once, joining forces with him. The Etruscan
Army embarked: heaven was with them and fate's embargo
Lifted, now they followed a foreign commander. Aeneas'
Ship led the line; on its prow were Phrygian lions surmounted
By Ida, most dear to the Trojan refugees, for a figurehead.
Here was stationed the hero Aeneas, calculating
The changeful factors of war. Pallas stayed close at his left side,
Inquiring about the stars by which they steered through the dark night,
Then asking Aeneas to tell his adventures on land and sea.
    Now, Muses, throw Helicon wide and inspire my poetry to speak of
The host that followed Aeneas from the Etruscan shore
Upon that night, manning the ships which rode the seaways.
    Massicus led a squadron, sailing in his bronze-beaked vessel,
The *Tiger*; his contingent, a thousand strong, had come from
Clusium and the town of Cosae; their arms were a deadly
Bow and a light-weight quiver of arrows slung over the shoulder.
Grim Abas came too, his whole detachment in glittering armour,
A gilded image of Apollo gleaming upon his poop:
Populonia had given him six hundred of her sons,
Expert fighters all; Ilva had furnished three hundred—
That isle so rich in mines of inexhaustible iron.
Third came Asilas, a medium between mankind and the gods,
A master at divining from the entrails of sacrificed beasts,
The stars in the sky, the songs of birds, the presage of lightning:
He hurried to war a thousand spearmen in close formation;
Etruscan Pisa, whose founders had come from the river Alphaeus,
Had raised them for him to command. Then followed the handsome

Astyr,

[*Lines 143–180*]

211

Confident in his charger and many-coloured accoutrements.
Three hundred more, who were all of one mind in their wish for battle,
Came from their homes in Caere, from the country around the Minio,
The ancient town of Pyrgi and malarial Gravisca.

I must not pass over Cinyras, most valiant leader in war
Of the Ligurians, or Cupavo with his small force
And swan's plumes waving above his crest—a symbol of his father's
Transformation, and thus a reproach to Cupid and Venus;
The legend being that his father, Cycnus, in grief for beloved
Phaethon, was consoling his sorrowful heart with song
Beneath the shady leaves of poplars, once Phaethon's sisters,
When he took on soft plumage, yes, snow-white as old age,
And left the earth behind and sang his way to the stars.
His son was sailing now with a band of other young men,
Oaring onwards a great ship, the *Centaur*, which trod the waves
In towering bulk, its figurehead threatening the water below
With a huge rock, its long keel furrowing through the deepsea.

There too was Ocnus, who'd whipped up a force from his native
land:
He, the son of the Tuscan river and the seeress Manto,
Founded the city of Mantua and gave it his mother's name—
Mantua, rich in its forefathers, who were not all of the same stock:
Three clans it had, each clan ruling over four townships,
With Mantua, by reason of its Etruscan blood, as the capital.
Five hundred from here had taken up arms against Mezentius:
They sailed in warships following a figurehead of the river
Mincius wreathed with the grey-green rushes of Lake Benacus.
Aulestes drove wallowing on, his hundred men tugging hard at
The sweeps and thrashing the waves; the sea's face foamed as they
churned it:
His ship was the giant *Triton*, the sound of whose conch affrighted
The dark-blue water; its dipping figurehead was the hairy
Trunk of a man to the waist, below the belly a great fish;
The water foamed and gurgled under that monster's breast.
So many the chosen princes who sailed in thirty ships
Cutting the sea with their bronze prows, to the relief of the Trojans.

And now had the daylight gone from the sky, and the gentle Moon's
Night-riding horses were pacing halfway across the heavens.
Aeneas, whose anxiety allowed him no rest, was doing

[*Lines 181–217*]

212

A trick at the helm and handling the sheets himself on the ship's stern,
When, in mid-passage, a marvel—an argosy of his own ones
Came to meet him; the nymphs, the ships that kindly Cybele
Had turned into nymphs and bidden to have a divine power in
The deep, came swimming up abreast, cleaving the waves,
As many as once had been moored by their bronze beaks to the shore.
From afar they knew the hero, and dancing wreathed around him.
Cymodoce, the one who was most skilled at speaking,
Followed behind, and gripping the stern with her right hand, raised up
Her body, while her left hand silently paddled the water.
Then she startled him, saying:—
                    Are you on the alert, Aeneas,
O heaven-descended? Awake! Pay out the sheets! Run free!
It is we, your fleet, your barques built from the pinewood of holy
Mount Ida, but now we are sea-nymphs. When treacherously the
                                                    Italian
Attacked us with fire and steel, we had to hurry and break
Your moorings, though we hated to do it. All over the sea
We've been looking for you. The Mother took pity and changed us
                                                    into
What you now see, to be goddesses, living our lives in the deep.
But your son, Ascanius, beleaguered within the walls and
                                                    entrenchments,
Is heavily under fire from the furiously fighting Italians.
By now the Arcadian cavalry, with a stiffening of Etruscans,
Are at the rendezvous. Turnus is firmly resolved to prevent them
Linking with the besieged, to intercept and attack them
With his own squadrons. Up, then, and when the dawn comes, order
Your comrades at once to be roused to arms, and take the invincible
Gold-rimmed shield which the Lord of Fire himself has given you!
To-morrow's light—these are no empty words I am speaking,
Do not suppose it—shall see the Italians slaughtered in great heaps.

So saying, and dropping away, she gave the tall poop a push with
Her right hand—an expert propulsion. The ship fled over the waves
Faster than any javelin or wind-swift arrow could fly.
The other ships crowded on speed when they saw it. Trojan Aeneas
Was mystified and astonished, yet the omen heartened him greatly.
Gazing up at the vault of heaven, he uttered a short prayer:—
    O gracious lady of Ida, mother of the gods, who rejoice in
    [*Lines 218–252*]

213

Dindymus, turreted cities, lions harnessed in couples,
Be now my guide in the battle! Be near and divinely prosper
This omen! Be with your Phrygian sons, O goddess, and bless them!

No more did he say; but even as he spoke, the returning day
Was streaming back in full flush of light, routing the darkness.
Now for a start he ordered his men to ready themselves—
Their hearts and equipment—for combat, and to obey his signals.
And now, as he stood high up in the stern-sheets, Aeneas held
His Trojans and their encampment in view: so he lifted his shield with
His left hand and made it flash. The Dardans upon the walls there
Raised a great shout; their fighting spirit revived at this new hope,
Their fire was redoubled: so it is when under the dark clouds
The cranes flying back to the Strymon announce their approach, and
trail their
Bugling cries as they swim through the air ahead of the South wind.
But Turnus and the Italian commanders thought it a strange thing
Until, looking round, they saw ships backing up to the beach
And the whole sea one swarm of vessels running towards them.
The peak of Aeneas' helmet was blazing, flame poured from its lofty
Crest, and the golden boss of his shield spurted huge flashes:
It was as when on some cloudless night you see a comet
Glowing, blood-red and ominous, or the fiery Dog-star rising
Which glooms the sky with sinister light and carries with it
Drought and pestilence to suffering humanity.
Yet the gallant Turnus' confidence was unimpaired—he reckoned
To occupy the beaches before them and beat off the landing-forces.
He spoke to raise their spirits, he even rebuked his men:—

This is what you have hoped and prayed for—to break them in
hand-to-hand combat!
Brave men have the very spirit of war in their hands. Let each of you
Now remember his wife and his home, remember the great
And glorious deeds of our fathers. We'll meet the foe right at the
sea's edge
While he's in a flurry, just disembarking, his foothold precarious.
Fortune always fights for the bold.

So Turnus spoke; then considered whom he should lead in this onset
And whom he could delegate to carry on with the siege.

Meanwhile Aeneas was landing his men by assault gangways
From the high sterns of the ships. Many watched for the backwash

[*Lines 253–288*]

214

Of a swell that had spent its violence, then boldly jumped into the
shallows;
Others slid down the oars. Tarchon, eyeing the beaches,
Noticed a point where no shoals were heaving and roaring with
breakers,
But the seas ran up and spread out over the shore, unbroken,
And quickly changed course towards it, crying out to his comrades:—
Now then! Rise to the stroke! Row hard, my gallant lads!
Lift the ships! Hurl them forward! Let's make a gash with our bows in
That enemy land! Let our keel gouge out a trough for itself there!
I don't care if the ship breaks up on the foreshore yonder
Once we have got a grip on the land.
As soon as Tarchon
Had shouted these words, his crews all tugged on the oars together
And ran their ships in a smother of spray at the Latin shore
Until the bows were lodged on dry land and the keels wedged there,
Undamaged all—all except Tarchon's ship: this galley,
Striking a shoal, ran aground on the ridge of a treacherous sandbank
Where she hung balanced awhile, see-sawing and slapping the waves,
Then broke her back, tipping out her crew into the water;
Splintered oars and floating thwarts got in their way,
And the waves' backwash sucked at their feet as they struggled
shorewards.

Turnus reacted with speed and decision, aggressively throwing
His whole force at the Trojans, blocking the beach against them.
Trumpets rang out. Aeneas led the assault on the yeoman
Ranks—an auspicious start for the fray, mowed down the Latins
And killed Theron, a giant of a man, who had had the nerve
To attack him: Aeneas' sword pierced a joint of his bronze corselet,
The tunic stiff with gold, and mortally opened his side.
Next he slew Lichas, who had been ripped from the womb of his dead
Mother, and consecrated to Phoebus because, as a babe,
He'd survived that perilous knife. Nearby, Aeneas put down
To death tough Cisseus and huge Gyas, who were laying about them
With clubs: no use to them now was the weapon of Hercules, though,
Nor their own strength, nor the spirit of Melampus, their father,
who'd been
The companion of Hercules during all his difficult labours
On earth. Now, see! while Pharus is boasting aloud like a novice,

[*Lines 289–322*]

215

Aeneas hurls a javelin right into his bawling mouth.
Cydon too, the golden down of youth on his cheek still,
Poor Cydon, who'd come here to be with Clytius, his latest love,
Would have fallen pitiably to the Trojan's sword and lain there
Oblivious of all his youthful loves, his ruling passion,
Had not his brothers, the offspring of Phorcus, interposed
Themselves in a solid body; seven they were, and seven
Spears they threw, some of which glanced harmlessly off from Aeneas'
Helmet and shield, while the rest were deflected by guardian Venus
So as merely to graze him. He now called out to his close friend,

Achates:—

  Pile me up weapons here! Each one I throw shall find its
Billet in an Italian, each weapon that once on the plains of
Ilium lodged in a Greek.

                    Then, snatching up a great spear,
He hurled it: that flying spear whacked through the bronze of Maeon's
Shield, shattered his breastplate, shattered the breast as well.
Alcanor goes to support his brother, holds up with his right arm
The tottering Maeon; a spear drives through that arm, and onward
Goes streaking still upon its bloody course, but Alcanor's
Arm is lifelessly dangling by the sinews from his shoulder.
Now Numitor, pulling out the spear from his brother's body,
Aimed it at Aeneas; but this time it was not allowed to
Strike its target—it merely grazed the thigh of Achates.
Now Clausus, from Cures, came up, all confident in his youthful
Physique, and hit Dryops under the chin—a long shot with a hardwood
Spearshaft, which went deep in, transfixing his throat and at one stroke
Depriving him of voice and life itself: so Dryops
Struck the ground with his forehead and vomited up thick gore.
Clausus laid low, as well, one way or another, three Thracians
Of the exalted line of Boreas, and three whom their father,
Idas, had sent from their native Ismarus. Now Halaesus
Ran up with his Auruncans; Messapus, the son of Neptune,
Renowned for his chargers, arrived in support. Each army strains
In turn to dislodge the other. The battle rages on Italy's
Very doorstep. As in high heaven the opposing winds
Battle with one another, equal in strength and spirit,
Wind to wind, cloud to cloud, wave to wave locked and unyielding;
Doubtful the issue—one long thrust and counterthrust, neither

[Lines 323–359]

216

Side budging. Just so did the ranks of Troy and Latium clash
Together, foot to foot, man to man locked in the mêlée.
    But on another sector, where a torrent had scattered about
The terrain, rolling boulders and bushes torn up from its banks,
Pallas observed his Arcadians turn tail and the Latins pursuing:
The broken ground here had led them for once to dismount from
                                                            their horses,
But they were not accustomed to fighting on foot. So he tried the
                                                            one thing
Left him to try in such a grave situation, and sought to
Revive their morale with a mixture of pleading and harsh rebuke:—
    Where are you running to, men? I call on you—by your brave deeds,
By the name of your king Evander, by the wars we have won, by
                                                            my own
Ambition which now is stirring to rival my father in glory—
Don't put any hopes on retreating! We must break our way through
                                                            the foe
With cold steel. There, where they mass against us in greatest numbers,
Is the route by which our dear country bids you and me to return to
                                                            her.
No gods are after us: we are men, hard pressed by enemies
Who also are men, with two hands and mortal lives, like us.
Look! that great barrier of sea cutting us off, and no room
Left for flight now! What shall it be—the sea, or Troy?
    With these words, Pallas hurled himself into the thick of the foe.
First to confront him was Lagus, led by unfair fate to
The encounter. Him, as he wrenched up a stone of immense weight,
Pallas hit with a spear-throw, nailing him just where the spine
Is joined to the ribs on either side, then started to pull out
His spear, which was stuck in the bone. Hisbo, who hoped to get him
While he was stooping, failed: for, as he ran in, full of rage
At the bitter death of his comrade, and reckless, Pallas was ready
And struck first, burying his sword in the lungs distended with anger.
Next he went for Sthenius, and Anchemolus, a man of
Rhoetus' ancient line, who had lain with his own stepmother.
Larides and Thymber fell too on Italian soil:
They were twin brothers, exactly alike, the sons of Daucus—
Their parents could not tell them apart, and with happy affection
Mistook them. But Pallas now created a dreadful difference
    [Lines 360–393]

217

Between them, for his sword swept off the head of Thymber,
While Larides—his severed right hand groped to find
Its owner, the half-alive fingers twitching, clutching at the sword-hilt.
The Arcadians, stung by Pallas' rebuke and witnessing these
Outstanding feats, now charged at the foe in shame and anger.
Then Pallas picked off Rhoeteus as he whirled past in a two-horse
Chariot. Ilus won a certain reprieve by that;
For Pallas had aimed his strong spear at Ilus from a distance,
But Rhoeteus received it, coming between as he fled from the gallant
Teuthras and his brother Tyres; he pitched from the chariot
And drummed upon the Italian ground with his heels, dying.
Just as, in summer-time, when the winds he has prayed for have risen,
A shepherd may light fires at intervals over the heathland;
All of a sudden the interspaces catch fire, an unbroken
Line of crackling flame is spread across the broad acres;
He sits and reviews the exultant flames like a conqueror:
Even so did the brave hearts of Pallas' men all rally and weld
Into one, and they backed him up. But that quick-moving fighter,
                                                    Halaesus,
Came forward to meet them, crouching tensely behind his shield.
He killed Ladon, Pheres and Demodocus; his flashing
Sword lopped off the right hand of Strymonius, who was making
A thrust at his throat; he struck Thoas in the face with a stone,
Smashing the skull into fragments spattered with blood and brains.
His father, presageful of fate, had hidden Halaesus in a forest;
But when he was old, near death, his eyes glazing and whitening,
The Fate-spinners laid their hands upon him, and made him a victim
To Evander's weapons. Pallas now went for Halaesus, first praying:—
    O father Tiber, grant this spear which I poise to throw
Good luck! May it find its way through the stubborn heart of Halaesus!
Your sacred oak shall be graced with the armour I strip from him.
    The god gave ear to this prayer. Halaesus, who was shielding
Imaon, alas uncovered his own breast to Pallas' weapon.
    But Lausus, who was a major factor in war, allowed
No panic amongst his men at Pallas' killings. He first slew
Abas, who'd been a problem baffling the opposition
And holding them up. Many Arcadians went down and Etruscans,
Trojans too—warriors the Greeks had not destroyed.
Equal in force and leadership, the armies close. Support troops

[*Lines 394–431*]

Press up to strengthen the front line: so thick the mêlée, they can
                                                                    hardly
Move weapon or hand. Here Pallas strains and shoves, here Lausus
Struggles to meet him: the two are of much the same age, and both
Uncommonly handsome; but fate had forbidden that they should ever
Return to their own homelands. The ruler of great Olympus
Did not, however, allow these two to confront each other:
Their fates await them—how near!—at the hands of greater foes.
   Meanwhile Turnus was warned by his guardian sister to hurry
To Lausus' aid; so he cut through the fray in his speeding chariot.
When he got there, he called out:—
                              You can stop fighting now.
I am going alone against Pallas: he is my meat, and mine
Alone. I wish his father was here to witness the duel.
   He spoke; and his comrades withdrew from the field of battle, as
                                                                    bidden.
But when the Rutulians moved back, young Pallas, amazed by that
                                                                    arrogant
Order, stood tongue-tied a moment, surveying the mighty bulk of
Turnus, and truculent, looking him up and down at a distance,
Then he hurled back these words in the teeth of that haughty prince:—
   I shall soon be renowned for winning the arms of an enemy general
Or dying a glorious death: my father can take either.
To hell with your threats!
                              So saying, he moved out onto the field.
The blood of his Arcadians grew chill, and their hearts numb.
Leaping down from his chariot, Turnus prepares for close combat
On foot. As a lion who has espied, from some high point of
Vantage, far off on the plain a bull spoiling for battle,
He bounds forward; yes, that was what Turnus' oncoming looked like.
Pallas, as soon as he reckoned his foe was in range of a spear-cast,
Was first to move, hoping that luck would side with one who dared
To take on a powerfuller man, and praying thus to high heaven:—
   Hercules, I implore you, by the welcome my father gave you,
The table you shared, though a stranger, help me in this great
                                                                    enterprise!
Let Turnus, dying, behold me strip off his bloodstained armour,
And let his closing eyes acknowledge me as his conqueror!
   Hercules heard the lad. He repressed a terrible groan
   [*Lines 432–464*]

219

That rose from deep in his heart, gave way to hopeless tears.
Then the Father of heaven spoke these kindly words to his son:—
    Every man's hour is appointed. Brief and unalterable
For all, the span of life. To enlarge his fame by great deeds
Is what the brave man must aim at. Beneath Troy's lofty battlements
Fell many sons of the gods; aye, there Sarpedon among them
Fell, who was my son. Turnus too is summoned
By his fate, and is nigh to the destined finish of his life.
    So Juppiter spoke, then averted his eyes from the land of Italy.
But Pallas hurled a spear, putting all his strength behind it,
And plucked his sword, flashing, out of the hollow scabbard.
That skimming spear went home high up, where shield and armour
Protect the shoulder, and actually piercing the rim of the shield,
Just managed to graze in the end the mighty body of Turnus.
Turnus now gave himself plenty of time to poise and aim at
Pallas his steel-tipped, oaken spear; as he threw it, he shouted:—
    Watch out, and see if my spear does not go deeper than his went!
    Pallas' shield, for all its layers of iron and bronze,
For all the protective layers of bull's hide that reinforced it,
Was broken through in the centre by the impact of Turnus' quivering
Spearpoint, which drove on to pierce the breastplate and then the breast.
Pallas wrenched out the weapon warm from the wound: it was no
                                                                good;
His blood and his life ebbed, through the same channel, at once.
Hunched over the wound, he fell, his armour clanging above him—
Fell with his bleeding mouth to the enemy soil, dying.
Turnus straddled above him and spoke:—
    Remember well what I say, you Arcadians, and tell your king
I send him back his Pallas, a dead man; Evander deserved it.
What compensation there is in a tomb, what comfort in burial,
He can have. He'll find he has paid dear enough for making friends with
Aeneas.
            So saying, he pressed his left foot hard on the back of
The corpse, and tore off the sword-belt, a thing of immense weight,
Engraved with a legendary crime—that family of brothers foully
Murdered upon their wedding-night, the bed-chambers swimming
                                                                in blood;
Eurytus' son, Clonus, had worked it in rich gold chasing.
This belt was now taken by Turnus for spoils, and delighted his heart.
                                                    [*Lines 465–500*]

Ah, mind of man, so ignorant of fate, of what shall befall him,
So weak to preserve moderation when riding the crest of good fortune!
For Turnus a time is coming when he'd give anything
To have left Pallas unharmed, and will loathe this day and the spoils
It brought him. But Pallas' comrades clustered around him, laid
His corpse on a shield and bore it away, lamenting and weeping.
What grief, what pride his father would feel at his homecoming!
To-day had been his baptism in war, to-day his end;
Still, he had left behind him a trail of Italian dead.

    This calamity came to the ears of Aeneas now, not as a rumour
But through an official message to tell him his allies were right on
The brink of disaster, were broken and needed succour immediately.
Mowing down all who stood in his way, like a demon he carved out
A broad swathe with his sword through the foe; his objective was

                                                Turnus,

Insolent from his last killing. He seemed to see Pallas, Evander,
The banquet—the first he'd been welcomed to here in this land as a

                                               stranger,

The hands he had clasped—to see them before him. So now he captured
Alive four warrior sons of Sulmo and four whom Ufens
Had reared, designing to sacrifice them to the ghost of Pallas
And sprinkle his funeral pyre with the blood of these captive youths.
Next in his anger he tried a long spear-shot at Magus,
Who ducked adroitly, so that the vibrant projectile flew over him,
Then clutching the knees of the Trojan, babbled out prayers for

                                            mercy:—

    By the shade of your sire and by all your hopes for Ascanius' future,
I implore you, don't kill me, preserve me for my son's sake and my

                                            father's!

There's a fine palace, it's mine, and deep below it are buried
Talents of chased silver; I've plenty of gold, too—wrought
And unwrought gold. The Trojans don't have to depend upon killing
Me to win the day: one life will not make any difference.

    Magus had spoken. Aeneas gave him his answer, thus:—
    Those many talents of silver and gold you tell me about—
Keep them for your children! Such courteous bargains in war
Turnus was first to abjure, just now, when he killed Pallas.
That's what my father Anchises thinks, and my son Ascanius.
    So saying, Aeneas gripped the man's helmet in his left hand,
    [*Lines 501–535*]

Bent his head back, while he pleaded, and drove the sword home in
                                                            his throat
Up to the hilt. Nearby was Haemon's son, a priest of
Apollo and Trivia, wearing the wreath and sacred headband,
Resplendent from head to foot in his dress and distinctive
                                                            accoutrements.
Him did Aeneas meet on the field, send flying and strike down,
Then, standing over him, killed him, palled him in darkness: Serestus
Collected and bore off the dead man's arms, as a trophy for Mars.
Now the enemy ranks were stiffened by Caeculus, a man
Of Vulcan's line, and by Umbro who came from the Marsian hills.
Aeneas stormed against them. His sword lopped off the left arm
Of Anxur, and with that arm the round shield fell to the ground.
Anxur had just said something big, thinking his prowess
Would equal his boasting; maybe he was building castles in the air
And had seen every prospect of living to a ripe old age.
Next moment, in glittering armour, Tarquitus bounded forth,
The son of the nymph Dryope, by Faunus, lord of the woodlands,
And stood in the path of the raging Aeneas; who, drawing his spear
                                                            back,
Pinned Tarquitus' ponderous shield to his corselet with a thrust:
Then, as he begged for mercy, uselessly babbling, Aeneas
Struck off his head, sent it rolling, and pushing away the still warm
Trunk of the man, stood above it, saying these pitiless words:—
    Lie there, you terrible warrior! Your lady mother shall never
Inter you, commit your remains to the tomb of your ancestors.
You're for the carrion birds; or else you'll be chucked in the sea
For the waves to dispose of, the hungry fishes to suck your wounds.
    At once he went in chase of Antaeus and Lucas, front-rank
Soldiers of Turnus, brave Numa, and the ginger-haired Camertes
Whose father was generous Volscens, the biggest of all Italian
Landowners, and governed Amyclae, where noone might sound the
                                                            alarum.
Even as Aegaeon, whom legend relates to have had a hundred
Arms and hands, to have breathed out fire from fifty mouths and
Fifty chests, to have fought against Juppiter's thunderbolts
With fifty identical shields clanging and fifty swords,
Just so did Aeneas, once he had whetted his steel with blood,
Storm over the battlefield irresistibly. Look, how he goes at
                                    [*Lines 536–570*]

222

Niphaeus' four-horse chariot—head-on at him and his horses!
They, when they see his giant strides and hear him bellowing
Hideous threats, wheel round in panic and bolt away
Towards the shore with the chariot, tipping their master out of it.
Meantime Lucagus charges into the fray on his chariot
Drawn by two white horses, his brother Liger beside him
As driver, and he himself whirling his sword with furious purpose.
Aeneas could not abide the way they came charging at full pelt;
Made for them; stood in their path, a giant, his spear at the ready.
Liger cried:—

These aren't the horses of Diomed or Achilles' chariot before you!
You aren't on the plains of Troy! No, this very spot is now going
To see the end of the war, and of you!

They were flung to the winds—
Those crazy words of Liger. The Trojan hero's reply was
Not to reply in words, but to hurl his spear at the enemy.
Lucagus, leaning right forward and lashing the horses on
With the flat of his sword, now took up position for combat, his left

foot

Advanced: as he did so, Aeneas' spear passed through the rim
Of his shining shield, at the bottom, then penetrated his left groin:
He was knocked out of the chariot, and rolled on the ground, dying.
Aeneas the true addressed these bitter words to his victim:—

Lucagus, you're not betrayed by your chariot horses' running
Too slowly, or shying away from some bodiless enemy shadow:
It's you who abandoned them, jumping down from the wheels.

So saying,
He gripped the horses' bridles. Poor Liger slid down from the chariot,
And quite unnerved held out imploring hands to Aeneas:—

Sir Trojan, have pity, I beg you, and spare my life—I entreat you
By your own soul, by the parents who gave the world such a great

man!

He'd have gone on beseeching, but Aeneas broke in:—

Your language
Was different just now. You're to die. Brothers should stick together.
Then he broached the heart of Liger, the crypt of life, with his blade.
Such were the killings done all over the field by the Dardan
Leader, who stormed like a river in spate or a black cyclone.
Finally prince Ascanius and the Trojan garrison made

[*Lines 571–604*]

A successful sortie from their encampment. The siege was lifted.
  Meanwhile, uninvited, Juppiter spoke to Juno:—
  Sister and most beloved consort of mine, it's Venus,
Just as you thought—you were not mistaken in so thinking—
Who buoys up the Trojan cause; it is not their own resilient
Strength, their warlike temper and steadiness under fire.
  Juno meekly replied:—
                                    My fairest husband, why
Do you tease me? I am sick-hearted, and overawed by your stern words.
If my love had the influence on you that once it had,
And still should have, you would surely not refuse this to Juno,
You the all-powerful—that I might at least convey my Turnus
Out of the battle and keep him unscathed for Daunus, his father.
As it is, let him die and atone with his patriot blood to the Trojans—
Although he can trace his origin back to the gods (for Pilumnus
Was his grandfather's grandsire), although he has often loaded
Your altars with a wealth of offerings, a lavish hand.
  To her, the lord of Olympus on high made this brief answer:—
  If it's a short reprieve from death, a mere breathing-space
For one who is doomed, that you ask; if you realise fully my meaning;
You may snatch Turnus away to escape his impending fate
For a little. So far I may indulge you. But if your petition
Conceals some further demand on my goodwill, if you imagine
The war's result is being changed or affected, your hopes are vain.
  And Juno replied, in tears:—
                                    What if your will should grant
What your words grudge, and long life be assured, after all, for Turnus?
As it is, though he's done no wrong, a hard end awaits him, or else I am
Wide of the mark. Would rather I were deluded by empty
Fears, and you—as you can—might think again, alter your policy!
  When she had spoken, Juno at once came down from the heights of
Heaven, cloud-enshrouded, riding upon the storm,
And made for the Trojan lines and Laurentine camp. Out of thin mist
She supernaturally fashioned a strengthless and insubstantial
Wraith, to look like Aeneas—a miracle apparition;
Hung it with Trojan weapons, faking the shield and the plumed
Helmet the hero wore; endowed it with lifelike tongue,
An automaton's speech; and made it mimic the gait of Aeneas.
It resembled the phantom figures that flit, they say, after death,

                                    [*Lines 605–641*]

Or the dream-images that seem real when we are sleeping.
Well, that figure gleefully stalked out in front of the fighters,
Provoking the foe with its weapons, uttering loud taunts.
Turnus went for it, hurled from a distance a whirring spear
At the phantom, which, wheeling about, retreated from him. Then
                                                            Turnus
Really believed that Aeneas had shirked a fight and was running.
Bemused by this, he began to nourish unjustified hopes:—
    Aeneas, where are you off to? Don't welsh on your marriage contract!
I'll give you the land you have crossed the seas to find—six feet of it.
    Turnus, shouting these words, and brandishing his sword, pursued,
Not knowing that what so thrilled him was only a *doppel-gänger*.
Now it happened a ship was lying, moored to the lofty side of
A rocky mole, with its gangway and rope-ladders all in position—
The ship which had brought king Osinius here from the shores of
                                                            Clusium.
This way the apparition of fleeing Aeneas hastened
And plunged into hiding. Turnus, following swift on its heels,
Surmounted all obstacles and bounded across the high gangway.
The instant he was aboard, Juno cut the cables
And whisked out the unmoored vessel upon a receding wave.
But Aeneas kept challenging the man who had vanished to fight him:
Many the foes he slew as he scoured the field after Turnus.
Then did his double, that tissue of air, try to hide no longer,
But soaring aloft was soon absorbed into the dark clouds.
Turnus, far out at sea now, was driven on by the gale:
He had no idea of the truth, no gratitude for his deliverance;
Kept looking back; stretched out both hands to heaven in prayer:—
    Father almighty, do I deserve to incur so grave
A reproach? to be punished so sorely? Was this your will and your
                                                            judgment?
Where and from what am I being taken? I cannot fathom
This running away, its means or its end. How can I face
Laurentum again, my town and stronghold? What of the men who
Followed my flag, all left to die?—such a death, I can't speak of it,
I'm so ashamed—all scattered now, I can see them and hear
Their groans as they fall. What am I to do? What grave would be
                                                            deep enough
Now to hide my dishonour? Oh, rather, you winds, take pity
    [*Lines 642–676*]

225

And dash this vessel on rock or reef—from my heart I implore you—
Pile it up on some merciless quicksand, anywhere
Beyond the ken of my people, the reach of my shameful story!
    So Turnus spoke, and his mind was all one surge and backwash—
Whether to fling himself on his sword in desperation
At such a disgrace, and drive the cruel blade through his ribs,
Or throw himself into the deepsea and try to swim back to the shore
Of the bay, so he might once more wade in at the Trojan soldiers.
Three times he began to attempt either alternative; three times
Great Juno held him back, and, pitying him, prevented it.
Onwards he went through the deep, with wave and current behind him,
Until he brought up at the ancient town of his father, Daunus.
Meanwhile, prompted by Juppiter, Mezentius dashingly took
Turnus' place in the fight and attacked the exultant Teucrians.
The Etruscans closed in upon him: with all their hatred, with all
Their fire-power they concentrated on him, on him alone.
He, like some rocky cliff that juts out into the wild sea,
Exposed to the tempests' fury and the full force of the waves,
Outstaying the threats, the concerted violence of sea and sky,
Standing immovable there—so Mezentius stood, and laid low
Hebrus, son of Dolichaon, Latagus, fleet-footed Palmus:
Latagus he got with a stone, a regular chunk of
Mountain, full in the mouth and face; while Palmus he hamstrung
And left to wallow disabled, giving his armour to Lausus
To wear on his own person and stick the plumes on his helmet.
He killed Evanthes, too, a Phrygian, and Mimas,
The friend and coeval of Paris, born to his mother, Theano,
And his father, Amycus, on the same night that Hecuba,
Pregnant with fire, gave birth to Paris: Paris, he sleeps
In his native soil; but Mimas is buried, a stranger, in Italy.
Now, like a boar which the hounds have driven down from the
                                                    mountains,
Snapping at his heels—a boar that has sheltered for years on pine-
                                                    crowned
Vesulus, or one that has skulked in the Laurentine fenland
Feeding upon the reed beds—but now it is in the toils of
The hunters, at bay, ferociously snorting, its shoulders bristling,
And none of them has the nerve to get his blood up and go closer,
But from a safe distance they assail it with yells and missiles—

[*Lines 677–713*]

Just so, of all who cherished a righteous wrath at Mezentius,
Not a single one had the courage to draw his sword and close with him;
No, they stood off, shouting, hurling weapons, baiting him.
But he, undaunted, unflurried, turned all ways to confront them,
Setting his teeth, while the spears bounced off his back like raindrops.
From the ancient township of Corythus had come a man of Greek
origin,
Acron, a refugee, who had left his betrothed there, unwed still.
Mezentius spotted him far off in the thick of the battle, wearing
His lady's favours—a purple garment and plumes of crimson.
Then, like a famishing lion which pads to and fro through the jungle,
As often happens, compelled by crazed hunger, and when he has
marked down
Some timorous goat, it may be, or a stag with its antlers pricked up,
Exults, huge jaws agape, hair standing on end, and crouches
Over the kill, claws deep in the flesh, his ravenous muzzle
Horribly steeped with gore—
Just so did Mezentius eagerly spring right into the thick of
The foe, and felled poor Acron, who dying drummed with his heels
On the darkening ground and stained with his blood the broken spear.
Mezentius now would not cheapen himself by killing Orodes,
Who was running away, with a spear-cast, a wound in the back:
instead,
He ran to cut off and meet him face to face, confronted him,
Mastered him, not by underhand means, but hand to hand.
Then he planted his foot on the fallen, strained at his spear, and cried:—
    Comrades, here lies tall Orodes, one of our biggest obstacles!
    His friends took up the cry of triumph with one great shout.
But the dying Orodes said:—
                    My death will be avenged.
You have not long to rejoice in your triumph, whoever you are;
For a like fate awaits you, the same earth shall cover you later.
    Now Mezentius, smiling but angry too, replied:—
    Die then! Leave my future to the father of gods and king
Of mortals!
                    With these words, he plucked his spear from the body.
Unkind repose, the iron sleep weighed down Orodes'
Eyes: his eyelids closed for everlasting night.
Caedicus slew Alcathous, Sacrator slew Hydaspes,
    [Lines 714–747]

227

Rapo slew Parthenius and the very powerful Orses;
Messapus slew Clonius and Erichaetes, the son of Lycaon—
The one while he lay on the ground, his bridleless steed having
stumbled,
The other in combat on foot. Agis, the Lycian, had ridden
Forward; but Valerus, skilled in the fighting mode of his fathers,
Unhorsed him. Thronius fell to Salius, he to Nealces
Famed both for javelin work and the arrow that kills at a distance.
  Now the hard hand of the War-god was dealing out impartially
Death and agony: either side had its ups and downs,
Its killings and fallen, alike; but neither dreamed of retreating.
In the halls of Jove the gods felt pity for all that pointless
Fury, to think that men should inflict such pains on their fellows.
Saturnian Juno and Venus sat, well apart, looking down
Where pale Tisiphone raged among the embattled armies.
But now Mezentius, shaking his mighty spear, strode forth
Over the field like some tornado. As great Orion
Moves forward, cleaving his way, with his feet treading the floor
Of the deepest mid-ocean, his shoulders overtopping the waves;
Or, when he's carrying back from the hills some venerable ash tree,
Walking upon the ground he buries his head in the cloud-base—
So, with his giant weapons, Mezentius advanced.
On the other side Aeneas, seeing him there in the long
Column, went out to meet him. Mezentius, undismayed,
Awaited his heroic foe, stood firm and massive:
Then, judging by eye the moment Aeneas would come within spear-
range:—

  May this right hand, which is god to me, and this spear I am poising
Bring me luck now! Lausus, I'll clothe you in armour stripped from
This brigand's corpse; you shall be a living trophy, I vow,
Of my victory over Aeneas.
                        He spoke. At long range his spear
Went whistling, but ricocheted from the shield of Aeneas to pierce
Good Antores, who stood nearby, between his thigh and his ribs—
Antores, a friend of Hercules, who had come on a mission from Argos,
Attached himself to Evander and settled in a town of Italy.
Felled by a weapon meant for another, he now gazed up at
The sky, and his last moments were filled with thoughts of dear Argos.
Aeneas the true then hurled his spear, which went through the convex

[*Lines 748–783*]

Triple-bronze face of the shield, its layers of linen, its innermost
Backing composed of threefold bull's-hide, and lodged low down
In Mezentius' groin; but it failed to drive home deep. So Aeneas,
Elated to see his enemy bleeding, promptly drew
His sword from its scabbard and went for the dazed man with furious
                                                          energy.
Lausus, seeing this happen, groaned deeply in sympathy
For his beloved father, and tears rolled down his cheeks.
How could I pass over in silence the heroic action of Lausus
And the hard death befell him?—he's worthy of fame, and we
May credit such deeds because long tradition allows us to do so.
Mezentius was giving ground, crippled and sorely encumbered,
With his enemy's spear, stuck fast in his shield, dragging behind him,
When Lausus, his son, leapt forward and intervened in the combat:
Just as Aeneas was rising on tiptoe to slash Mezentius,
Lausus thrust out his own sword, parried the blow, and held him
In check. His comrades hailed the action with a loud shout,
And while the father drew back under cover of Lausus' shield
They tried to beat off Aeneas with volleys of missiles fired
From a distance. Aeneas, baffled and angry, kept his guard up.
It was like when the storm-clouds burst, scattering down their shrapnel
Of hailstones; all the ploughmen and labourers have dispersed
Hurriedly from the fields, and the traveller is sheltering somewhere
In safety—beneath a river-bank, maybe, or a cornice of rock—
While the downpour drenches the earth; and they wait for the sun to
                                                          come back
And let them get on with their work. Aeneas, snowed under with missiles
From every angle, endured the blizzard of war and waited
For it to be spent, taunting and threatening Lausus the while:—
    Why rush upon death like this? You're too rash, fighting out of
                                                          your class;
And your loyalty's tempting you to your ruin.
                                        But Lausus continued
His crazy defiance. And now the Trojan commander's rage
Boiled up more deeply, now the Fate-spinners passed through their
                                                          fingers
The last threads of Lausus' life; yes, Aeneas drove his strong sword
Right through the young man's body, and buried it there to the hilt.
It penetrated his light shield, frail armour for so aggressive
    [*Lines 784–817*]

229

A lad, and the tunic his mother had woven of pliant gold,
And soaked it with blood from his breast. Then the soul left the body,
Passing sadly away through the air to the land of shadows.
But when Aeneas beheld the dying boy's look, his face—
A face that by now was strangely grey—he felt pity for him,
And a deep sigh escaped him; he stretched out his hand to Lausus,
Who had conjured up for his mind's eye a picture of filial devotion:—
   Poor lad, what now can I give you, to show how I honour your
                                       brave deed,
Or worthy of such a fine character? What can Aeneas do?
These arms you were so proud of, keep them; also, for what
It is worth, I give you back to the ashes and shades of your fathers.
At least it shall soften the edge of your piteous death for you,
That the great Aeneas caused it.
                       What's more, he rebuked the hesitant
Comrades of Lausus, and lifted the body, its neatly ordered
Hair befouled with blood, and gave it into their hands.
   Meantime, beside the stream of Tiber, the father of Lausus
Was cleansing his wound with water, as he reclined with his back
Propped up against a tree-trunk. His bronze helmet is hung
On a branch nearby, and his heavy accoutrements rest on the grass.
Round him the bodyguard stands: Mezentius, sick and gasping,
Eases his neck, and the beard flows down to cover his chest.
He keeps on asking about his son, keeps sending messengers
Bearing commands from an anxious sire to recall him from battle.
But Lausus' friends were bearing his lifeless body, in tears,
On his shield—a heroic lad laid low by a wound from a hero.
Mezentius, who had a premonition of evil, sensed
Their grief from afar. He sullied his grey hair with dust, extended
To heaven his clasped hands, and clung to his son's body:—
   My son, was I so eager to go on living that I
Allowed you to take my place, to take the enemy's sword—
You, my own son? Oh, that I should have been saved by these wounds!
Alive because you are dead! Ah, god, the bitterness
Of death comes home to me now at last! the wound goes deep!
For I have tarnished your name with my own disrepute, as well,
Since I was driven from the throne of my fathers in execration.
Long had I owed my country, my people who loathed me, atonement.
I was the guilty one. Would I had died a thousand deaths!
                             [*Lines 818–854*]

Instead, I live on, mankind and the light of day still unrelinquished.
But leave them I will.

                So saying, he struggles up onto his wounded
Thigh; and although the deep wound drains his strength and hampers
                                  him,
Will not give in, but orders his horse to be brought. His treasure
And comfort this animal was: he had ridden it out of every
Battle, victorious. Now he addressed the sorrowing beast:—
  Rhaebus, we have lived long, if anything can be called long
In human affairs. To-day you shall bear back triumphantly
Aeneas' head and his bloodstained armour, sharing with me
Revenge for the pangs of Lausus; or else, if that end is beyond
Our strength, we shall fall together. Brave steed, you would never
                                consent,
I know it, to have a new master—a Trojan, least of all.
  He spoke; then, mounting the beast and settling himself on its back
As so often he'd done, bronze helmet glinting and horse-hair plume
Flaunting, he took sharp-pointed lances in either hand.
Thus armed, he went into the fray at full gallop. His heart was seething
With deep shame and the very ecstasy of grief,
With love driven wild by loss, and awareness of his own valour.
Now he called out "Aeneas", in a loud voice, three times.
Aeneas recognised that voice, and prayed with a glad heart:—
  So may the Father of heaven and glorious Apollo grant it!
To it, then! Start the fight!
  Without more words, spear levelled, he went to meet Mezentius,
Who cried:—
                Do you think to frighten me, now you have taken my
                                  son,
You murderer? That was the only way you could really destroy me.
I'm not afraid of death, nor yet will I spare your gods.
Enough! I have come to die; but first, here are some presents
I've brought you.

                So saying, Mezentius hurled a spear at his foe,
Another then, and another, sending them in as he wheeled round
Aeneas in a wide circle; but the gold-bossed shield withstood them.
Three times he galloped, anti-clockwise, around his vigilant
Enemy, shooting: three times the Trojan hero pivoted,
His bronze shield bearing an ever-increasing harvest of javelins.
  [*Lines 855–887*]

Then, tired of these long-drawn defensive tactics and pulling out
                                                            spearpoints,

Finding himself hard-pressed in such an unequal combat,
Aeneas, after much thought, at last rushed forward and hurled
His spear, to strike Mezentius' charger right in the forehead.
The beast reared up and hung there; its forefeet pawed at the air,
Its rider was unseated: then the horse came down on top of him,
Pinned him, and lay there, its shoulder put out and its head drooping.
The shouts of Trojans and Latins roared like flames in the sky.
Aeneas ran up, unsheathed his sword, stood over Mezentius,
And said:—
                    Where is that hot-head Mezentius now, and all his
Brutal ferocity?
                    The Tuscan, recovering consciousness,
Gazing up at the sky, gulping the air, answered:—
   Harsh foe, you need not rail, or waste words on your deadly purpose.
No crime in killing: I never supposed there was, when I made war.
Mercy is not in the bond my Lausus made between us.
I ask but one thing—if the conquered has any right to a favour—
Allow my body interment. I know I'm beset by my people's
Bitter hatred. I ask you, protect my remains from their fury,
And let me rest in the same sepulchre as my son.
   He spoke, and deliberately offered his throat to the sword, and
                                                            received it.

His life went out in waves of blood all over his armour.
                                            [*Lines 888–908*]

BOOK XI

Night came and went. Aurora rose up, leaving the ocean.
Aeneas, although he felt a pressing duty to make time
For burying his friends, and was greatly distressed by the death of
Pallas,
First, at daybreak, fulfilled the vows he had made for victory.
Lopping the branches all round from a giant oak, he erects it
Upon a mound, and dresses the trunk with gleaming armour
He'd stripped from the enemy general, Mezentius, as a trophy
To the great War-god. He fastens up the blood-dabbled plumes,
The broken-off spears of his foe, the breastplate which had been struck
And pierced in twelve places; upon the left side he secures
The shield of bronze, and hangs from the neck the ivory scabbard.
Then, for his field commanders were all mustered around him
Closely, he made his triumphant comrades a rousing speech:—
    Gentlemen, we've performed our hardest task; for the rest
We need have no apprehension. Here are the spoils, our first-fruits,
From an insolent king, Mezentius: he's here in these arms my sword
won.
Now we must march on Latium's capital and king.
With courage make ready to fight, work out the war in your minds,
So that there'll be no hitch, no unpreparedness, the moment
The gods say   Lift your standards and lead the troops out of camp —
No delays through the over-caution that comes from a faltering
purpose.
But first, let us commit to earth our unburied comrades,
For that is the only honour the world of the dead acknowledges.
Go now, and pay your last respects to those gallant hearts
Who shed their blood to win us this Italy for our homeland:
Before anything else, convey to Evander's mourning city
The body of Pallas, our brave, good comrade, whom a dark day
Stole from us and plunged in the bitter waters of death.
    Thus spoke Aeneas, weeping; then he retired to his tent door
Where old Acoetes watched over the lifeless body of Pallas
[*Lines 1–30*]

233

Which had been laid there: Acoetes had served as squire to Evander
In the old days in Arcadia; but then, beneath a less fortunate
Star, he went as an aide to his dear foster-son, Pallas.
All the servants were gathered round, and a crowd of Trojans,
With Trojan women whose hair streamed loose in the manner of
                                                    mourning.

But when Aeneas entered the lofty door, they raised
To heaven a loud, long sound of keening, and beat their breasts;
The royal tent was one great moan of grief and wailing.
Aeneas, looking at Pallas' head on the pillow there,
The snow-white face, the open wound in his young breast
Made by the spear of Mezentius, spoke amid rising tears:—

   Poor lad, alas that Fortune, in the hour she smiled on me,
Grudged me one thing—your life—and would not let you behold
My kingdom or ride back to your father's home in triumph!
How different from all I promised Evander to do for you,
That day I left him, when he embraced me and sent me forth
To my imperial destiny! He felt some fear, and warned me
How dangerous was the foe, how tough the people I'd fight with.
This very moment—who knows?—quite beguiled by a groundless
                                                    hope,

He may be paying his vows and loading the altars with offerings;
While we, with mourning tributes useless to him, attend
Dead Pallas, who now owes nothing to any of the gods in heaven.
Evander, poor man, shall see his son buried, and break his heart.
So much for our triumphal return that he is awaiting!
So much for my solemn promise! But at least Evander will not
Look on a son wounded in cowardly flight, or pray for
A death made accursed by the son's living on in dishonour. Alas,
What a tower of strength is lost to Italy, lost to Ascanius!

   When he had made lamentation, Aeneas bade them lift up
The piteous corpse, and choosing a thousand men from his whole
Army, detailed them to form the solemn cortege and to share in
The tears of the bereaved Evander—small consolation
In such great grief, but one that was due to a sorrowing father.
Others quickly construct a resilient wickerwork bier,
Wattling switches of oak and shoots from the arbutus tree,
Then shade the built-up bier with a canopy of foliage.
Now they are laying young Pallas aloft on that country bed;

[Lines 31–67]

234

And he resembles a flower plucked by a girl's fingers—
A gentle violet, perhaps, or a fainting hyacinth—
Whose sheen and shape are not yet lost, not yet departed,
Though mother earth no longer can give it sap or strength.
Aeneas now brought out two purple robes that were richly
Brocaded in golden thread: Sidonian Dido had made them
With her own hands, in the old days, interweaving the fabric
With threads of gold, and giving all her heart to the work.
In one of these robes he sadly wrapped Pallas—a farewell gesture,
Hooding with it the hair that would soon be burned to ashes:
He made a great heap, as well, of spoil they had won in the battle
Against the Laurentines, and had it borne in a long procession—
Horses and weapons, too, they had taken from the enemy.
Manacled captives there were, consigned to be gifts to the dead—
Victims whose blood would be sprinkled upon the altar flames.
He bade the leaders themselves to carry tree-trunks adorned with
Enemy armour, the names of the fallen foes attached to them.
Forlorn Acoetes, feeble and old, was supported along,
Beating his breast with his fists, tearing his cheeks with his nails,
And often prostrating himself full length upon the ground.
There were chariots in the cortege, splashed with Italian blood.
Behind them paced Pallas' war-horse, Aethon, without its trappings:
It wept as it walked—yes, big tears were rolling down its muzzle.
Others bore the helmet and spear of Pallas; the rest of
His armour, victorious Turnus had taken. Now followed a phalanx
Of mourners—Trojans, all the Etruscans, Arcadians bearing
Their arms reversed. When the files of his comrades had gone some
distance
Forward, Aeneas stopped, sighed heavily, then spoke:—
   The same dread fate of war summons me hence to weep
For other dead. Brave Pallas, salute for evermore!
For evermore, farewell!
                    Aeneas said nothing further,
But turned towards the ramparts and made his way into camp.
   Envoys had just arrived from the capital of Latium,
Decked in olive branches and bringing a plea that Aeneas
Hand over to them their fallen, whose bodies lay everywhere
On the field, and let them bury the dead in a common grave:
One could have no quarrel, they said, with men defeated and lifeless;
   [*Lines 68–104*]

235

They'd once been his hosts, had promised his men their daughters,
                                                    and therefore
He should show mercy. Aeneas courteously granted the plea—
He could not well reject it—and said these words besides:—
    It was indeed a malignant fate that involved you Latins
In such a terrible war, and caused you to flout our friendship.
You ask me to make peace with the dead, whom the fortunes of battle
Have killed: believe me, I'd like to make peace with the living equally.
I would not be here, but that destiny said it should be my home.
It is not your people that I'm at war with, only your king,
Who broke off relations with me, put faith in the weapons of Turnus.
Fairer if Turnus had stayed to face the death which your friends met.
If he's so keen to force an issue and drive out us Trojans
By fighting, he ought to have met me here in single combat:
The better man, or the one heaven favoured, would have survived.
Go now, and burn your unfortunate comrades upon the pyre.
    Aeneas had spoken. The envoys were taken aback, could find nothing
To say for a while, but silently searched one another's faces.
Then Drances, an old man, no friend to the young prince, Turnus,
Who always indulged his dislike by speaking against him, began
To answer Aeneas thus:—
                                    Sir Trojan, great your fame
And greater your deeds. What words can I find to extol your glory?
Your fairness, your feats in battle—which is the more remarkable?
Most gladly we shall report in our city what you have just said:
Moreover, if circumstance makes it possible, we shall unite you
With king Latinus. Let Turnus look for his own alliances.
Nay, we'll delight to help you build the great walls of your destined
City, and bear on our shoulders the stones for the second Troy.
    So Drances spoke, and his colleagues all voiced their entire agreement.
A twelve-day truce was arranged; under its mediation
Trojans and Latins wandered amicably together
Over the wooded heights. Ash trees rang with the blows
Of axes, and the soaring spires of pine trees were felled;
There was no end to the splitting of oakwood and fragrant cedar
With wedges, the carting away of rowans in creaking wagons.
    And now winged Rumour came, first herald of great grief,
To Evander's ears, to his palace and all his city—Rumour
                                              [*Lines 105–140*]

236

D.W.Whitfield.

Which only just now was reporting that Pallas had beaten the Latins.
Hurriedly seizing funeral torches—an antique custom—
The Arcadians ran to their gates: the long, torchlight procession
They formed shone like a broad parting across the fields.
The Trojan cortege moved on to meet them: the mourning columns
Merged into one. When the mothers saw it enter the city,
Their shrieking ran like wildfire through the afflicted streets.
No force on earth could restrain Evander now. He rushed out
Into the crowds, and as soon as the bier was set down, prostrated
Himself upon Pallas, clung to the body, weeping and moaning.
For a while grief choked him: at last he just managed to find his voice:—
    Oh, Pallas, this was not the promise you gave your father—
That you'd be careful how you ventured into the grim fight!
But I knew too well how great is the lure of glory in battle
For a young man, how sweet to win fame in his first engagement.
Bitter your youth's first-fruits, harsh your initiation
Into this war so near home! Alas that not one of the gods
Gave ear to my vows and prayers! My blessed wife, how lucky
You were to die before such anguish could come upon you!
But I have lived on, exceeding my natural term—lived on
For what?—to survive my own son. Why didn't I march with our
                                                              Trojan
Allies, and fall to the enemy's fire? Would *I* had perished,
And this cortege was carrying me, not Pallas, home!
Yet, Trojans, don't think I am blaming you, or our pact, or the joining
Of our right hands in friendship. What has happened—fate surely had it
In store for my old age. But though an untimely death
Was awaiting my son, I'll be proud that he died leading the Teucrians
Into Latium, with thousands of enemy dead to his credit.
Besides, I could not grace you with a worthier funeral, Pallas,
Than this which Aeneas the true, the mighty Trojans, the generals
Of the Etruscans and their whole army are giving you.
They bear great trophies, symbols of those who fell by your hand.
You too, Turnus, would be here—a trophy, a giant tree-trunk
Adorned with arms—had your age and the strength of your years
                                                      been no more than
My son's. But why do I let my own tragedy keep you Trojans
From war? Go forth, and forget not to take back these words to your
                                                              king;

[*Lines 141–176*]

237

Tell him I linger on, though I care not for life now Pallas
Is gone, to receive the debt which he knows is owing to father
And son—vengeance on Turnus: it's the sole task that remains for
His courage and luck to accomplish. I ask it, not to gladden
My life—that were wrong—but to bring the good news to my son in
                                                    the Underworld.

Meanwhile Aurora had lifted her cordial light above
Suffering humanity, and the daily round began again.
Pyres were built up on the shore of the bay by lord Aeneas
And Tarchon now. Each, after his own traditional usage,
Brought hither his dead. They applied to the pyres the funereal torches,
And smoke rolled up, spreading out and palling the sky above.
Clad in their gleaming accoutrements, they marched three times around
The blazing pyres: three times they circled the melancholy
Flames of the dead, on horseback, and uttered the cries of mourning.
With tears the earth was sprinkled, their armour was wet with tears.
A lamentation of men arose, and a bray of trumpets.
Now some of them threw on the flames equipment which had been
                                                    taken
From the enemy dead—helmets, fine swords, bridles, and chariot
Wheels that had scorched into battle; while others were throwing the
                                                    shields
And unlucky weapons of their own fallen—familiar objects.
They were sacrificing oxen all round to the god of death,
Slaughtering bristle-haired swine and sheep, for which they had scoured
The countryside, to lay on the burning pyres. The whole length of
The shore, they look at their comrades burning, keep watch beside
Those charred pyres: nothing can drag them away, till dewy night
Unrolls a heaven thickly jewelled with sparkling stars.

Some distance off, the dejected Italians too had built
Countless funeral pyres: such numbers of dead there were,
They buried some on the spot, lifted up others and bore them
Into adjacent fields or sent them back to their city;
While for the rest, a huge indiscriminate pile of corpses—
They burnt them, uncounted, anonymous. All round about, the desolate
Countryside was dotted with pyre after blazing pyre.
When a third dawn had peeled the chill darkness off the sky,
Sadly they swept the ashes and bones into a heap from
The smouldering pyres, and built up a barrow of still-warm earth
                                    [*Lines 177–212*]

238

Above them. But in the houses of wealthy Latinus' city
The noise of mourning was loudest, greatest the long-drawn agony.
Mothers, sick-hearted brides, loved sisters bewailing their brothers,
Children whose fathers had fallen, here in the city were cursing
The war that had brought them ruin, the betrothal of Turnus that
                                                            caused it.
Let him who claims for himself this realm and sovereign power here—
Let him, they cry, decide the issue in single combat.
Drances aggravates this vindictively, making it known
That Turnus, and Turnus alone, is called on, is challenged to fight.
All the same, there was much support for Turnus, expressed in
Various arguments: the queen's great name protected him;
Also, his fame and the trophies he'd won told in his favour.
   In the middle of these cross-currents, when partisan feeling had
                                                            reached
High pressure, to crown it all, the envoys returned with their answer
From Diomed's city, in deep depression. For all the pains
They had taken, they'd got nowhere: Diomed was impervious
To presents, to gold, to urgent entreaties; he said the Latins
Must look for allies elsewhere, or come to terms with Aeneas.
Latinus himself collapsed under his load of anguish:
The wrath of the gods, the new graves in front of his eyes, told him
Heaven's will was beyond dispute and Aeneas had fate behind him.
Therefore Latinus convened a privy council, commanding
The foremost of his people to appear in his lofty palace.
They came together, their numbers crowding the streets as they flocked
To the royal home. Latinus, the eldest and wielding supreme
Authority, sat in their midst, a gloomy look on his face.
And now he bade the envoys returned from the Aetolian
City to make their report, and to set out in full detail
What Diomed had replied. Absolute silence followed
As Venulus, obeying the king, began to speak:—
   Citizens, we accomplished our journey, surmounting all its
Hazards: we saw Diomed in his Argive settlement,
And pressed the hand which wiped out the country of Ilium.
He was building a city, Arpi, named after his father's people,
On land he had won in war round about Apulian Garganus.
Entering his palace, we sought and were given a personal interview:
So we presented our gifts to him, told him our names and nation,

[*Lines 213–249*]

What had brought us to Arpi and who had invaded our country.
Diomed heard us out, then replied, with an equable mien:—
You people of ancient Italy, from the kingdom of old Saturn,
So blessed by fortune, what ill wind is troubling your calm regime
And driving you to provoke war, who have no experience in warfare?
All we who profaned with the sword the land of Ilium—I leave
Aside what we went through during the battles beneath Troy's walls,
And our heroic dead engulfed in the Simois—all of us
Suffered condign and terrible retribution, wherever
We went, so that even Priam must pity us: look at the storm that
Wrathful Athene raised, wrecking Ajax on Cape Caphereus
In Euboea. After that war, driven to wide-apart coasts,
Menelaus, the son of Atreus, was exiled far away
At the pillars of Proteus, Ulysses beheld the Cyclops of Aetna.
Neoptolemus' kingdom partitioned, Idomeneus' home broken up—
Why talk of them?—or the Locrians compelled to settle in Africa?
Agamemnon himself, the leader of our Greek expedition,
Fell at the hands of his damnable wife in the first hour of
His homecoming, for an adulterer lurked behind conquered Asia.
Look how the gods have grudged me a sight of the wife I long for
And beautiful Calydon—stopped me returning to my home altars!
Even now I'm pursued by things of ill omen, dreadful
To look at: my own lost comrades, changed into birds, made off
To the sky—an uncanny retribution they suffer, haunting
The streams, and the cliffs are loud with their melancholy cries.
What else could I expect but horrors such as these
From the moment I raised my sword to the person of a divinity,
Wounding the hand of Venus, committing a sacrilege on her?
No, no, don't push me into another war like that!
No quarrel have I with the Teucrians since Troy's annihilation,
Nor does it give me pleasure to recall those bad old days.
As for the presents you've brought me out of your native land—
Give them instead to Aeneas. We've faced his tigerish weapons,
Have met him hand to hand. Believe me, I know from experience
How he springs at you, with his shield up, how his spear comes at
        you like
A hurricane. If two other champions of equal calibre
Had risen in Troyland, the Dardans would have stormed up to the
        cities

[*Lines 250–286*]

Of Greece—aye, fate had changed sides and it's Greece would be
mourning to-day.
That we stayed so long investing the walls of stubborn Troy,
That victory kept on eluding the Greeks and came not until
The tenth year, was due to the efforts of Hector and Aeneas.
Both were outstanding in courage and feats of arms; but the latter
Stood first in devotion of heart. I advise you, make terms with him
As best you may: don't risk fighting it out on the battlefield.
Good king, you have heard the reply king Diomed sent, and with it
The views he expressed about this great war that we are engaged in.

The envoys had barely finished, when a mutter of conflicting
Comment arose among the uneasy Italians: so, when
A torrent is checked by boulders, it frets against them and babbles,
And the banks on either side resound with chattering water.
As soon as they had calmed down and their anxious murmurs were
silenced,
The king, first invoking heaven, spoke from his lofty throne:—
I could wish, and it would have been better, gentlemen, that we
had reached
Some decision ere now on so crucial a matter—not had to call
A meeting at a time like this, when the enemy's at our gates.
We are waging an ill-advised war, fellow-citizens, with a people
Of heavenly descent, unconquerable: no amount of fighting
Wears them down; though beaten, they never relinquish the sword.
If you had any hopes of an armed alliance with the Aetolians,
Resign them. Our only hope is in ourselves, and you see
How slim it is. That, apart from Diomed's refusal,
Our fortunes are a total wreck, is plain and palpable.
I am not blaming anyone: whatever a people's valour
Could do, was done: our realm put all it had into the struggle.
Give me your close attention while I explain briefly
What seems to me, though I'm not sure, best to do in our present
dilemma.
I possess land along the Tiber—it's been Crown property
From ancient times—stretching westwards far, right up to and over
The Sicilians' frontier: Auruncans and Rutuli farm it, working
The stony hills with the plough and grazing their roughest slopes.
Let us cede the whole of this area, with its pine-covered mountain
ridge,

[*Lines 287–320*]

241

To gain the goodwill of the Trojans. Let us draw up a treaty, fair to
Both sides, and invite them to partner us in the kingdom.
If they want it so much, let them found a city and settle down here.
But if they intend to possess themselves of the land of some other
Nation, and are at liberty to leave this soil of ours,
Let us build them twenty ships of Italian oak—or more,
If they can man them: all the raw material lies
At the water's edge; they can say what class of ships and how many
They want: we will supply the bronze, the labour, the shipyards.
Further, to take our proposals and ratify the agreement,
I would send a hundred envoys, men of our most distinguished
Families: they should offer the olive branch to Aeneas,
Bearing as presents gold and ivory, a talent of each,
With the chair and purple robe—the insignia of my kingship.
Now express your own views. Our affairs are desperate. You must
                                                    mend them.

   Then Drances, hostile as ever to Turnus, whose high renown
Pin-pricked him with sour envy to intrigue against him—a man
Influential through his wealth, an able speaker, but no
Lion at fighting; one whose advice in debate was accounted
Weighty; a force in political faction—(his well-born mother
Gave him great pride of race; there was nothing to say of his father)—
Drances got up, and stoked the high feeling there with a speech:—
   Your gracious Majesty, the issue you ask our advice on
Is crystal-clear and does not require our comments. Everyone
Admittedly knows what this crisis demands, but they shrink from
                                                    expressing it.
Let *him* but allow us to speak and refrain from his usual blustering,
Him whose unlucky star and perverseness of mind have caused—
No, I *will* speak, though he mortally menaces me with his violence—
Have caused the death of so many of our brightest captains, and
                                                    drowned
The whole city in mourning, while he, confident of his own get-away,
Attacked the Trojan encampment and scared with his weapons the
                                                    blue sky.
You should add one more to those many presents you bid us take
And promise to the Dardan people—just one thing more, most gracious
Of kings; and let not anyone's intransigeance have the power to
Prevent you giving your daughter in honourable marriage

                              [*Lines 321–355*]

242

To an excellent man, thus cementing a peace between us for ever.
But if our hearts and minds are obsessed by terror of Turnus,
Let us implore and beseech him in his infinite grace to stand down,
And restore to his king and country the marriage-rights he lays claim to.
O head and source of these disasters to Latium, why
Are you always thrusting her luckless folk into obvious peril?
Fighting will not save us: it's peace that we all demand of you,
Turnus, and with it the one pledge of peace that cannot be broken.
I, whom you claim to be hostile to you—well, what if I am?—
I take the lead in imploring you—look at me! Pity your people!
Strip off your pride! Admit yourself beaten, and go! We have seen
Enough deaths, in this rout, have unpopulated our countryside.
But, if you lust for glory, if you're so hardy of heart,
And if you're so set upon a royal bride, a king's palace,
Be bold, trust in your own strength, and face Aeneas in combat.
Good god! are we, we no-account souls, to litter the plains,
A multitude unburied and unmourned, so that Turnus
May marry the heir to the throne? Yes, you, if you've anything in you,
Any of the fighting spirit of your fathers, look at me, answer
My challenge!
     The impulsive, intransigeant Turnus blazed up in rage at this speech:
He gave a groan of anger, then passionately broke out:—
     Words, words, words! You've always plenty of them, Drances,
When war is asking for deeds. Let a council be summoned, and you
Are the first to appear. But we don't want big talk from an armchair

                                                                          critic
Like you just now in this House, while our battlements still keep
The foe at arm's length, and the moat is not yet swimming in blood.
Go pounding on with your usual rhetoric, and accuse me
Of cowardice, Drances—you whose strong right hand has inflicted
Such wonderful slaughter upon the Trojans, and set up notable
Trophies all over the battlefield. There's nothing to stop you trying
What real courage can do: you needn't go far, I assure you,
To find the enemy; they are massed all round our walls.
Are we going to meet them? What, no move from you? Is your

                                                                      bellicose
Spirit permanently confined to a windy tongue and a
Clean pair of heels?
     [*Lines 356–391*]

243

So I'm to "admit myself beaten"? You clot, could anyone really
Argue I'm beaten, after he'd seen the Tiber in spate with
Trojan blood, and the whole house of Evander prostrate,
Root and branch, and his Arcadians stripped of their arms?
Bitias and huge Pandarus did not find me a weakling,
Nor the countless men my conquering arm despatched to Hades
When I was shut up in the enemy's walls, with their ramparts around
me.

"Fighting will not save us": you're raving! Keep those morbid
Forecasts for yourself and Aeneas! Ah, go on creating
Alarm and despondency everywhere, cracking up the immense strength
Of a twice-conquered nation and slandering our own army!
You'll be telling us next the Myrmidon generals are all quaking
At the Phrygian forces—Diomed and Larissaean Achilles—
And Aufidus river is scampering back from the Adriatic.
Yes, and look how this artist in scheming gives out he's in terror of
threats

From me, thus using fear to sharpen the edge of his calumny!
Don't be alarmed, I would never degrade myself by taking
A life like yours: you can keep it, tucked up in your cowardly breast.
Now, sire, I revert to you and the problems you've laid before us.
If you have no more faith in the armed forces, if we
Are really abandoned by all, if to suffer a single reverse
Means our whole cause is lost and there's no chance of recovery,
Then let us lay down our arms and helplessly sue for peace.
Yet I would that some gleam of our traditional valour would show
itself!

I would esteem that man most fortunate in his exertions
And noblest in soul of us all, who, rather than witness so shameful
An end, has fallen and died, has bit the dust once for all.
But suppose we have resources and manpower still untapped,
Potential allies left among the peoples of Italy;
Suppose, too, that the Trojans have paid for success with heavy
Losses—they had their dead all right, the same storm blasted
Both sides:—then why are we fainting in the first lap of the war
And disgracing ourselves? Why tremble before the trumpet has blown?
Time, and man's versatile efforts over the shifting years,
Have often changed things for the better: fortune's vicissitudes
Make fools of us often, and then set our feet again upon firm ground.

[*Lines 392–427*]

Diomed and his Aetolians will give us no help, you say:
Yes, but we have Messapus and heaven's favourite, Tolumnius,
And captains sent by many peoples; great glory, too,
Will attend the flower of Latium and the Laurentine fields.
Then there's Camilla, from the illustrious Volscian nation,
Leading her regiment of horse, her squadrons blooming in bronze.
But if the Trojans demand to fight with none but me—
If such is your will, and otherwise I'm ruinous to our cause—
Victory has not been such a total stranger to me that
I'd refuse any venture which held out such great possibilities.
Though he's Achilles' equal and carries weapons, as he did,
Made by Vulcan himself, I'll go out and face Aeneas
With all my heart. I, Turnus, second in courage to none of
Our ancestors, solemnly vow my life to you and Latinus
Whose son I would be. Aeneas challenges me alone?—
I welcome it. Whether it's heaven's wrath or honour and glory that's
                                                              in it,
I would not let Drances be martyr to one or crowned with the other.
    So the Italians were hotly debating these controversial
Issues. Meanwhile Aeneas moved out of camp and advanced.
Through the palace a messenger hurried, spreading great consternation
Around him, so that the whole town was seized with panic: he said
The Trojans and the Etruscan forces were sweeping down from
The Tiber in battle formation, deploying across the plain.
At once the populace rose up, their minds in confusion, their feelings
Shocked, but their temper aroused by strenuous excitement.
Wildly they clamour for action. To arms! the young men shout;
While the senators gloomily weep and mutter. A monstrous din
Went up now all over the town as men argued and wrangled together:
So it is when a flock of birds have alighted upon
The tree-tops in some wood, or the fish-haunted river Padusa
Resounds with the harsh screaming of swans till its pools are a bedlam.
Turnus, seizing the opportunity, cried:—
                                        Fellow-citizens,
Talk on—that's right—and tamely sing the praises of peace,
Though the enemy's launched an offensive against us!
                                        Without a word more
He whirled away and ran out from the high-vaulted chamber:—
    Volusus, order the Volscian squadrons to stand to arms,
    [Lines 428–463]

245

And lead forth the Rutuli! Messapus, Coras and your brother,
Get your cavalry moving, deploy them out in the open!
Let every approach to the city be blocked, and the turrets manned!
The rest will be under my orders, to counter-attack where I tell them.
    At once from all over the city they raced up to line the battlements.
Meanwhile Latinus adjourned the meeting and left, postponing
His grand design, depressed and upset by what had just happened:
He censured himself severely for not accepting Aeneas
Of his own free will, or attaching him to the Crown through marriage.
Now they are digging trenches in front of the gates and bringing up
Stones and stakes. The hoarse trumpet blares the alarum for bloody
Battle. Around the walls there is stretched a motley chain
Of women and boys; the supreme ordeal calls upon everyone.
Now, a great throng of mothers about her, the queen is driving
Uphill to the temple and heights of Pallas Athene: she bears
Offerings, and has beside her the girl, Lavinia, the cause of
These terrible evils, sitting with eyes prettily downcast.
The mothers pass into the temple, fill it with smoke of incense,
And mournfully utter a prayer as they stand at the door of the
                                                            sanctuary:—

    O puissant in arms, O regent of war, Tritonian maiden,
Break with your hand the spear of the Trojan marauder, and lay him
Prostrate upon our soil, yea, let him fall in the gateway!
    Turnus, enraged, is eagerly girding himself for battle.
Now he has donned the breastplate whose scales of rugged bronze
Glow like embers, and fastened the gold greaves on his legs:
Head still unhelmeted, he has strapped the sword to his side
And is running down from the citadel heights, a flash of gold,
And exults in anticipation of coming to grips with the enemy.
So, when a horse has broken its tether and galloped away from
The paddock, free at last, out on the open plains,
Look how he makes for the meadow where herds of mares are grazing,
Or else he plunges into some well-known stream, as he loves to,
Then leaps out, and throwing his muzzle high, so the mane is tossed
Over neck and shoulders, he whinnies in wild exhilaration!
Camilla hastened to meet him, leading the Volscian squadrons:
Right at the gate the princess jumped down from her horse, and the
                                                                whole
Contingent, taking their cue from her, dismounted smartly

[*Lines 464–500*]

And stood beside their horses: then did Camilla say:—
    Turnus, the brave are surely entitled to feel self-confidence;
Therefore I dare and I promise to engage the mounted brigade of
Aeneas, and meet the Etruscan cavalry single-handed.
Let me be the first to encounter the hazards of war, while you
Remain with the infantry here and guard the walls of the town.
    Eyes fixed on the redoubtable Camilla, Turnus answered:—
Princess, Italy's proud of you. How can I ever express
Or prove my gratitude? But I know your spirit's above
All thoughts of recompense, so share this task with me.—
I had got wind, and now my reconnaissance has confirmed it,
That Aeneas has actually thrown forward a wave of light-armed
Horsemen to sweep the plain, while he moves on the town himself
Over the deserted mountain heights, through a pass.
I am planning an ambush, to block both ends of the glen with troops
Where his route is a sunken road through heavily-wooded terrain.
You are to meet the Etruscan cavalry and engage them:
You will have the gallant Messapus with you, the Latin squadrons
And the troops of Tiburtus. Take over command, and thus share the
                                      task with me.
    So saying, he briefed Messapus and the other allied commanders
In similar terms for the fight, then moved against the enemy.
There is a winding glen, a place cut out for ambush
And bloody stratagems: hill-slopes enclose it on either flank,
Darkening it with dense leafage: to reach it, you pass down a narrow
Track, through a bottleneck—a nasty, confined approach.
Overlooking this from above, at the summit on either side,
Are plateaux, invisible from beneath—a sound position
Whether you wanted to charge down the slopes at the enemy's flanks
Or to sit tight on the ridge and roll down boulders upon him.
Turnus arrived at this spot by a route he knew well, occupied it,
Disposed his men in the woods there—a dangerous threat to Aeneas.
    Meanwhile, in the abodes of heaven above, Diana
Was speaking to swift-footed Opis, one of the sacred band
Of nymphs who attended her, and in a despondent tone
Was saying:—
             Camilla goes forth to war and its savagery.
She's dear to me, girl, beyond all others; and yet our weapons
She's girding on cannot save her. Ah yes, this is no new love,
   [*Lines 501–537*]

247

Shaking the heart with sweet surprise, that I am feeling.
Listen. When Metabus left the ancient town of Privernum,
Expelled by the people, who hated his tyrannous use of power,
He smuggled out with him, as he fled through the street-fighting,
His baby daughter, to be a companion in exile; he named her
After her mother, Casmilla, just changing the name to Camilla.
Carrying her against his breast, he made for the mountains—
A long ridge, wooded and lonely: pursuers were close behind him,
And Volscian soldiers were skimming round to cut off his retreat.
All at once, as he fled, there was the Amasenus
In front of him, running bank-high, in full spate after a recent
Cloudburst. He is eager to swim for it, but is held back
By love and fear for the infant he tenderly carries. Casting
About in his mind, of a sudden this desperate remedy dawns on him:
Taking the mighty spear he had with him for self-defence—
A solid, gnarled, well-seasoned piece of wood—he fastened
The baby to its shaft, cocooning her first in bark
From a cork tree, and fixed her right at its point of balance for
                                                                throwing;
Then poised the spear in his huge hand, praying aloud to heaven:—
    O kindly Diana the Virgin, patron of woodlands, I,
Her father, vow this child to your service. Yours the first weapon
She holds to, a suppliant, fleeing the foe. I invoke you, O goddess—
Accept her for yours, whom now I commit to the chancy breezes.
    So saying, he drew back his arm and sent the spearshaft spinning.
The waters roared beneath: over the racing river
The spear went whirring; upon it, hurtled poor little Camilla.
But Metabus, since a great pack of pursuers was now drawing closer,
Dived into the stream, and triumphantly plucked from the turf on
                                                                the far side
The spear, with his babe still attached—his present to Diana.
No city offered him home or shelter: he'd not have accepted it
Anyway, being averse to civilisation: instead
He lived out his life among shepherds in desolate mountain country.
Here, in the thickets, the tangled coverts where wild beasts prowled,
He nursed the baby girl on milk drawn from the breast of
A brood-mare, milking the teats into her delicate mouth.
But as soon as the child had found her feet and learnt to walk,
Metabus put a pointed javelin in her hand

[Lines 538–574]

248

And slung a bow and a quiver across her little shoulder.
Instead of a golden clasp for her locks, and a trailing robe,
A tiger-skin hooded her hair and cloaked her from head to foot.
Even then, her soft, child's hand could hurl miniature weapons;
And, whirling the sling around her head by its twisted thong,
She could bring down a white swan or a crane from the river Strymon.
There were many mothers in the Etruscan cities who vainly
Sighed for her as a daughter. She was well pleased to serve
Diana alone, to remain a virgin for ever, worshipping
Chastity and the chase. Would she had not succumbed to
Desire for such service as this, or attempted to challenge the Trojans!
Then she'd be one of my train still, and I could love and protect her.
But come, since a bitter, untimely doom is surely upon her,
Glide down from the sky, Opis, and visit the land of Latium
Where, under no lucky star for her, grim battle is toward.
Take my bow and quiver: draw out an avenging arrow:
With it, exact retribution in blood for me from the man who
Wounds and profanes her hallowed flesh—Italian or Trojan.
Then I shall bear away in the womb of a cloud her piteous
Body, her weapons intact, to a grave in her own country.
    Diana had spoken. Opis swooped rustling down from above
Through the light airs of heaven, wrapped in a dark storm-cloud.
    Meantime the enemy force approaches the walls of Latium—
The whole brigade of cavalry, with its Etruscan officers,
Moving in squadron formation. Over the plain's expanse
The chargers prance and neigh, swerving this way and that
As they fight the restraining curb. The field is all iron, one endless
Bristle of lances; the plains flash with uplifted weapons.
Against them move Messapus, the swift-riding Latins, Coras
With his brother, and the wing led by the maiden Camilla:
These now emerge on the plain and range themselves opposite; hands
                                                   drawn
Well back, they hold the lance in rest or brandish the javelin.
Warriors advancing, horses neighing—the moment kindles.
And now each side had moved forward into spear-range, and there
Halted. Then with a sudden yell they all charged, spurring
Their maddened horses, and hurled as they charged volleys of weapons
Which stormed as thick as a blizzard, darkening the very sky.
Tyrrhenus and gallant Aconteus rode each at the other incontinent,
  [*Lines 575-612*]

249

Lances in rest; were the first to meet, to crash with a noise like
Thunder, and fall: their horses collided, head on, so that breast
Was broken and shattered on breast: the impact unseated Aconteus
And hurled him afar, like a meteorite or a great stone fired
From a catapult; he died before he hit the ground.
At once the formations were thrown into disorder: the Latins
Wheeled round and galloped towards the walls, with their shields
behind them.
The Trojans pursued hotly, Asilas leading their squadrons.
Then, as they neared the gates, the Latins raised the war-cry
Again, and pulled at the sinuous necks of their horses, to turn them.
So now the Trojans went back a long way in flight, with loose reins.
It was like the to-fro rhythm of the sea, when a wave runs forward,
Comes charging against the shore, rides over the rocks in a smother
Of spray, and drenches the sand far up on the beach where the swell
breaks;
Then rapidly draws away, the force of its undertow sucking
The pebbles back, swirls out, grows shallow, is gone from the shore.
Twice the Etruscans drove to the walls the fleeing Rutuli,
Twice galloped back, looking over their shoulders, with shields held
behind
For protection. But when the opposing forces clashed for a third time,
The lines were locked together, and each man marked his man:
Then the groans of the dying were heard—it was all a welter of blood,
A tangle of weapons and bodies, with mortally-wounded horses
Plunging amid dead riders: bitterly swelled the struggle.
Orsilochus dared not meet Remulus hand to hand,
But threw a spear at his charger, which lodged under its ear:
Driven mad by the blow, the unendurable pain of this wound,
The horse reared up its great chest, its forelegs thrashing the air,
And Remulus was hurled to the ground. Catillus struck down
Iollas and Herminius—a man of great courage, a giant
In shoulder and trunk, whose auburn hair was unhelmeted
And his shoulders bare; he had no terror of wounds, so much
Of himself he exposed to the enemy. Driven through his broad
shoulders,
The spear stuck, quivering, and doubled him up with agony.
Everywhere streams the dark blood. They struggle; they deal out doom
With the sword, and offer themselves to a glorious death in the combat.

[*Lines 613–647*]

250

Right in the thick of the slaughter, with one breast bared for the fray,
Like an Amazon was exulting the archeress, Camilla.
Now she delivers a quick fire of whippy javelins, now
Unwearied she whirls a powerful battle-axe with her right hand.
Tapping her shoulder, hung the gold bow, Diana's weapon.
Even when she was driven back and in flight, she loosed
Her shafts at the foe as she fled, turning the bow round to shoot them.
Her bodyguard kept close about her—the maiden Larina,
Tulla, Tarpeia who brandished a battle-axe of bronze—
Italian girls, whom the godlike Camilla had chosen to grace her
Retinue: good supporters they were in peace and in war.
They resembled the Amazon women of Thrace when they go to battle
In blazoned armour, their horse-hooves stamping the frozen river
Thermodon, escorting queen Hippolyta, or the martial
Penthesilea when she returns from a war in her chariot,
A woman-host with crescent-shaped bucklers screaming around her
In triumph. Ferocious Camilla, whom first did your hand lay low,
Whom last? How many men did you strike to the earth, dying?
Euneus was the first, Clytius' son: her long
Pinewood spear crashed through his unguarded chest as he faced her:
Coughing up streams of blood, Euneus fell; he bit
The ensanguined earth, and dying, he spun round on his wound.
Next she killed Liris, and Pagasus over him: one had been thrown
When his horse was stabbed in the belly, and was gathering up the
                                                                    reins;
The other was stretching his free hand to help the dazed man to his
                                                                    feet:
Side by side they fell headlong. Camilla killed, too, Amastrus,
Hippotas' son, and flung spears with a long follow-through from a
                                                                    distance
At Tereus and Harpalycus, Demophoon and Chromis:
For every single missile the princess aimed and threw,
A Phrygian warrior fell. Far off, queerly accoutred,
Was riding the hunter, Ornytus, upon his Apulian steed:
He wore for battle the hide of a bullock swathed about his
Broad shoulders, while his head was helmeted in a wolf's mask
Whose gaping mouth with its white-fanged jaws served for a visor:
A rustic hunting spear was his weapon. Ornytus turned,
With horsemen everywhere round him, overtopping all by a head.
    [*Lines 648–683*]

251

She caught him—no difficult task in the jam of a routed formation,
Pierced him, and over his body spoke these unmerciful words:—

Did you think you were hunting game in your own forest, Etruscan?
The day has come when a woman's weapons shall hurl your people's
Boasting back in their teeth. Never mind, you will go to the shades of
Your fathers with one piece of glory—you fell by the hand of Camilla.

Next she killed Orsilochus and Butes, two great champions
Of Troy. Butes she hit with a spear, while he was turned
Away, just where the rider's neck showed between helmet
And breastplate, where the shield hangs down from the left shoulder.
Orsilochus she fled from, riding in a wide circle,
Then tightening her circle, tricked him, herself became the pursuer.
Now, standing up in the stirrups, she hacked her strong axe through
                                                                his armour
And bones, though he begged and prayed for mercy, sending in blow
Upon blow: warm brains from his cloven skull spattered his face.
A warrior, the son of Aunus, an Apennine farmer, now happened
Her way, stood rooted to earth by shock and panic at seeing her:
Not least of Ligurian tricksters he, while fate allowed him
To cheat. When he saw it was too late now to avoid an encounter
Or to divert Camilla's onset by running away,
He tried to take her in with guileful provocative words,
Beginning thus:—

                    You're a woman, but must you rely on a strong steed
To win you distinction? Get rid of that chance to escape, and meet me
Fair and square on the ground—if you dare—yes, fight me on foot:
You'll soon find out who is bluffing and boasting, and who'll be
                                                            undone by it.

Stung by these words to bitter resentment, Camilla, in high rage,
Gave up her horse to a comrade, and fearlessly faced him on foot
With no advantage in weapons—drawn sword and unblazoned shield.
The Ligurian, however, believing he'd gained his ends by this ruse,
Promptly wheeled round his horse and started away—the coward—
In flight, plying the fleet-footed steed with his iron spurs:—

Deluded fool, you have over-reached yourself with your own
Conceit! You think you're a smart boy, but all the smooth tricks you
                                                            have learnt
From your folk won't get you back to your crooked father or save you!

So saying, Camilla ran, swift as a bush-fire, after him,

[*Lines 684–718*]

252

Headed him off, stood full in his horse's path; then seizing
Its reins, she took her revenge deep in the blood of her enemy.
With the same ease will a falcon, prophetic bird, take off from
A crag to pursue the dove which is flying high overhead,
Will catch it, seize it, slash out its bowels with hooked talons,
So blood and a scatter of feathers come floating down from the sky.
   But the Father of gods and men, aloft on the heights of Olympus,
Did not observe these events with an indifferent eye.
He inspired the Etruscan, Tarchon, to fight with greater ferocity,
Spurred him roughly on, whetted the edge of his anger;
So Tarchon rode amongst the wavering formations,
The slaughter, goading his squadrons with shouts of abuse and
                                  encouragement,
Calling each man by name, and rallied his broken forces:—
   Can nothing shame you, Etruscans? Will you never snap out of
                                    your lethargy?
What are you scared of? Why this shocking display of cowardice?
So now a woman can send you flying and rout our proud ranks!
What are your swords meant for? Why carry arms and not use them?
You're vigorous enough where girls are concerned and tussles in bed,
Or when a dance is on and the curved flute of Bacchus invites you;
Well, keep your strength for the banquet, the groaning table, the
                                   wine cups—
If guzzling is all you care for—and wait till the priest has announced
Good omens, and you can picnic off the rich meat of the sacrifice!
   So saying, he spurred his charger into the fray, as ready
To risk his own life as his men's lives, and swept like a cyclone on
                                  Venulus.
Tearing him off his horse, Tarchon furiously galloped
Away, with his right arm clamping the man to the saddle in front
                                  of him.
All the Latins turned their eyes on the spectacle. Shouts
Went up to the sky. Now Tarchon streaks over the plain like wildfire,
Carrying the man and his weapons: he breaks off the business end of
His enemy's spear, and with it probes for a joint in his armour
Through which he can give him the death-blow: but Venulus fights
                                  back
To hold off Tarchon's hand from his throat, pitting strength against
                                  violence.

   [*Lines 719–750*]

It was like when a golden eagle soars aloft with a snake
In its grip, twined round its feet, held fast by the claws that impale it:
But the snake, though wounded, writhes about with its whip-like coils,
And its scales stand up on end, and it hisses in fury, rearing
Its head to strike; while, fiercely as ever, the bird's hooked beak
Darts at the lashing snake, and its pinions thrash the air.
Just so did Tarchon triumphantly bear off his prey from the ranks
Of Tiburtines. Fired by their general's success, the Etruscans followed
His lead, and charged. Now Arruns, that fateful and fated man,
Circled round the fast-riding Camilla, javelin in hand, cleverly
Anticipating her movements, seeking the best way to strike.
Wherever the berserk princess rode in the thick of the mêlée,
There Arruns would appear, shadowing her unobtrusively:
When she withdrew from some successful foray at the foe,
This warrior stealthily wheeled his swift horse and kept contact with her.
Hefting his sure-as-doom spear—nothing would foil him—he tried for
One opening after another, circling and circling about her.
It befell that Chloreus, a one-time priest in the service of Cybele,
Showed at a distance, the shining Phrygian armour conspicuous,
Spurring his foam-flecked mount, which wore a horse-cloth—a hide
Armoured with scales of bronze, like plumage, and buckled with gold.
Chloreus himself, resplendent in dusky, exotic purple,
Was shooting Cretan arrows from a bow of Lycian make:
Golden the bow this warrior carried, and gold the helmet
He wore; his mantle was made of linen, a saffron colour,
And a red-gold brooch held fastened its rustling folds; his tunic
And oriental trews were embroidered with golden thread.
Whether she wished to hang up his Trojan arms in a temple
Or to strip off his gold and wear it herself, Camilla
Picked out this man from the mass of combatants there, and trailed him,
Blind to all else, in full cry, recklessly ranging amid
The battle, on fire with a woman's desire for another's finery.
Now had come Arruns' chance, at last. From where he was lurking
He lifted his spear, poised it, prayed to the heavens above:—

    Most worshipful god, Apollo, guardian of blest Soracte,
Where we, your chief devotees, heap up in your honour the blazing
Pine logs and walk through the midst of the flames, sure in our faith,
Treading the high-piled embers as we perform your rites—
Apollo, puissant in battle, grant that I may rub out

[*Lines 751–789*]

254

This stain on our escutcheon! I ask no spoils, no trophy
Of her defeat; it is not loot that I want: I'll be famous
For other deeds: let me but strike down this pestilent fury,
And I will gladly return home, taking no credit for it.

    Apollo silently gave his assent to one part of Arruns'
Prayer, but the rest he tore up and threw to the four winds.
He granted his wish to take Camilla off guard and deal her
A mortal wound; but that ever he should return to his own land,
He granted not—those words were snatched away on the breezes.
So, when the spear of Arruns went whistling from his hand,
The Volscians turned their fiercely expectant minds and eyes,
All, upon the queen Camilla. She was oblivious—
No wind, no sound of the hurtling weapon she got: next moment
The spear went into her body, just under the naked breast,
And stuck there, deeply drinking the maiden blood where it lodged;
In consternation her friends rushed up and caught their queen
As she collapsed. Most frightened of all was Arruns: in fear
Mingled with exultation, he fled; he would not trust his
Weapon, or dare to face Camilla's, a moment longer.
Just as, before the armed pursuers can get on his trail,
Some cowardly wolf, which has killed a shepherd or a big steer,
Makes rapidly off, avoiding the beaten paths, to hide in
The mountains; and knowing quite well he has done wrong, he runs to
The wooded heights, with his quivering tail between his legs—
Even so did Arruns remove himself from their view, all wrought up,
And vanished into the ruck of the fighters, glad just to escape.
Camilla, dying, tugged at the spear; but its iron blade,
Deep in her body, was firmly fastened between the ribs there.
She is sinking, faint from loss of blood: her fainting eyes
Are glazed with the frost of death: the colour ebbs from her face.
Now, with her last breath, she spoke to Acca, a girl of
Her own age, one who had been her confidante and of all
Her companions was the truest. These were the words she spoke:—

    Acca, dear, I can do no more. This bitter wound
Is the end of me. Shadows are falling, it's growing dark all round me.
Make your best speed and bring this last message of mine to Turnus—
He must take my place here and fight the Trojans off from the city.
Now, good-bye.

               So saying, she loosed her grip on the reins
  [*Lines 790–827*]

255

And helplessly slid to the ground. Then, little by little, her body
Grew numb and released its hold upon life; her neck was drooping,
Her head bowed down to victorious death: she let go of her weapons,
And with a moan her protesting spirit fled to the shades.
Then, oh, then a terrific outcry arose, the welkin
Rang, and the fight grew fiercer because of Camilla's death.
All the Teucrian force, the Etruscan captains, Evander's
Arcadian squadrons—all of them—launched a concerted attack.

But Opis, Diana's observer, had long been watching the fight,
Unflinching, from where she sat on a high mountain-top.
Now when she beheld from afar Camilla, right there in the yelling
Mêlée of warriors, struck down and dying a piteous death,
Opis heavily sighed and spoke with deepest emotion:—

Ah, cruel, too bitterly cruel, poor lass, the forfeit you've paid
For having dared to challenge the Teucrian host in battle!
You lived alone in the wildwood, you served Diana and carried
Our quiver upon your shoulder; but none of this saved you now.
Still, your mistress has seen that you shall not be left dishonoured
In death's last hour; your dying shall be a famous thing
Among the nations—they shall not say you were unavenged.
Whoever it was that wounded and desecrated your body
Shall get the death he deserves.

Under that mountain height
There was a huge barrow, the tomb of an old Laurentine
King, Dercennus, lying beneath the shade of holm-oaks.
First, then, the beautiful nymph, with a movement swift as light,
Came and stood here, from the top of the mound looking out for

Arruns.

When she saw him, shining in armour and swelling with idle vanity,
She said:—

Why are you moving away? Come over here,
Come deathwards, come and receive the reward you deserve for killing
Camilla! Yes, you're a wretch, but you'll die by Diana's weapons.

So saying, the Thracian nymph took from her quiver of gold
A flighted arrow, and stretched her bow, aiming at Arruns:
She drew the string right back, till the ends of the curving bow
Had almost met, her hands level, the left supporting
The arrow's point, the right hand drawing the string to her nipple.
Next moment, Arruns heard the whizz of a shaft, the whirring
[*Lines 828–863*]

256

It made through the air, and the arrow pierced him that very same
instant.
His comrades, unconcerned, left him gasping and moaning
With his last breath on the dust of the plain—an inglorious end,
While Opis winged her way back to the heights of Olympus.
Their mistress fallen, Camilla's light brigade were the first
To fly; then the Rutulians and gallant Atinas broke
In panic; detachments left leaderless, officers who had lost touch with
Their troops, now wheeled away and raced back to the cover of the
walls.
There was no holding the Trojans' deadly, remorseless pressure,
However hard you fought, no standing against them. The Latins,
Slinging their unstrung bows on weary shoulders, retired,
And as they galloped away the hammering hooves shook the dry flats.
A dust cloud, dark and whirling, rolls up to the city walls,
Where mothers stand in the watch-towers and, as they gaze forth, beat
Their breasts; the shrieks of women go up to the heavens above.
Those who first poured in through the open gates at a gallop
Had a crowd of the enemy hard on their heels, even riding amongst
them,
And did not escape a cruel death: at the actual gateways,
Within the walls, and worse—in the houses where they took refuge—
They were speared, and breathed their last. Some of them shut the
gates,
Barring their comrades out, and for all their appeals, dared not
Admit them to the city. A tragic slaughter ensued
Between those defending the gates and their own friends fighting to
enter.
Of those shut out, in full view of their weeping parents, one lot
Were tumbled into the moat by the pressure of those in panic
Behind them, while others with loose rein were blindly riding full tilt
Into the solid doors that stood in their way, and ramming them.
The mothers themselves, on the battlements—they had seen Camilla's
example,
And genuine love of their country showed them the way—with the
utmost
Energy hastened to hurl down missiles, impulsively making
Tough poles of oak and fire-hardened stakes do the work of cold steel:
Eager they were to be first to die in defence of the city.
[*Lines 864–895*]

257

Meantime desperate tidings came to the ears of Turnus
While he lay in the woods, for Acca brought word of the grave
                                                        disaster—
How the Volscian forces had been wiped out, and Camilla had fallen;
How the foe were attacking fiercely, the battle had gone their way
And they'd swept all before them; panic now lapped at the town walls.
Turnus in anger—for so the stern will of Jove required—
Moved off from his menacing ambush among the trees on the hillside.
He had scarcely marched out of sight of that place and reached the plain
Below, when Aeneas entered the pass, now unobstructed,
Surmounted the ridge and debouched from the dark woods with his
                                                            army.
So both of them, leading their columns, were rapidly marching towards
The city, with no great interval between them. At one and the same
Moment Aeneas descried at a distance ahead the plain
Smoking with dust, the Laurentine forces moving across it,
And Turnus became aware of the armed array of relentless
Aeneas, heard the tramp of feet and the snorting of chargers.
They would have joined battle and fought it out immediately,
But that the roseate sun now dipped his weary steeds in
The Iberian sea, and day was darkening to night. So both of them,
Camping outside the city, consolidate their positions.

[*Lines 896–915*]

BOOK XII

When Turnus saw that the Latins were crushed by defeat and in lowest
Spirits—saw, too, that all eyes were upon him as if demanding
That now he should make good his promise, he burned with a mood
                                      all the more
Uncompromising; his temper sharpened. Just as an African
Lion, when he's received a bad wound in the breast from the hunters,
Then at last becomes really dangerous, gleefully tosses
The shaggy mane from his neck, and uncowed snaps at the assailant's
Arrow stuck in him, breaks it, roars with his mouth all bloody:
So Turnus looks; his violent intransigeance kindles and mounts up.
Now, with an outburst of passion, he speaks to Latinus, saying:—
   I am not holding back. Those yellow Trojans have no cause
To swallow their words or renounce their agreement, as far as I am
Concerned. I shall fight him. Make ready the rites and frame the terms.
Either this hand of mine will send that Dardan, that runaway
Asiatic, to hell—the Latins may sit and look on at us—
And with my sword I'll wipe out the slur on our people's good name,
Or he'll have Lavinia in marriage and the rest of you in subjection.
  Latinus would not be rushed off his feet: he replied equably:—
  Prince, I admire your spirit; but the higher your passionate courage
Rises, the deeper and more attentively I must ponder
What's best; I have to be cautious and weigh all sides of the question.
You own the realm of your father, Daunus, and many cities
You've captured in war; while I have gold, and am not close-fisted.
Are there not other unmarried girls of good birth in Latium
And the Laurentine land? To speak with brutal frankness
And lay all my cards on the table—please take to heart what I'm saying—
I never had the right to promise my daughter to any
Of her old suitors: both oracles and popular feeling forbade it.
But, overborne by my affection for you, by our kinship
And the tears of my grieving wife, I disregarded all vetoes:
I cheated Aeneas of his bride, and took up arms in a bad cause.
What a disastrous war has resulted from this, you can see,
  [*Lines 1–32*]

259

And how great are the evils, Turnus, which you are the first to suffer.
Twice beaten in full-scale battles, we can hardly hold this town now—
Italy's last hope. The Tiber is still running warm with
Our blood, and our people's bones are blanching the plain all over.
My mind yaws like a madman's, for ever washed back to the same
point.

If I'm prepared to make friends with the Trojans, on Turnus' death,
Why don't I end the conflict while he is still alive?
Think what your Rutulian kinsmen, what all Italy
Would say, if I were responsible for Turnus getting killed
(God save the mark!) through his desire to marry my daughter.
Reflect how war can change men's fortunes. Be sympathetic
Towards your old father who grieves for you, cut off as he is in his
native

Ardea.
      These words made no impression at all upon Turnus'
Intransigeance—nay, it increased, the cure only inflamed it.
As soon as he was able to speak, he began like this:—

    The anxiety you show for me, most gracious king, I implore you
For my sake to discard: let me purchase fame with death.
I am no weakling, sire, I too can rain blows and deliver
Fusillades; men bleed when I wound them—same as Aeneas:
His goddess mother will not be on hand, concealed in mere shadow,
To cover his flight with a cloud delusive as woman herself.

    But the queen, greatly alarmed by this new turn of the struggle,
Clung to the hot-headed Turnus, weeping, knowing her death near:—

    By these tears of mine, by whatever love and respect you feel
For me, I implore you, Turnus—since you are my one hope now,
Sole stay of my sad old age; since Latinus' honour, authority
Rest in your charge; but for you we should collapse altogether—
One thing I beg, give up this idea of fighting the Trojan.
Whatever hazards await you in such a duel, the same
Await me too: if you die, then will I quit a life
I hate; Aeneas shall not be my son, nor I his captive.

    Lavinia listened while her mother was speaking: tears
Flowed down her burning cheeks, suffused with a deep crimson
Blush that spread all over the glowing face. Imagine
A piece of Indian ivory stained with a blood-red dye
By a craftsman, or a bouquet of white lilies blended with many

[*Lines 33–68*]

260

Red roses: that was how the hues in the girl's face looked.
Turnus, deeply moved by love, gazed hard at Lavinia.
More eager than ever to fight, he spoke to the queen briefly:—
  Please do not send me forth to the tough encounter before me
With tears and with such defeatist, ominous words, Amata.
If I'm to die, it's not in my power to postpone the hour of it.
Idmon, act as my herald and take this word to the Phrygian
Despot—it won't amuse him: as soon as to-morrow's dawn
Rides up the sky in its rosy car and flushes it, let him
Not lead the Teucrians against us, let there be armistice
For Trojans and Rutuli, while he and I settle the war
Between us: that fight shall decide who is to have Lavinia.
  When he had finished speaking, he quickly withdrew to his own
                                                          place
And called for his horses, happy to see them neighing before him—
Those steeds, more dazzling white than snow, swifter than winds,
Which Orithyia herself had graciously given to Pilumnus.
The charioteers stand busily round them, slapping their resonant
Barrels with open hand, and comb the luxurious manes.
Turnus then put over his shoulders a corselet stiff with
Gold and pale orichalc, at the same time fitting on ready
His sword, his shield, and the helmet with sockets to hold its red crest.
The sword had been made for Daunus, his father, by the Fire-lord's
Own hands, who had tempered the white-hot blade in the waters of
                                                          Styx.
Now he snatched quickly up his powerful spear, which was leaning
Against a mighty column in the central courtyard (he'd won it
As spoil from Auruncan Actor), and shouted aloud as he shook
The vibrating shaft:—
                  Ha! now is your chance, my spear! You have never
Failed me when I have called on you. Actor, a great champion,
Carried you once. Now Turnus hefts you. Together we'll bring
That Phrygian pansy down, tear open and rend off
His corselet by main force; we'll dabble in the dust those love locks
He crisps and dolls up with curling-tongs and smarms with perfumed
                                                          grease!
  He was wildly wrought up, so burning for battle that all his countenance
Seemed to shoot sparks, and darts of fire to come from his fierce eyes.
So it is when a bull bellows out its first terrible challenge to combat,
  [*Lines 69–103*]

261

And practises throwing all its fury into its horns
By goring trunks of trees, butts at the air in anger,
Paws and tosses the sand as a prelude of coming battle.

    Aeneas the while, a grim figure in the arms his mother had brought
                                                 him,
Was whetting no less his desire for the fight, and keying himself up
With anger, glad of the chance to settle the war on these terms.
Now he comforts his friends and the dreadfully anxious Ascanius
With things the fates have told him, bids officers take to Latinus
A definite answer and to dictate the conditions of peace.

    The morrow's dawn was just beginning to shower its light on
The mountain-tops, and out of the deepsea the sun's horses
Were starting to climb and breathing the day from uplifted nostrils,
When Trojans and Rutuli paced out on the plain, beneath
The great town walls, the lists for the combat and made them ready,
Setting up braziers and altars of turf to the gods they both worshipped
In the middle of the arena. Some, wearing the priestly aprons
And garlanded with field herbs, were bringing fire and spring water.
Now the Italian army moved off, surged out through the gates
Marching in close column. From the other side the Etruscan
And Trojan forces streamed on, with their diverse equipment,
Heavily armed and in formation, as if for the stern
Arbitrament of battle. Amongst the assembled thousands
The captains move about, haughty in gold and purple—
Mnestheus of the Assaracan line, valiant Asilas,
Messapus too, the tamer of horses, the scion of Neptune.
When the signal is given, each side retires to the area allotted it;
Planting their spears in the ground, they lean their shields up against
                                                 them.

Then the women came running out excitedly, with the unarmed
Civilians and frail old men, to throng the towers and the roofs of
The houses, while other spectators stood by the tall gateways.

    But Juno, looking forth from the eminence which to-day
We call the Alban hill (then, it had neither name
Nor fame), was attentively gazing at the Laurentine ranks,
And the Trojan, arrayed upon the plain, and Latinus' city.
At once she addressed Juturna, the sister of Turnus, deity
Speaking to deity, she being goddess of lakes and sounding
Rivers; for Jove himself, king of high heaven, had conferred

                                      [*Lines 104–140*]

This office on her in return for the maidenhead he had ravished:—
    Water-spirit, most dear to my heart, pride of the rivers,
You know that, of all the Italian maids who have mounted into
The unrewarding bed of large-hearted Jove, I have singled
You out and gladly promoted you to a place in heaven:
I must tell you what pain is in store for you, lest you blame me for
                                                            causing it.
As far as fortune seemed to allow and the Fate-spinners granted
That Latium's affairs should go well, I have shielded your walls and
                                                        your brother.
But now I see he is facing a destiny loaded against him:
The day of doom is here, the enemy's hand is upon him.
I cannot endure to look on at this duel or its preliminaries.
If you dare do anything more effective to aid your brother,
Do it: *you* may. You and he may yet have a chance, poor souls.
    She had hardly finished speaking when Juturna burst into tears
And violently struck her beautiful breast, three times and again.
Saturnian Juno cried:—
                        This is no time for weeping.
Hurry, and if there's a way, rescue your brother from death!
Or start them all fighting, arrange that this embryo peace be stillborn!
I am behind you, whatever you venture.
                                        With such encouragement
Juno left her, bemused, unsettled, in agony of mind.
    Meantime the kings came forth, Latinus, heroic of stature,
Riding a four-horse chariot, his temples crowned and brilliant
With coronet of twelve gold rays, an emblem of
His ancestor the Sun, while Turnus rode behind a
White pair, swinging a couple of broad-bladed javelins.
Over there, lord Aeneas, father of the Roman nation,
Bright in the armour from heaven, his shield like a star flashing,
Moves out of camp, with Ascanius beside him, the other hope
For Rome's great future: a priest, clothed in immaculate vestments,
Has led up the young of a bristly boar and with it an unshorn
Two-year-old sheep, and brought the beasts to the flaming altars.
The heroes, turning their eyes towards the rising sun,
Sprinkle the salted meal from their hands, cut off with a knife
The victims' forelocks, and pour libations from bowls on the altars.
Then did Aeneas the true, drawing his sword, pray:—

    [*Lines 141–175*]

263

Let the Sun witness my invocation now, and this Earth
For whose sake I have endured to go through such terrible travails,
And you, Father almighty, and you, Saturnian Juno,
Kindlier-disposed to me now, I hope and pray; and you,
Famed Mars, whose providence governs and shapes all wars:
And I call upon Springs and Rivers, on all the dread powers of the sky
Above us, and every deity haunting the cobalt sea—
If so it be that the victory goes to Italian Turnus,
It's agreed that the vanquished side shall withdraw to Evander's city;
Ascanius shall quit this soil, and my people shall never renew
The war thereafter, or challenge Latium with the sword.
But if victory falls to me in this fight—as I deem more likely,
And may the assent of the gods confirm me in so believing!—
I shall not make the Italians a subject race to the Trojans,
Nor do I seek this realm for my own: let both our peoples,
Unconquered, as equal partners be joined in a league for ever.
The gods and the hallows I'll give: Latinus shall keep, as my father,
His arms and his rightful authority. The Trojans shall build for me
My city walls, and Lavinia shall give her name to the city.
  Aeneas spoke first, like that. Then did Latinus follow,
Gazing up at the heavens, stretching his right hand towards them:—
  I too, Aeneas, swear by Earth, by Sea, by Sky,
By Apollo and Diana, by Janus-facing-both-ways,
By the power of the Underworld gods and the shrine of Dis, the
                                                      merciless:
May the Father, whose lightning sanctions our treaties, hear me!
I touch the altar, I call on the fire and the godhead between us:
Never, for us Italians, shall this peace treaty be broken,
However things betide, no force of circumstance make me
Swerve from it of my own free will, not even though a flood
Should melt all earth into sea and heaven be dissolved in hell;
As sure as this sceptre of mine, which I hold in my right hand, never
Could put out new shoots and be dressed in light leaves to give men
                                                      shade,

Once it was cut away from low down on its parent tree
In the forest, shedding its twigs and foliage to the knife:
It was a growing thing, but the hand of a craftsman encased it
In elegant bronze and made it the sceptre of the kings of Latium.
  So, in full view of the princes assembled, they ratify

[*Lines 176–212*]

264

The treaty between them in these terms. Then are the ceremonial
Victims solemnly sacrificed, hard by the fires, their living
Entrails torn out, and the altars loaded with high-piled dishes.

But for some time the Italians had been in a vacillating,
Uneasy state of mind, thinking the fight an unfair one;
All the more now, when they saw from close up that the principals
were not
Equally matched for it. Turnus heightened the feeling, as mutely
He went to the altar, and humbly worshipped with downcast eyes—
They noticed how pale he was too, how wasted his cheeks had become.
As soon as his sister, Juturna, perceived that the mutters of unrest
Were growing, that public opinion was wavering and irresolute,
Into the crowd she moved, assuming the likeness of Camers,
A man of distinguished family, whose father was widely renowned for
His valour, and who was himself a most active soldier; she went
Into the ranks of the Rutuli, a definite plan in her head,
And started a whispering campaign with remarks like this:—

Aren't you ashamed, you Italians, at risking one hero's life
To save an army like ours? Are we not equal in numbers
And strength to the foe? Arcadians and Trojans—look, they are all
there,
With the doom-ridden Etruscans intent upon Turnus' death.
Why, if half of us fought them, they'd hardly have men to equal us.
Turnus shall mount on wings of fame to the gods whose altars
He vows his life to, and live on the lips of men for ever;
But we shall lose our country and have to obey those arrogant
Masters, because we choose to sit here now and do nothing.

More and more did these words inflame the mood of resentment
Among the Rutulian soldiers; muttering crept through the ranks:
Even the Laurentines and Latins began to change their attitude.
Men who'd been dreaming of rest from the struggle, of going about
Their affairs in peace, now wanted to fight, prayed that the treaty
Be void, and felt pity for Turnus in his unfair predicament.
Here Juturna threw in a heavier weight, a delusive
Portent, giving a sign from the skies above, which worked on
The minds of the Italians more strongly than anything else.
A golden eagle, Juppiter's bird, aloft in the red sky,
Was chasing a pack of water-fowl, which uttered clamorous sounds

[*Lines 213–248*]

265

As they flew before it: suddenly swooping down to the water,
It greedily seized a magnificent swan in its hook-like claws.
The Italians grew tense as they watched. Now the whole flock of
                                                        water-fowl
Wheeled from their flight, screaming—a regular marvel to see—
And darkening the sky with their wings, closed up, a cloud of them,
                                                        mobbed
The eagle, and drove it before them, until, overborne by their fury
And the sheer weight of its burden, it weakened, dropping the victim
Into the river below, and fled to the cover of a cloud.
This, of course, the Rutulians hailed with shouts as an augury;
Their hands flew to their sword hilts. Tolumnius, the augur, at once
                                                        cried:—

    This, aye this was what I have often prayed for! I mark
And acknowledge this sign from above. Out with your swords and
                                                        follow me,
You downtrodden folk, whom, like a flock of birds at his mercy,
A greedy adventurer terrorises, and violently plunders
Your coasts! Now *he*'ll have to fly, sail far away and take cover
Out on the deep. Close up your ranks, then, with one accord,
And fight to defend the prince whom that bird of prey has seized.

    So saying, he ran forward and launched a weapon right at
The foe: his spear of cornel-wood cut through the air, whining,
Accurate in aim. At once a great roar went up; all the rows of
Spectators broke out in a frenzy of uncontrollable passion.
That spear flew on. Now it happened nine brothers stood in its path—
Young men of splendid physique, all were the sons of Arcadian
Gylippus by one faithful wife, an Etruscan woman:
One of these, a handsome fellow in shining armour,
Was hit by the spear, at his waist, where his stomach was chafed by
                                                        the belt
Heavily sewn at the buckle which clasped it tightly together.
It skewered him through the ribs, and laid him dead on the brown sand.
His brothers, crazy with grief, brave as they come, in a body
Charged at the foe head down, unsheathing their swords or snatching up
Iron-tipped javelins. The army of the Laurentines
Ran forward to meet them; and then, once again, streamed forth a
                                                        great flood
Of Trojans, of Caeretans, and Arcadians with blazoned arms.

                                                [*Lines 249–281*]

266

All are devoured by one passion, to fight it out with the sword.
The altars stood dismantled: a whirling barrage of missiles
Darkened the sky like a storm-cloud, the blizzard of iron grew thicker.
The bowls and the fires were removed from the altars. Latinus himself,
Now the treaty was void, picked up the images of his defeated
Gods, and fled. Men harnessed their chariot horses or leapt
Astride their chargers, and raced with drawn swords to the fray.
Messapus, eager to tear up the treaty, rode at Aulestes,
A Tuscan king, who bore the insignia of his kingship,
And frightened him into receding: Aulestes, reeling backwards,
Unluckily tumbled over an altar behind him and fell
On his head and shoulders. Messapus was up to him in a flash
With his lance, and towering above him on horseback, fiercely
                                                    stabbed down
At him, for all his entreaties, with the massive weapon, and cried:—
    He's had it! This best of victims I've sacrificed to the gods.
    The Italians ran to the spot and despoiled the still-warm corpse.
As Ebysus came at him, ready to strike, Corynaeus, full in
His path, snatched up a red-hot brand from an altar and thrust
The blaze of it into his face: the man's great beard caught fire
And gave off a smell of singeing: Corynaeus followed it up
By gripping the hair of his dazed antagonist in his left hand,
Bringing a knee up against him and thrusting him hard to the ground,
Then slashed him in the side with his tempered blade. Podalirius
Bore down with uplifted sword on Alsus the shepherd, just as he
Charged through the missiles there in the front rank: Alsus, however,
Swung back his axe and bisected his enemy's head from brow
To chin, so that his armour was spattered with blood all over.
Unkind repose, the iron sleep weighed down Podalirius'
Eyes: his eyelids closed for everlasting night.
    But Aeneas the true, his head unhelmeted, put out his right hand
Which held no weapon, and shouted appeals to his own comrades:—
    Where are you off to? Why this sudden outbreak of violence?
Pull yourselves together! The truce has been made and its terms
Are all fixed now: I am the only man who's allowed to fight.
Leave it to me, and no more of this panicking! I will confirm
The pact with my arms; the rites we've performed make Turnus my
                                                    business.

    Even as he spoke, before he'd finished appealing, an arrow—
    [*Lines 282–318*]

267

Imagine it!—winged its way towards him, whizzing: nobody
Knows who drew the bowstring, who sent that arrow flying,
Who won, whether by accident or heavenly aid, such glory
For the Italians: noone claimed the renown for so splendid
A feat, or ever boasted of having wounded Aeneas.
When Turnus saw Aeneas retire from the field, and his officers
Gravely disturbed, with a sudden access of glowing confidence
He called for his weapons and horses, proudly leapt up at one bound
Into his chariot, and fought to control the plunging team:
Then, careering about the field, he killed many brave warriors,
Bowled many over, mortally wounded, knocked down whole ranks
                                                                with
His chariot wheels, sent a quick fire of spears at the fleeing enemy.
As, by the banks of icy Hebrus, ensanguined Mars,
Driving his horses at full pelt, clangs out on his shield the alarum
Of war: the horses are furiously galloping over the broad plains,
Faster than South wind or West; their drumming hooves make the
                                                              furthest
Regions of Thrace reverberate: Fear, with its louring visage,
Angers and Stratagems speed on in the train of the War-god—
Exultant as this now, Turnus is lashing on through the battle
His horses, streaming with sweat: he tramples over the horribly
Slaughtered foe, while showers of blood fly out from beneath
The galloping hooves as they stamp the sand into bloody paste.
Sthenelus now he killed, Thamyrus, Pholus—the first
From a distance, the other two at close quarters: he killed with spear-
                                                                casts
The sons of Imbrasus, Glaucus and Lades, brought up by their father
In Lycia; he had equipped them with arms equally suitable
For close fighting on foot or charging on wind-swift horses.
On another sector Eumedes hurled himself into the fighting,
The war-famed son of that Dolon widely renowned of old,
Having his grandsire's name, the courage and strength of his father
Who once, for venturing into the Danaan camp as a spy,
Demanded that his reward should be nothing less than Achilles'
Horses: but Diomed gave him a very different reward for
His daring—a dead man cannot aspire to the team of Achilles.
Well, Turnus noticed Eumedes far off on the open plain,
And hitting him first with a long-range javelin shot, drove over,
[*Lines 319–354*]

Pulled up his pair of horses, leapt down from the chariot, straddled
The fallen, dying man, and putting his foot hard down
On his neck, twisted the sword out of his hand, to plunge its
Glittering blade deep into his throat; then spoke these words:—
    Lie there, measure out with your length, you Trojan, the land of
                                                     Hesperia
You wanted to grab by aggression. This is the pay-off they get
Who dare to take arms against me: thus do they found their city.
    Then, hurling his spear, he sent Asbutes to keep him company,
Chloreus and Sybaris, Thersilochus and Dares,
Thymoetes too, who had fallen, pitched over his horse's head.
As when a northerly gale from Thrace is roaring over
The Aegean, and driving shorewards rank upon rank of waves,
And clouds go flying in the sky where squalls of wind have flailed them,
So the formations give way, the ranks turn round and run
Wherever Turnus cleaves a path, carried on by his own
Momentum, his plumes fluttering in the wind of the chariot's passage.
Phegeus, enraged at this onset and Turnus' arrogant shouting,
Now threw himself in the chariot's path; and seizing the foam-flecked
Bridles of the frenzied horses, he wrenched them off their course.
As gripping the yoke, he was dragged along, the broad-bladed lance
Of Turnus found his unshielded side, broke through the joint of
His corselet where it was thrust, and gave him a slight flesh-wound.
But Phegeus turned on his foe, shield up, and was trying to get at him,
To draw his sword and make a fight of it, when the wheel,
With the impetus of the hurtling chariot behind it, sent him
Spinning and crashed him to earth; Turnus at once followed up with
A sword slash between the helmet's lower rim and the top of
The corselet, which took off his head and left his trunk on the sand.
    Now while the victorious Turnus littered the battlefield
With dead, Aeneas, bleeding, was helped into camp by his best friend,
Achates, and by Mnestheus, Ascanius beside them: he leant
Heavily on his tall spear at every other step.
Bitterly chagrined he was; he strove to pluck out the head of
The broken arrow, told them to give him a rough and ready
Treatment—to cut out the barb with a sword, open up the flesh
Where it was lodged so deep, and get him back into the fighting.
At this point Iapis, the son of Iasus, came up: this man
Was specially dear to Apollo, who, seized by intense passion
    [*Lines 355–392*]

For him, had delightedly offered him once his own arts, his own powers—
Of divination, of music, of shooting the swift-flying arrow.
Iapis, to lengthen the life of a father desperately ill,
Elected the knowledge of healing herbs, the science of medicine,
Choosing to practise an art which has little status, in obscurity.
Aeneas, chafing and fuming, stood there propped on his giant
Spear, a great crowd of soldiers about him, with young Ascanius
Grieving, himself unmoved by their tears. Now the aged Iapis,
With sleeves rolled up and gown close-girdled, as doctors have them,
Rapidly tried many methods, applying the curative herbs
Of Apollo; but all were useless, and vainly too did he work
To coax the arrowhead out of the wound in the grip of his forceps.
Fortune gave him no clue, nor did his patron, Apollo,
Assist him; and all the time the terrible roar of battle
Was mounting, disaster nearing. The fighters saw no sky
But a canopy of dust; the enemy horsemen charged closer; and missiles
Fell thickly right in the camp. The din of warriors fighting
And falling as they struggled went hideously up to the heavens.
Now Venus, greatly distressed by her son's unmerited suffering,
With a mother's solicitude plucked, from Ida in Crete, a root of
Dittany, full-grown, with down on its leaves and a crimson
Flower: the plant is one not unfamiliar to wild goats,
Which get relief from it when they've been stuck by an arrow.
Putting a veil of mist around her, the goddess brought
This herb and made an infusion of it, in a cauldron, with sparkling
Water—none saw her doing it—adding drops of the juice
Of health-giving ambrosia and fragrant panacea.
The aged Iapis bathed the wound with that infusion,
Quite unaware of its provenance: at once, as might be expected,
The pain all went and the flow of blood from the deep wound stopped.
So then the barb came away in his hand—no force was needed—
And fell out: Aeneas' strength was renewed, he was strong as ever.
Iapis immediately roused up their fighting spirit by shouting:—
    Jump to it! Fetch our commander his weapons! Don't stand about
                                                                    there!
This cure has been brought to pass by no human means, no medical
Mastery of mine. It is not my skill that has saved you, Aeneas.
One greater, a god, is behind it, restores you for deeds yet greater.
    Aeneas, thirsting for battle, irked by delay, had put on

[*Lines 393–430*]

270

His golden greaves—left leg, right leg; now he brandished his spear.
As soon as the corselet was on and the shield at his side in position,
He folded his son, Ascanius, in a mailed embrace; and lightly
Kissing his lips through the helmet's open visor, he said:—

From me you may learn courage and what real effort is;
From others, the meaning of fortune. To-day this hand will see
You're protected in war, and take you to where war's prizes are found.
Be sure that, when you have grown to your full manhood, you do not
Forget; but rather, dwelling upon your kinsmen's example,
Be inspired by your father Aeneas, your uncle Hector.

When he had spoken, Aeneas sallied forth in his might,
Shaking his massive spear, Antheus and Mnestheus with him—
A close-packed column of warriors rapidly moving forwards
And leaving the camp deserted. Then was the plain a flurry
Of blinding dust, and the ground thrilled with the tramp of feet.
Turnus, upon a rampart opposite, saw them advancing;
The Italians saw it, and tremors of icy fear pervaded
Their inmost hearts. Before any of the Latins, Juturna heard
That marching sound and knew what it meant, and fled in terror.
Aeneas raced on, his column sweeping and darkening the plain.
As when a storm has burst and a cyclone strides across
The sea towards the land, and forewarned from afar the hearts of
Poor countrymen are appalled—that storm is going to fell
Their trees and flatten their growing crops, create havoc everywhere;
Gusts, blowing in from the sea, trumpet the gale's approach—
So did the Trojan commander launch a frontal attack
On the enemy, with his men all rallying to him, compact in
Arrowhead formations. Thymbraeus struck down big Osiris,
Mnestheus killed Arcetius, Achates killed Epulo,
Gyas killed Ufens; even the augur, Tolumnius, fell—
He who had been the first to fire at the Trojan ranks.
A din rose up to the sky, as the Rutuli, routed in their turn,
Took to their heels and fled over the field in a cloud of dust.
Aeneas was not concerned to slaughter these fugitives, nor did he
Follow up such as opposed him, foot to foot, or were threatening
To shoot at him: Turnus alone was his quarry; for Turnus he peered
Through the fog of battle, tracking him, calling on him to fight.
Shaken by fear of this, the warrior maid Juturna
Pushed out of Turnus' chariot his driver, Metiscus, who stood

[*Lines 431–469*]

271

With the reins about him: striking the pole, he fell to the ground
And lay far in their wake. Juturna, taking his place and transformed to
His likeness—in voice, physique, armour—now handled the rippling
reins.

Just as a blue-black swallow flits through the villa of some
Rich lord, weaving a skein of flight in the fine big halls as she
Gathers up crumbs of food, tit-bits for her chirruping nestlings—
You can hear her twittering, now through the empty colonnades,
Now by the tanks in the garden: so Juturna went darting
Amid the foe, her chariot flying all over the battlefield.
Now here, now there she gave them a glimpse of her conquering
brother,
But allowed no encounter—next moment she's off and safely away.
Aeneas, for all that, followed their mazy trail, determined
To meet him; he dogged Turnus through all the confusion of battle,
Shouting his challenge. Whenever he set eyes on his enemy
And tried to outmatch the speed of those galloping horses by running,
So often Juturna steered the chariot away at a tangent.
What was Aeneas to do? He was at a loss, undecided,
With different ideas ebbing and flowing across his mind.
Just then Messapus, who carried two whippy javelins, pointed
With steel, in his left hand—a fighter quick off the mark—poised one
And with unerring aim hurled it straight at Aeneas.
He stood his ground, and covering up behind his shield,
Sank down upon one knee; but the flying javelin took off
The peak of his helmet, shearing away the crest from its top.
Aeneas then got really angry: his hand had been forced by
Their treachery. Seeing that Turnus had driven off, well out of reach,
He repeatedly called to witness Jove and the altar of the broken
Treaty, and then at last went in at the foe, with the flood-tide
Of battle behind him, gave rein to the pent-up fury within him,
And terribly unleashed a fierce, indiscriminate slaughter.
Have I the inspiration now to do justice to so many
Horrors, to such a gamut of carnage—the deaths of captains
Driven all over the field by Turnus now, and now by
The Trojan prince? Juppiter, was it your will that nations,
Destined to live at peace for ever, should clash so bitterly?
Well, the first combat to hold up the Trojans' assault, though not
For long, was when Aeneas met the Rutulian, Sucro:

[*Lines 470–506*]

He got him soon in the side, where death comes quickest, driving
His merciless sword through the ribs, the palisade of the chest.
Turnus, unhorsing Amycus and also his brother Diores,
Went for them on foot, nailed one with his long spear as he advanced,
Struck down with his sword the other; then cut off both their heads
And drove away with those blood-dripping heads attached to his

chariot.

Aeneas despatched Talos, Tanais and the brave
Cethegus, all three at one killing, and slew the dejected Onites,
A man of Theban stock, his mother's name Peridia.
Turnus killed the brothers who'd come from Apollo's land
Of Lycia; also Menoetes, a man who loathed war, but that didn't
Help him—he was Arcadian, a fisherman living in humble
Circumstances near the waters of Lerna, a stranger
To the mansions of the great, the son of a tenant-farmer.
You know how it is when fires have been kindled on either side
Of a wood that is dry as tinder, dense-grown with crackling laurel;
Or when from the mountain heights two torrents, foaming in spate,
Come rapidly roaring down and race towards the sea,
Leaving behind them a trail of devastation: Aeneas
And Turnus tore through the battle with the same violence. Now
Does an eagre of wrath sweep them, their hearts now cannot contain it
Or imagine defeat; they charge on the enemy's weapons at full power.
Murranus, who was sounding off about his ancestors,
The whole of his ancient pedigree traced through the kings of Latium,
Was struck by a rock which Aeneas whirled at him, and sent flying
Out of his chariot full length on the ground: the wheels rolled him

forward

Under the traces and yoke of his horses, which trampled him down
With a flurry of galloping hooves, and no thought for their master's

life.

Turnus encountered Hyllus charging and yelling out savage
War-cries; he flung a spear at the man's gold-helmeted head:
The weapon pierced the helmet of Hyllus and lodged in his brain.
His strong arm did not preserve the bravest of the Arcadians,
Cretheus, from Turnus: nor did his gods protect Cupencus
When Aeneas came his way, but he took the cold steel full in
The breast, poor fellow—his bronze shield could not arrest the blow.
Now the Laurentine plain saw Aeolus perish too,

[*Lines 507–542*]

273

His body sprawling upon the ground—that Aeolus
Whom all the armies of Greece had never been able to bring down,
Nor even Achilles who overthrew the kingdom of Priam:
Here he came to the finish; he had a fine home at Lyrnesus
Under Mount Ida, a fine home, but he sleeps in Laurentine soil.
The whole of each army had now been thrown into the battle—
All the Latins and Trojans, Mnestheus and gallant Serestus,
Messapus, the tamer of horses, brave Asilas, the whole
Etruscan division, Evander's Arcadian cavalry squadrons.
They struggled, with every man putting all he had into the struggle;
No hanging back, no respite: they fought to the death everywhere.

   Then did his lovely mother put into the head of Aeneas
That he should move on the city, divert his men to a sudden
Assault on its walls, and surprising the Latins, disorganise
And defeat them. Scouring the various battle sectors for Turnus,
And looking all round him, this way and that, he viewed the city
Untouched by all this fighting, peaceful and undisturbed.
At once his imagination was lit by the thought of a greater
Battle. He called up Mnestheus, Sergestus and brave Serestus,
His staff, and took his stand on a hillock: the rest of the Trojan
Force gathered to him, tight-packed, but did not ground their shields
Or spears. Then, standing above the ring of warriors, he said:—

   I want my orders obeyed instantly. Juppiter's with us.
My plan may surprise you, but that must be no excuse for
                                                 half-heartedness.
Look at the city, the cause of this war, the seat of Latinus'
Power!—unless they admit they are beaten and owe us obedience,
This day I'll destroy it and raze its smoking roofs to the ground.
Do I have to wait until Turnus feels like facing the ordeal
Of combat? is willing to meet me again, after once being beaten?
Here is the heart, the centre of this cursed war, my men.
Get torches! Hurry! Fire shall exact the terms of the treaty.

   Upon these words, they all are seized by an equal enthusiasm,
Get into wedge formation, drive solidly at the walls.
In a moment ladders appear, incendiaries the same instant.
Some of them run to the several gates, cut down the guards there;
While others darken the sky with a covering fire of arrows.
Aeneas, in the forward party, stretches his right hand
Up at the battlements, loudly rebukes Latinus, and calls

                                        [*Lines 543–580*]

The gods to witness that once again a fight is forced on him,
Twice the Italians have broken a treaty and been the aggressors.
The citizens' nervous excitement bursts out into violent dissension,
One party demanding the gates be unbarred, the town thrown open
To the Trojans, and Latinus himself haled onto the walls:
The others took arms and ran to the defence of their city.
So, when a shepherd has traced a swarm of bees to their chamber
Deep in some porous rock, and filled it with acrid smoke,
The bees within, alarmed for their community, scurry
About the wax castle, and raise their temper with high-pitched buzzing:
Black, pungent smoke rolls through their cells; the hollow rock
Is all one inward humming; smoke trickles out from its crannies.

    A further calamity now befell the war-weary Latins,
Shaking the town to its very foundations, and causing great grief.
The queen, looking forth from her roof-top, saw the advance of the foe,
Their assault on the walls, the flaming material flung at the houses,
But nowhere the Rutuli, no opposition from Turnus.
She believed, alas, that her warrior had lost his life in the desperate
Fighting. The shock and anguish of this unsettled her mind:
Crying out that she was the cause, she only to blame for disaster,
Talking wildly, distracted by paroxysms of grief,
Death in her heart, she tore the crimson gown she was wearing
And hung from a beam the noose that would horribly make an end
                                        of her.

When the poor Latin women got word of this calamity,
Led by the queen's daughter, who tore at her flower-bright tresses
And rose-petal cheeks, they soon were all of them in a frenzy
Of grief around her: the palace resounded with lamentations.
From there the appalling story spread through the city everywhere.
All were dismayed: Latinus, rending his clothes, went about
In a daze at the tragic end of his wife and his city's downfall,
Sprinkling upon his grey head handfuls of unclean dust,
And censured himself severely for not accepting Aeneas
Of his own free will, or attaching him to the Crown through marriage.

    Meanwhile, at the far side of the plain, Turnus is fighting,
Pursuing a few stragglers, but not with such spirit now,
With less and less enjoyment in the action of his horses.
Borne on the wind, there came to him now an outcry, vague
But frightening: he strained his ears; he had to listen; he heard

[*Lines 581–618*]

275

The sound of a city in tumult, a murmur of no good cheer:—
    O god! What is all that noise coming from the distant city?
What has happened to shake the walls with such sounds of grief?
    So Turnus spoke, and wild with anxiety reined up his horses.
Whereat his sister who, still in the likeness of Metiscus,
His charioteer, was controlling the horses and driving the chariot
Countered his thoughts by saying:—
                              Let us pursue those Trojans:
That way lies the path to immediate victory, Turnus.
Others there are to defend the town, and quite competent for it.
Aeneas is battling and fully committed against the Italians,
Let us deal merciless havoc upon the Trojans here.
You'll win as much glory as he, and have no fewer dead to your credit.
    Turnus replied:—
    Sister, I recognised you long ago, the first moment you cleverly
Caused the pact to be broken, embroiled yourself in this war;
And I'm not deceived now by this mortal disguise of yours. But who
                                                        was it
Sent you down from Olympus to go through so great an ordeal?
To witness the hard death your unfortunate brother must die?
For what can I do? What chance or warrant have I of survival?
I have seen Murranus—and noone is left whom I love so well—
A champion slain by a wound from a champion fighter, fall
Before my very eyes, calling on me for aid.
The ill-starred Ufens died, rather than look upon
Our dishonour: the Trojans now possess his corpse and his armour.
Am I to let our homes be destroyed—the one disaster
I have been spared—and not give the lie to Drances' slanders
By fighting? What? Turn my back? My country to see me a runaway?
Death is not all that dreadful. You Shades, be kind to me,
Since now the Powers above have taken their goodwill from me.
I shall come down to you, a soul unstained, with no cowardice
Upon my conscience to make me unworthy of my great ancestors.
    He'd barely finished when Saces came racing up on his lathered
Horse, having ridden right through the enemy, though he was wounded
By an arrow full in the face: he cried out to Turnus for aid:—
    Turnus, you are our last hope, pity your people and save them!
Aeneas attacks like a thunderbolt, threatens to batter down
The citadel of the Italians and blast us with total destruction.

                                          [*Lines 619–655*]

Already they're shooting up fire at our roofs. The Latins look to you,
Pray to you. King Latinus debates with himself, uncertain
Which alliance to favour and whom to have for Lavinia.
And listen—the queen, your most trustworthy supporter, has died
By her own hand: she was frightened out of her wits, and killed herself.
Messapus and gallant Atinas alone, in defence of the gates,
Are holding our men together. Around them, on flank and front,
The hostile formations are pressing, a thick-set bristling crop of
Cold steel, while you're joy-riding over these empty fields.
    The picture of their changed fortunes struck Turnus dumb,

                                        bewildered him.
Speechless and staring, he stood there, his heart in a violent conflict,
Torn by humiliation, by grief shot through with madness,
By love's tormenting jealousy and a sense of his own true courage.
As soon as the mists parted and he could think again clearly,
He turned his blazing eyes upon the walls, in great
Distress of mind, looked back at the city there from his chariot.
He saw a whirling spire of flame which was leaping upwards,
Wave after wave, through the floors of a turret, had got a firm grip

                                        on it:
Turnus had built this turret himself, a solid construction
Of planking, with wheels to move on, and gangways rigged aloft:—
    The fates are too strong for me, sister—I see it now. Don't hold

                                        me back;
Let me go where God and my own unmerciful fortune call me.
I am resolved to fight Aeneas, to bear whatever
Bitterness death holds for me. You shall not see me disgraced
Any longer. Just let me indulge this madness of mine ere I die.
    So saying, Turnus at once leapt down to the ground from his chariot,
And leaving his sister sorrowing, dashed through the enemy, ran
The gauntlet of fire, his impetus breaking a way through their midst.
Even as a boulder that rolls straight down from a mountain summit,
Dislodged by a gust of wind—a cloudburst has washed away
The soil it was fast in, perhaps, or the passage of time has loosened it;
Down, with terrific momentum, the huge thing insensately bounces
Over the ground, steep down, carrying trees, flocks, men
Before it: just like this did Turnus speed to the city,
Scattering the foe from his path, and run to the walls where the earth

                                        was

[*Lines 656–690*]

277

Most deeply drenched with blood and the air screeched with missiles.
He held up his hand as a signal, shouted for all to hear:—

Rutuli, put up your weapons! Cease fire, you Latins! Whatever
The issue is, I shoulder it. Better that I redeem
For you the breaking of the treaty, and decide all, in a duel.

So then they drew apart, leaving a space in the midst for the combat.
But lord Aeneas, as soon as he heard the name of Turnus,
Hurried away from the walls, from the towers he was then attacking,
Broke off the whole engagement, impatient of any delay,
Overjoyed at the prospect of meeting Turnus; and terribly clashed his
Sword on his shield. Gigantic as Athos he looked, as Eryx,
As our own Appennine range when a storm roars in its oak trees
Dancing their leaves, and its snowy peaks soar joyfully skywards.
Now did the Rutuli, the Trojans and all the Italians
Excitedly gaze at their two champions—those who were up on
The battlements, and those who were thumping the walls below
With a ram. All laid down their shields. Latinus himself marvelled
To see those giants, born in different parts of the world,
Now met together to fight it out in single combat.
They, as soon as the lists were cleared on the open plain,
Exchanged spear-shots from a distance and then advanced at a run
Into the fight and met with a clang of their bronzen shields.
Earth groaned beneath the encounter: the sword strokes rained so fast
You could not see which hits were lucky and which were skilful.
As on the ranges of Sila or a plateau of Taburnus
Two bulls charge at each other, head on, determined to fight
To the death; the herdsmen have backed away from the combat in
terror,
And the whole herd stands mute with fear, the heifers wondering
Which will be lord of the forest and sultan of all the herd:
The two bulls furiously tussle, wounding each other repeatedly,
Horns straining together and butting, blood running down
Their necks and shoulders in streams; the woodland rings with their
bellowing:
Equal to this was the fray between Trojan Aeneas and Turnus
Of Italy: shield against shield, they collide with the sound of a
thunderclap.
Juppiter holds the scales in his own hand: empty, they balance:
And then he puts in the scales the different fates of the two men,

[*Lines 691–726*]

To see which weight sinks down, meaning defeat and death.
Turnus sprang forward that moment, thinking he saw a safe opening,
Rose on tiptoe, whirled up his sword, and with all his strength
Behind it, struck. The Trojans and the excited Latins
Cried out. Both sides were tense, keyed-up. But the treacherous blade
Snapped—yes, right in midstroke it failed the fiery Turnus,
Left him no choice but to flee. When he realised he was disarmed
And the sword-hilt he held was not even his own, he ran like the wind.
The story goes that, when he was mounting in haste for battle
Behind his chariot team, he snatched up the sword of Metiscus,
His driver, instead of his father's blade, being blind with excitement.
That sword was good enough to deal with the routed Trojans:
But it was only a mortal blade; so, when it struck
On armour made by the Fire-god, it shivered to bits at the blow,
Like brittle ice, and its fragments lay glittering on the brown sand.
So Turnus in desperation tried this way and that to escape
Out onto the open plain, running in circles erratically,
Since all about him the Trojans had formed a ring, and besides
A wide-spreading marsh cut off one escape-route, the steep walls
another.

Aeneas pursued the while, though hampered and slowed down
At times by the arrow-wound he had received in his leg:
Still, he pressed hard and hotly upon his panting foe.
It was like the scene when a hound has got a stag cut off by
A river, or headed off by the nets with their crimson feathers
Which scare it: the hound, baying, follows up close on its heels;
The quarry, frightened both by the snares and the river-bank's steepness,
Turns on its tracks again and again; but the spirited staghound
Sticks to it, jaws agape—has he got it?—you'd think he had got it,
The way his teeth snap like a trap, but he's bitten the air and is baffled.
Then what a din arose! The river-banks and the marsh pools
Echoed and echoed all round, the sky roared with the shouting.
Even as he fled, Turnus cursed the Rutulians who stood there,
Calling on men by their names, demanding they give him his own
sword.

Aeneas stopped that by threatening immediate death for any
Who went near Turnus, terrorised the already unnerved Rutulians
By swearing he'd wreck their whole city; kept on in spite of his wound.
Five times the pair ran in a circle, then changing direction, returned

[*Lines 727–763*]

On their own tracks: no light-hearted sporting event it was, though—
The prize they ran for being the very life-blood of Turnus.
Now it happened a bitter-leafed wild olive, sacred to Faunus,
Had stood here—a tree from of old held in great reverence by sailors
Who, when they'd escaped from drowning, would hang on its boughs
their offerings
To the Laurentine god, hang up the clothing they'd vowed him.
But the Trojans, to clear the arena for the two combatants,
Had removed the trunk of this tree with no regard for its sanctity.
Here, in the stump, was sticking Aeneas' spear: the momentum
Of flight had carried it here and wedged it firm in the tough wood.
Aeneas now strained every muscle in an attempt to extract
The weapon, wanting to catch with a missile the foe he could not
Catch up by running. Turnus cried out in extremity of fear:—
    Faunus, I beg you, take pity! Dear native earth, hold fast to
That spear! Remember how I have always paid you reverence,
And how the Trojans profaned you to clear the field for our combat!
    This prayer to the god for help did not fall upon deaf ears.
Aeneas, though long he struggled, bent over the tough-grained stump,
Could not by any effort manage to free his spear
From the bite of the wood. While he fought and strained with
violent exertions,
The nymph Juturna, changing again into Metiscus
The charioteer, ran forward and gave her brother his own sword.
Venus, annoyed that the nymph was granted such freedom of action,
Approached and tore out the spear from the deep grip of the tree stump.
Now in high heart the two champions, their arms and their spirits
restored,
One with his trusted sword, one erect and aggressive holding
His spear, stand facing each other, breathing hard, in the lists.
    Meantime the king of all-powerful Olympus addresses Juno
As she looks down at the combat out of a golden cloud:—
    My wife, how shall it end now? What more is there you can do?
For you know, and admit the knowledge, that Aeneas is called of
heaven
As a national hero, and fate is exalting him to the stars.
What are you planning? Why do you linger here in the chill clouds?
Was it right that Aeneas, the heaven-born, should be hurt by the
hand of a mortal?

[*Lines 764–797*]

Or that Juturna should give back the missing sword to her brother—
Ah yes, without you she was powerless—and strengthen the loser's hand?
Then yield to my persuasions, give up the long feud now at last!
No more of the hidden rancour that so consumes you, the sullen
Recriminations your sweet lips have troubled me with so often!
This is the end, I say. You had power to harry the Trojans
All over lands and seas, to kindle accursed war,
Bring tragic disgrace on a king's home and drape a betrothal in
mourning.

I forbid you to carry the feud any further.
So Juppiter spoke.
Juno, the daughter of Saturn, with lowered eyes, replied:—
It is because your wishes, great consort, were known to me,
That I have reluctantly given up Turnus and quit the earth.
Otherwise I'd not be sitting apart here and putting up with
Every humiliation: no, armed with flame, I'd be there
In action, dragging the Trojans into a fatal fight.
I admit I encouraged Juturna to go and help her unfortunate
Brother, approved of her acting more boldly still to preserve him;
But not that she should use her bow and shoot at the Trojans:
This I swear by the source of the inexorable river,
Styx—the one dreadful and binding oath for us heaven-dwellers.
And now I do truly yield; I give up the fight—I am sick of it.
One thing, and no ruling of fate forbids you to grant it, I do
Entreat, for Latium's sake and the dignity of your own kin:
When they make peace through a prosperous—aye, let it be so—a
prosperous
Marriage, and when they are making agreements and laws to unite
them,

Do not command the indigenous Latins to change their ancient
Name, to become Trojans and to be called the Teucrians:
Allow them to keep the old language and their traditional dress:
Let it be Latium for ever, and the kings be Alban kings;
Let the line be Roman, the qualities making it great be Italian.
Troy's gone; may it be gone in name as well as reality.
The creator of man and of all things replied to her with a smile:—
Jove's sister you are indeed and the second child of Saturn,
So powerful the tides of wrath sweeping within your breast!
But come, there was no need for this violent emotion; calm yourself.
[*Lines 798–832*]

281

Willingly I grant what you ask: you have won me over.
The Italians shall keep their native tongue and their old traditions;
Their name shall not be altered. The Trojans will but sink down in
The mass and be made one with them. I'll add the rites and usage
Of Trojan worship to theirs. All will be Latins, speaking
One tongue. From this blend of Italian and Trojan blood shall arise
A people surpassing all men, nay even the gods, in godliness.
No other nation on earth will pay such reverence to Juno.

    The goddess bowed and agreed, glad now to change her whole

                                                      policy,
Passed forthwith from the sky, leaving her place in the clouds.

    This being accomplished, the Father brooded awhile on another
Question—how to detach from her brother's side Juturna.
Two demon fiends there are, called by the name of Furies,
Whom darkest Night brought forth at one and the same birth with
Hellish Megaera, breeding all three alike with the twining
Coils of serpents and giving them wings like the wind. These creatures
Attend on Juppiter's throne, at the house of heaven's stern Ruler,
Ready to stab fear into the hearts of anguished mortals
Whenever the king of the gods is dealing out pestilences
And hideous death, or affrighting guilty cities with war.
Juppiter now sent one of these demons hurrying down from
Heaven, to confront Juturna with a forbidding omen.
Off she flew, and swiftly was borne to earth in a whirlwind.
Just as an arrow flies through the clouds from a bowstring—a shaft
Whose tip some Parthian or Cretan archer has doped with a deadly
Poison, and then shot it; fatal the wound it will give—
Whirring and unsuspected it flies through the mirk of the clouds:
So sped the spawn of Night upon her way to the earth.
When she could see the Trojan lines and Turnus' army,
She suddenly dwindled and changed into the shape of that small owl
Which often at night, when noone's about, perches on tombs
Or gables, and hoots for hours disquietingly through the darkness.
Thus transformed, the Fury flittered about the face of
Turnus, screeching, and kept on bumping his shield with her wings.
The thing was so uncanny that he went numb with fear
And his hair stood on end, and the voice died in his throat.
But Juturna recognised from afar the creaking wings of
The demon. It broke her spirit: she rent her dishevelled hair,

                                      [*Lines 833–870*]

Scratched at her cheeks and beat her breast in grief for her brother:—
    Oh, Turnus, what can your sister do for you now? What worse
Remains for this much-tried heart? I have used all my powers
To save you. But how can I face a manifestation so dreadful?
No, no, I give up the fight now. I tremble—oh, spare me your terrors,
You sinister bird: I know the beat of your wings, I know that
They sound the tocsin of death, and Jove's high purpose has given
These high-handed orders. So thus he requites me who took my
                                            virginity?
Why did he make me immortal? disfranchise me from the common
Law of death? But for that, I could end my terrible anguish
This very moment, and go through the shades with my poor brother.
I immortal! What joy can I have from immortal life,
Bereft of my brother? Alas, that nowhere may earth yawn deep
And let me go down to the ghosts below, for I am a deity!
    So saying, the goddess veiled her face in her grey-green mantle,
And heavily sighing, vanished into the depths of the river.
    Aeneas moved up on his enemy, hefting and flashing his spear
Which was huge as a tree, and shouted out with extreme ferocity:—
    Turnus, you'll get no more reprieves. Are you still recoiling?
It's cold steel now, hand to hand, not fleetness of foot, that will tell.
Try all the transformations of Proteus! Summon up
Your powers, whether of courage or magic! Take wings, if you like,
And shoot straight up to the stars, or go to ground in the deep earth!
    Turnus, shaking his head, replied:—
                            It's the gods and Juppiter's
Enmity frighten me, not your sneers or your bloodthirsty speeches.
    Without a word more he looked round and his eyes alit on a huge
                                            stone—
A huge old stone which for years had been lying there on the plain
As a boundary mark between fields, to prevent disputes about
                                            ownership.
Hardly could twelve strong men, of such physique as the earth
Produces nowadays, pick up and carry it on their shoulders.
Well, Turnus pounced on it, lifted it, and taking a run to give it
More impetus, hurled this stone from his full height at Aeneas.
But as he moved, as he ran, as he raised his hands, as he threw
That boulder, for him it was just as if somebody else were doing it.
Ice-bound were his veins, and his legs felt like water.
    [*Lines 871–905*]

283

So too the stone he hurled, flying through empty air,
Failed to make the distance, fell short of its objective.
But, as it is in a nightmare, when sleep's narcotic hand
Is leaden upon our eyes, we seem to be desperately trying
To run and run, but we cannot—for all our efforts, we sink down
Nerveless; our usual strength is just not there, and our tongue
Won't work at all—we can't utter a word or produce one sound:
So with Turnus, each move he bravely attempted to make,
The unearthly demon brought it to nothing. Now did his feelings
Veer this way and that in distraction: he gazed at the city, the Rutuli;
Faltered with fear; trembled at the weapon menacing him.
He could see no way to escape and no way to get at Aeneas;
His chariot, his sister who drove it, were nowhere to be seen.
So Turnus faltered: the other brandished his fateful spear,
And watching out for an opening, hurled it with all his might
From a distance. The noise it made was louder than that of any
Great stone projected by siege artillery, louder than
A meteorite's explosion. The spear flew on its sinister
Mission of death like a black tornado, and piercing the edge of
The seven-fold shield, laid open the corselet of Turnus, low down.
Right through his thigh it ripped, with a hideous sound. The impact
Brought giant Turnus down on bent knee to the earth.
The Italians sprang to their feet, crying out: the hills all round
Bayed back their howl of dismay, far and wide the deep woods
                                                        echoed it.
Turnus, brought low, stretched out a pleading hand, looked up at
His foe in appeal:—
                I know, I've deserved it. I'll not beg life.
Yours was the luck. Make the most of it. But if the thought of a
                                                        father's
Unhappiness can move you—a father such as you had
In Anchises—I ask you, show compassion for aged Daunus,
And give me back to him; or if that is the way it must be,
Give back my dead body. You have won. The Italians have seen me
Beaten, these hands outstretched. Lavinia is yours to wed.
Don't carry hatred further.
                        Aeneas stood over him, poised
On the edge of the stroke; but his eyes were restless, he did not strike.
And now what Turnus had said was taking effect, was making him
                                                [*Lines 906–940*]

284

More and more indecisive, when on his enemy's shoulder
He noticed the fatal baldric, the belt with its glittering studs—
How well he knew it!—which Turnus had stripped from young
                                                    Pallas after
He'd killed him, and put on himself—a symbol of triumph and doom.
Aeneas fastened his eyes on this relic, this sad reminder
Of all the pain Pallas' death had caused. Rage shook him. He looked
Frightening. He said:—
                        Do you hope to get off now, wearing the spoils
You took from my Pallas? It's he, it's Pallas who strikes this blow—
The victim shedding his murderer's blood in retribution!
   So saying, Aeneas angrily plunged his sword full into
Turnus' breast. The body went limp and cold. With a deep sigh
The unconsenting spirit fled to the shades below.
   [*Lines 941–952*]

APPRECIATION

by

JOHN POLLARD

Everyone has heard of Virgil. Many people have read him in the original Latin. Few, however, are aware of his unique place in literature or of man's debt to his poetry.

Among those who appreciated the contemporary importance of a Roman poet who had lived two thousand years previously were the handful of scholars and men of culture who founded the Virgil Society in 1943. The date of the society's founding is significant. It was during the period of the war described so graphically by Sir Arthur Bryant as the " Turn of the Tide. " There was now, at last, a gleam of hope, like the star seen by Aeneas when Troy was in flames and prospects seemed darkest.

> A sudden crash of thunder, and a shooting star slid down
> The sky's dark face, drawing a trail of light behind it.

It was felt by some that even if the war were won the traditional culture of western Europe was in danger. As the symbol of that culture they chose the poet Virgil, for reasons that will appear. Other choices were open to them, Homer, Dante, Shakespeare, Milton, to mention only four of the more obvious candidates. Why then did they choose Virgil ?

It was not, of course, his subject-matter that proved Virgil's greatness. Far from it. The *Eclogues*, his earliest work, based on the *Idylls* of Theocritus, resembled the latter in that they were often trivial in theme and content, while their successor, the *Georgics*, was concerned with the mundane details of agriculture and farming. The *Aeneid* itself was but a long propaganda epic, a conscious boost of Roman greatness, based on the hackneyed tale of the Trojan War and the wanderings of one of its least distinguished heroes. Such a work would hardly seem likely, on the face of it, to rival Homer or even the epic poets who succeeded him, let alone

289

move and inspire readers two millennia later in a way that Homer had never done.

What then distinguished Virgil both from his predecessors and contemporaries ? It was, in a word, his profound humanity. Virgil saw through the contemporary scene deep down into the universal principles which underlay and motivated men to a degree that no poet had ever done before, and expressed them in memorable phrases. In this he was helped by the terse and epigraphic nature of the Latin language, but the sentiments were uniquely his own. A familiar example is the line on the pity of war, quoted by C. Day Lewis in his Introduction to this edition. Aeneas, approaching Carthage, pauses to admire the carvings on the walls of Dido's temple and is both excited and saddened to recognise scenes from the Trojan War. Turning to Achates he observes, with brimming eyes:

> Here too we find virtue somehow rewarded,
> Tears in the nature of things, hearts touched by human transience.

These lines, vague in their scope and universality, strike, nevertheless, a responsive chord in the reader's emotions. For Virgil possessed the power of feeling through his characters, and making his readers feel in turn. This, though a commonplace in drama, is unparalleled and extraordinary in an epic poet. The lines, in fact, imply so much more than they do on the surface. Men must die. Most of what they do is futile. Glory is an illusion. All this and much more is latent in Virgil's terse phrase.

When the poet resorted to the brilliant subterfuge of showing Aeneas a vision of his future descendants, it was inevitable that they should include among his own contemporaries, the recently and tragically dead. The Emperor Augustus had placed all his hopes on the young Marcellus, his nephew and son-in-law, who died in his twentieth year. When his sad form appears at the end of the sixth book of the *Aeneid*, Anchises comments amid welling tears:

> Alas, poor youth! If only you could escape your harsh fate!
> Marcellus you shall be.

But no one can escape death. Not even Eurydice could, though Orpheus descended to the underworld to save her. The reader in fact feels for all young men cut off from their prospects in youth's bright Maytime.

Again, when Aeneas and the Sibyl embark on their Stygian journey, Virgil prefaces his description with the words:

> Dimly through the shadows and dark solitudes they wended,
> Through the void domiciles of Dis, the bodiless regions.

Taken at its face value there is nothing particularly remarkable about the passage. Aeneas and the Sibyl are only dimly visible as they enter the dark cave. But we are conscious of something more. The hero and his guide are entering the place of the Dead, a privilege vouchsafed to few before. It is thus only fitting that they should appear to assume some of the characteristics of the underworld denizens whose realm they are invading. Then again the world of spirits is not a real world at all, but a figment of the imagination, as the poet reveals when Aeneas comes out through the ivory gate:

> There are two gates of Sleep: the one is made of horn,
> They say, and affords the outlet for genuine apparitions:
> The other's a gate of brightly-shining ivory; this way
> The Shades send up to earth false dreams that impose upon us.

" Dark solitudes " too are expressive of the loneliness of man vis-a-vis the universe, as well as of Aeneas in unfamiliar surroundings. Virgil's vision, in effect, transcends more than one level of reality at a time, and in this lies his greatness.

It is sometimes said that Virgil, like Shakespeare, was a product of his age, and there is obviously truth in the assertion. He was born at a time when the Latin language was destined to achieve perfection; when the tardy Roman imagination was stirred by events as never before, and the hopes of a peaceful millennium seemed on the point of realisation. It was the Golden Age of Latin literature, the age of the sportive, witty Catullus, who loved too long and too well, of the gifted, gloomy scientist Lucretius, who

291

were jointly responsible for the break-through in Latin poetry, which Virgil was destined to mould and perfect. Next came his great contemporaries Tibullus, the gentle lover of the countryside, Propertius, poet of passion in all its grisly realism, Horace, author of reflective and noble odes, Ovid, the light-of-love, amoral and debonair, and finally the poet-historian, Livy. There were others, like Cornelius Gallus, whose works have failed to survive, and still others like Manilius, the poet of astronomy who failed to avoid mediocrity, or Bavius and Maevius whom no one admired. For to be born in a great age does not guarantee genius, as some of Shakespeare's contemporaries bear witness. For all that, the Golden Age was a remarkable era which produced remarkable men as well as the greatest names in Latin literature.

Why the age of Augustus should have been prolific in literary talent is hard to say, except—and perhaps this was the crucial factor—that it happened to coincide with the attainment of maturity by the Latin tongue. The parallel with Shakespeare is, in fact, unreal, because Latin never achieved the riotous blossoming of English at the end of the Elizabethan era, for it is essentially a staid and formal language, whose greatness lay in compression and simplicity.

But just as Shakespeare proved a giant among his contemporaries, so Virgil outshone the poets of the Golden Age. One reason may be because he attempted more, and so was better enabled to influence Latin. Greek epic had been dead since Apollonius of Rhodes attempted to revive it during the third century B.C., and although Ennius had given epic form to Roman history a hundred and fifty years earlier, no one had possessed the talent to rival Homer until Virgil wrote the *Aeneid*. In order the better to understand how he came to write it, it is necessary first to attempt to reconstruct his life.

Virgil was born on the Ides (the 15th) of October in 70 B.C. This was the date of the consulship of the brilliant general Pompey, and of Crassus, the richest man in Rome. They were soon to be joined by the young Julius Caesar

1

Virgil as a young man, about the time he started his literary career in Rome. Idealized classical busts of this type tell little about the actual appearance of the subject.

2

A young shepherd of Lucania. Virgil celebrated the rural life in his first major pieces, the *Eclogues* and the *Georgics*. In the former he wrote, " ...a countryman should be concerned to put flesh on his sheep and keep his poetry spare."

3

A Roman teacher of rhetoric and philosophy. Virgil, born near Mantua, learned his Greek and Latin literature at Cremona and his rhetoric at Milan. By contemporary standards his education was very good.

4

A Roman farmhouse of about the first century A.D. Virgil's own beloved farm was confiscated in 42 B.C. to make room for Octavian's veterans. In the *Eclogues* he wrote: "But poems stand no more chance, where the claims of soldiers are involved, than do the prophetic doves if an eagle swoops upon them."

5
A very early funeral terracotta shows a peasant with his oxen. In writing about farming, Virgil managed to raise a pedestrian subject to great poetic heights.

and so renew the anarchy which characterised the dying years of the Republic, and initiate a fresh era of civil war.

Virgil's birthplace was the hamlet, or township of Andes, which lay only three miles from Mantua in Cisalpine Gaul. " Mantua begot me " the poet proudly proclaimed in his epitaph, while in the *Aeneid* he referred to:

> Mantua, rich in its forefathers, who were not all of the same
> stock.

The modern town of Pietole possesses the Italian equivalent of " The Virgil Arms, " but this, of course, does not prove that it occupies the site of the original Andes. All the same, despite the fact that the landscape has changed in the interim, there is general agreement on the identification. The local river was the Mincius, and in the same passage in *Aeneid* X, Virgil imagines, achronistically, Etruscan warriors sailing down it to Aeneas' aid:

> They sailed in warships following a figurehead of the river
> Mincius wreathed with the grey-green rushes of Lake Benacus.

How far the scenery of his homeland contributes to an author's genius is debatable. The country of Virgil's birth was flat, tranquil, fertile and full of " peaceful rivers, soft and slow "; Virgil's affections clung very strongly to his early home, and at the beginning of the third *Georgic* he promises to build a poem-temple beside Mincius' stream:

> And there in the green meadow I'll build a shrine of marble
> Close to the waterside, where the river Mincius wanders
> With lazy loops and fringes the banks with delicate reed.

Nevertheless Virgil appears to have forsaken his home forever at the age of thirty, and neither Mantua nor Andes witnessed the composition of his greatest poems.

Virgil's nationality has been much disputed, not to say distorted, by all kinds of people anxious to claim him for their own. Like his neighbour Catullus, he was clearly not a Roman, and it is possible that he was not even Italian either. French writers have argued that he possessed a Celtic temperament, and there is no gainsaying the fact that he lived in Cisalpine Gaul. We are told that his complexion was extremely swarthy, which has been interpreted as denoting that he derived from pre-Celtic stock. Certainly the plain of Lombardy had been the scene of a great mingling of races through the ages, including Ligurians, Venetians, Etruscans and Gauls. Virgil's father belonged to the family of Vergilii, and his mother to the Magii, a name found in southern Italy as well as in the north. On the whole it might seem that Virgil was of Etruscan ancestry. Mantua, at any rate, was predominantly Etruscan, as the poet himself acknowledges in the passage already mentioned:

> Three clans it had, each clan ruling over four townships,
> With Mantua, by reason of its Etruscan blood, as the capital.

The origin of the Etruscans is much disputed, though they left many impressive archaeological remains. Six centuries before Christ they were a considerable power north of the Tiber. Subsequently they provided Rome with the Tarquin dynasty, but the people revolted against their foreign tyrants, who inspired the kind of hate that the English felt for the Normans, and threw them out. As the power of the Etruscans waned, that of Rome grew, and by the end of the fifth century they were no longer formidable. The Etruscans were not of Italic stock, and although their language can be read, being written for the most part in Greek characters, it cannot be deciphered or understood. It appears, in fact, to be non-European, and there may well be substance in the tradition that they came originally from Lydia in Asia Minor. The Etruscans were much concerned with the after-life, and from them the Romans derived many of their religious beliefs and much of their ritual.

There is hardly any agreement on Virgil's social standing. Several of the ancient biographers state that he was of peasant stock, and that his father was an industrious apprentice who had married his master's daughter. His maternal grandfather was said to have been a deliverer of court summons—in effect a policeman—while his father is constantly described as a potter. It is possible that Virgil's father, like Horace's, was a freedman who had once been a slave, though this is never suggested in the fragmentary biographies.

We are told on the other hand that Virgil assumed the toga of manhood (between the ages of fifteen and seventeen) which suggests that he came of a family of standing. Also he possessed a considerable estate, which was later confiscated and divided, we are told, between no less than sixty ex-servicemen. How then did the tradition that his father was a potter arise ? As the remains of ancient pottery kilns have been discovered in the neighbourhood of Pietole it seems probable that his father possessed considerable clay estates. In other words he may well have been a master potter who prospered in late Republican times. The tradition that Virgil was a peasant could have arisen from the *Eclogues,* in which many of the characters are rustic types.

The biographers' description of Virgil's appearance tallies with that preserved on the famous African mosaic. It was discovered near Carthage, and although it long postdates Virgil it is thought to have been copied from a contemporary or near-contemporary portrait. Virgil was tall of stature, swarthy in complexion and with rustic features, and so he appears in the mosaic. He is represented there as writing the eighth line of the *Aeneid:*

Muse, do you recollect for me the reasons...

which is appropriate in the context as he is flanked by two Muses. His face is decidedly not that of a conventional poet, which lends weight to its probable authenticity. The toga and shoes also seem in keeping, as according to Horace and others he was untidy and ungainly, paying little attention to the style of his clothes. On the other hand a contemporary minor poet pays tribute to the remarkable beauty of his voice, which he wishes he could borrow to recite his verses and make them sound memorable. Not all poets, of course, are favoured with fine speaking voices, to mention only Shelleys' unearthly cackle.

Virgil was painfully shy, and if recognised in the street would take refuge in a neighbouring house. He was also slow of speech, and broke down when he attempted to orate in public. His poor health was shared by his two brothers, neither of whom survived youth. This might account for his vein of melancholy and sad, whimsical humour. In character he was delightful, good-tempered, unenvious and scholarly, praising the good and criticising no one. His favourite saying, culled from Euripides, was " Friends have everything in common. " In the *Journey to Brundisium* his friend Horace describes a shy, self-effacing, wholly loveable person, untypical of the harsh Roman world.

Virgil enjoyed a sound education by contemporary standards. At the age of twelve he was sent to school in Cremona, where he was thoroughly drilled in Greek and Latin literature. Probably he lodged with his mother's family, but of this we cannot be sure. On assuming the toga he removed to Milan, where he began the conventional, but barren, training in rhetoric. Finally, and perhaps inevitably, he went to Rome, during an appalling political crisis. During Caesar's absence in Gaul the rebellious gang-leader Clodius, brother of Catullus' beautiful and notorious lady-love, intrigued in his interest and that of the other two Triumvirs, Pompey and Crassus, and succeeded in securing the outspoken and liberal-minded Cicero's banishment. Later Clodius was killed in a scuffle with the rival gangster Milo, who claimed to be acting in the Senate's, i.e. the Republican interest against the would-be dictators. Anarchy ensued, Pompey was requested by the Senate to restore order, and Crassus suffered disaster fighting against the Parthians. This brought Caesar and Pompey into head-on collision, and in 48 B.C. Pompey was defeated at the Battle of Pharsalus in northern Greece, leaving Caesar undisputed master of the world. Virgil was then twenty-two, of university age, and studying the philosophy of Epicurus in Siro's school. He also, we are told, studied astronomy and medicine, and his poor health doubtless saved him from entanglement in politics or the public events from which his sensitive spirit rebelled. All the formal knowledge he acquired, in addition to his wide-ranging antiquarian interests, he was destined to pour into his poetry. With his interests he combined a boundless capacity for work, which in the end was destined to kill him. Between the ages of eighteen and twenty-eight, the formative period of his life, we lose sight of the poet entirely. Some think that the

6
Maecenas, patron of the arts and Virgil's friend and protector. A close friend to the Emperor Augustus, Maecenas encouraged Virgil in his literary career.

7

Odysseus and his companions listen to the song of the sirens. Odysseus, or Ulysses, plays an important role in Virgil's *Aeneid*. Moreover the Roman ship shown in this mosaic must have been the type that carried Virgil to Greece just before his death.

8
Remains of the Imperial palaces on the Palatine hill in Rome. Virgil must often have frequented the palace of Augustus, who encouraged him in his writing of the *Aeneid* and often asked for readings of each portion as it was completed.

minor poems, known collectively as the " Virgilian Appendix," belonged to this period, when he experimented in subject and metre. But the correct attribution of the poems has never been satisfactorily settled, and some are certainly spurious.

The turning point in Virgil's life came with the confiscation of his farm in 42 B.C., to make room for Octavian's veterans. Matters had moved fast since Pompey's death. First Caesar was murdered. Then followed the political alliance between the young and astute Octavian and the roué Mark Antony which ended in the defeat of Brutus and Cassius at Philippi. When Antony retired to the east his wife and brother attempted to seize power. But Agrippa, Octavian's able commander, reduced the rebel army, bottled up in Perusia, and forced it to capitulate. Although Antony's brother was spared, the grim legend arose that Octavian sated the soldiers' blood-lust by sacrificing 300 knights and senators to the shade of his adopted father Caesar. Virgil hated bloodshed, but the *Aeneid* demanded battles, and some have considered that the more gory descriptions, including the single and shocking example of threatened human sacrifice in Book X, were inspired by these events.

Although Virgil possessed powerful friends in his fellow-poet Cornelius Gallus, whom Octavian had put in charge of land distribution in northern Italy, and Asinius Pollio, the governor of Transpadane Gaul, it is by no means certain that he recovered his farm. Pollio himself was the author of tragedies and histories, who had been in his youth a friend of Catullus and had later become intimate with both Horace and Virgil. It was Pollio who launched Virgil on his literary career by suggesting he write the *Eclogues*.

The *Eclogues*—literally " Selections " or Bucolics— " Poems about herdsmen " were basically escapist in inspiration. Public life had entered and shattered Virgil's private life, and these poems expressed his reaction:

> Tityrus, here you loll, your slim reed-pipe serenading
> The woodland spirit beneath a spread of sheltering beech,
> While I must leave my home place, the fields so dear to me.
> I'm driven from my home place.

Such are the opening lines of the *Eclogues*, a poignant lament for the lost farm he loved so well.

Other poems are sportive or light in tone, but he returns to his farm in the penultimate eclogue:

Moeris

We're down and out. And look how Chance turns the tables
on us—
These are *his* goats (rot them!) you see me taking to market.

Lycidas

Can this be true ? I had heard that all the land, from the place
where
That spur with its gentle slope juts out from the recessive
Hill-line, as far as the water and the old beech-trees with
Their shattered tops—all this had been saved by Menalcas' poetry.

Moeris

So you heard. That rumour did get about. But poems
Stand no more chance, where the claims of soldiers are involved,
Than do the prophetic doves if an eagle swoops upon them.

In other words Virgil's reputation as a poet had so far failed to save his farm. Indeed he hints that his protests had all but cost him his life:

Indeed, but for a raven which croaked from a hollow ilex
On my left hand, and warned me to stop this last dispute
Whatever it cost, neither I nor Menalcas would be alive now.

In the *Eclogues* Virgil honours his friends, and in particular Gallus and Pollio, to whom the tenth and fourth are dedicated. The fourth is remarkable in that it prophesies the return of the Golden Age of Greek legend when men lived in peace and innocence:

Ours is the crowning era foretold in prophecy
Born of Time, a great new cycle of centuries
Begins. Justice returns to earth, the Golden Age
Returns.

The Christians were not slow to see in the eclogue a prophecy of the Saviour's birth, though it possessed a far more mundane origin. A child is to be born, though to

whom is not clear, but at any rate during Pollio's consulship.
The tone of the poem is certainly Messianic, though not
without humorous incidents:

> We shall stop treating wool with artificial dyes,
> For the ram himself in his pasture will change his fleece's colour,
> Now to a charming purple, now to a saffron hue,
> And grazing lambs will dress themselves in coats of scarlet.

In the *Eclogues*, in a sense, Virgil was merely playing at
the game. He did not yet feel up to coping with a protracted
theme, and contented himself with imitating the charming
" Little Pictures " which the Sicilian Theocritus had composed, for the most part, in the broad accents of his native
Doric Greek, two hundred years before. It was a sound
choice. The " Idylls " gave scope for his love of nature,
of expressing his gratitude to the men of power on whom
his safety depended, of exercising his wry humour and
trying his hand at subjects both trivial and grand. The
Eclogues are not always easy to follow, for the pointed asides
and loaded contemporary references are sometimes as dark
to us as Shakespeare's sonnets. But the high quality of the
poetry there is no gainsaying, or of the poet, who confesses
that he had greater things in view:

> When I commenced poet, my Muse was not ashamed
> To live in the woods and dally with lightweight pastoral verse.
> Next, kings and wars possessed me; but Apollo tweaked my ear,
> Telling me, " Tityrus, a countryman should be
> Concerned to put flesh on his sheep and keep his poetry spare. "

The success of the *Eclogues* brought Virgil to the notice
of Octavian's influential friend and counsellor, Maecenas.
Maecenas, according to Horace, could trace his ancestry
back to Etruscan kings, had accompanied Octavian at
Philippi, and had become one of the Emperor's closest
friends. Though he never held public office, Octavian
entrusted him with diplomatic missions and actually appointed him his deputy during his absences from Rome.

The agricultural theme of the *Georgics* was in accordance
with Octavian's policy of " back to the land " after the Civil

War. Virgil acknowledges his debt to Maecenas' encourage-
ment in the second line, and to Octavian somewhat later in
the prelude:

> You too, whatever place in the courts of the Immortals
> Is soon to hold you—whether an overseer of cities
> And warden of earth you'll be, Caesar, so that the great world
> Honour you as promoter of harvest and puissant lord
> Of the seasons...

The flattery is fulsome to modern taste, and derived from
the emperor-worship paid to the Ptolemies in the courts
of Egypt since the days of Alexander the Great.

If Virgil had a model for the *Georgics* it was Hesiod's
epic, *The Works and Days*. *The Works and Days* belong to the
earliest period of Greek literature and are full of wise counsel
and agricultural advice. But the treatment and topics are
different, and although he consulted many other works,
including Greek didactic poems, his older contemporary
Lucretius, and even prose treatises on husbandry, the
Georgics in the end remained uniquely his own.

It is not easy to account for the perfection of the *Georgics*.
Farming is at best a pedestrian topic, but Virgil was able
to raise it to a higher power. He saw beneath the ploughing
and horse-breeding and bees deep down into the world of
nature:

> Then rooks, the guttural talkers, three times or four repeat
> A clear cool note, and often up there in the treetop cradles
> Charmed by some unfamiliar sweet impulse we cannot guess at
> Gossip among the leaves: they love, when rain is over,
> To visit again their baby brood, their darling nests.
> It's not, to my belief, that God has given them
> A special instinct, or Fate a wider foreknowledge of things;
> But, when the weather's changing, when the wet atmosphere
> Shifts and a sky dripping from the south wind condenses
> What was rare just now and rarefies what was condensed,
> New images possess their mind, impulses move
> Their heart other than moved them while the wind was herding
> the clouds.

Man too, and his part in nature intrigued him, and the moral
implications of work:

300

9

An Attic vase of the fifth century B.C. shows Aeneas escaping from the burning city of Troy with his father, Anchises, on his back. Virgil built his *Aeneid* from legends of Aeneas's wanderings that had long been current.

10

A miniature from one of the oldest medieval manuscripts of the *Aeneid* shows Laocoon entwined by the serpents. As Virgil wrote: " They fastened upon Laocoon, as he hurried, weapon in hand, to help the boys, and lashed him up in their giant whorls."

11-12
The love story of Aeneas and Queen Dido of Carthage (shown here in a Pompeian wall painting) raises the *Aeneid* to a high level of compassion. Very little is left today of Dido's Carthage on the shores of North Africa except some ruins and the desolate, rock-strewn shoreline.

Unless you make war on the weeds relentlessly with your mattock
And scare the birds away, and pare with a bill-hook the dark-
ening
Overgrowth of the country, and the rain has come to your call,
Vainly alas you will eye another man's heaped-up harvest
And relieve your own hunger by shaking an oak in the woods.

The poet's sense of humour is as evident in the *Georgics* as in the *Eclogues*, but usually with deeper overtones.

The first three books of the *Georgics* deal with soil and weather, the culture of the vine and cattle and horse rearing. The fourth, which deals with bee-keeping, ends with the tragic tale of Orpheus, who descended to the underworld in search of his wife, told in poetry of a beauty unmatched even in the high passages of the *Aeneid*:

And now he's avoided every pitfall of the homeward path,
And Eurydice, regained, is nearing the upper air
Close behind him (for this condition has Proserpine made),
When a moment's madness catches her lover off his guard—
Pardonable, you'd say, but Death can never pardon.
He halts. Eurydice, his own, is now on the lip of
Daylight. Alas! he forgot. His purpose broke. He looked back.
His labour was lost, the pact he had made with the merciless king
Annulled. Three times did thunder peal over the pools of Avernus.
"Who," she cried, "has doomed me to misery, who has doomed
us?
What madness beyond measure? Once more a cruel fate
Drags me away, and my swimming eyes are drowned in darkness.
Good-bye. I am borne away. A limitless night is about me
And over the strengthless hands I stretch to you, yours no longer."
Thus she spoke: and at once from his sight, like a wisp of smoke
Thinned into air, was gone.

So the story-teller was born, and Virgil felt ready to tackle the *Aeneid*.

By the time Virgil had completed the *Georgics*, which took six years, Octavian had vanquished his last rival, Antony and his Egyptian paramour Cleopatra at the battle of Actium. Henceforth he ruled supreme, assuming the title of Augustus, and bringing the promised era of peace whose advent Virgil had prophesied in the fourth *Eclogue*.

Virgil wrote the later *Georgics* at Naples, and recited them to the Emperor at nearby Atella in 29 B.C. But the time had come to embark on the great epic which he had had so long in incubation. The *Aeneid* was written partly as a tribute to Augustus, but mainly to glorify Rome. It is clear from the *Eclogues* that the poet was aware that it was in him to do it, and writing them and the *Georgics* had given him the practice he required. The genius, of course, was there from the beginning. The handling of the verse displays the touch of the master, as clearly as do Mozart's earlier compositions. But the handling of big themes, against a vast canvass of events and characters, demanded a process of trial and error in advance, and this the two earlier works had given him. Virgil's hesitation was doubtless partly temperamental. Had he been Lucan he would have embarked on the *Aeneid* right off. But Lucan was a revolutionary who joined a conspiracy against Nero and perished in the attempt, whereas Virgil was rooted in the establishment. It was the difference between Shelley and Tennyson, and it is significant that whereas Tennyson idolised Virgil, Shelley preferred the surface brilliance of Lucan to the depth and humanity of the Augustan poet.

Latin, to the unskilled, is an intractable language, far more intractable than Greek. The Romans were aware of this, and although the fragments which have survived from the Republican period not seldom have force and dignity, Ennius, the first poet to attempt these, found it hard to capture the freedom and speed of the Greek epic hexameter in the stolid medium of Latin. Lucretius, much later, was more successful, though handicapped at the outset by the rigours of his scientific theme. Despite this his poetry sometimes attains great heights, which were admired and imitated by Virgil. Catullus, for all his wit and brilliance, was not at his best in epic verse, which still tended towards the artificial and monotonous. Yet Virgil echoes him from time to time.

In some ways it must have seemed impossible to improve on Lucretius at his best, but the evolution of the Latin hexameter had still some way to go and Virgil added the crowning touch. It was in his handling of verse in patterns that Virgil displayed his mastery, and in the evocative and haunting use of words. Often, or even usually, the words or phrases are derived from other poets, in the true classical tradition, but the new combinations are infinitely more affecting than the old and the feelings expressed are not the same.

Before he could start on his task Virgil was faced with the problem of mastering and moulding the evidence. Legends about Aeneas' wanderings were contradictory and tenuous and these had to be arranged in a consistent story. It had to be Aeneas, because he alone of all the Trojan heroes was, according to Homer, destined to survive the fall of Troy and refound the Trojan dynasty. According to a later tradition he actually reached Italy, which meant that the Romans could claim Trojan ancestry and their longed-for place in legend. Furthermore Julius Caesar believed that his family descended from Aeneas' son, Iulus, and since Venus was Aeneas' mother his lineage was immortal.

The Emperor Augustus was Caesar's great nephew and adopted heir, so he too had a powerful claim to immortality. Such was the tendencious and prosaic background to the poem. How then did it itself achieve immortality and greatness? It was, of course, what Virgil made of the material at his disposal. Mere history is never sufficient for a creative genius and in the love story of Dido and Aeneas the poet let his imagination roam. He let it roam even further when Aeneas visits the realms below and sees a vision, not of the past as Odysseus did in Homer, but of the future greatness of Rome. It was a brilliant subterfuge and moved Augustus' wife Octavia so painfully that when she heard Virgil recite the lines, already quoted, about her dead son Marcellus, she is said to have fainted. It was indeed a sign of the *Aeneid*'s greatness and popularity that Augustus required the poet to give him frequent readings as each portion was completed.

The *Aeneid* is divided into twelve books, which tend to alternate curiously in their degree of emotional appeal. The first book, though not generally regarded as one of the greatest, captivates the reader by its narrative skill and the meeting of Dido and Aeneas. Virgil makes use of standard Homeric artifices, such as introducing Venus in the guise of a human being and cloaking the hero and his companion in mist. The scenes again depicted on Dido's temple look forward to the following book and we are prepared for the un-epic sensitivity of Virgil by the great line already discussed:

> Tears in the nature of things, hearts touched by human transience.

In the second book Aeneas describes the fall of Troy in a memorable series of scenes and flashbacks. As Homer's narrative ended short of the climax, Virgil turned to later accounts for his material. Once again his feeling for the dramatic and human touch stood him in good stead. Laocoon's mysterious, unjust end, hints at the ruthless, cynical aspect of the gods:

> They fastened upon Laocoon, as he hurried, weapon in hand,
> To help the boys, and lashed him up in their giant whorls.
> With a double grip round his waist and his neck, the scaly creatures
> Embrace him, their heads and throats powerfully poised above him.
> All the while, his appalling cries go up to heaven—
> A bellowing, such as you hear when a wounded bull escapes from
> The altar, after it's shrugged off an ill-aimed blow at its neck.
> But now the twin monsters are gliding away and escaping towards
> The shrine of relentless Minerva, high up on our citadel,
> Disappearing behind the round of the goddess' shield, at her feet
> there.

For a moment we forget Laocoon, and his fearful doom. We feel sorry for the innocent bull, done to death for no fault of its own, and at a deeper level still for the cruelty in man and in nature.

We sympathise again with old Priam, fumbling with his armour in a vain attempt to withstand the fury of Pyrrhus. But he is as doomed as the white-haired members of the Perusian senate, butchered by Agrippas' legions:

> Even as he spoke, he dragged the old man, trembling,
> And sliding in the pool of his son's blood, right to the altar;

13
The blinded Polyphemus looking for Aeneas. Fifteenth Century French enamel from the workshop of the "Master of the *Aeneid*."

14
Aeneas meets Latinus, an episode from Virgil's *Aeneid* as painted by
a fifteenth century artist. The *Aeneid* was immensely popular through the
Middle Ages and the Renaissance.

15
A fine late fifteenth century woodcut shows Virgil and Maecenas wandering together through the latter's gardens.

16

An ornament from a fifteenth century box, cameo on shell, illustrates
an episode from a popular legend about Virgil.

Twined Priam's hair in his left hand, raised with his right the
flashing
Sword, and sank it up to the hilt between his ribs.

The rest is destruction and slaughter. All seems lost, as it
must have seemed during the darkest hours of the Civil War.
Yet there is still hope. Aeneas receives a sign from heaven
and escapes with his family and followers from Troy.

Book III is as exciting as the Odyssey on which it is based,
filled with incident and spine-chilling adventure. Most
important, Aeneas learns from Apollo's oracle a report
which is later confirmed by Calaeno, the Harpy, and by
Priam's surviving son Helenus, that his goal is Italy.

The fourth book is devoted to the love affair between
Aeneas and Dido, and Aeneas', to our eyes, heartless desertion of the queen. In fact Virgil aimed to make even Roman
eyes weep at the tragedy of a man torn between love and
duty. For a Roman there could be only one way out of the
dilemma, and if it wasn't the way of romance this wasn't
Virgil's fault. Even Homer, of course, wasn't entirely objective, though it is sometimes argued as if he was. Achilles
is full of self-pity, and Agamemnon of pride, but Homer
rarely condescends to the near-histrionics of some of the
speeches of Dido. But then Virgil had not only Apollonius
of Rhodes' fiery Medea as a model and other episodes in the
Greek epic of the Argonauts, but all the passionate heroines
of Greek tragedy as well. In effect Dido is not a Greek
heroine at all, but an emotional, warm-blooded Roman
woman. Both she and the love affair were Virgil's own
creation, and together provide the greatest emotional experience in all western literature.

> Then did almighty Juno take pity on her long-drawn-out
> Sufferings and hard going, sent Iris down from Olympus
> To part the agonized soul from the body that still clung to it.

Why, we ask, must such things be? And it is Virgil that
makes us ask.

Book V is concerned with the funeral games held in
honour of Aeneas' father Anchises. It is replete with effort
and brutality. Yet we mourn for the dove tied to the masthead, which so nearly gets away:

> And marking the dove up there in the blue, exultantly clapping
> Its wings, he shot, and transfixed it before it could reach cloud
> cover.
> Stone-dead the dove came down, leaving its life in the regions
> Of air—came tumbling down with the arrow still stuck through it.

So often in life the dove fails to get away.

The sixth book of the *Aeneid* is the greatest book in Latin, and indeed perhaps any literature. It is so because it describes the imponderable mystery of death in terms that anyone can understand. The underworld it describes is admittedly the underworld of classical myth, but Virgil succeeds in presenting it in universal terms. Above all it is a great adventure, far more detailed and exciting than its Homeric counterpart. Men have invented cave myths from time immemorial, and believed in ghostly guides like the Sibyl. The separation by water of the living and the dead, the crossing of the water by favoured heroes possessed of a talisman like the golden bough, occur in the Babylonian epic of Gilgamesh as well as in modern Malekulan legend. Virgil could not know this, but the founts from which he drew flowed from a common psychological source. That is why they are important today, because all men in all ages have believed these things.

Did Virgil invent the Golden Bough ? Apparently he did. There is certainly nothing like it in the rest of ancient literature. But then Virgil was deeply read in antiquarian lore, and possibly he was familiar with some tradition of which we have no knowledge. It is certainly a talisman of great power, without which entry to the underworld is barred:

> Yet none is allowed to enter the land which earth conceals
> Save and until he has plucked that gold-foil bough from the tree.

It does not strike us as strange that the dead have rules, or that to do the impossible demands special precautions, because we have long been conditioned to expect and accept such requirements in fairy tales. The sixth *Aeneid*, of course, is a fairy tale, but also a vision of man's aspirations. The great Romans yet to be born are all very impressive, if you happen to be a Roman, and in particular a Roman of birth or standing. But everyone yearns to meet their nearest and dearest in the world of shadows, and in this Aeneas succeeds. He is closer to Anchises, his father, than to anyone, and what more affecting than that he should find him,

> Deep in a green valley

He also meets Dido, but she, not unreasonably, gives him the cold shoulder:

> At last she flung away, hating him still, and vanished
> Into the shadowy wood where her first husband, Sychaeus,
> Understands her unhappiness and gives her an equal love.

In the seventh book Aeneas sails up the Tiber mouth, then, if not now, a beautiful spot:

> Around and above, bright-plumaged
> Birds whose habitat is the river banks and channel
> Charmed the air with their song.

But war was the fate prophesied by the Sibyl, and Aeneas finds himself engaged in a struggle for the hand of a local princess with her headstrong Italian lover. It is Homer's *Iliad* all over again, complete with the horrors of battle. The combatants marshall, but we only remember one of them, the fair Camilla:

> A warrior maid, her woman's hand unaccustomed to womanly
> Tasks—to the distaff, the basket of wool; a girl, but hardy
> To face the horrors of battle and to catch up with the winds.
> She could have skimmed along the blades of an unmown corn-
> crop
> Without so much as bruising their tender ears as she ran.

Yet she is doomed we feel, doomed to die like everything fair and young.

The eighth book describes the famous battle between Hercules and the monster Cacus, and also brings Aeneas to the site of Rome. This was a clever move on the poet's part, and enabled him to refer to many of the future city's most famous features hundreds of years prior to its founding. Finally he described the scenes on the hero's shield, which deal again with the pageant of future history. There is

Augustus himself winning the battle of Actium, accompanied by Minerva, Neptune, and Mars himself, for the gods, as in Homer, join in the battle. The book closes with the enigmatic reflection that in taking up his shield Aeneas shouldered his destiny.

Book IX emphasises both the glory and the tragedy of war in which young men must die. Nisus and Euryalus are inseparables. They plan a raid and wreak great slaughter, but pay the inevitable penalty:

> Let's stop! (Nisus says) It will be light soon, and light is no
> friend to us.

But Euryalus has clearly gone beserk and when the pair are finally halted it's too late. Not even Nisus' attempt at self-sacrifice works, when he tries to rescue Euryalus:

> Here! I am standing here! I did it!

Virgil, though he'd never been a soldier, knows what happens on the battlefield and makes us mourn for the waste of war, the wars that we knew as well as his.

Book X continues the carnage, apart from the opening conclave of the gods. Throughout the *Aeneid* the gods have proved in the main heartless and hostile, though none so implacable as Juno, who hated all Trojans with a scorned woman's fanaticism, ever since Paris the Trojan had awarded the prize for beauty to Venus, Aeneas' mother. She had been in the main responsible for the Italian War in rousing Allecto, a fiend from Hell. When Venus accuses her before almighty Jove, the father, as ever, remains impartial. Is there an impartial power in the universe? Even if there is it is subservient to fate. So Jove acknowledges:

> I am king to all, and impartial.
> Fate will settle the issue.

And so the conference ended.

In book XI Arruns slays Camilla, as Achilles had once slain Penthesilea, the Amazon queen. But to slay a woman no matter how doughty is the mark of a coward, and Arruns slinks away like a wolf:

17
A portrait of Virgil painted by the Flemish artist, Joos van Gent. This
is one of a series of paintings of twenty-eight famous men, executed about
1476.

18

Aeneas lands on the shores of Italy, an episode from the *Aeneid* painted with romantic fervour by an early sixteenth century artist. As a subject for illustration, Virgil and his *Aeneid* almost rivalled Homer and the Bible.

19

A statue of Virgil, drawn by the fifteenth century Italian artist, Andrea Mantegna. Mantegna was intensely interested in the details of classical antiquity, and was an expert on archaeology, which explains the loving detail of this drawing.

20

The title page of an edition of the *Aeneid*, dated 1529, which was the
work of the famous early French printer, Jehan Petit. The amusing
drawings seem to have little relation to the subject matter of the *Aeneid*.

> Some cowardly wolf, which has killed a shepherd or a big steer,
> Makes rapidly off, avoiding the beaten paths, to hide in
> The mountains; and knowing quite well he has done wrong, he
> runs to
> The wooded heights, with his quivering tail between his legs.

Such was the end of the babe whom her father had once saved by tying her to the shaft of a javelin and hurling her across a river. There is a touch of Virgil's wry humour here, even in the midst of tragedy.

The twelfth book has the power of *Lear* or Beethoven's ninth symphony. The poet was doubtless tiring, and although his powers were not yet impaired, there is a harsh and brittle quality about the writing, relieved only by Juturna's solicitude:

> She had hardly finished speaking when Juturna burst into tears
> And violently struck her beautiful breast, three times and again.

It is a long book, longest of all, as if Virgil was reluctant to end his task. In the end Juno agrees to accept the Trojans' new destiny, and Juturna is forced by a demon to desert her brother. From that moment his end is inevitable. The gods have turned against him and Turnus must die. So Aeneas slays him, but even in death his soul protests:

> The body went limp and cold. With a deep sigh
> The unconsenting spirit fled to the shades below.

Such is the experience of the *Aeneid*. Inevitably some portions affect us more than others and on the whole we react better to the first six books than to the last six, and least of all to the last three. But then on the whole we prefer the *Odyssey* to the *Iliad* because, apart from the slaying of the suitors it takes place in an atmosphere of peace. But Rome was not the product of peace but of war, and this Virgil makes his readers feel. That the same poet who wrote the slight *Eclogues* and in praise of the countryside in the *Georgics* could have written so movingly and realistically of war is perhaps extraordinary and unexpected. But Virgil lived through a time of war, and was familiar with its horrors. He could not ignore it, so he set out to describe it in the kind of grisly detail which appealed to the ancients. Nowadays we still like to read about war, but without the gory details.

The Romans had stronger stomachs, and Virgil, for all his sensitivity, remained a Roman at heart.

Before revising the *Aeneid* Virgil set out on a long-delayed visit to Greece. He got as far as Megara before his health broke down, and he was easily persuaded to return in Augustus' train. He died at Brundisium and was buried in his beloved Naples, but not before issuing instructions that the *Aeneid* should be burnt. Fortunately for posterity his executors, Varius and Tucca, declined to accede to his last request, and despite minor imperfections and infelicities the poem remains a monument to the Latin language and some of the noblest thoughts of men.

News of the *Aeneid* leaked out long before it was finished, as the contemporary poet Propertius bears witness:

> Give way, Roman writers, give way ye Greeks too,
> Something is coming to birth greater than the Iliad.

Immediately it was published it became a popular school text book, and has remained so down to this day; but perhaps this was more of a misfortune than an advantage, as it was read for the wrong reasons. It provided not only a good literary training, but the speeches were found useful for instruction in rhetoric.

Lucan's bizarre effects in the long epic on the Civil War between Caesar and Pompey, which he wrote under Nero, owe nothing to Virgil, and although Statius and Silius Italicus worshipped at his tomb in Naples, their inferiority to their great master is everywhere patent. Their contemporary, Valerius Flaccus, achieved more success, but the penumbral effects were lacking. Virgil's immense influence was nevertheless virtually total, even among prose writers. Seneca, the philosopher, is forever quoting him, while the pointed, lofty style of Tacitus, the historian, owed much to his use of Virgil's language. Yet, just as there was never another Homer though many poets attempted to emulate him, so there was never another Virgil. Neither Calpurnius Siculus nor Nemesianus, two hundred years later, succeeded in recapturing the spirit of the *Eclogues*, and Claudian, who flourished during the last days of the Roman empire, for all his remarkable command of Latin, was in effect flogging a dead horse.

St. Augustine wept for Dido, and during the fourth century the learned commentaries and disquisitions of Servius, Donatus and Macrobius continued to stimulate interest in the greatest of Latin poets. During the Middle Ages Virgil assumed the unlikely roles both of magician and romantic hero. His deeds (and misdeeds!) were carefully recorded in the popular Latin work known as *The exploits of the Romans*, as well as in the French *Virgil's amazing deeds*. The *Aeneid* became an allegory of love during the Renaissance, and it was Virgil whom Dante chose to guide him to Beatrice.

Spenser, Milton, Dryden, Gray, Pope, Gogarty and, above all, Tennyson, were perhaps most influenced by Virgil among British poets. The absurd practice of composing poems by rearranging lines from Virgil persisted for upwards of a thousand years. It was far more barren and certainly less educative than the practice of writing Latin verses— either free, or as translations of English poems—practised in the schools and universities during the nineteenth century. Sometimes such efforts were attended with remarkable results, as when Benjamin Hall Kennedy, the famous headmaster of Shrewsbury School, gave the boys a half-holiday in honour of a copy of verses that were deemed " worthy of Virgil . "

The custom of opening the *Aeneid* at random, as if consulting an oracle, began a century after Virgil's death and lasted down to Charles the First. Probably it arose from the ancient practice of consulting the Sibylline books, as the Sibyl played such an important part in the *Aeneid*.

Different periods and different people have regarded Virgil in different ways, yet all have paid tribute to his supremacy as a poet. Though times change, Virgil does not, and it is as a symbol of eternal values that he was, and still is, relevant today. Above all, he gives hope for the future. When disaster struck Aeneas, he looked for a guiding sign and found it. This has been Virgil's message to bewildered humanity through the ages.

SOURCES OF THE ILLUSTRATIONS

This book, designed by
Werner Schelling
is a production of
Edito-Service S.A., Geneva

Printed in Switzerland

R 1